AF540576

Women, Challenges and Advancement

INTERNATIONAL ENCYCLOPAEDIA OF WOMEN-3

WOMEN, CHALLENGES AND ADVANCEMENT

Editors

Dr. DIGUMARTI BHASKARA RAO

Chairman

Mrs. DIGUMARTI PUSHPA LATHA

Executive Member

Care Welfare Society, Guntur- 522006

Andhra Pradesh, India.

1999

DISCOVERY PUBLISHING HOUSE

New Delhi-1100 02

First Published-1999

ISBN 81-7141-496-6

Published by:
DISCOVERY PUBLISHING HOUSE
4831/24, Ansari Road, Prahlad Street,
Darya Ganj, New Delhi-110 002 (*INDIA*)
Phone: 3279245
Fax: 91-11-3253475

Printed at:
Tarun offset Printers
Maujpur, Delhi-53

Contents

Foreword

Women and men are equal in every human concern in this World. They are equally competing in almost all spheres of work and power and are equally achieving the set goals. Culture, economy and polity may be barriers to women in certain parts of the globe, still women are marching ahead with great conviction and confidence to keep themselves on par with their counter parts in every affair..

This International Encyclopaedia of Women is touching every area concerned to women. Volume 1 explains the status of the world's women, Volume 2 discusses the role of education in women's empowerment, Volume 3 discusses the challenges and advancement of women, Volume 4 outlines the family health, and Volume 5 presents the details of the international instruments applicable for the development of women.

This Encyclopedia will meet the requirements of planners, researchers, educationists and activists.

DR. DIGUMARTI BHASKARA RAO
MRS. DIGUMARTI PUSHPA LATHA
R.V.R COLLEGE OF EDICATION
NAGARJUNA UNIVERSITY,
GUNTUR 522006 (INDIA)

Acknowledgements

We are thankful to the United Nations and its various commissions, agencies, divisions and departments, the UNESCO, Paris, the UNESCO Institute for Education, Hamburg, the United Nations Centre for Human Rights, Geneva, the UNESCO, Dakar, the International Institute for Population Sciences, Bombay, the Organisation of African Unity; and the United Nations Information Centre, New Delhi for extending their kind cooperation in providing us with the necessary material on our request for the preparation of this International Encyclopaedia of Women.

Volume 1 of the Encyclopaedia contains the material taken from *The World's Women 1995: Trends and Statistics*, United Nations. We thank Prof. Ann Marie Erb-Leoncavallo, Associate Information Officer, Department of Public Information, United Nations, New York for sending the above cited material along with some other valuable documents with the necessary permission to cite material with due credit.

Volume 2 contains the material obtained from Carolyn Medel-Anonueva, ed., *Women, Education and Empowerment: Pathways Towards Autonomy*, UNESCO Institute for Education, Carolyn Medel-Anonueva, ed, *Women Reading the World: Policies and Practices of Literacy in Asia*, UNESCO Institute for Education, Namtip Aksornkool, *Daughters of the Earth,* UNESCO; Cynthia Guttman, *In Our Own Hands,* UNESCO; *The African Conference on the Empowerment of Women through Functional literacy and the Education of the Girl Child*, Kampala: We thank Prof. Cendrine Sebastiani, Publications Department, UNESCO Institute for Education; Prof. Francoise Pinzon, Global Action Programme on Education For All, UNESCO; The Organisers of the African conference on the Empowerment of Women for sending the material for use in our work.

Volume 3 contains the material obtained from *Worldwide Facts and Statistics About the Status of Women,* Committee for the '95 World conference on Women, *Women: Challenges to the Year 2000,* United Nations; *Fourth World Conference on Women, The Advancement of*

Women: Notes for Speakers, United Nations, etc. We are thankful to the concerned Personnel of United Nations Department of Public Information, New York, United Nations Information Centre, New Delhi; Committee for the '95 World Conference on Women, New York; and East- West centre, Honolulu for their kind material support.

Volume 4 contains the material obtained from International Institute for Population Science, *National Family Health Survey (MCH and Family Planning) India, 1992-93*, IIPS. We are thankful to the IIPS, Bombay, Government of India; East-West Centre, and Population Research Centres in India for their valuable cooperation.

Volume 5 contains the material taken from *The International Bill of Human Rights*, United Nations, *Discrimination Against Women: The Convention and The Committee*, UN Centre for Human Rights, Geneva, *Harmful Traditional Practices Affecting the Health of Women and Children*, UN Centre for Human Rights, *The Nairobi Foreword-Looking Strategies for the Advancement of Women*, United Nations (as adopted by the World Conference to Review and Appraise the Achievements of the United Nations Decade for Women: Equality, Development and Peace, Nairobi, Kenya, 15-16 July 1995), and *The Flatform for Action*, United Nations, We are thankful to the United Nations for using these international instruments on women.

We are also thankful to many scholars, researchers, teachers, administrators and friends working on women around the globe who helped us in gettings the necessary information and material on women to prepare this International Encyclopaedia of Women.

Dr. Digumarti Bhaskara Rao
Ms. Digumarti Pushpa Latha

OVERVIEW OF THE WORLD'S WOMEN

Issues of gender equality are moving to the top of the global agenda but better understanding of women's and men's contributions to society is essential to speed the shift from agenda to policy to practice. Too often, women and men live in different worlds—worlds that differ in access to education and work opportunities, and in health, personal security and leisure time. *The World's Women 1995* provides information and analyses to highlight the economic, political and social differences that still separate women's and men's lives and how these differences are changing.

How different are these worlds? Anecdote and misperception abound, in large part because good information has been lacking. As a result, policy has been ill-informed, strategy unfounded and practice unquestioned. Fortunately, this is beginning to change. It is changing because advocates of women's interests have done much in the past 20 years to sharpen people's awareness of the importance of gender concerns. It is changing because this growing awareness has, by raising new questions and rephrasing old, greatly increased the demand for better statistics to inform and focus the debate. And it is changing because women's contributions—and women's rights—have moved to the centre of social and economic change.

The International Conference of Population and Development, held in Cairo in 1994, was a breakthrough. It established a new consensus on two fundamental points:

—Empowering women and improving their status are essential to realizing the full potential of economic, political and social development.

—Empowering women is an important end in itself. And as women acquire the same status, opportunities and social, economic and legal rights as men, as they acquire the right to reproductive health and the right to protection against genderbased violence, human well-being will be enhanced.

The International Conference on Population and Development drew together the many strands of thought and action initiated by two decades of women's conferences. It was also the culmination of an active effort by women's groups to lobby international forums for women's issues. At the United Nations Conference on Environment and Development in Rio de Janeiro in 1992, nongovernmental organizations pushed for understanding the link between women's issues and sustainable development. At the World Conference on Human Rights in Vienna in 1993, women's rights were finally accepted as issues of international human rights.

At the Population Conference and later at the World Summit for Social Development, held in Copenhagen in 1995, the terms of discourse shifted. Not only were women on the agenda—women helped set the agenda. The empowerment of women was not merely the subject of special sessions about women's issues. It was accepted as a crucial element in any strategy seeking to solve social, economic and environmental problems. And building on the advances made in the recognition of women's human rights at the World Conference in Vienna, women's human rights became a focus of the debate in Cairo. The rights approach, advanced by women's groups, was added to the core objectives of development policy and the movement for women's equality.

To promote action on the new consensus, this edition of *The World's Women* builds on the first, presenting statistical summaries of health, schooling, family life, work and public life. Each has to be seen in proper context, however. Yes, there have been important changes in the past 25 years and women have generally made steady progress, but it is impossible to make sweeping global statements. Women's labour force participation rates are up in much of the world, but down in countries wracked by war and economic decline. Girls' education is improving, but there are hundreds of millions of illiterate women and girls who do not complete primary schooling, especially in Africa and southern Asia.

It is also important to look at a range of indicators. Women's political participation may be high in the Nordic countries, but in employment Nordlc women still face considerable job segregation and wage discrimination. Women's higher education may be widespread in western Asia, but in many of those countries there are few or no women in important political positions and work opportunities are largely limited to unpaid family about.

It is also important to look at a range of indicators. Women's political participation may be high in the Nordic countries, but in employment Nordic women still face considerable job segregation and wage discrimination. Women's higher education may be widespread in western Asia, but in many of those countries there are few or no women in important political positions and work opportunities are largely limited to unpaid family labour.

The World's Women presents few global figures, focusing instead on country data and regional averages (see the box on regional trends). There are myriad differences among countries in every field and *The World's Women* tries to find a meaningful balance between detailed country statements and broad generalization. Generalizations are primarily drawn at the regional and subregional levels where there is a high degree of uniformity among countries. For all the topics covered, *The World's Women* has tapped as many statistical sources as possible, with detailed references as a basis for further study. Specialized studies are used when they encompass several countries, preferably in more than one region, so as to avoid presenting conclusions relevant in only one country.

Indicators relevant to specific age groups are crucial to understanding women's situation. The Programme of Action of the International Conference on Population and Development identified equality for the girl-child as a necessary first step in ensuring that women realize their full potential and become equal partners with men. This edition of *The World's Women* responds to this concern by highlighting the experience of the girl-child. Evidence of prenatal sex selection and differences in mortality, health, school enrolment and even work indicates that girls and boys are not treated equally.

The experience of the elderly is more difficult to describe from the few available data. Although elderly people constitute a valuable component of societies' human resources, data on the elderly are insufficient for regional generalizations. Considering that the number of elderly are growing rapidly in all regions, this gap needs to be addressed.

Regional trends

Latin America and the Caribbean

* Fertility has declined significantly—dropping 40 per cent or more over the past two decades in 13 of the region's 33 countries. The total fertility rate has fallen from 4.8 to 3.2. But adolescent fertility remains high—13 per cent of all births are to mothers below age 20. In Central America, 18 per cent.

* Maternal mortality has declined in most countries of Latin America but the incidence of unsafe abortion in South America is the highest in the world.

* Literacy has reached 85 per cent or more across most of the region, and girls outnumber boys at both secondary and tertiary levels of education.

* Latin America's recorded labour force participation rate for women (34 per cent) is low, but in the Caribbean it is much higher (49 per cent).

* Latin America's and the Caribbean are as urbanized as the developed regions, with 74 per cent of the population in urban areas. But the rate of growth is much higher—2.5 per cent a year compared with 0.9 per cent—which strains housing, water and sanitation and other infrastructure.

Sub-Saharan Africa

* Minimal progress is seen in the basic social and economic indicators. Health and education gains have faltered in the face of economic crises and civil strife. Literacy remains the lowest in the world, 43 per cent of adult women and 67 per cent of adult men, and the difference between women's and men's literacy rates is the highest.

* Fertility is the highest in the world at about six children per woman.

* Women's labour force participation has dropped throughout the past two decades—the only region where this occurred.

* Urban areas are growing at a rate of 5 per cent a year, but with new housing and economic growth at a standstill, many live in poverty and squalor. Africa's urban migrants are predominantly male, shifting the sex ratio in rural areas to 106 women per 100 men.

* Estimated HIV infection rates continue to soar, and unlike any other region, the per centage of women infected with HIV is estimated to be as high if not higher than the per centage of men. In Uganda and in Zambia, the life expectancy of both women and men has already declined because of the disease, and eight other countries are beginning to see similar effects.

Northern Africa and western Asia

* In the past two decades, many countries in the region have invested in girl's education—bringing the primary -secondary enrolment ratio for girls to 67 in northern Africa (from 50 in 1970) and 84 in western Asia, and raising women's literacy to 44 per cent in the region. But women's illiteracy in northern Africa remains high, and girls' enrolment still lags behind boys."

* Women are entering the labour force in increasing number—up from 8 per cent in 1970 to 21 in 1990 in northern Africa and from 22 to 30 per cent in western Asia. Still, these numbers are the lowest in the world. Also low is women's share of decision-making positions in government and business.

* Marriage among girls aged 15--19 has declined significantly in northern Africa and to a lesser degree in western Asia—from 38 per

cent to 10 per cent in northern Africa and from 24 per cent to 17 per cent western Asia. Teenage fertility, however, remains fairly high.

* Fertility—which was traditionally high—has declined significantly in the past 20 years, especially in northern Africa. It remains high (with total fertility rates over 5) in several countries in western Asia. These countries also have low female literacy.

Southern Asia

* Many health and education indicators remain low. Although it has risen by 10 years in the past two decades, life expectancy remains lower in southern Asia than in any other region but sub-Saharan Africa—58 for both women and men. Equal life expectancies are also exceptional—in all other regions, women have an advantage of several years.

* One in 35 women dies of pregnancy-related complications. Maternal mortality has declined but still remains high.

* Nearly two thirds of adult women are illiterate and the per centage of girls enrolled in primary and secondary levels of schooling is far below all other regions except sub-Saharan Africa.

* Women continue to marry early—41 per cent of girls aged 15-19 are already married—and adolescent fertility remains high.

* More women are counted in the labour force but most are still relegated to unpaid family labour or low-paying jobs. Although women's representation at the highest levels of government is generally weakest in Asia, four of the world's 10 current women heads of state or government hold office in this region.

Eastern and South-eastern Asia

* Development indicators continue to improve. Infant mortality has declined significantly in south-eastern Asia in the past two decades.

* Literacy is nearly universal in most countries for men but not for women. However, girls and boys now have nearly equal access to primary and secondary education.

* Adolescent marriage rates in eastern Asia are the lowest in the world—only 2 per cent of women and less than 1 per cent of men aged 15-19 are married—and household size is shrinking.

* Eastern Asia reports the largest average decline in fertility, from 4.7 to 2.3, and its contraceptive use now exceeds that of developed regions. Fertility has also declined in south-eastern Asia, but is still generally higher than in eastern Asia.

* Women's participation in the labour force is as high as in developed regions—approximately 55 per cent.

Developed regions

* Basic health and education indicators generally indicate high levels of well-being but in eastern Europe some show signs of deterioration. Currently, women in 13 countries have a life expectancy of 80 years of more and 11 more countries are expected to reach that level after the year 2000. Men's life expectancy has increased little during the past two decades in eastern Europe, however, partly due to a rise in death rates for middle--aged men. Women's life expectancy in eastern Europe has increased much less than in other regions.

* Fertility continues to fall—from 2.3 in 1975 to 1.9 in 1995. But teenage pregnancy is relatively high in some countries—Bulgaria, the Republic of Moldova, Ukraine and the United States.

* Traditional family structure and size are changing. People are marrying later or not at all, and marriages are less stable. Remarriage rates have dropped—especially for women—and single parent families now make up 10—25 per cent of all families. The population is ageing and becoming increasingly female as it does.

* Women's labour force participation increased significantly for regions outside of eastern Europe from 38 per cent in 1970 to 52 per cent in 1990. In eastern Europe, where women's labour force participation was already 56 per cent in 1970, the increase was small (to 58 per cent).

* Women continue to earn less than men—in manufacturing, women's average wage is three quarters that of men's. And women and men tend to work in different jobs—women in clerical, sales and services, and men in production and transport. And men commonly do work which is accorded higher pay and status. For example, the majority of school administrators are men while most teachers are women, and the majority of hospital consultants are men while most nurses are women.

* Women work longer hours than men in the majority of these countries—at least 2 hours longer than men do in 13 out of 21 countries studied. Much of the unpaid work is done by women—for example, women contribute roughly three quarters of total child care at home.

Education for empowerment

In the Programme of Action of the International Conference on Population and Development, education is considered one of the most important means to empower women with the knowledge, skills and self—confidence necessary to participate fully in development processes. Educated women marry later, want fewer children, are more likely to use effective methods of contraception and have greater means to improve their economic livelihood.

Through widespread promotion of universal primary education, literacy rates for women have increased over the past few decades—to at least 75 per cent in most countries of Latin America and the Caribbean and eastern and south—eastern Asia. But high rates of illiteracy among women still prevail in much of Africa and in parts of Asia. And when illiteracy is high it almost always is accompanied by large differences in rates between women and men.

At intermediate levels of education, girls have made progress in their enrolment in school through the second level. The primary—secondary enrolment ratio is now about equal for girls and boys in the developed regions and Latin America and the Caribbean and is approaching near equality in eastern, south—eastern and western Asia. But progress in many countries was reversed in the 1980s, particularly among those experiencing problems of war, economic adjustment and declining international assistance—as in Africa, Latin America and the Caribbean, and eastern Europe.

In higher education enrolments, women equal or exceed men in many regions. They outnumber men in the developed regions outside western Europe, in Latin America and the Caribbean and western Asia. Women are not as well represented in other regions, and in sub—Saharan Africa and southern Asia they are far behind—30 and 38 women per 100 men.

The Framework for Action to implement the World Declaration on Education for All states that it is urgent to improve access to education for girls and women—and to remove every obstacle that hampers their active participation. Priority actions include eliminating the social and cultural barriers the discourage—or even exclude—girls and women from the benefits of regular education programmes.

Seeking influence

Despite progress in women's higher education, major obstacles still arise when women strive to translate their high—level education into social and economic advancement. In the world of business, for example, women rarely account for more than 1 to 2 per cent of top executive positions. In the more general category of administration and management including middle levels, women's share rose in every region but one between 1980 and 1990. Women's participation jumped from 16 to 33 per cent in developed regions outside Europe. In Latin America, it rose from 18 to 25 per cent.

In the health and teaching professions—two of the largest occupational fields requiring advanced training—women are well represented in many countries but usually at the bottom levels of the status and wage hierarchy.

Similarly, among the staff of an international group of agriculture research institutes, women's participation at the non—scientific and trainee levels is moderate, but there are few women at management and senior scientific levels.

The information people receive through news papers, radio and television shapes their opinions about the world. And the more decision—making positions women hold in the media, the more they can influence output—breaking stereotypes that hurt women, attracting greater attention to issues of equality in the home and in public life, and providing young women with new images, ideas and ideals. Women now make up more than half of the communications students in a large number of countries and are increasingly visible as presenters, announcers and reporters, but they remain poorly represented in the more influential media occupations such as programme managers and senior editors.

In the top levels of government, women's participation remains the exception. At the end of 1994 only 10 women were heads of state or government; of these 10 countries only Norway had as many as one third women ministers or subministers. Some progress has been made in the appointment of women to ministerial or subministerial positions but these positions are usually tenuous for them. Most countries with women in top ministerial positions do not have comparable representation at the subministerial level. And in other countries, where significant numbers of women have reached the subministerial levels, very few have reached the top. Progress for women in parliaments has also been mixed and varies widely among regions. It is strongest in northern Europe, where it appears to be rising steadily.

Missing from this summary is women's remarkable advance in less traditional paths to power and influence. The importance of the United Nations Decade for Women and international women's conferences should not be underestimated, for these forums enabled women to develop the skills required for exercising power and influence, to mobilize resources and articulate issues and to practise organizing, lobbying and legislating. Excluded from most political offices, many women have found a voice in non—governmental organizations (NGOs) at the grass roots, national and international levels. NGOs have taken issues previously ignored— such as violence against women and rights to reproductive health—and brought them into the mainstream policy debate.

Since the women's conference in Nairobi in 1985, many grass—roots groups have been working to create new awareness of women's rights, including their rights within the family, and to help women achieve those rights. They have set agendas and carved out a space for women's issues.

And as seen in recent United Nations conferences, NGOs as a group can wield influence broad enough to be active partners with governments in deciding national policies and programmes.

Reproductive health-reproductive freedom

With greater access to education, employment and contraception, many women are choosing to marry later and have fewer children. Those who wait to marry and begin child—bearing have better access to education and greater opportunities to improve their lives. Women's increased access to education, to employment and to contraception, coupled with declining rates of infant mortality, have contributed to the worldwide decline in fertility.

The number of children women bear in developed regions is now below replacement levels at 1.9 per women. In Latin America and in most parts of Asia it has also dropped significantly. But in Africa women still have an average of six children and in many sub—Saharan African countries women have as many or more children now than they did 20 years ago.

Adolescent fertility has declined in many developing and developed countries over the past 20 years. In Central America and sub—Saharan Africa, however, rates are five to seven times higher than in developed regions. Inadequate nutrition, anaemia and early pregnancies threaten the health and life of young girls and adolescents.

Too many women lack access to reproductive health services. In developing countries maternal mortality is a leading cause of death for women of reproductive age. WHO estimates that more than half a million women die each year in childbirth and millions more develop pregnancy—related health complications. The deteriorating economic and health conditions in sub—Saharan Africa led to an increase in maternal mortality during the 1980s, where it remains the highest in the world. An African woman's lifetime risk of dying from pregnancy-related causes is 1 in 23, while a North American woman's is 1 in 4,000. Maternal mortality also increased in some countries of eastern Europe.

Pregnancy and childbirth have become safer for women in most of Asia and in parts of Latin America. In developed countries attended delivery is almost universal, but in developing countries only 55 per cent of births take place with a trained attendant and only 37 per cent in hospitals or clinics. Today new importance is being placed on women's reproductive health and safe motherhood as advocates work to redefine reproductive health as an issue of human rights.

The Programme of Action of the International Conference on Population and Development set forth a new framework to guide government actions in population, development and reproductive health—and to measure and evaluate programmes designed to realize these objectives. Instead of the traditional approach centered on family planning and population policy objectives, governments are encouraged to develop client —centered management information systems in population and development and particularly reproductive health, including family planning and sexual health programmes.

Fewer marriages—smaller households

Rapid population changes, combined with many other social and economic changes, are being accompanied by considerable changes in women's household and family status. Most people still marry but they marry later in life, especially women. In developing regions, consensual unions and other non-formal unions remain prevalent, especially in rural areas.

As a result of these changes, many women— many more women than men—spend a significant part of their life without a partner, with important consequences for their economic welfare and their children's.

In developed regions, marriage has become both less frequent and less stable, and cohabitations is on the rise. Marriages preceded by a period of cohabitations have clearly increased in many countries of northern Europe. And where divorce once led quickly to remarriage, many postpone marriage or never remarry.

Since men have higher rates of remarriage, marry at an older age, and have a shorter life expectancy, most older men are married, while many older women are widows. Among women 60 and older, widowhood is significant everywhere—from 40 per cent in the developed regions and Latin America to 50 per cent in Africa and Asia. Moreover, in Asia and Africa, widowhood also affects many women at younger ages.

Between 1970 and 1990 household size decreased significantly in the developed regions, in Latin America and the Caribbean and in eastern and south—eastern Asia. Households are the smallest in developed regions, having declined to an average of 2.8 persons per household in 1990. In eastern Asia the average household size has declined to 3.7, in south—eastern Asia to 4.9. In Latin American countries the average fell to 4.7 persons per household, and in the Caribbean to 4.1. In northern African countries household size increased on average from 5.4 to 5.7.

In developed countries the decline in the average household size reflects an increase in the number of one—person households, especially among unmarried adults and the elderly. In developing regions the size of the household is more affected by the number of children, although a shift from extended households to nuclear households also has some effect.

Household size remains high in countries where fertility has not yet fallen significantly—for instance, in some of the African and western Asian countries.

Work—paid and unpaid

Women's access to paid work is crucial to their self—reliance and the economic well—being of dependent family members. But access to such work is unequal between women and men. Women work in different occupations than men, almost always with lower status and pay.

In developing countries many women work as unpaid family labourers in subsistence agriculture and household enterprises. Many women also work in the informal sector, where their remuneration is unstable, and their access to funds to improve their productivity is limited at best. And whatever other work women do, they also have the major responsibility for most household work, including the care of children and other family members.

The work women do contributes substantially to the well—being of families, communities and nations. But work in the household—even when it is economic—is inadequately measured, and this subverts policies for the credit, income and security of women and their families.

Over the past two decades, women's reported economic activity rates increased in all regions except sub—Saharan Africa and eastern Asia, and all of these increases are large except in eastern Europe, central Asia and Ocean. In fact, women's labour force participation increased more in the 1980s than in the 1970s in many regions. In contrast, men's economic activity rates have declined everywhere except central Asia.

The decline in women's reported labour force participation in sub—Saharan Africa stands out as an exception—dropping from a high of 57 per cent in 1970 to 54 per cent in 1980 to 53 per cent in 1990.

In 1990 the average labour force participation rate among women aged 15 and over ranged from a high of 56—58 per cent in eastern and central Asia and eastern Europe to a low in northern Africa of 21 per cent. The participation rates of men vary within a more limited range of 72—83 per cent. Because so many women in developing countries work in agriculture and informal household enterprises where their contributions are underreported, their recorded rates of economic activity should be higher in many cases. The estimated increase in southern Asia—from 25 per cent of women economically active in 1970 to 44 per cent in 1990—may be due largely to changes in the statistical methods used rather than to significant changes in work patterns.

Although work in subsistence production is crucial to survival, it goes largely underreported in population and agricultural surveys and censuses.

Most of the food eaten in agricultural households in developing countries is produced within the family holding, much of it by women. Some data show the extent of women's unreported work in agriculture. In Bangladesh, India and Pakistan, government surveys using methods to improve the measurement of subsistence work, report that more than half of rural women engage in such activities as tending poultry or cattle, planting rice, drying seeds, collecting water and preparing dung cakes for fuel. Direct observation of women's activities suggests that almost all women in rural areas contribute economically in one way or another.

The informal sector—working on own -account and in small family enterprises—also provides women with important opportunities in areas where salaried employment is closed or inadequate. In five of the six African countries studied by the Statistical Division of the United Nations Secretariat, more than one third of women economically active outside agriculture work in the informal sector, and in seven countries of Latin America 15-20 per cent. In nine countries in Asia the numbers vary—from less than 10 per cent of economically active women in western Asia to 41 per cent in the Republic of Korea and 65 per cent in Indonesia.

Although fewer women than men participate in the labour force, in some countries—including Honduras, Jamaica and Zambia—more women than men make up the informal sector labour force. In several other countries, women make up 40 per cent or more of the informal sector.

In addition to the invisibility of many of women's economic activities, women remain responsible for most housework, which also goes unmeasured by the System of National Accounts. But time—use data for many developed countries show almost everywhere that women work at least as many hours each week as men, and in a large number of countries they work at least two hours more than men. Further, the daily time a man spends on work tends to be the same throughout his working life. But a woman's working time fluctuates widely and at times is extremely heavy—the result of combining paid work, household and child—care responsibilities.

Two thirds to three quarters of household work in developed regions is performed by women. In most countries studied, women spend 30 hours or more on housework each week while men spend around 10 hours. Among household tasks, the division of labour remains clear and definite in most countries. Few men do the laundry, clean the house, make the beds, iron the clothes. And most women do little household repair and maintenance. Even when employed outside the home, women do most of the housework.

Efforts to generate better statistics

The first world conference on women in Mexico in 1975 recognized the importance of improving statistics on women. Until the early 1980s women's advocates and women's offices were the main forces behind this work. Big efforts had not yet been launched in statistical offices—either nationally or internationally.

The collaboration of the Statistical Division of the United Nations Secretariat with the International Research and Training Institute for the Advancement of Women (INSTRAW) —beginning in 1982—on a training programme to promote dialogue and understanding between policy makers and statisticians, laid the groundwork for a comprehensive programme of work.

By the time of the world conference in Nairobi in 1985 some progress was evident. The Statistical Division compiled 39 key statistical indicators on the situation of women for 172 countries, and important efforts at the national level included the preparation of *Women and Men* in Sweden, first published in 1984 and with sales of 100,000.

Since Nairobi numerous developments have stregthened and given new momentum to this work. The general approach in development strategy has moved from women in development to gender and development. The focus has shifted from women in isolation to women in relation to men—to the roles each has, the relationships between them and different impacts of policies and programmes.

In statistics the focus has likewise moved from attention to women's statistics to gender statistics. There now is a recognition, for example, that biases in statistics apply not only to women but also to men—in their roles as husbands and fathers and in their roles in the household. That recognition reaches beyonds the disaggregation of data by sex to assessing statistical systems in terms of gender. It asks:

—Do the topics investigated on statistics and the concepts and definitions used in data collection reflect the diversities of women's and men's lives?

—Will the methods used in collecting data take into account stereotypes and cultural factors that might produce bias?

—Are the ways data are compiled and presented well suited to the needs of policy makers, planners and others who need such data?

The first World's Women: Trends and Statistics, issued in 1991, presented the most comprehensive and authoritative compilations of global indicators on the status of women ever available. The book's data have informed debates at international conferences and national policy meetings and provided a resource to the press and others. Its publication greatly contributed to the understanding of data users and created, for the first time, a substantial global audience for statistical genderbased information. This audience has demanded, in turn, more and better data. The book also stimulated more work on the compilation of statistics and led to The World's Women 1995 being prepared as an official conference document for the Fourth World Conference on Women in Beijing in 1995.

As gender issues receive greater priority in the work programmes of international organizations, support to the Statistical Division of the United Nations Secretariat and to national efforts to improve this work have gathered strength at UNFPA, UNICEF, UNDP, WFP, UNIFEM and INSTRAW, among others, ILO, FAO, WHO, UNESCO and UNHCR are also rethinking statistical recommendations and guidelines in their work to better understand women's activities and situations, and products of this change are evident in The World's Women 1995.

The World's Women 1995 shows considerable development in the statistics available on women and men—and in ways of presenting them effectively. But it also points to important needs for new work—to be addressed in the Platform for Action of the Fourth World Conference on Women. Some problems identified by the first world conference—such as the measurement of women's economic contribution and the definition of the concepts of household and household head—are still unresolved. But significant improvements have been made in many areas. Data users know much more today than 20 years ago about how women's and men's situations differ in social, political and economic life. And consumers of data are also asking many more questions that are increasing the demand for more refined statistics. Still other areas not commonly addressed in the regular production of official statistics have only begun to be explored: the male role in the family, women in poverty and women's human rights, including violence against women.

Important in today's more in-depth approach are:

—Identification of the data needed to understand the disparities in the situation, contributions and problems of women and men.

—Evaluation of existing concept and methods against today's changed realities.

—Development of new concepts and methods to yield unbiased data.

—The preparation of statistics in formats easily accessible to a wide array of users.

None of this is easy—or without cost. Every step requires considerable efforts and expertise. All require integrated approaches that pull together today's often fragmented, specialized efforts and take a fresh look at methods and priorities—in, say, education, employment, criminal justice, business, credit and training. All require a broader, more integrated treatment of social and economic data. And all require special efforts to improve international comparability. But required above all—for true national, regional and global assessments of the social, political and economic lives of women and men—is agreement on what the key issues are and support for how to address them.

The objectives is always to produce timely statistics on women and men that can inform policy, refine strategy and influence practice. After two decades of efforts, improved gender statistics are doing much to inform policy debate and implementation. But to proved truly effective monitoring at all leaves requires continuity and reinforcing the dialogue between statisticians and the consumers of statistics—policy makers, researchers, advocates and the media.

ed efforts to improve international comparability—is required both for the national, regional and global assessments of the social, political and economic lives of women and men—is agreement on what the key issues are and support for how to address them.

The objective is always to produce timely statistics on women and men that can inform policy, refine strategy and reflect on practice. After two decades of efforts, improved gender statistics are doing much to inform policy debate and implementation. But to prove truly effective, monitoring at all levels requires continuity and reinforcing the dialogue between statisticians and the consumers of statistics—policy makers, researchers, advocates and the media.

WORLDWIDE FACTS AND STATISTICS ABOUT THE STATUS OF WOMEN

Introduction

Women perform an estimated 60 percent of the world's work but own only one percent of the world's land and earn just 10 percent of the world's income.

The first United Nations world conference on women convened in Mexico City. Prior to that conference, almost no research had been done nor were statistics available that could support the position that there were serious problems worldwide related to equity for women.

The following statistics are a telling sample of facts taken from the massive body of research done by UNDP (United Nations Development Programme) to illustrate the plight of women worldwide. They were also culled from a variety of other sources, including articles appearing in the New York Times; the Chicago Tribune; Self Magazine; Reuters; The Guardian: Vital Signs 1995 (Worldwatch Institute); The Progress of Nations (UN Children's Fund publication); The American Woman 1990-91 (Women's Research and Education Institute); From Cairo to Beijing (Pew Global Stewardship Initiative); and PRB Media Guide to Women's Issues 1995 (Population Reference Bureau).

Poverty

* Almost 1/2 of poor families in the US are supported by single women with an average income 23% below the poverty line. The growth of single-parent homes headed by women has contributed to the feminization of poverty.
* The feminization of poverty is a growing phenomenon. The immediate cause is the migration or desertion of the male head of household

so the burden of family support falls on women.

* 1/4 of families worldwide are headed by women.
* Women constitute nearly 60% of the world's one billion poor. Rural women living in absolute-poverty rose by 50% over the last two decades.
* Out of 1/3 billion people living in absolute poverty, over 70% are women.
* In countries with economies in transition, women have become the major victims of unemployment with a 14% unemployment rate as compared to 9% among men.
* There are 4 times as many widows as widowers worldwide, many ill, elderly, and living in poverty.

Education

* Women continue to be denied equal quality education especially in science and technology.
* In Pakistan, as recently as 1990, 72% of secondary vocational schools barred women.
* Women represent 2/3 of more than one billion adult illiterates who have no access to basic education. The majority live in rural areas.
* 2/3 of adult women in Southern Asia are illiterate.
* In sub-Saharan Africa, South Asia, Latin America and the Caribbean, less than 1/2 the female entrants in Grade 1 finish Grade 5.
* Girls' enrollment in primary school has reached parity with boys in most regions, but not in Africa or Asia—out of more than 900 million illiterate adults, two out of three are women.
* The rate of female illiteracy in Rumania is 35%—twice that of men
* On average, by the age of 18, girls have received 4.4 years less education than boys.

Health

* Annually, 1/2 million women die from pregnancy complications and 100,000 from unsafe abortions.
* Women now constitute 40% of HIV- infected adults worldwide.
* In Bangladesh, Maldives, and Nepal, female life expectancy is lower than that of the male.
* A pregnant African woman is 180 times more likely to die than a Western European pregnant woman.
* In some African countries, the chances that a woman entering her reproductive years will not survive them is 1 in 6 because almost 1/2 the births are delivered by untrained birth attendants.

* In Sub-Saharan Africa, unlike any other region, the percentage of women infected with HIV is as high if not higher than men.
* In the Republic of Korea, only half as many girls as boys were brought for measles immunization after a small fee was introduced.
* In South Africa, 1,000 pregnancies are terminated legally and between 42,000-167,000 pregnancies are terminated illegally.
* In Albania, the maternal mortality rate, (57 per 100,000 live births), is the highest in Europe.
* Fertility is Sub-Saharan Africa is highest in the world at about six children per woman.

Violence

Violence against women emerges as a truly universal issue, crossing cultural, geographical, racial, class, religious, and ethnic boundaries. Existing laws in many countries offer only limited protection for women. Domestic violence is often regarded as a "private family matter"

* A woman is beaten every 18 minutes and raped every 6 minutes in the U.S. More women are injured in domestic violence incidents than in car accidents, rapes and muggings put together.
* 3-4 million women are battered each year worldwide.
* Battered women are 12 times more likely to commit suicide than other women.
* 1 in 6 woman are victims of rape in industrialized countries.
* Reports from France indicate that 95% of its victims of violence are women, 51% at the hands of their husbands.
* 1/5 to 1/2 of women experience some degree of domestic violence during marriage worldwide.
* In Uganda, a husband's right to "control" his wife by beating is recognized in customary law. Beating are often supervised by neighbours and relatives so that they do not exceed a "reasonable" threshold.
* More than half of all murders of women in Bangladesh, Brazil, Kenya, Papua New Guinea and Thailand were committed by present or former partners.
* In 1993, 14,000 Russian women died because of family violence and another 56,000 were wounded.
* Under Bolivian law, lesions caused by husbands in domestic violence are punishable only if they incapacitate the women for more than 30 days, Bolivia specifically permits the maltreatment of women by all male relatives, (husband, father, brother, brother-in-law, son, etc.), so long as wounds produced are not "grave". The maximum sentence

for wife abuse is 30 days of community service.

* In Brazil, husbands have a customary "right to honor" which he may preserve by beating, or even killing his wife, if circumstance so warrant. The "honor-defense" has been a successful plea in approximately 80% of wife-murder cases.
* In Haiti, Paraguay and Venezuela, criminal law excuses the murder of a woman by her husband if she is caught in the act of adultery. This does not apply to a husband caught in a similar situation.
* In Bangladesh, India and Sri Lanka, in cases of rape, a woman's character and sexual history are pertinent evidence and the burden of proof, establishing lack of consent, falls largely on the woman.
* In rape cases in Pakistan, "Four pious males" must witness complete penetration and testify in court. If witnesses are not available and if a woman's accusations of rape cannot be corroborate, her statements can be used as a confession of illicit sex, punishable by death under the Hadood Ordinance of 1979.
* Testing for genetic defects is used to determine the sex of an unborn child which may be aborted if it is a girl in several countries.
* In rural China, women are still sold to husbands they never met. One in three wives report being beaten by her husband at one stage of marriage.

Armed and other conflicts

* Women and their dependents constitute 80% of the world's 23 million refugees, suffering physical disabilities, lifetime traumas from witnessing atrocities, homelessness, illiteracy, illness, and poverty.
* Women traditionally have no role in decisions leading to confiicts but are left to maintain families.
* Women are often victims of torture, disappearance and systematic rape as a weapon of war. At the same time, they have had no input in decisions regarding internal and regional conflicts.
* The vast majority of millions of homeless refugees in the Sub-Shara are women and children.

Economic Disparity

Job opportunities for women have generally been confined to clerks, sales persons, maids, household worker and the informal sector. They receive lower wages than men for equal work and drop in and out of labor forces because of child bearing and rearing responsibilities.

* $ 11 trillion is missing from the global economy each year because

of unpaid housework, childcare, agricultural and other labour performed by women.

* Wages for women lag behind men for similar works in ALL countries—(the average is 30-40% less than men for comparable work).
* In the UK, women earn on average 70% of men's wages; in Kenya, 74%; in Brazil, 51%; in the Republic of Korea, 51%; in Japan, 43%.
* Women work longer hours than men in almost all countries except Peru. Women put in 12% more time than men in market activities and household work taken together. In rural areas, total work time is much longer (around 20%) than in urban areas.
* In Sub-Saharan Africa, women's labour force dropped over the past 2 decades, the only region where this occurred.
* 95% of street food vendors in Nigeria are women.
* The largest informal sector activity employing women is subsistence agriculture.
* In rural areas of developing countries, women devote more than 10 times as many hours as men, (9.7 hours versus 0.9 hours), collecting fuelwood and water.
* In N. Africa and western Asia women are entering the labour force in increasing numbers, but they are still the lowest in the world.

Governance and Politics

* In 1993, there were only six female heads of government worldwide.
* Worldwide, only 1 elected politician in 9 is a woman.
* Over 100 countries worldwide have no women in parliament at all.
* The highest number of women in the US Congress at any one time was during the 1961-62 session, when 20 served.
* Only six out of 185 member countries of the UN have a woman Permanent Representative.
* Women represent only 22% of total diplomatic staff in UN missions.
* There is better parliamentary representation in developing nations, (12%) than in industrialized nations, (9%).
* Female representation in government: Latin American/Caribbean countries (10%); Sub-Saharan (8%); Middle East/North Africa (3%); S. Asia (5%); East Asia/Pacific (9%); industrialized countries, (18%).
* Baharain, Kuwait and the United Arab Emirates continue to deny women the right to vote or stand for election.
* In the US, women in the current Congress comprise slightly over 11% in the House and 7% in the Senate.
* In Eastern Europe, women's participation in parliament dropped sharply, (from 22% in 1987 to 6.5% in 1993), largely as a result of

the collapse of communism and the elimination of quotas for women in parliament.

National and International Institutions

* National institutions for the advancement of women lack financial and human resources to perform adequately, disseminate information, or develop educational programs in almost every nation.

Human Rights

* Women are often unable to exercise their rights due to lack of awareness of international and national laws plus no commitment by governments and communities to uphold them.
* In many countries, such as Canada, husbands may apply for citizenship for a foreign-born spouse after one year of marriage, but wives must wait two years.
* A husband's consent is necessary for his wife to obtain a passport but not vice-versa in countries such as Egypt, Morocco, and Saudi Arabia.
* Women cannot leave the country without their spouse's permission but men can in Iran and Saudi Arabia.
* Men can bring foreign-born wives and children into Switzerland and other countries but women don't have the same right.
* Married women are under permanent guardianship of their husbands and have no right to manage property in many countries including Botswana, Chile, Lesotho, Namibia, and Swaziland.
* Husbands can restrict wife's outside employment but wives have no such right in several countries.
* A father's presence is mandatory at his daughter's marriage but not at his son's in several middle Eastern countries.
* Women cannot remarry for six months after a divorce but men can in Japan.
* Under Muslim law, daughters inherit only 1/2 the son's share.
* Under Hindu law, women have no right to inherit paternal property.
* Women have no right to abort in cases of rape or incest in many countries around the world.
* Women married to foreigners cannot transfer citizenship to husbands though men can do so in a similar situation in Algeria, Bahamas, Egypt, Morocco, Turkey and Yemen.
* Africa women produce 78% of the continent's food (meat as well as staple grains)—on subsistence plots to which the vast majority hold no title. They receive only 2-13% of the technical assistance and training.

* In Bangladesh, women wage-earners in poor households have only 1.3 meals a day as compared to 2.4 eaten by men.
* When poverty threatens or strikes, women's assets are often sold before those of men in the developing world.
* Dowry related abuse is common in many countries. The most extreme is "bride burning", where women are burnt to death (usually in a kitchen, to make it seem like an accident with a stove) by husbands or in-laws.
* A 1993 police study in the Philippines found that 80% of rape reports and data on other forms of violence against women, such as battering, harassment or verbal abuse, were omitted from police records and crime index tables. (Since that study was released, more than 160 women's desks have been established in police stations, staffed by over 275 policewomen).

Mass Media

* Media in most countries provide distorted, stereotyped images of women.
* Women's share of jobs is consistently low, (under 25% in Africa, Asia and Latin America, and the Caribbean for press and broadcasting; 30% for press and 36% for broadcasting in Europe).
* A ten-country UNESCO study shows that only 1.4% of TV news items deal with women's issues.
* In Asia, news decisions are still made by men even if news is reported and edited by women. Most 'soft sections', (weekend supplements, health, culture and education) are almost exclusively run by women whereas defense, commerce and foreign affairs are largely male strongholds.
* Out of 200 organizations studied in 30 countries (The World's Women: Trends and Statistics: 1970-1995) only seven were headed by women.

Environment and Development

* Women account for 1/2 the food production in developing countries
* In some African countries, women have to walk 10 kilometers or more to fetch water and fuel.
* In India, women rovide 75% of the labor for transplanting and weeding rice, 60% for harvesting and 33% for threshing.
* Much soil conservation in East Africa over the past decades has been done by women.
* Deforestation has created hardships on women forced to trek up

mountains for water each day in several countries, like the Himalayas, Mozambique and Senegal.

* Millions of women spend many hours a day walking long distances for supplies of unsafe water. And it is usually women who cope with family illness that results from drinking it. Infected water in Africa and Asia is responsible for diseases such as guinea worm disease, infecting approximately 3 million adults and children.

The Girl Child

* In the US, increasing levels of sexually-transmitted diseases have been reported among children under 14.
* The US rate of teenage pregnancy is the worst among industrialized nations at nearly 12%—one million girls per years.
* Girls constitute the majority of 130 million children worldwide who have no access to primary school.
* 1/3 of women worldwide report sexual abuse during childhood or adolescence.
* An estimated 85-114 million girls suffer forced genital mutilation worldwide. Most live in Africa, a few in Asia and, in recent years, cases have been reported in Europe, Canada and the US, where several immigrant African populations have settled.
* In some countries, testing for genetic defects is used to determine the sex of an unborn child which may be aborted if it is a girl.
* In India's match factories, girls below the age of 15 work for up to 10 hours a day.
* Poverty is the parent of child prostitution since children are often sold into prostitution for money.
* An estimated one million children are forced into child prostitution annually, with the majority being girls, Asia has the most child prostitutes.
* In Italy, a child prostitute, not the adult client is held legally and criminally responsible.
* The Aids epidemic has led to increased demand for child prostitutes. The accepted client superstition is that the younger the child, the smaller the risk of exposure to the Aids virus. This is not true.
* 1/2 women give birth before the age of 18 in several African countries where the maternal death rate is three times higher for teenage mothers than for women in the 20-29 age group.
* Although genetic testing for sex selection and aborting female foetuses has been banned in India under recent legislation and in China since January 1995, it is still a lucrative underground business in

these countries.

* In some countries, a bias in favour of males determines nutritional intake. The typical girl in these countries, according to UNICEF's 1989 Annual Report, receives 20% fewer calories than her brother and is more likely to be malnour rished. In one rigion of India girls were 4 times more likely than boys to suffer from acute malnutrition, and 40 times less likely to be taken to a hospital.
* In southern Asia, 41% of girls aged 15-19 are already married and adolescent fertility remains high.

Worldwide Breakthroughs since the first United Nations Women's Conference held in 1975

"Over the past 20 years, doors to education and health have opened rapidly for women, but the doors to economic and political power are barely ajar."

—*Mahbub ul Haq*, former Pakistani finance minister and principal author, UNDP Annual Report, 1995.

* The most dramatic movements toward equity for women over the past twenty years has been made in developing countries. Two countries that have made considerable progress towards protecting women's rights and establishing legal equality between women and men are Tunisia and India.
* Females advanced twice as fast as males in literacy and school enrollment in developing countries.
* With scarce resources and a strong political commitment, China raised women's literacy rates from virtually complete illiteracy 50 years ago to more than 82% literacy among adult women.
* Twelve other developing countries raised female literacy by more than 30 points in the last twenty years and several of the world's poórest nations have achieved females literacy rates of 75% or more.
* Between 1970 and 1990, the former People's Democratic Republic of Yemen, one of the poorest countries in the world, experienced the fastest increase in female school enrollment at the rate of 17% annually.
* In the U.S., 21% of state legislators are now women-a five-fold increase since 1969.
* Women's life expectancy increased nine years in developing countries, 20% faster than the increase in men's.
* Maternal mortality rates nearly halved worldwide.
* In industrial countries, the proportion of women administrators and

managers has nearly tripled from 15% in 1970 to 40% in 1990.

* In many Nordic countries, near-equality is being achieved by women who are accessing economic and political opportunities.
* In September, 1994, Sweden voted women into 41% of its parliamentary seats—currently the world's highest. The incoming government also appointed women to 7 out of the 17 available cabinet positions.
* Bangladesh has 30 national seats reserved for women and the highest percentage of women parliamentarians in South Asia.
* Contraceptive use has increased substantially over the last two decades with more than 1/2 of married women in the developing world using modern contraceptives in 1990 compared to less than 1/4 in 1980.
* Three million children have been saved each year through the extension of basic immunization facilities developed during the last two decades.
* More than 1/3 of the labour force in Latin America and Caribbean countries is female.
* Female representation in parliaments in East Asia is twice the level achieved in the industrial world.
* In South Africa, in the struggle against apartheid, approximately 30% of the members of the now ruling ANC were women. They campaigned for, and succeeded in getting the government to set aside August 9 as National Women's Day.

LEGAL LITERACY: PUTTING AN END TO DISCRIMINATION

Discrimination still persists in all countries—sometimes blatantly, often in subtle nuances and ingrained attitudes. Yet, looking back over time, there has been progress. Amongst both women and men, gender equality is gradually acquiring a legitimacy of its own. This new sense of awareness has been heralded by many as the ground swell of a major social revolution.

The Legal concept of gender equality

In the context of international human rights, the legal concept of gender equality is enshrined in the 1948 *Universal Declaration of Human Rights, as well as in the 1979 United Nations Convention on the Elimination of All Forms of Discrimination against Women.*

The Convention, which has been ratified by over 100 countries, states clearly and unequivocally that "discrimination against women violates the principles of equality of rights and respect for human dignity"[1].

Often described as an "international bill of rights for women", this Convention provides for women's civil rights and their legal equality in all fields. It is the only international human rights treaty to affirm the reproductive rights of women and to target culture and tradition as influential forces shaping gender roles and family relations. It also establishes an agenda for national action to end discrimination. This multidimensional approach makes the Convention a landmark treaty in the struggle to end discrimination based on sex.

The legacy of tradition

Once upon a time, women enjoyed a wide range of rights, including access to citizenship, education and political power. In ancient Egypt, Celtic Britain and Japan, for example, queens and empresses ruled their empires while men served in subordinate roles. Women also had the right to own property and money: Spartan women owned two thirds of the land, Arab women owned herds which were tended by their husbands, Egyptian women could charge their spouses interest on money lent to them, and Babylonian women had exclusive rights over their dowries.[2]

Marriage was a contract between equal partners that guaranteed each party's individual rights. Women had the right to divorce, in which case they got custody of the children and were entitled to alimony. An ancient Egyptian marriage vow even seems matriarchal given modern biases. The man's vow was as follows: "I bow before your rights as a wife. From this day on, I shall never oppose your claims with a single word. I recognize you before all others as my wife, though I do not have the right to say you must be mine, and only I am your husband and mate. You alone have the right of departure...I cannot oppose your wish wherever you desire to go....."[3]

Women in these societies were not restricted to the home but enjoyed substantial physical and sexual freedoms. Their rights were enshrined in social custom and legal codes. Most importantly, women were aware of these rights and exercised them fully.

However, the fabric of society was altered with the advent of monotheistic religions which were often interpreted in ways that devalued and subjugated women[4]. To cite some extreme examples of the kind of distortions which resulted in discrimination: "A woman's heaven is under her husband's feet", according to one Bengali proverb. "The body of a woman is filthy, and not a vessel for the low", [5] Buddha was quoted to have said. "Blessed art thou, O Lord our God, King of the Universe, who has not made me a woman",[6] is attributed to one Hebrew prayer. "A necessary object, woman, who is needed to preserve the species or to provide food and drink", wrote Thomas Aquinas, for "man is above woman as Christ is above man. It is unchangeable that woman is destined to live underman's influence, and has no authority from her lord."[7]

As a result, women were stripped of their rights before the law, including: the right of choice and security in Marriage; the right to property and inheritance; the right to control their bodies; the right to education and, in some cases, employment; as well as the right to their individual identities. The incorporation of women's objectification within the legal codes and laws legitimized their subordination. The social conditioning upon which the entrenchment of women's inferior status depended plunged them into a virtual non-status. In effect, the law became an instrument of control, inhibiting access to economic and social resources, as well as to political power, while sanctioning social values that upheld discriminatory structures and relations.

Equality in Theory, Inequality in Practice

Against this backdrop, it is not surprising that despite significant progress in the status of women vis-a-vis the law in recent years, equality continues to elude the vast majority of women. Even though all developed countries have adopted legislation or constitutional provisions to ensure women's equality under the law, in practice discrimination persists. As George Orwell put it in *Animal Farm*: "All animals are equal, but some animals are more equal than others."[8]

This metaphor accurately reflects the discrepancy between the equality guaranteed women by law and their actual status in society. The right to vote, reforms in family law and legislation on equal pay have not always translated into better conditions for women, nor have they necessarily improved the quality of their lives. A case in point is Bangladesh, where constitutional equality and affirmative action programmes exist on paper, yet the statistics reveal a grim picture: namely, that Bangladeshi women are worse off than most other women in the world.[9] In a global comparison of the status of women based on indicators of health, marriage and children, education, employment and social equality, prepared by the Population Crisis Committee, Bangladesh received the lowest score.[10]

The underlying reasons for the discrepancy in the status of women are as varied as they are complex. Firstly, discriminatory or unjust laws continue to be passed. Secondly, even where legal reforms exist, governments often lack the political and economic commitment to enforce them. In spite of the creation of women's ministries or other specialized agencies in many countries around the world, women's issues invariably remain a low priority. Social structures often reinforce biased attitudes in applying the law. Thirdly, when prejudice is deeply ingrained in the social fabric, new laws pertaining to women's issues are slow to be implemented without continued public pressure. Cultural beliefs and traditions that discriminated against women may be officially discredited but continue to flourish at the grass-roots level. Often, old laws are not repealed to make way for new legislation. Fourthly, personal, customary and religious law often conflict with civil law and end up outweighing government policies. Fifthly, most countries lack empirical data on the law and how it functions in society, which is crucial for any change in the legal system.

Lastly, but most importantly, legal reforms have often been adopted in a vacuum, without actually involving those concerned or mobilizing public opinion as a whole. As a result, many women, particularly in the developing world, are not even aware of their rights before the law or else do not understand the legal and administrative process well enough to be able to exercise those rights.

Thus, the first step towards the elimination of discrimination and the empowerment of women lies in educating them on the existence and extent of their legal rights. In Sierra Leone, a project entitled "Literacy and Civil Education for Women" is training 2,000 women on constitutional rights and duties.[11] Similar legal literacy programmes aimed at reaching people at the grass-roots level could make all the difference in translating legal and constitutional equality into reality.

The next step would be to offer women free legal services to ensure protection of their rights. Some 45 countries—30 of them in the developing world—already provide such services.[12]

However, it is not yet clear how many women actually benefit from them, given problems of access and dissemination of information, which are particularly accentuated in rural areas of developing countries. Judging from the case of China, however, which successfully set up advisory agencies at the county level in 1983 to provide women with legal counsel, such schemes could be highly effective.[13]

A concerted and systematic world-wide effort is imperative to promote legal literacy and to create the requisite legal infrastructure to forge links between individual women and national machineries in each country.

Finally, it is essential that men learn to recognize and respect women's equality before the law. "No fundamental change in favour of women is possible without a massive change in male attitudes," argues Dr. Nafis Sadik, Executive Director of the United Nations Population Funds. "This is more than a philosophical point: men control the legal, administrative and financial systems which effectively deny a vast number of women the right to own land, inherit property, establish credit, enter the professions or rise in business."

Sex stereotypes

Sex stereotyping, possibly the most effective propaganda instrument of the patriarchal status quo, is among the most firmly entrenched obstacles to the elimination of discrimination and is largely responsible for the denigration of the role and potential of women in society. Traditional male/female roles have been deeply ingrained and glorified in language, education, the mass media. advertising and the arts to such an extent that even women have become desensitized to their own inferior portrayal.

Language being the primary means of communication the world over, it is a good point of departure for any discussion of sex stereotypes. Compare and contrast the definitions of woman and man in the 1975 edition of Roget's Thesaurus, English Words and Phrases:

> "Women, Eve, she; petticoat, skirt; girl, virgin, maiden....ma'am, *spinster,* co-ed, undergraduette; lady; bride, matron....*spouse;* mother......*parent;* wench, lass, nymph; dame....*teacher;* blonde, brunette; sweetheart, bird....*loved one;* moll, doll, broad, mistress.....*loose woman;* quean, *shrew virago, amazon."*

> "**man**, he, virility, manliness, masculinity, manhood; mannishness, virginity, gynandry; he-man, cave-m.; gentleman, sir, esquire....*title;* wight, fwllow, guy, blade, bloke, beau, chap. cove, card, chappie, johnny, buffer; gaffer, goodman, male relation.....*kindmsn,*....parent.....*youngster,*..... son-ship,....spouse; bachelor; stag party, menfolk."

The difference in criteria and in the associations evoked by each definition is striking in the above entries. While those of **man** are essentially dynamic and laudatory, the definitions of **woman** speak for themselves.

Even more eloquent is the definition in the **Oxford English Dictionary**: **Woman**: "with allusion to qualities generally attributed to the female sex, as mutability, capriciousness, proneness to tears; also to their position of inferiority or subjection (phr. to make a woman of, to bring into submission)."[14]

It should hardly be surprising then that society's perceptions of women are for the most part negative. At best, women are perceived as mothers and "angels at the hearth", their professional and other capabilities going virtually unnoticed. Often, they are considered no more than housewives or dispensable sex objects. If they are clever, they can earn a reputation for their "charm, beauty, frivolity, {and} fragility".[15]

Significantly, even before the law, the judiciary may be influenced by these biases: "It is well known that women in particular and small boys are liable to be untruthful and invent stories,"[16] argued judge Sutcliffe of the Old Bailey as recently as 1976. This point was even more forcefully illustrated at a 1988 trial examining a gang rape case involving a 30 year old Italian woman, in which the defense declared, "All women are liars, it's a known scientific fact."[17]

The above examples of male perceptions of women underscore the extent to which women's contributions to society have been ignored and downplayed in modern times in sharp contrast to a demographic finding from the United Nations Decade for Women which said that women constitute half the world's population, perform two thirds of the world's work, but receive only one tenth of its income and own less than one one-hundredth of its property.

Sex stereotypes and social prejudices which influence legislation are all the more inappropriate considering that traditional male/female roles and male-headed families are no longer the norm. An estimated one third of households around the world are now headed by women. In the Caribbean, women constitute up to 50 percent of all heads of households and in parts of sub-Saharan Africa the figure is 45 percent. [18]

Despite rapid changes in the socio-economic structure of the family, sex stereotypes will persist unless they are counteracted. Beginning with the family unit itself, equal rights and responsibilities require that sex stereotypes be banished from labour legislation, thereby enabling women to integrate work and family-a step that will encourage men to share the household burden. Language and the law must also get rid of sex stereotyping, and school textbooks and curricula must be systematically revised.

Discrimination in Marriage and the Family

Many women in the developing world have no choice of whom or when they will marry, when they will begin to bear children or how large their families will be. In addition, while men may divorce easily, women can only rarely initiate divorce. To date, only 22 countries (most in the industrialized world) have granted women equal rights with men in matters of marriage, divorce and family property.

Women actually marry as children in many developing countries. In five Latin American states, the legal age for marriage is 12 years for females, and in another nine it is 14 years. In Africa, five countries allow girls to marry at the age of 15.[19] Some countries like Kenya have no legal age for marriage. However, even where a minium legal age for marriage exists, it is not always enforced. In India, for example, even though the law sets the legal age for marriage at 18, some 10 million girls under 11 years old get married each year.[20] Such early marriages severely restrict the range of options available to these "child brides" and may trap them prematurely within a web of poverty, illiteracy, repeated child bearing and social marginalization.

In much of the developing world, marriage and divorce laws supersede women's rights to own land, thus virtually disinheriting them. In Asia, the vast majority of women are landless as a result of discriminatory divorce and inheritance laws that do not give them access to land owned by men. In the Middle East, women are not legally autonomous individuals but need a male "guardian" to act for them in all legal transactions, including property acquisition and transfer, and applications for loans and credit. In 12 countries, the law does not allow women to seek employment, open a bank account or apply for a loan without the husband's authorization.[21] Several Islamic countries have tried to modernize family law, but reforms had an impact only where an effort was made to inform women of their rights and provide them with legal counsel.

In 1985 the Nairobi Forward-looking Strategies reiterated demands for equal status legislation with regard to marriage and its dissolution, stating that "Marriage agreements should be based on mutual understanding, respect and freedom of choice. Careful attention should be paid to the equal participation and valuation of both partners so that the value of housework is considered equivalent of financial contributions."[22]

The fact that women are most discriminated against by those with whom they are most intimate and in whom they have placed the most trust points to the urgency of exerting pressure on governments around the world to enforce women's equality in both civil and criminal law.

Discrimination in Society

The adverse effects of discrimination within marriage and the family are compounded by the economic and political discrimination which persists in society.

In the realm of economics, legislation to facilitate women's access to the means of production, paid employment, training and promotion, as well as laws guaranteeing protection and sound working conditions, have been implemented to various degrees in many countries. Some nations have even incorporated the principle of equality of opportunity in their constitutions, while others have adopted laws prohibiting discrimination in the workplace.

"[Legal] reforms should guarantee women's constitutional and legal rights in terms of access to land and other means of production and should ensure that women will control the products of their labour and their income, as well as the benefits from agricultural inputs, research, training, credits and other infranstructural facilities," stated the 1989 **World Survey on the Role of Women in Development**. [23] However, such far-reaching reforms have yet to be fully implemented anywhere in the world.

With regard to political discrimination, when the United Nations was founded in 1945, women had the right to vote on an equal basis with men in only 31 countries. Although there has been great progress, women are not yet fully enfranchised worldwide. Pockets of resistance persist. For example, in 1991 there was still one country, Kuwait, in which men had the right to vote but it was explicitly denied to women. Yet this fundamental right to vote has not automatically spurred equal representation for women in local, state and national decision-making bodies nor has it given women true political power.

A more complete discussion of the economic and political dimensions of discrimination is contained in chapters 5 and 6.

Towards the year 2000: Empowering women—

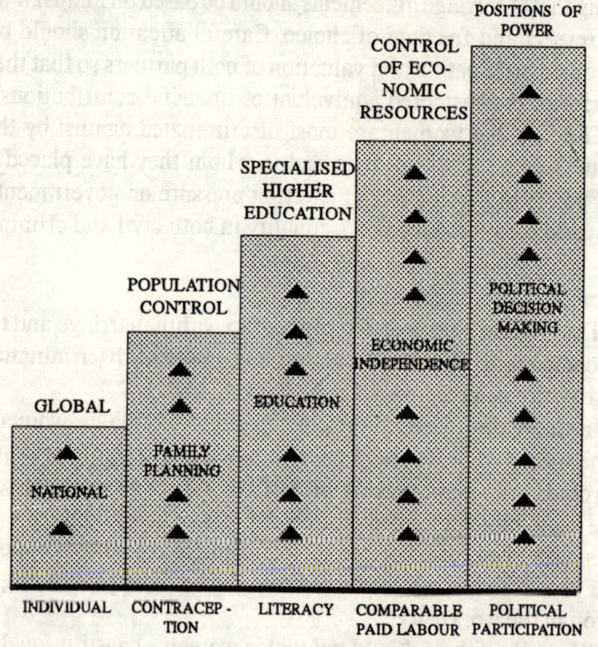

Women and the Laws in the 1990s

In order to establish an internationally recognized legal framework for women's equality, it is essential for all countries to ratify and implement the *Convention on the Elimination of All Forms of Discrimination against women*. This is an important commitment, for, as the Nairobi

Forward-looking Strategies pointed out, "Legislative enactment is only one element in the struggle for equality, but an essential one as it provides the legitimate basis for action and acts as a catalyst for societal change." [24]

A Committee on the Elimination of Discrimination against Women has been established to monitor implementation of the Convention. With the support of national governments, women's groups and non-governmental organizations, extensive legal literacy campaigns should be undertaken or intensified to reach urban as well as rural areas to inform both men and women of women's rights.

Latin America's progress in terms of legal provisions in favour of women, as well as in terms of mobilizing public opinion behind reforms, is encouraging. Today, all South American countries, with the exception of Suriname, have ratified the *Convention on the Elimination of All Forms of Discrimination against Women*. Brazil's new constitution has abolished discriminatory measures against women with regard to land ownership, social security benefits and retirement. Colombia is considering legislation which will remunerate part-time work and maternity leave. In Nicaragua, Legislation stipulates that both parents must share the responsibilities of children and housework.[25]

Yet, while constitutions may guarantee equal political rights, that does not guarantee equality between husbands and wives in other realms, as a recent study of four Latin American and Caribbean countries confirmed. Discrimination in civil law was pervasive. For example, with regard to common law unions, common property and inheritance were not clearly demarcated by the law. In Brazil, wives who were physically abused by their husbands had no legal protection, and men could invoke the "honour defense" in court to justify murdering their wives or daughters. Although the Brazilian Superior Justice Tribunal, in a landmark decision, recently rejected the honour defense as a valid legal argument, woman activist Elaine Matozinho argued that "lawyers will continue to try to convince [the jury] that the victim is the guilty one, that she is responsible for her own murder."[26]

Therefore, it is clear that in order to progress in the elimination of legal discrimination, governments must revise constitutions, laws and civil and labour codes to eliminate the legal basis for discrimination and to eradicate obstacles that do not allow women to participate in society on an equal basis with men. In addition, affirmative action programmes which link individual women with official machinery, such as offices of ombudsmen and other services giving them access to legal redress, should be established.

Social pressure, however, will continue to constitute a formidable obstacle, especially in traditional societies where inequalities are deeply ingrained in the social fabric and popular culture. As Tina Anselmi of Italy argued at the Nairobi Women's Conference, "it is not enough to change the spirit".[27] Legal literacy can go a long way towards enabling women to change the letter of the law, one must also change the spirit of the laws, exercise their rights and play a key role in the transformation of attitudes and social values.

Already, there are some positive signs. Recent reports show that women's portrayal in the media around the world is improving, albeit slowly. Substantive articles on women now appear on the front pages of newspapers; stories about successful businesswomen are becoming regular features in the mass media. In India, women scientists, writers and artists are beginning to be recognized, while in Africa, migrant women who have left their villages to make a better life for themselves and their children are popular feature subjects in the local press. [28] Also, in the United States, a growing number of television programmes are focusing on men's role as fathers—a new phenomenon which reflects the changing role of the male in many Western societies. This trend is bound to have a profound effect on men's perception of women, as well as on women's perception of themselves.

But the battle is far from won. While overall progress in women's legal rights has been heartening in recent decades, the ongoing effects of the economic crisis of the 1980s threatens to slow down or even reverse these gains. As preexisting economic inequalities intensify, goverments allocate fewer resources for women's issues, and the sense of urgency abates before an onslaught of other priorities. In addition, religious fundamentalism and ethnic revivalism in some countries are creating new obtacles to women's struggle for equality.

LEGAL CHALLENGES TO THE YEAR 2000

Governments and non-governmental organizations must mobilize behind the Convention in order to accelerate the process of legal equality between men and women and to make legal literacy a priority around the world. The tide of democratization sweeping over much of the world could well serve as a catalyst for enforcement of women's equality, if enough pressure is brought to bear upon governments for stricter adherence to already existing laws and conventions and if the challenge is answered to:

* Increase awareness among men and women of women's rights under

international conventions and national laws

* Strengthen national machineries for the advancement of women
* Ratification by all countries of the *Convention on the Elimination of All Forms of Discrimination against Women*
* Ensure equal rights for women under national laws
* Guarantee enforcement of laws safeguarding women's equality; introduce affirmative action incentives and penalties for nonadherence
* Abolish all forms of slavery and prostitution of women
* Establish a legal minimum age for marriage and ensure the mutual consent of both parties, as well as the woman's right to retain her own nationality
* Guarantee the right of all women independently to buy, sell, own, inherit and administer property and other resources
* Provide legal protection of women's equal access to land ownership, credit, training, investment and income
* Establish national machinery in all countries to implement and monitor progress towards women's equality and to provide a mechanism for redress of grievances.

NOTES

1 *Convention on the Elimination of All Forms of discrimination against Women* (DPI/993), United Nations Department of Public Information, November 1989.

2 Rosalind Miles, *The Women's History of the World*, (London: Palladin, p.48.

3 Egyptian marriage contract as recorded by Greek historian Diodorus, in Miles, op. cit., p. 49.

4 Miles, op. cit., chapter 4.

5 Quoted in Miles, op. cit., pp. 102 and 103.

6 Fidelis Morgan, *A Misogynist's Sourcebook*, (London: Jonathon Cape, 1989), p. 41.

7 Ibid., 183 and p. 17.

8 George Orwell, *Animal Farm*, 1945, in John Bartlett, Familiar Quotations.

9 *The World's Women*: 1970-1990: *Trends and Statistics*, United Nations, prepared by the Statistical Office of the Department of International Economic and Social Affairs and the Division for the Advancement of Women, New York, 1991, p. 7.

10 *Poor, Powerless and Pregnant*, Population Crisis Committee, Population Briefing Paper No. 20, and Wall chart, Washington D.C., June 1988.

11 *Literacy: Tool for Empowering Women*, (UN Focus, DPI/1075), United Nations Department of Public Information, New York, 1990, pp. 3-4.

12 Review and Appraisal: Part 1-General Development. World Conference to Review and Appraise the Achievements of the United Nations Decade for Women, Kenya, July 1985, cited in *The State of the World's Women*, United Nations Department of Public Information, 1985, p. 17.

13 *1989 World Survey on the Role of Women in Development*, United Nations Office at Vienna, Centre for Social Development and Humanitarian Affairs, New York, 1989, p.94.

14 Morgan, *A Misogynist's Sourcebook*, op. cit., p. 59.

15 As described by men in Cote d'Ivoire, in a study conducted during the United Nations Decade for Women, *The State of the World's Women*, op., cit., p. 16.

[16] Morgan, op. cit., p. 204

[17] Ibid., p. 204

[18] *The State of the World's Women*, United Nations Department of Public Information, New York, 1985, p. 76.

[19] *The State of the World Population 1990*, United Nations Population Fund, p. 15.

[20] Lawasia, June 1987, p. 6.

[21] Review and appraisal, op. cit., cited in *The State of the World's Women*, op. cit., p. 17; 1989 World Survey on the Role of Women in Development, op. cit., p. 299.

[22] *Nairobi Forward-looking Strategies for the Advancement of Women*, para. 73, p. 22, in Report of the World Conference to Review and Appraise the Achievements of the United Nations Decade for Women: Equality, Development and Peace, Nairobi, 15-26 July 1985, (United Nations publication, Sales No. E. 85. IV.10).

[23] *1989 World Survey on the Role of Women in Development*, op. cit., p. 93.

[24] *Nairobi Forward-looking Strategies for the Advancement of Women*, para. 43.

[25] *1989 World Survey on the Role of Women in Development*, op. cit., p. 93.

[26] *Time Magazine*, New York, I April 1991, p. 50.

[27] *UN Chronicle Perspective*, 1985, p. v.

[28] *1989 World Survey on the Role of Women in Development*, op. cit., pp. 292-293.

WOMEN'S HEALTH: A VITAL PREREQUISITE

WOMEN'S HEALTH: A VITAL PREREQUISITE

This bleak and poignant Truism is grim reality for more than half a million women around the world who die from complications in pregnancy, childbirth and unsafe abortions annually. Another 5 million to 7 million each year become handicapped or crippled from uterine prolapse, incontinence, infertility and other childbirth-related health impairments.[1] Ill health, much of it related to women's reproductive functions, remains one of the most important obstacles to women's development in most of the Third World.

"Over 60 per cent of all women and girls in the world live under conditions which threaten their health.....", declared a recent briefing paper entitled *Poor, Powerless and Pregnant*.[2] The ramifications of ill health for women, their families and their communities are far-reaching, given the direct correlation between a woman's health and her productivity, her capacity to care for her children properly, and her contribution to the socio-economic development of her community.

THE GLOBAL HEALTH BOOM

Over the three decades between 1950 and 1980, female health improved substantially as a result of sharp declines in the incidence of infectious and parasitic diseases, improved access to safe water, sanitation and primary health care, and better nutrition. Life expectancy at birth for women rose from 44 years in 1950 to 61 years in 1980, with the most dramatic increase recorded in Asia where life expectancy rose from 45 to 63 years for women. [3] At the same time, the average birth rate in developing countries fell from 5.9 children per mother in 1950 to 4.1 in 1980, with the most significant declines recorded in Latin America, the Caribbean and Asia. [4] Average infant mortality rates also declined from 163 per 1,000 live births in 1950 to 91 in 1980.[5]

To augment these gains, in 1978 the World Health Organization (WHO) launched a global campaign: "Health For All by the Year 2000". Its objective was the provision of global primary health care, which could solve three quarters of the world's health problems. The campaign identified improved water and sanitation, basic nutrition, immunization, and training of primary health care workers as top priorities. Women's health was not to be dealt with in a vacuum, however, argued WHO: "The anchor of our strategies for health development should relate to all-round improvements in the status of women and children, who form the majority of the population.[6]

Women as primary health care providers

The WHO campaign recognized women as the foremost providers of primary health care. In the developing world, three quarters of all health care is provided by the family, and especially by women. It is the women who fetch water, prepare meals, and feed and nurse their children, in addition to caring for the disabled, the elderly and ill members of the extended family. Mothers are also usually the ones to take their children to the health centre when they are ill or need to be immunized and they are the ones who purchase medicines. Women teach their families about hygiene and cleanliness and help introduce new health-related technologies to their communities. It is also women who bear the brunt of the responsibility for family planning.

On the community level, women form the majority of professional health workers, from traditional midwives and village healers in developing countries to nurses in the industrialized countries. In Honduras and Sierra Leone, 80 and 75 per cent of children respectively are delivered by midwives.[7]

Clean Water, Sanitation and Nutrition

In the developed world, safe water and sanitation became accessible to the vast majority of the population by the 1960s. Developing regions lag behind: 25 per cent of the people in cities and 71 per cent of rural dwellers in the developing world (excluding China) do not have access to clean drinking water, while 47 per cent of urban inhabitants and 87 per cent of the people living in rural areas are without safe sanitation, according to WHO estimates. Due to rapid population growth, these numbers are constantly rising.

The fact that the provision of water, sanitation and nutrition are women's responsibility in most developing countries gives these tasks a gender dimension that needs to be taken into account. For example, every day rural women in developing countries must walk long distances to provide their families with fresh water for drinking and cooking, as well as for cleanliness and hygiene—an exhausting task which constitutes only one of many daily responsibilities in these women's lives. In the Baroda region in India, women spend about 7 hours per week fetching water, while in rural Senegal, women spend up to 17.5 hours per week drawing and carrying water.[8] Often, the water these women draw is unsafe: an estimated 80 per cent of all disease in the world is attributed to the lack of clean drinking water and sanitation. In an attempt to remedy this acute problem, the United Nations launched the International Drinking Water Supply and Sanitation Decade in 1980.

Recalling that rural women in developing countries are the most disadvantaged in terms of access to health care, WHO's "Health for All by the Year 2000" campaign underscored the importance of primary health care workers, who began reaching women in remote areas for the first time. In addition, nutrition programmes designed to meet the needs of women were set up in 50 countries. Food supplements for pregnant women reduced the incidence of low birth weight among infants by as much as three quarters in Guatemala and other developing countries.[9]

The Effects of the Economic Crisis

The economic crisis of the 1980s, coupled with the remedial structural adjustment and stabilization programmes impeded efforts to supply clean drinking water and sanitation. It also dealt a severe blow to the health care services of developing countries, where existing facilities were still only rudimentary. Thus, economic obstacles, exacerbated by rapid population growth, undermined the objectives of "Health for All by the Year 2000". Instead,

- Some 37 of the world's poorest countries cut their health budgets by half in the mid-1980s. Africa suffered most of all the developing regions.[10]
- Ghana's per capita health expenditure in 1982 was only one fifth its 1975-76 level, while Uganda reduced its health budget from 5 per cent of total government expenditures in 1972 to 2 per cent in 1986.[11]
- At least one third of Asian and Latin American countries also re-

duced their public expenditures devoted to health.

These cuts are hard to justify in countries which increased military expenditures during the same period. Thus, while in 1960 only two African countries, Egypt and Ethiopia, spent more for the military than for health and education combined, by 1986 the list also included Angola, Burundi, Chad, the Sudan, Ugandá and Zaire[12]—some of the continent's poorest countries.

Overall, the 1980s—called by many the "lost decade"—witnessed a notable decline in the provision of health care for people in developing countries, especially for those most at risk: women and their dependent children. "Women's health has been adversely affected by increased hours of work and by reduced availability of food and health care facilities. Less healthy women are less efficient and this reduces their productivity in each of their roles, thereby diminishing national income and national welfare," a recent report of a Commonwealth Expert Group on Women and Structural Adjustment elaborated. [13]

Nutrition levels for women and girls deteriorated, while infant, child and maternal mortality rates (which had declined steadily over the last few decades) now increased. In Ethiopia, Ghana, Kenya, Liberia, the Niger and the Philippines, female life expectancy declined-by as much as 7 per cent in Liberia. [14] Essential drugs became prohibitively expensive or else were no longer available. Doctors and nurses often quit after not having been paid their salaries for months. Some governments also introduced medical fees or cost-sharing schemes which meant that health care became inaccessible for many poor families in the developing world. Women—who have special health needs due to their reproductive function, their generally greater longevity and their role as care givers—suffered most, both from the economic crisis and from its bitter "cure".

Maternal Mortality

According to the United Nations *World Economic Survey 1990*, for women living in poorer parts of the world, maternal mortality augments the already existing risk of premature death by at least one third, and in some remote areas by as much as 85 per cent. [15] While maternal mortality has been virtually eliminated in the industrialized world, one out of every two deaths among women of reproductive age in parts of South Asia is pregnancy-related, [16] bringing the total number of maternal deaths in the region to just under one third of a million each year. In Africa, a woman of child bearing age has a 1:20 chance of dying in childbirth, in sharp contrast to a woman in an industrialized country whose risk stands at 1:2000.

MATERNAL MORTALITY

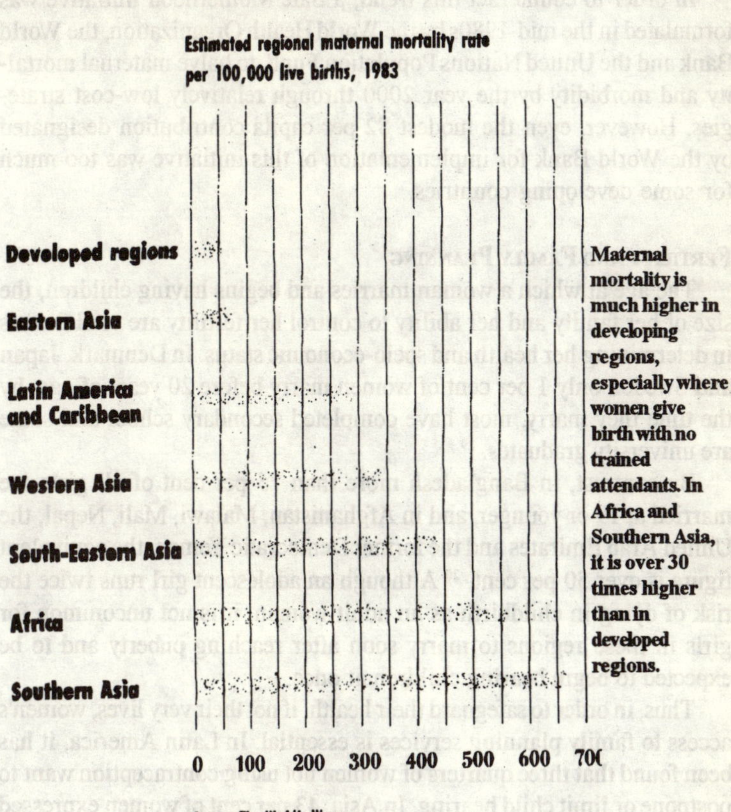

Women in developing countries often have too many children, too close together, both too early and too late in their reproductive lives.[17] According to the 1989 *World Survey on the Role of Women in Development*, for the first time in decades, the 1980s saw alarming increases in maternal and infant mortality in some developing countries, [18] Where most women have no access to family planning, pre-natal check-ups or emergency health care in case of complications in childbirth. Fully 99 per cent of the 500,000 annual maternal deaths recorded occurred in developing countries where almost half the births are delivered by traditional, untrained birth attendants.

In order to counteract this trend, a Safe Motherhood initiative was formulated in the mid-1980s by the World Health Organization, the World Bank and the United Nations Population Fund, to halve maternal mortality and morbidity by the year 2000 through relatively low-cost strategies. However, even the modest $2 per capita contribution designated by the World Bank for implementation of this initiative was too much for some developing countries.

Fertility and Family Planning

The age at which a woman marries and begins having children, the size of her family and her ability to control her fertility are vital factors in determining her health and socio-economic status. In Denmark, Japan and Sweden only 1 per cent of women marry before 20 years of age; by the time they marry, most have completed secondary school and some are university graduates. [19]

By contrast, in Bangladesh more than 75 per cent of all girls are married at 19 or younger, and in Afghanistan, Malawi, Mali, Nepal, the United Arab Emirates and the former Democratic Yemen, the equivalent figure is over 50 per cent. [20] Although an adolescent girl runs twice the risk of dying in childbirth as an adult woman, it is not uncommon for girls in these regions to marry soon after reaching puberty and to be expected to begin bearing children at once.

Thus, in order to safeguard their health, if not their very lives, women's access to family planning services is essential. In Latin America, it has been found that three quarters of women not using contraception want to postpone or limit child bearing. In Asia, 43 per cent of women expressed a similar wish, and in Africa the equivalent figure was 27 per cent. [21] Yet, a recent survey found that in at least 28 countries and areas, mostly in Africa and Asia, less than one third of married women practice contraception. [22]

Once within the legal bond of marriage, women's inferior status in many parts of the world does not permit her to control her own fertility. A vicious circle is set in motion whereby women cannot use contraceptives without their husbands' permission but are afraid to bring up the subject because contraception is often associated with prostitution and infidelity. "The inability to control child bearing can increase women's vulnerability and dependence in marriage, since even in countries with child support laws, many divorced or abandoned women have little or no income from former spouses," according to a recent report on the repercussions of uncontrolled fertility.[23]

While the past three decades have recorded considerable progress in individual family planning and government-sponsored population programmes, a veritable population explosion is effectively neutralizing these gains. If present growth rates continue in Africa, the continent will double its population every 22 years. By the year 2030, a total African population of 2.6 billion is anticipated, a four-fold increase from the current total of 650 million. Southern Asia is projected to account for nearly one third of the total increase in world population by the year 2000. [24] Against this backdrop, health care cuts effects as a result of the economic crisis and structural adjustment programmes have further undermined women's access to family planning and made birth control an unaffordable luxury for most families. The repercussions of this population explosion on the health of African and Asian women is likely to be disastrous.

Malnutrition on the increase

Malnutrition affects one in four people and is a major cause of death among women in developing countries. During the 1980s, nutritional standards deteriorated in 25 countries, and in some cases women suffered disproportionately in relation to men.

Nutritional anemia makes women susceptible to disease, exacerbates fatigue, reduces their working capacity in the workplace and at home, and is particularly dangerous for pregnant women. In industrialized countries, 11 per cent of women from nutritional anemia. In Africa and much of Asia, up to two thirds of pregnant women are anaemic. [25] In addition, 7 out of 15 developing countries examined in a recent report recorded a rise in the proportion of low-birth-weight babies in the first half of the 1980s.[26]

During the 1980s, a combination of factors—including government removal of food subsidies, a subsequent increase in the prices of basic foodstuffs, a decrease in real wages and soaring unemployment—created extremely adverse conditions in many developing countries. Under these circumstances, it was almost always the women who adjusted their lives to absorb the brunt of the burden. This usually meant they had to work longer hours just to keep their families afloat. This "invisible adjustment" jeopardized women's health as well as that of their children.

For poverty-striken, female-headed house-holds in developing countries, a sudden hike in the price of staple foods can make all the difference between subsistence and starvation. In Zambia, deaths related to malnutrition rose by 20 per cent between 1981 and 1987. Malnutrition rates rose by 50 per cent in Ghana and Peru in the first half of the 1980s.[27] Bolivia, the Dominican Republic, Jamaica, Peru and Uruguay witnessed rising malnutrition in children under five years of age during the same period.

AIDS AND GENITAL MUTILATION

Recent cutbacks in health care coincided with the emergence of a new threat to women's health: acquired immunodeficiency syndrome (AIDS). Worldwide, 3 million women are infected with the human immunodeficiency virus (HIV) and, during the 1990s, according to WHO, AIDS will kill about 2 million women, the majority in sub-Saharan Africa. While in industrialized societies the threat has so far been more immediate for homosexual men, the incidence of HIV-positive women is rising steadily. In Africa, where according to one estimate, 1 in 20 people will be infected with AIDS by the year 2000, [28] the male-to-female ratio of seropositives is about equal. In Latin America, one in 500 women is already infected with HIV, while in Asia, over the last three years alone, up to 200,000 women may have been infected.[29] AIDS is also taking a heavy toll on women in cities across Western Europe, sub-Saharan Africa and North and South America.

"By the end of the 1990s, the number of women infected with HIV which causes AIDS may well double as heterosexual transmission becomes the predominant mode of spread of the virus in most parts of the world", reports WHO. It has been estimated that adult and child mortality rates will soar in some regions, wiping out the gains of past decades. Another dimension of the tragedy of this disease is the orphans it leaves behind: in Africa alone, there will be 10 million AIDS orphans by the year 2000.[30]

The most insidious form of discrimination, and a pressing health problem for women in the developing world, is genital mutilation—or female circumcision—as it is sometimes called. An estimated 80 million women in Africa alone, million more in the Middle East, in addition to some African and Middle Eastern populations residing in Europe, are victims of genital mutilation intended to ensure chastity and fidelity. At great risk to the physical and mental health of young girls, clitoridectomy and mental health of young girls, clitoridectomy and infibulation are often performed without even rudimentary hygienic facilities and often result in dangerous, even fatal, haemorrhages, subsequent complications in childbirth, chronic infection, incontinence and painful sexual intercourse.

Although this traditional practice is illegal in several African countries, the social pressure for female circumcision is enormous, as uncircumcised women are not considered eligible for marriage. Thus, this practice often persists, largely because there has been little concerted efforts to educate the public and to raise awareness about the physical and psychological risk of the operation.

HEALTH:
A MALE PRIVILEGE?

Even though women are the main providers and brokers of family and community health, largely as a result of pre-existing inequalities, their own health needs are almost everywhere inadequately addressed. In societies where boys are more valued than girls, the latter are more likely to be affected by reduced access to health care. [31] In parts of South Asia, discrimination is reflected in the female infant and child mortality rates, which are higher for girls than for boys, even among wealthier Asians. [32] For example, in Bangladesh girls have a 70 per cent higher mortality rate than boys.[33] It is also reflected in the fact that in some countries girls are less likely to be taken to the hospital than boys.

Food is not always equally distributed among family members. In some regions, and especially in South Asia, men and boys eat first; whatever is left is then distributed among the women and girls. Invariably, the latter eat less food which is of inferior quality and nutritive value. As a result, girls in developing world are more than four times as likely to be malnourished as boys.[34] These practices are aggravated when family incomes shrink: women tend to suffer even more deprivation. [35] In some Amazon communities, over twice as many women suffer from malnutrition as men.[36]

There are, however, even more sinister forms of discrimination to be found in the practices of female infanticide (which occurs in China, India and certain Arab States), and bride-burning and dowry deaths, especially in India, where pre-arranged marriages have a long tradition. When a woman leaves her home on her wedding day, when she is told, "Now only your dead body can leave your husband's house". As far as the in-laws are concerned, the bride may be little more than a source of status and dowry income. Thus, if marriage goes bad, the husband's family may decide to "get rid of the problem by getting rid of the bride", since the death of a wife frees a man marry again without the inconvenience of divorce proceedings.[37]

In some countries, the amniocentesis test (created to reduce the risk of handicapped babies)is used to determine the sex of the unborn child, which, if it is a girl, may be aborted. In 1984-85 alone, some 16,000 female foetuses were aborted in a single Bombay clinic, following amniocentesis.[38]

Even within the family, a less dramatic but equally all-pervasive prejudice against females is evident. One of the most universal daily forms of discrimination is illustrated by the "double day" worked by women around the world: doing housework as well as a full day as agricultural or wage labourers. Men, on the other hand, whose working day ends with their departure from the job or the fields, contribute only a negligible amount of time to housework. Under this burden of multiple responsibilities, over-worked women often do not have time to rest and routinely neglect their health. It is not uncommon for women to ignore treatment until they are gravely ill due to lack of time to visit a health centre. The alleviation of women's multiple workload and equal sharing of household chores are finally being recognized as important developmental and legal issues.

The cumulative result of all these discriminatory practices may be reflected in the difference in longevity for men and women in some regions. In many industrialized countries, including Canada, Hong Kong, Japan and Norway, women have an average life expectancy at birth of 80 years—seven years longer than men. In most developing countries, however, the gap between male and female life expectancy is considerably smaller. In Egypt, Haiti and Iraq, the gap between male and female life expectancy is only slight.[39] In India and Pakistan, life expectancy at birth is the same for men and women, while in Bangladesh, Bhuttan, the Maldives and Nepal, women actually have lower life expectancies than men.[40]

Discrimination also affects women within the medical profession itself. Whereas women constitute the majority of primary health care workers and many have been trained as traditional midwives, there is great reluctance within the medical profession to grant women decision-making representation commensurate with their actual numbers. Allocation of three quarters of the health care expenditures in developing countries is under the jurisdiction of hospitals and doctors, leaving women who are midwives and primary health care workers little financial authority.[41] In addition, since sex stereotypes designate medicine as a male profession, few families encourage female children to become doctors.

Women and Health in the 1990s

Calls from the international community for "adjustment with a human face" in the late 1980s put the adverse effects of austerity policies into sharp focus, particularly as they affected health and education. In some cases, in order to mitigate the severe impact of austerity policies, special programmes were adopted focusing on clean water, sanitation, safe child bearing, nutrition programmes and family planning services. Nevertheless, women's special health needs continue to be ignored or, at best, inadequately addressed in such programmes. Thus, sexual discrimination in health care persists.

"The long-run consequences of malnutrition and ill health, particularly among women and young girls, can be very serious," the Commonwealth Expert Group on Women and Structural Adjustment observes. "A recent survey showed that it could take up to two generations for a young girl to 'wash out' the effects of a period of severe malnutrition, since weaknesses in her own reproductive system could influence those of her children and grandchildren, even if they were well fed and received good health care." [42]

Health Challenges to the Year 2000

Despite negative trends over the last decade, the set-backs in women's health that occurred in the 1980s could be counteracted if the following measures are immediately adopted:

- Improve women's and girl's health by ensuring them access to adequate maternal health care, family planning and nutrition
- Increase national health budgets to allow for free primary health care, maintenance and improvement of existing health facilities, improved clean water and sanitation facilities and subsidized prescribed medications
- Earmark national funds for research and provision of family planning devices
- Ensure access to family planning and the right of each woman to decide on the number and spacing of her children; actively discourage child bearing at too early an age
- Reduce maternal mortality through provision of adequate pre-and post-natal health care, including nutrition for pregnant and lactating mothers
- Campaign for equal sharing of domestic responsibilities between men and women
- Protect women's equal access to health services, especially for female children, the disabled and elderly women

- Increase life expectancy for women to at least 65 years in all countries
- Introduce a global immunization against the six major communicable diseases of childhood: tuberculosis, diphtheria, poliomyelitis, measles, tetanus and whooping cough
- Impose severe penalties for pre-and post-natal female infanticide
- Eliminate the traditional practice of female circumcision
- Guarantee access to protective measures against contraction of AIDS and other sexually transmitted diseases; provide counselling and support services for AIDS victims and their families.

Notes

1 Dr. Nafis Sadik, Investing in Women: The focus of the 90s, United Nations Population Fund, 1989, PP: 9-10.

2 *Poor, Powerless and Pregnant*, op. cit., p. 3.

3 *Engendering Adjustment for the 1990s*, Report of a Commonwealth Expert Group on Women and Structural Adjustment (London: Commonwealth Secretariat, 1989), 18.

4 Ibid., p. 19.

5 Ibid., p. 18.

6 *The State of the World's Women*, op. cit., p. 12

7 Ibid., p. 14

8 *The World's Women: 1970-1990: Trends and Statistics*, op. cit., Table 5.6, p. 75.

9 *The State of the World's Women*, op. cit., p. 12.

10 Sadik, op. cit., p. 1.

11 *Engendering Adjustment for the 1990s*, op. cit., p. 69, and *Africa News, World Bank*, 1 May, 1989. Decimal figures have been rounded to the nearest number.

12 *The World's Women: 1970-1990*, op. cit., Table 2.10, p. 37.

13 *Engendering Adjustment for the 1990s*, op. cit., p. 72.

14 Ibid., Table 3.7, p. 84.

15 *World Economic Survey 1990*, Department of International Economic and Social Affairs, United Nations, New York, 1990, p. 16.

16 Ibid.

17 *The World's Women*: 1970-1990, op. cit., p. 59.

18 *1989 World Survey on the Role of Women in Development*, op. cit., pp. 6 and 41.

19 *Poor, Powerless and Pregnant*, op. cit., p. 59.

20 Ibid.

21 Sadik, op. cit., p. 3.

22 *The World's Women*: 1970-1990, Table 4.10 p. 61.

23 *Poor, Powerless and Pregnant*, op. cit., p. 10.

24 The state of the world Population 1990, op. cit., p. 1.

25 *The World's Women: 1970-1990*, op.cit., p. 58.

26 *Engendering Adjustment for the 1990s*, op. cit., p. 27.

27 Ibid., p. 70.

28 Sadik, op. cit., p. 15.

29 *WHO Features*, No. 151, November 1990.

30 Ibid.

31 *1989 World Survey on the Role of Women in Development*, op. cit., p. 26.

32 *Poor, Powerless and Pregnant,* op. cit., p. 3.
33 *Women in Developing Countries: Invisible Victims of the Economic Crisis,* (DPI/1014), United Nations De Department of Public Information, Novermber 1989, p. 4.
34 *Notes for Speakers* (DPI/989), United Nations Department of Public Information, 1989, p. 76.
35 *Women 2000,* Review and Appraisal 1990, Division for the Advancement of Women, No. 2, 1990, p. 6.
36 Ibid.
37 *The New York Times,* 3 May 1991.
38 *The Guardian, London,* 11 April 1986.
39 *Poor, Powerless and Pregnant,* op. cit., p. 3; and World Economic Survey 1990, p. 15.
40 *Poor, Powerless and Pregnant,* op. cit., p. 3.
41 *The State of the World's Women,* 1985, op. cit., p. 14.
42 *Engendering Adjustment for the 1990s,* op. cit., p. 70.

WOMEN'S EDUCATION: KEY TO EMPOWERMENT

Mythologies around the world have ascribed to women the supreme literacy achievements of creating alphabets and inventing language. "Goddess of the Logos, Mother of the Gods, One with Creating, thou art Intelligence, the Mother of Science...." begins the Hindu prayer to the mother of Krishna. Queen Isis has been credited with conferring the alphabet on the Egyptians, as did Medusa on Hercules in Greece, while the Indian goddess-priestess Kali invented the Sanskrit alphabet. Even the world's first novel., *The Tale of Genji,* was written by Lady Murasaki in eleventh century Japan.[1]

These scattered examples show that women were once at the centre of the world of learning before patriarchal dictates denied them the right to education, condemning them to centuries of intellectual obscurantism. Yet, even after education became a requirement for men—though it remained a forbidden fruit for women almost everywhere—a few unique women succeeded in circumventing formidable obstacles to excel in all fields of learning.

Illiteracy: A Lifelong cul-de-sac

According to the United Nations Educational, Scientific and Cultural Organization (UNECSO), in 1990, 26.5 per cent of the adult population of the world (948.1 million) were illiterate. Of that number, 346.5 million were men (i.e. 19.4 per cent of the male population) while 601.6 million were women (i.e. 33.6 per cent of the female population). The numbers were even more striking for developing countries, where the illiteracy rate for women stood at 45 per cent.[2]

For these women, illiteracy compounds their other problems, contributing to their marginalization within the family, the workplace and public life. It accounts for the fact that women have often not benefited from socio-economic and technological progress. Illiterate women are invariably caught in a vicious circle of poverty, repeated child bearing, ill health and powerlessness, lacking the means to break out of their predicament: education.

The direct correlation between literacy, health, economic and political power and the exercise of informed choice, especially for women, cannot be emphasized enough. Education decisively determines a woman's access to paid employment, her earning capacity, her overall health, control over her fertility, family size and spacing, and the education and health of her family. For example, it has been found that women with seven years or more of education tend to marry on average four years later and have 2.2 fewer children statistically than women with no schooling. [3]

Education also plays a crucial role in child survival. In Ghana, women with no education are twice as likely to lose children as mothers with primary schooling and four times as likely as mothers with secondary education. [4] In Indonesia, mothers who have not received any education are three times more likely to lose children under five than mothers with some schooling.[5]

In addition, education helps women over-come social prejudice, take control of their lives and assume a status and identity beyond child bearing, thereby allowing them to participate more fully in the public life of their community. It opens up wider horizons, creates new opportunities and, most importantly, empowers women with choice. And, last but not least, education is the single most important weapon to combat sexual stereotyping and discriminatory attitudes towards women.

The Education Avalanche

The dramatic global increase in school enrolment between 1950 and 1980, striking especially in developing countries, was tantamount to a revolution that promised to sweep away illiteracy, improve the quality of life of millions of the world's people and decisively change the course of women's lives. Massive investments in social services meant that education budgets in-creased seven-fold in the developing world and four-fold in industrialized countries, while all countries adopted universal primary education as a fundamental goal. Primary schools swelled to include girls who had virtually been excluded until then in many developing countries, while modest but significant enrolment increases for girls in secondary schools and in higher education courses were also recorded.

ILLITERATE WOMEN

In Africa and Southern and Western Asia, over 40 per cent of young women are still illiterate. Although illiteracy rates for young women fell between 1970-1990, they are still much higher than those for young men.

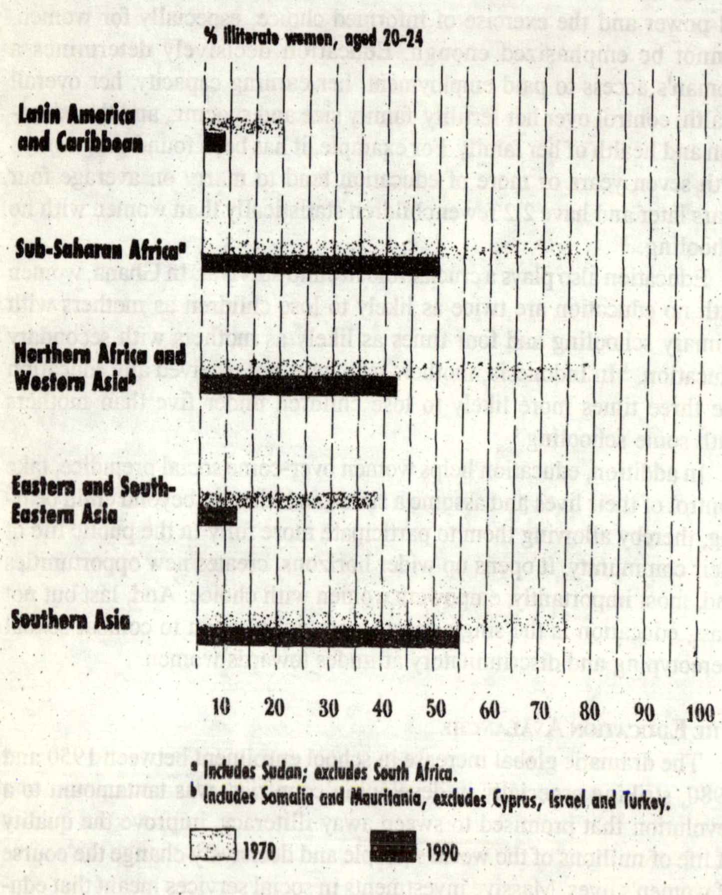

[a] Includes Sudan; excludes South Africa.
[b] Includes Somalia and Mauritania, excludes Cyprus, Israel and Turkey.

Source: The World's Women

The educational gains for girls and women at all levels were impressive. The world adult female illiteracy rate fell from 45 per cent in 1960 to 35 per cent in 1985. Female enrolment in primary schools in the developing world was as high as 44 per cent by 1980, up 7 per cent from 1950. [6] Near universal primary school enrolment had been attained in Latin America and much of Asia. Girl's enrolment in secondary schools increased from 24 per cent in 1950 to 40 per cent in 1980.[7]

Throughout this entire period, women continued to close the gap with men, not only in secondary school enrolment but also in university. Today there are more women than men enrolled in higher education in several countries, according to UNESCO sources. For instance, in 1990 in Qatar, there were 202 women per 100 men in university, in Dominica, there were 200 women per 100 men; likewise, in Lesotho 172 per 100, in Mongolia 149 per 100, in Panama 136 per 100, in Bulgaria 124 per 100, and in Portugal 113 per 100.[8] Yet, the gap between male and female literacy rates grew as illiteracy rates for men fell faster than for women, highlighting the fact that access to education continued to be easier for males than for females.

Women have also made great progress in the teaching profession and, after decades of improvement, half or more of first-level teachers around the world (excluding Africa) are women. In Asia and the Pacific, 49 per cent of first-level teachers are now women, compared to 38 per cent in 1970; in Africa, 39 per cent are now women, compared to 28 per cent in 1970.[9]

The Effects of the Economic Crisis on Education

The economic crisis of the 1980s and the remedial structural adjustment programmes adopted by developing countries under the auspices of international financial institutions abruptly slowed and, in some instances, actually reversed the steady progress of preceding decades. Preexisting inequalities experienced by women worsened during the economic crisis and women suffered disproportionately from the cuts in education. Rapid population growth also contributed to the rise in the total number of illiterate women—a trend which is expected to continue into the twenty-first century.

According to the United Nations Children's Funds (UNICEF), the world's least developed countries slashed their education budgets by 25 per cent per capita during the 1980s in order to deal with the debt crisis; Latin America and the Caribbean effected the largest cuts. [10] In Jamaica, per capita real expenditure on education was cut by about one third from

1980 to 1985.[11] Bolivia and Costa Rica cut their education expenditures by over 45 and 41 per cent respectively.[12]

The deterioration of education programmes became most acute in many African nations which had made great strides after achieving independence. Some countries virtually eliminated education from their budgets: Zaire, one of the world's poorest countries with one of the highest illiteracy rates, slashed its education budget from 15.2 per cent of total government expenditure in 1972 to 0.8 per cent in 1986.[13] As school buildings and equipment decayed, teachers' salaries were devalued up to 10 times as a result of spiralling inflation, and school fees were introduced in many countries. The dramatic fall in per capita income often meant that parents could not afford the transportation costs or the school supplies their children their children required. Reports of schools operating without desks, blackboards, slates or books became common; some African communities, in a desperate attempt to provide even a minimum of learning for their children, created makeshift outdoor schools with volunteer teachers, most of whom were women.

The impact of the global economic crisis and subsequent efforts at adjustment on the availability and quality of education has yet to be fully assessed, but as Adebayo Adedeji, former Executive Secretary of the Economic Commission for Africa, recently warned, "If things continue like this, Africa will have more illiterate people as a proportion of the population than at independence"—a scenario which will have disastrous consequences for the continent's future, for as Adedeji put it: "How can you develop an illiterate society?[14]

During the 1980s, as a result of the economic crisis:

- Some 16 low-income and 14 middle-income countries with ongoing structural adjustment programmes experienced falling ratios of primary school enrolment. In the first category, female enrolments were most severely affected in Somalia, Togo and Mali where rates fell by 40, 18 and 15 per cent respectively. In the second category, Yemen, Chile and Costa Rica were most affected.[15]
- Improvements in secondary education enrolments slowed down in much of Asia and Africa,[16] and in several countries there was a lower enrolment for girls than for boys among the poorer strata of society.
- In six Latin American countries, education deteriorated both in quantitative and qualitative terms.[17]
- Drop-out rates increased in several countries as a result of the introduction of school fees.

Girls are often the first to suffer from these set-backs since female education is not a priority among families, local communities and governments. If a family is to choose which child will continue its education, preference is invariably given to boys, in the belief that their chances for employment are better than girls'. Hard-pressed parents also tend to take their girls out of school to help them with domestic work and child care, or else to marry them off. In addition, rapid population growth and shrinking education budgets in many developing countries mean that there are not enough schools to accommodate the school-age population, which expanded 1985. [18] Again, girls are the first to be excluded.

The introduction of school fees in developing countries already suffering from declining per capita incomes further undermined girls' access to education. Moreover, as social services available to women deteriorated during the 1980s, their workload increased along with their financial responsibilities, and education became and additional burden. In Uganda, for instance, about a third of mothers now pay school fees that were previously taken care of by their spouses. [19] Even where education is free, however, the cost of basic school items can be prohibitively expensive for poor families: in 1985, Zambian parents had to allocate over one fifth of their per capita income per child for basic school supplies [20]—an insurmountable financial burden considering that these families generally average six or seven children.

Rural Women: When Education interferes with survival

Rural societies, which depend heavily on women for their survival, are especially resistant to educating them. In Afghanistan, for instance, the illiteracy rate for women in rural areas is 93.8 per cent, versus 56.4 per cent in cities. In Benin, 92.1 per cent of rural women are illiterate compared to 59 per cent of urban women.[21]

Rural women tend to have more children, be poorer, and, in their struggle to survive, have little or no time and energy to spare on adult literacy programmes. Children of female-headed households in rural areas are often put to work in order to ensure the survival of the family. According to a study published in 1984, in India, even though 60 per cent of rural children were enrolled in primary school, after five years only 16 per cent of the girls continued to attend classes, as opposed to 35 per cent of the boys. [22] Survival needs aside, rural women are also more likely to encounter resistance from within the family to their pursuing an education: an educated woman might pose a threat to her husband and upset the family status quo.

Recession in the Developed World

In the industrialized world, following the education boom of previous decades, the economic recession of the late 1970s came as a shock. It was tackled with cut-backs which struck a severe blow at the quality of the entire educational system, from primary schools to universities.

Female enrolment in adult literacy and education programmes in industrialized countries also suffered, while university enrolments reportedly declined as fees skyrocketed and the availability of scholarships declined drastically. In the United Kingdom, educational grants which were previously the right of every national became restricted; in the United States, the cost of university education became prohibitively high for many middle-class families.

The Gender GAP

The gap between literacy rates for men and women has decreased significantly in developing countries, especially in Latin America over the past 20 years, and particularly for young women under 24 years of age. In some regions, illiteracy rates for young women have been cut in half. In Latin America and the Caribbean, the percentage of illiterate young women aged 20-24 in 1970 was 19.4; by 1990, it had fallen to 8 per cent. In sub-Saharan Africa (including the Sudan but excluding South Africa), the equivalent figures are 80.3 and 49.2 per cent; in Eastern and Western Asia, illiteracy among young women fell from 37.9 to 12.2 per cent. [23]

Despite this progress, however, today there are considerably more illiterate women than men in most parts of the world, particularly in Africa and Eastern and South-Eastern Asia where the ratio approaches 2 to 1 in certain regions. Furthermore, the gap between male and female literacy remains high in most of the developing world, especially for adult women living in rural areas. Even in Europe, where only 2 per cent of the population is illiterate, there are twice as many women as men who cannot read and write.

One of the primary reasons for the education gap is that girls are brought up and educated only for "traditional occupations". Social custom often accounts for the popular belief that girls do not need an education since they will marry and raise children rather than work at a job outside the home where educational qualifications are required. "[A girl] has the additional disadvantage of being born into a world that does not even expect her to succeed, a world that perhaps does not really want her to succeed, a world that has been systematically schooling her for failure", argued the 1985 State of the World's Women. [24] Having always been excluded from education, many women have come to believe that their abilities are restricted to cooking, cleaning and minding children—all of which are crucial, yet unpaid and undervalued tasks.

Such beliefs have been reinforced by sexist stereotypes which are pervasive in textbooks and curricula from elementary schools to universities. Consider the following Introductory Logic exercise:

"Exhibit the logical form for the following sentences by translating them into the notation of the predicate calculus:

a) Susan is feather-brained
b) Janet is feather-brained
c) All women are feather-brained
d) No man is feather-brained
e) Some men are not feather-brained
f) John is not feather-brained" [25]

Girl's secondary school enrolment lags behind boys' in much of Asia and Africa, and in Southern Asia the discrepancy is particularly striking, with only 40 girls per 100 boys enrolled at secondary level. [26] In Afghanistan, only 9 per cent of girls are enrolled in secondary school, while in Pakistan the equivalent figure is 17 per cent. [27]

Girl's enrolment in vocational and technical training schools is also very low. As an increasing number of women around the world seek paid employment, vocational and technical training becomes all the more significant.

The gap in male/female university enrolment continues to be very wide in most countries. Furthermore, female enrolment in science, engineering, business and law is especially low. There has been little progress in the promotion of women in university level teaching. For example, a recent investigation into the male to female ratio of tenured professors at Harvard University in the United States found that there were 161 tenured male professors as opposed to less than half a dozen women. [28] Such examples of education-related discrimination point to the fact that education should not be dealt with in isolation but as part of the advancement of the status of women as a whole.

Educating Women for the Future

As a result of the set-backs that the economic crisis inflicted on education during the 1980s and the criticism of the devastating effects of adjustment and stabilization policies in much of the developing world, special measures to mitigate the adverse effects of structural adjustment programmes on education were adopted in the late 1980s. However, women have been largely absent from such programmes. Ghana's model Programme of Action to Mitigate the Social Costs of Adjustment (PAMSCAD), designed to cushion the impact of adjustment among the hardest high—the urban poor, retrenched civil servants and small-scale farmers—is no exception.

Tacking the current regression in education, particularly in the developing world, should be a component of sustainable development strategies in the 1990s, considering that:

- About 75 per cent of women aged 25 and over cannot read and write in much of Asia and Africa. [29]
- In some countries, illiteracy is virtually pandemic. In Burkina Faso and Somalia, only 6 per cent of adult women are literate, while in Afgahnistan and Nepal the figures are 8 and 12 per cent respectively. [30]
- In Africa, primary school enrolment was only 76 per cent in 1987 (84 per cent for boys and 68 per cent for girls). [31]

Education Challenges to the Year 2000

Educating women is a high return investment in socio-economic development for society as a whole since, by educating a woman, one is in effect reaching and entire family. At present, however, this simple equation appears to go unrecognized by development planners and governments alike. If the recorded negative trend in female school enrolment is to be reversed and the gender gap closed over the next decade, it is imperative that governments, as well as the private sector:

- Make a concentrated world-wide effort to end illiteracy among females by the year 2000
- Create incentives aimed at achieving equal literacy rates for males and females; measure progress towards the goal of universal literacy and numercy by the year 2000
- Intensify efforts towards universal primary education during the 1990s by making education a priority concern
- Revise all textbooks to eliminate sex stereotyping and to include the contributions of women to civilization
- Improve secondary education for girls, especially in rural areas, by introducing double shift or single-sex schools in regions where gender segregation discourages female education; provide incentives to families for girls to remain in school

- Guarantee equal access to quality education and training in all subjects and at all levels; provide preferential treatment or financial subsidies which would facilitate female access to male-dominated universities
- Promote more women teachers at secondary and university level, encouraging them to act as role models and mentors for female students
- Increase the salary scale and status of the over all teaching profession, from kindergarten to university, in recognition of the fact that education is a vital key to the quality of life
- Encourage women to select male-dominated occupations and desegregated the curricula; improve training in the sciences, the mathematics, as well as in vocational, technical and business subjects, for girls and young women
- Provide convenient access to adult education for women, including child care facilities and night classes
- Develop adult legal, economic and political literacy programmes to augment basic literacy and numeracy

NOTES

1 All four examples cited in Rosalind Miles, *The Women's History of the World* (London; Palladin, 1990). pp. 128-129.

2 *1990: International Literacy Year*. UNESCO Information Document, June 1989.

3 *The State of the World Population 1990*, op. cit., p. 15.

4 World Bank study, cited in box 2.2, in *Engendering Adjustment for the 1990s*, op. cit., p. 43.

5 *The State of the World Population 1990*, op. cit., UNFPA, p. 15.

6 *Engendering Adjustment for the 1990s*, op. cit., p. 18.

7 Ibid.

8 *The World's Women*: 1970-1990, op. cit., Tablo 3.5, p. 48.

9 Ibid., Table 3.6, p. 48.

10 Mayra Buvinic and Sally W. Yudelman, *Women, Poverty and Progress in the Third World*, Headline Series, No. 289, Summer 1989, p. 14.

11 *Engendering Adjustment for the 1990s*, op. cit., p. 66.

12 Ibid., Table 3.4, p. 81.

13 *World Bank, Africa News*, 1 May 1989.

14 *Engendering Adjustment for the 1990s*, op. cit., pp. 27-28.

15 Ibid., Table 3.5, p. 82.

16 *1989 World Survey on the Role of Women in Development*, op. cit., p. 31.

17 *Engendering Adjustment for the 1990s*, op. cit., p. 27.

18 *World Economic Survey 1990*, op. cit., p. 192.

19 *Literacy: Tool for Empowering Women*, op. cit., p.2.

20 *Engendering Adjustment for the 1990s*, op. cit., p. 67.

21 *Literacy: Tool for Empowering Women*, op. cit., p. 1.

22 *The World's Women: 1970-1990*, op. cit., p. 2.

23 *The World's Women: 1970-1990*, op. cit., p. 3.2, p. 46.

[24] *The State of the World's Women*, op. cit., p. 15-16.
[25] Beginning Logic, 1982, cited in Fidelis Morgan, *A Misogynist's Sourcebook* (London, Jonathan Cape, 1989), p. 60.
[26] *The World's Women: 1970-1990*, op. cit., p. 3.4, p. 47.
[27] Ibid, and *Poor, Powerless and Pregnant*, op. cit., p. 5.
[28] *The New York Times*, 14 March 1990.
[29] *The World's Women: 1970-1990*, op. cit., Table 3.3, p. 47.
[30] *The State of the World Population 1990*, op. cit., Social Indicators.
[31] *World Economic Survey 1990*, op. cit., p. 10.

MAKING WOMEN'S WORK COUNT

Hypatia, who lived and taught in the city of Alexandria, was an astronomer, philosopher, mathematician and mechanical genius who invented, among other things, the astrolabe and the planisphere. In the year 415, she was ambushed, and killed for her beliefs. Her remains were burned and her documents, writings and other works destroyed. [1] One of many out-standing women scientists over the past 3,000 years, Hypatia has only recently been accorded the recognition she justly deserves.

Although this is a dramatic example of a woman who was outstanding in what has often been considered exclusively a man's field, women have worked alongside men for centuries. It is only as we approach the twenty-first century, however, that the realization dawns that women are a shadow workforce without whose contribution the economies of some countries, and certainly some communities, would founder.

Women's recent absorption into the paid workforce is something of a mixed blessing. On the one hand, it allows them to acquire skills and professional training, gives them access to new professional training, gives them access to new occupations and allows them to earn income. On the other hand, it has not automatically guaranteed them equal status. On the contrary, pay differentials between men and women persist. Women working in the informal sector continue to be invisible statistics, struggling against social, if not legal, impediments to their access to wage labour. As a result, women constitute a disproportionate number of those who are unemployed, underemployed, impoverished and subject to oppressive workplace practices. Despite gains in legislation and protection of rights, women continue to be "second-class citizens" in the labour force of every country in the world.

The Multiple Roles of Women

Within the household, the division of labour is such that men are seen to be the primary producers while women are the consumers and have overall responsibility for reproduction and domestic work. In effect, however, women fill thé multiple roles of both producers and consumers, in addition to being home managers, mothers and community organizers. [2]

Let us consider a typical household among the Beti people in southern Cameroon. Beti men work about seven and a half hours a day. They spend less than an hour on food-related tasks, about two hours on their cocoa plots, four hours on either beer or palm wine production, house building and repair or production of housing materials, and the rest on part-time work. In contrast, Beti women labour for 11 hours a day. Five hours are spent on food production, consisting of four hours providing for family needs and one hour producing surplus for the urban market. In addition, they devote three or four hours a day to food processing and cooking and two or more hours to water and firewood collection, washing, child care and tending the sick. In addition to their family specific duties, women are often involved in community projects, such as the installation of pumps, wells, schools and health care centres.[3]

In the above example, most conventional studies would count the male as the active labourer and the wife as simply a helper to her husband. Moreover, as tangible evidence of their status, the men would be credited with decision-making power.

Accounting for women's Economic Activity

In 1990, out of the 828 million women officially estimated to be economically active, 56 per cent lived in Asia, 29 per cent in the developed world, 9 per cent in Africa and 5 per cent in Latin America and the Caribbean. [4] However, the above statistics do not include much of the agricultural work in the developing world, nor do they include domestic work.

In the five years since the end of the United Nations Decade for Women, calls have intensified for a radical overhaul in the way women's work is measured. In 1982, the International Labour Organization (ILO) elaborated an international standard definition according to which "the economically active population includes all persons of either sex who provide labour for the production of economic goods and services. All work for pay or in anticipation of profit is included. In addition, the standard specifies that the production of economic goods and services includes all production and processing of primary products, whether for the market, for barter or for home consumption. [5]

In India, as a result of this redefinition of economic activity, initial estimates of only 13 per cent economically active women were revised upwards to 88 per cent using the new ILO criteria. [6]

However, even the ILO concedes that methodological problems persist in measuring certain aspects of women's work. By far the most "invisible" of all work done by women the world over, is domestic work, which continues to go unrecognized, unpaid, undervalued and largely ignored by the law despite its crucial importance to society. It has been argued that if domestic work were to be quantified, it would contribute up to 40 per cent of the gross national product of industrialized societies. [7] In Pakistan, a rural woman spends 63 hours a week on domestic work, and in the developed world, despite technological advances which greatly alleviate the hardship of domestic work, women work an average of 56 hours a week around the house. [8] Yet, social values are such that most women whose job description reads " housewife and/or mother" do not consider themselves economically active.

Female-Headed Households: No Longer the Exception

It is estimated that one third of the world's households are headed by women; [9] nearly half of women heading households in industrialized regions and at least a quarter in other regions are elderly; [10] in some rural areas of Latin America and Africa, the number of female-headed households reaches 50 per cent; [11] in areas where civil or military conflicts are in progress, the figure is closer to 80 per cent. [12] The underlying reasons for the greater incidence of female-headed households are two fold:

- *de jure* as a result of being single, divorced, or widowed;
- *de facto* due to long-term migration, economic crisis, refugee status or abandonment.

Women being incharge of the home in the absence of men is not a new phenomenon; it is simply unnoticed or unacknowledged. Women face a stigma in living alone, and even when they are obviously heading a household, recognition by the State is usually confined to some industrialized nations that have an extensive social welfare system. Around the world, female-headed households are subjected to further discrimination:

- In a region of Ghana, 59 per cent of house-holds are headed by women who had to for—feit land when they lost their husbands through death, divorce or migration; [13]

- In Zambia, the income of female-headed households was being taxed at a higher rate under the assumption that these women would be provided for by their husbands; [14]
- Even in pre-unification West Germany, retired women received, on average, only half of the pension men enjoyed.[15]

WOMEN WORK MORE

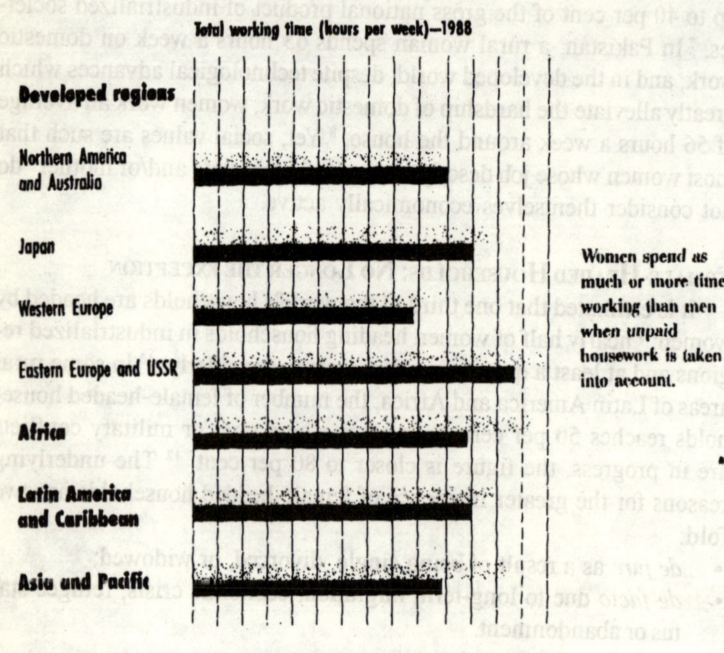

Source: The World's Women.

Economic conditions in female-headed households vary considerably, but often these women are the most impoverished and the most burdened by the multiple roles they bear. All too often, these households fall below the poverty line and contribute to the deepening feminization of poverty. About 70 per cent of the world's poor people are women, a recent study reported.[16]

WOMEN IN AGRICULTURE: ALL WORK AND NO PLAY.....

With startling new evidence, the United Nations Women's Decade exploded the myth that women in the developing world were only peripherally engaged in agricultural labour:

- In Africa, about 75 per cent of agricultural work is done by women, who also produce and market up to 80 per cent of the food. [17] Asian women account for half the agricultural labour force. And in Latin America and the Middle East, women are involved in a substantial amount of farming, as part of family chores or as a result of male out-migration.
- In Eastern Europe, half the agricultural labour force is composed of women.
- In some industrialized market-economy countries, women farmers work as long as 70 hours a week alongside the men, as shown by surveys in Spain and Turkey. In addition, they put in many hours of housework per week. [18]

As with domestic work, much of women's agricultural labour is overlooked because it is unpaid or because tradition goes against women being required to engage in farming or other economic activity. In the Andean countries, for instance, a 1976 survey put economically active women in the agricultural sector at 13 per cent.[19] A closer examination revealed that women were heavily involved in agricultural work and off-farm activities; Quechua women were not just helping their husbands, they often held the purse-strings by being in charge of all economic decision-making.[20] On the African continent, there are far more women than men doing unpaid agricultural work. In Mali and Ghana, the ratio is over 2 to 1; in Cameroon it is more than 3 to 1; and in Liberia, unpaid women working the land outnumber men by over 4 to 1 [21]

Since women's contribution to agriculture is concealed behind a veritable "grass curtain", women are rarely factored into development policy planning and adjustment measures. Agricultural projects and strategies are designed without consulting women. For example, in Nepal studies show that women provide between 66 and 100 per cent of labour in many agricultural activities and make 42 per cent of agricultural decisions. But a review of government projects in 1983 revealed that of all agricultural advisers trained to help villagers, only one was a woman, trained in home economics. [22]

Similarly, technology is usually geared to the needs of men, or ends up displacing women. In Sierra Leone, the tractors and tillers introduced to help with swamp rice cultivation made men's working-day shorter but increased women's workload by half, since more land was being cultivated and women were concentrated in planting and transplanting. [23]

In Asia, as a consequence of the Green Revolution, there is a higher demand for seasonal labour, leading to the marginalization of small tenant-farmers. The female share of the agricultural labour force has been falling, while growing landlessness has led to an increase in the proportion of women who are wage labourers . In India, 30 to 40 per cent of landless labourers are women. [24] In Bangladesh, women are increasingly seen working in rice fields or on road construction as poverty deepens and they seek wage labour. [25] In Malaysia and Sri Lanka, women account for half the seasonal workers on plantations. [26]

In Latin America, the tradition has been to employ men as farm labourers, who outnumber women engaged in paid agricultural work. Women are either hired at harvest time or work unpaid on family plots. In Africa, women's traditional land rights have been undermined by colonial policies while development projects have reinforced the problem by allocating land ownership to men. In Burkina Faso, until new reforms were introduced in the mid-1980s, all new tenancies were given to men, despite women's responsibility for growing all the family's responsibility for growing all the family's subsistence food. [27] In Kenya, a woman only has access to land if she has living husband or son. [28]

Women who work in the agricultural sector seldom have title to land, or access to credit, technology and extension services. Their situation is exacerbated by the fact that they are often the first to fall victim to growing population pressure on the land, to marginalization of the agricultural sector and to economic crisis and adjustment measures. Some United Nations economists have argued that African women, who are responsible for subsitence crops, have been particularly hard hit by adjustment policies that have boosted incentives for cash crops tended by men; many women are summoned to help with their husband's cash crops tended by men; many women are summoned to help with their husband's cash crops at the expense of their own food crops. Moreover, women are typically not given access to credit, fertilizers and other necessities.[29] The most desperate of rural women leave for urban areas where they are drawn into the undefined masses who eke out a living from informal economic activity.

WOMEN IN THE INFORMAL SECTOR: ON THE EDGE OF SURVIVAL

Leelaben Datania and her family have been vegetable vendors in Ahmedabad's Manek-Chowk Market for several generations. Her introduction to the Self-Employed Women's Association, or SEWA, a cooperative that as brought together women in the informal sector in Gujarat (India), Transformed her life. From vending vegetables to mobilizing women, she has now been trained in video techniques. The respect she has earned among her peers demonstrates the status that empowerment and organization can bring to the most impoverished, oppressed women in the workplace.[30]

The accomplishments of SEWA and many other organizations like it are hailed as a turning-point in the frustrating tale of women who have attempted to stand up and be counted, particularly when they are not armed with political power, legal literacy, education or skills. No evaluation of women and work is complete without a discussion of women who are neither waged agricultural or industrial labourers, nor professional or domestic workers.

Although not visible and organized, the informal sector is known to have expanded as a result of progressive urbanization, economic crises and adjustment policies, but remains clouded in mystery to statisticians. In recent decades, social scientists have conducted numerous studies of women in the informal sector but little analysis is available on a global or regional basis. The United Nations International Research and Training Institute for the Advancement of Women (INSTRAW) has investigated women's participation and production in the informal sector.

Income-generating activities taken up by women in the informal sector have expanded rapidly across Africa and Latin America as a result of formal sector entrenchment, unemployment, falling incomes and rising food prices. In Lima, Peru, women's share in the informal sector increased from 36 per cent in 1983 to 45 per cent in 1987. [31]

Many informal sector activities are the extension of agricultural work, such as processing and marketing of produce. Also, spin-off activities such as smoking and drying fish as an adjunct to the fishing industry, common in the Caribbean, or making clay utensils for storing food and water, or trading household goods, account for much informal activity is now carried out on a contract basis—in India, the rolling of "beedis", the poor person's cigarette, is thought to employ some 2 million to 3 million women.[32] In parts of Africa, including Cameroon, Liberia, Malawi, Mali and the Sudan, only 2 per cent of women are reflected in the paid labour force. [33] While such employment can greatly increase family income and may even bring women some independence, exploitation is widespread and job security non-existent.

WOMEN IN THE FORMAL SECTOR: THE PINK GHETTO

While women have benefited from equal rights legislation, they have also become victims anew of economic exploitation. It is not just unpaid housework that is either undocumented or grossly undervalued, as recent United Nations statistics reveal:

- On average, women around the world earn 30 to 40 per cent less than men for work of comparable value. [34]
- Women are on average paid less than men, even in industrialized countries such as the Netherlands or New Zealand, where they receive 77 to 79 per cent of men's wages for comparable work. The record is significantly better for women in Tanzania, who earn 92 per cent of what their male counterparts make, while in Egypt it is a lower 64 per cent. Japan is one of the lowest at 52 per cent. [35]
- Gemerally, women are a large part of the clerical, sales and services labour force but are largely excluded from manufacturing, transport and management. In the industrialized regions, women comprise 47 per cent of professional or technical workers, while they constitute 63 per cent of service or clerical employees. In Latin America, the corresponding figures are 49 and 58 per cent. [36]

Everywhere in the world women are found in jobs that are low-paying and of low social status. This "pink ghetto" is characteristic of every country, regardless of how much progress has been made in women's permeation of the professions, or in narrowing wage differentials, or even in acknowledging women's right to work. The pink ghetto is found not only in developing countries but even in the Nordic countries. Women's average earnings in the manufacturing or other sectors are a fraction of what men are paid in those same occupations. Similarly, when it comes to government service, women are rarely found in upper-grade posts:

- In the United States, 37 per cent of federal civil service employees are women but they occupy only 6 per cent of higher level posts; [37]
- Women constitute more than half of all public servants in France,

but they earn 19 per cent less than men since they occupy mostly lower level jobs;[38]

WOMEN EARN LESS

Women are paid on average less than men. The country samples be low show women's average wages as a percentage of men's.

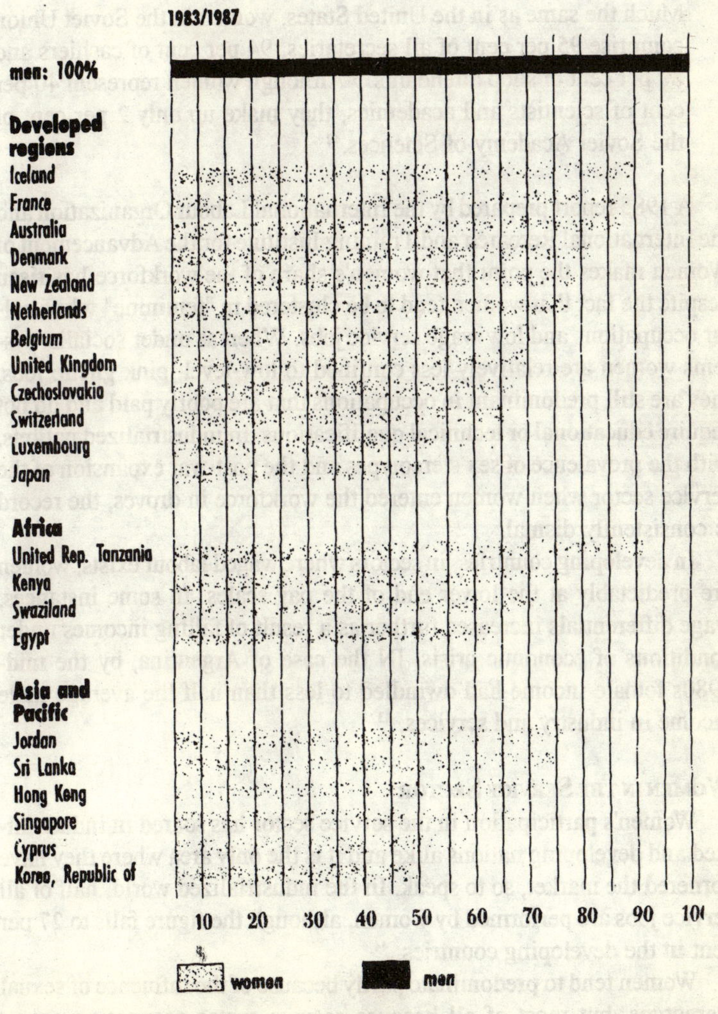

- Technical change affects women in unskilled jobs disproportionately: it has been estimated that, due to the introduction of micro electronics, 170,000 secretarial jobs will be lost in the United Kingdom by 1990; [39]
- In Japan, most women work in small companies with few benefits, In 1985, women were still earning only 52 per cent of what men earned; [40]
- Much the same as in the United States, women in the Soviet Union comprise 95 per cent of all secretaries, 94 per cent of cashiers and 80 per cent of shop attendants.[41] Although women represent 40 per cent of scientists and academics, they make up only 2 per cent of the Soviet Academy of Sciences.[42]

A 1985 report prepared by the International Labour Organization and the International Research and Training Institute for the Advancement of Women makes the point that women's share of the workforce has risen despite the fact that women tend to be clustered in "feminine" white collar occupations and low wage service jobs. Whereas under socialist systems women are relatively less confined to low-level, pink ghetto jobs, they are still predominant in occupations that are poorly paid and do not require educational or technical qualifications. In industrialized nations, with the prevalence of sex stereotypes and the post-war expansion of the service sector when women entered the workforce in droves, the record is consistently dismal.

In developing countries, in sectors where waged labour exists, women are predictably at the lower end of the pay scales. In some instances, wage differentials increased further as a result of falling incomes under conditions of economic crisis. IN the case of Argentina, by the mid-1980s female income had dwindled to less than half the average male income in industry and services.[43]

Women in the Service Sector

Women's participation in the service sector has soared in industrialized and developing nations alike and it is the only area where they have cornered the market, so to speak. In the industrialized world, half of all service jobs are performed by women, although the figure falls to 27 per cent in the developing countries. [44]

Women tend to predominate partly because of the influence of sexual stereotyps, but most of all because service sector occupation correspond neatly to women's traditional domestic roles:

- In the cities of Latin America, half of all working women are employed in the service sector, most as domestic servants; the figure rises to almost 60 per cent in Costa Rica; [45]
- In Morocco, despite a low percentage of women in the work force (20 per cent), they are usually employed as white collar government workers; [46]
- In Kuwait, more than 90 per cent of female workers before the Persian Gulf War were salaried employees and wage earners in the service sector, [47]
- Women account for 60 per cent of sales employees in the Philippine's service sector, [48]
- Between 1975-1985, women filled between 50 and 80 per cent of all service jobs in the 24 nations of the Organization for Economic Cooperation and Development; [49]
- In the United States, two thirds of all women are concentrated in lower paid, white collar jobs, earning on average only half of what men earn. Women constitute 99 per cent of all secretaries, 96 per cent of registered nurses and 94 per cent of bank tellers. [50]
- The picture is not so different in Eastern Europe where women account for three fifths of the service sector—in Hungary, 100 per cent of the typists and wage clerks are women, according to a 1982 report. [51]

Women in Industry

Two fifths of the world's workforce, or 1 billion people, are hitched to the machine that drives modern society. Although one in three of the world's paid jobs goes to women, they are only one quarter of those employed in industry. The factors that have triggered women's integration into the industrial sector are varied: they are usually related to mechanization, rapid urbanization, marginalization of the agricultural sector, a shrinking family income and the international division of labour, which draws certain manufacturing industries to locations in developing countries.

- In Eastern Europe, women are found in larger number in the manufacturing sector than anywhere else in the industrial world. In the Soviet Union, women account for 52 per cent of the workforce in the electronics industry and 67 per cent of those engaged in the manufacture of precision instruments. 52 In Hungary, almost 40 per cent of the industrial workforce was composed of women in 1983.[53]

- Between 1972 and 1980, women entered the job market in Italy at the rate of five women to one man. It was not until 1977 that the Italian Government passed an equal opportunity act making it illegal to discriminate on the basis of sex in the marketplace, whether in training, hiring, promotion, dismissal or pension. After 1977, the Fiat company made a decision to hire some 10,000 women for automobile assembly lines, formerly an exclusively male preserve. [54]
- In British industries, although the wage gap between men and women has narrowed, a wide differential still exists. In 1983, women earned 65 per cent of men's gross weekly wages. [55]
- French women have benefited from increasing legislative and administrative activity under a socialist government committed to making them aware of their rights. Thus, by 1984 female hourly earnings in non-agricultural occupations were 83 per cent of male earnings. [56]
- In Chine, labour segregation is so strong that in some industries, such as textiles, finance, commerce and tailoring , women comprise 80 per cent of the workers. [57] However, only 18.5 per cent of engineers are women. [58]

The boom in the industrial sector in Asia resulted in the number of women in industry growing by 104 per cent in the years between 196-1980, compared to a 70 per cent increase for men. [59] In countries like Brazil, India, Mexico and Nigeria which have experienced rapid growth by the manufacturing sector, women have been absorbed into certain industries, based on the assumption that they make a some docile and disciplined workforce. [60] The expansion of the Export Processing Zones, or EPZs, in these countries and in newly industrialized Asian countries (e.g. the Philippines, Sri Lanka, Thailand and Taiwan), has exploited cheap female labour, especially in the garment, textile and electronics industries. [61]

In developing countries, the introduction of new technologies has undermined subsitence farming, displacing women from traditional economic activity and speeding up their exodus to urban areas and the industrial sector. In industrialized nations, women's inclusion in the manufacturing sector results in a higher concentration of women in less skilled or in monotonous jobs, with lower wages and the threat of being displaced more easily than men. In France, women constitute only 1.8 per cent of skilled worker in the mechanical trades. [62] In Eastern Europe, women tend to be found in food processing and light industry, though they are present in the metal trades as well. ILO figures show that more than half of Bulgarian women industrial workers are employed in machine building, metal working, light industry and food processing. [63] The point is not to insist on their inclusion in high-risk or heavy industry, but to work towards their penetration into managerial and more technical positions, even as safety and working conditions are assured.

Legislating for Women in the Workplace

The International Labour Organization (ILO) has been in the forefront in building a body of law that protects women's equal rights in the workplace and safeguards against occupational hazards and discrimination. Many of its conventions pre-date the founding of the United Nations itself, while others require further action at the national level. Key achievements include:

- The 1951 Convention Concerning Equal Remuneration for Men and Women Workers for Work of Equal Value, ratified by 111 nations as of January 1991, is the principal international agreement requiring parties to promote equal remuneration for work of equal value. This is not the same as equal pay for equal work, another contentious principle; [64]
- The 1960 Convention Concerning Discrimination in Respect to Employment and Occupation promotes equality of opportunity and treatment in the workplace in order to eliminate any discrimination; it had been ratified by 110 countries as of January 1991. [65]

Legislation on maternity leave has met with less success if one judges by the 1955 ILO Convention on Maternity Protection, ratified by only 25 countries as of 1991. [66] Similarly, adherence to conventions on right work, women workers with family responsibilities or unfair termination of employment remains low. [67] Conventions adopted by the United Nations itself reinforce some of these instruments. The international Covenant on Economic, Social and Cultural Rights calls for equal pay for equal work and the right to promotion, while the Convention on the Elimination of All Forms of Discrimination against women urges equal remuneration, including benefits. As a result of the United Nations Decade for Women, the number of countries that enacted equal pay laws rose significantly. [68]

Governments can pay lip service to the low without translating legal niceties into reality; thus the ratification and stricter enforcement of existing conventions must become a priority in the 1990. Certain countries have already made some progress in this domain:

- In Italy, provision is made for women to work, making allowances for their domestic responsibilities; [69]
- Some Latin American countries, including Cuba, Ecuador and Nicaragua, have outlawed discrimination and called for equal rights and opportunities regardless of women's marital status, while many others provide maternal care and benefits; [70]
- Sweden is one of the few countries that has model provisions for parental leave, amounting to a total of nine months at 90 per cent of the mother's earnings, protection of her seniority and a guaranteed return to her job; [71]

Since labour legislation does not apply to the informal sector where the vast majority of women in developing countries work, discrimination persists and is difficult to root out. Frequently, agrarian reform has actually impaired women's rights by not recognizing women as heads of household or farmers, thereby excluding them from eligibility for loans, credit and title deeds. As a result, landlessness among women is on the rise, even in countries where women form the majority of the agricultural labour force.

Even in the formal sector, notwithstanding equal pay legislation, women almost always earn less than men for the same work or work of comparable value. Take agriculture in most of Asia and Africa, for example, where women's average daily wages for the main crops are 25 to 33 per cent less than those earned by men; [72] or Bangkok, where female wages in the informal sector are one third lower than those of males; [73] or Manila, where almost half the enterprises employing women pay them below the minimum wage. [74] Even in developed countries like Switzerland, women earn only 67 per cent of men's wages, while in Cyprus, the figure is 59 per cent. And in Japan, women are paid only 52 cents for every dollar earned by men. [75] Although translating the law into practice is often the major stumbling block, there may be some good news in that roughly 100 countries have adopted equal pay legislation, compared to only 28 countries in 1978. [76]

The Backlash of the "Lost Decade

Across much of Africa, Latin America and the Caribbean, the economic crisis of the 1980s and the World Bank/International Monetary Fund stabilization and adjustment programmes adopted to redress it, significantly worsened women's socio-economic position and standard of living. "Women have been at the epicentre of the crisis and have borne the brunt of the adjustment efforts," recently reported the Commonwealth Expert Group on Women and Structural Adjustment. [77]

Negative cumulative growth rates in gross domestic product per capita were recorded in 70 per cent of the countries in Africa, the Middle East and Latin America. This development, coupled with falling per capita incomes, soaring prices, interest rate hikes and drastic cuts in government spending, affected women in each of their roles. By placing further demands on women as products while reducing access to social services that supported women's other roles, structural adjustment programmes placed a disproportionate burden on women, reversing economic and social progress achieved over the past 30 years.

"In all developing regions, and recently even in some developed regions, growth in the female labour force has been undercut by economic recession," *The World's Women: 1970-1990* reports. [78] In some developing countries, poorer women are now working 60 to 90 hours a week to try to maintain their meagre living standards of a decade ago. "Women generally continue to be the last to benefit from job expansion and the first to suffer from job contraction—particularly in the stagnant or declining economies of Africa and Latin America and the Caribbean. In Africa, due to especially severe economic conditions, the growth in the female labour force has fallen well behind population growth." [79] Women—the victims of the economic crisis and adjustment strategies—have been negatively affected as employment, income and conditions of work deteriorated during the 1980s.

ADJUSTMENT WITH A FEMALE FACE

While the adverse effects of stabilization and adjustment programmes on women and vulnerable groups have recently been recognized by national governments and international organizations, women's needs and concerns have yet to be explicitly recognized in policy-making. Remedial schemes to mitigate the adverse effects of adjustment on women have generally been characterized as amounting to "too little, too late".

The Commonwealth Expert Group on Women and Structural Adjustment argued in a recent report that "effective adjustment requires the full participation of women. As producers, women's labour is critical to the output of food and labour-intensive manufactures, both of which are vital to the adjustment efforts, while their earnings are essential to contain the cuts in household incomes. Moreover, these income cuts, which currently form such a big part of adjustment, would have far worse effects on health and nutrition without women's domestic success of adjustment efforts and the minimization of social costs are critically dependent on the creative response of women."[80]

Governments need to keep in mind that narrowing economic disparities will go a long way towards eliminating social barriers. Women must be integrated into the main-stream development and adjustment programmes and their many roles and responsibilities have to be recognized so that they can manage the burden of holding up half the sky, and not more.

ECONOMIC CHALLENGES TO THE YEAR 2000

- Introduce special measures to increase the proportion of women involved in economic decision-making
- Establish specific training programmes, especially for women living in extreme poverty, to improve their condition
- Expand the definition of "economically active" persons to include women performing productive but unpaid tasks in developing countries
- Establish guidelines for gender disaggregated statistics so that women's work is clearly reflected
- Include women's paid and unpaid work in national accounts and economic statistics
- Guarantee equal employment opportunities; provide preferential treatment in the hiring of women until equal employment conditions are established
- Provide equal access to financial credit, family benefits and the right to participate in recreational, cultural and athletic activities
- Ensure that women with children have the right to work, to maternity leave and to other parental benefits
- Develop services to reduce women's child care and domestic workload, including incentives to employers to provide child care facilities for working parents
- Establish flexible working hours and parental leave to encourage the sharing of child care and domestic work between parents
- Guarantee equal pay for work of comparable value; encourage total gender desegregation of the workplace
- Ensure adequate welfare services (e.g. social security, pension and unemployment benefits)

NOTES

1 Margaret Alie, Hypatia's Heritage: *A History of Women's in Science from Antiquity to the Late Nineteenth Century* (London: Women's Press, 1990). pp. 41-32, 44-46.

2 *Engendering Adjustment for the 1990s*, op. cit., chap. 2, pp. 35-50.
3 Marilyn Waring, *If Women counted*, (San Francisco: Harper and Row Publishers, 1988), pp. 29-30.
4 *The World's Women: 1970-1990*: op. cit., p. 83.
5 Ibid., p. 85.
6 Ibid.
7 *Women: A World Report, A New Internationalist Book*, (New York: Oxford University Press, 1985), p. 4.
8 Ibid., p. 3.
9 *The World's Women*: 1970-1990, op. cit., p. 10.
10 Ibid., p. 9.
11 Ibid., p. 10.
12 Gender Planning in the Third World", *World Development*, November 1989, p. 1802.
13 Rhoodie, A Global Survey of the *Economic, Educational, Social and Political States of Women*, op. cit., p. 29.
14 United Nations Economic Commission for Africa, (E/ECA/REIWD/OAU/4), 1984.
15 United Nations information kit, World Assembly on Aging, Vienna, 1982.
16 *Economic and Social survey of Asia and the Pacific 1990*, published by the United Nations Economic and Social Commission for Asia and the Pacific, cited in Press Release NO. F/03/91, 8 March 1991, at the 47 session of ESCAP, Seoul, Republic of Korea.
17 *Women: A World Report*, op. cit., p. 16.
18 Ibid, p. 18.
19 World Labour Report, International Labour Organization, Geneva, 1985, p. 203.
20 *The Hidden Power of Women," Development and Cooperation*, German Foundation for International Development, January 1990, p. 12.
21 *Women: A World Report*. op. cit., p. 17.
22 Ibid, p. 19.
23 Ibid., 20.
24 *World Labour Report*, op. cit., p. 206
25 Ibid.
26 Ibid.
27 *Women: A World Report*, op. cit., p. 23.
28 Ibid.
29 *Women in Developing Countries*: *Invisible Victims of the Economic Crisis*, op. cit., p. 3.
30 "Video as a Tool in Training and Regionalizing: Experiences of Video SEWA", *Development*, Journal of the Society of International Development , February 1990.
31 *Women in Developing Countries*, op. cit., p. 3.
32 *World Labour Report*, op. cit., p. 206.
33 *Poor, Powerless and pregnant*, op. cit., pp., 6-7
34 *The World's Women* : 1970-1990, op. cit., p. 3.
35 Monitoring the Implementation of the Nairobi Forward-looking Strategies for the Advancement of Women, Report presented to the United Nations Commission on the Status of Women (E/CN.6/199/11), Vienna, February 1991.
36 Ibid.
37 Sara Rix (ed.), (New York: W.W. Norton, 1988), *The American Woman 19 88-1989*: A Status Report.
38 Rhoodie, op. cit., p. 208.
39 Equal Opportunitics Commission, London, 1980, as cited in Rhoodie, op. cit., p. 43.
40 *Christian Science Monitor*, 10 January 1985.

41 Rhoodie, op. cit., p. 439.
42 Ibid., p. 438.
43 Women in Developing Countries, op. cit., p. 2.
44 International Labour Office, Bureau of Statistics, as cited in Women: *A World Report*, op. cit. p 31.
45 *Five Studies on the Situation of Women in Latin America*, United Nations, New York, 1983, p. 170.
46 Rhoodie, op. cit, p. 358.
47 *Women in Economic Activity*, ILO, Geneva, 1986, pp. 66-67.
48 Rhoodie, op. cit., p. 358.
49 Ibid., p. 44.
50 Sylvia Hewlett, *A Lesser LIfe: The Myth of Women's Liberation in the USA*, (New York: Warmer Books, 1986). pp. 46-47.
51 *World Labour Report*, op, cit., p. 210.
52 Rhoodie, op., cit., p. 294.
53 Ibid., p. 177.
54 Bianca Becalli and Rita Invernizzi, *Women in Non-traditional Jobs, the Italian Case*, Paper presented at the Conference on the Empowerment of Women, Groningen, Sweden, 1984.
55 *Department of Employment Gazette, London*, October 1983.
56 Andree Michel (ed.), *Positive Action for the Benefit of Women*, Council of Europe, Strasbourg, 1986, Vol. 3, p. 16.
57 *Women at Work*, Trade Unions and Women's Employment, International Labour Organization, Vol. 1, Geneva, 1988, p. 45.
58 "Women Fighting Discrimination in Jobs and Schooling", *China Reconstructs*, March 1986, p. 35.
59 *World Survey: Women in Industrial Development* (A/CONF. 116/4), United Nations, Nairobi, July 1985.
60 "On the Global Assembly Line: Women and Multinationals", *Development: Seeds of Change*, April, 1984, pp. 31-32.
61 Ibid.
62 World Labour Report, op. cit., p. 211.
63 Ibid., pp. 211-212.
64 Women at Work, Vol. 2, ILO, 1987, pp. 34-40.
65 Ibid.
66 Ibid.
67 Ibid.
68 Rhoodie, op. cit., p. 76.
69 Ibid., p. 186.
70 David Ziskind, "Labour Law in Latin America Constitutions", *Comparative Labour Law*, University of California, Vol. 6. No. 1, Winter 1984.
71 Rhoodie, op. cit., p. 186.
72 *1989 World Survey on the Role of Women in Development*, op. cit. p. 94.
73 Ibid., p. 226.
74 Ibid.
75 *The World's Women*: *1970-1990*, op. cit., Table 6.9, p. 88.
76 Rhoodie, op. cit., p. 82.
77 *Engendering Adjustment for the 1990s*, op. cit., p. 5.
78 *The Worlds' Women*: 1970-1990, op. cit., p. 83.
79 Ibid.
80 *Engendering Adjustment for the 1990s*, op. cit., p. 32.

WOMEN IN POLITICS: MORE VOTES, MORE VOICES

Despite that little boy's view, women politicians, not to mention female prime ministers, are rare. Women who try to succeed in the world of politics discover that the hurdles they face, whether based on tradition, finances, ethnicity or organization, are compounded by the hurdle that is theirs by birth—that of gender. Thus, women's increased participation in mass politics over recent decades has been predominantly concentrated in the lower echelons of public administration, political parties and trade unions and has not been matched by the same presence at higher levels of policy-and decision-making.

Consider the following statistics:

- Although women constitute 50 per cent or more of the world's population, female representation in the highest circles of government is less than 10 per cent. [1]
- In 1990, only 3.5 per cent of the world's cabinet ministers were women. [2]
- Women hold no ministerial positions in 93 countries. [3]
- Women are completely absent from the four highest levels in government in 50 countries (5 in the group of Western European and other States, 8 in Latin America and the Caribbean, 21 in Africa and 16 in Asia and the Pacific).[4]
- Women similarly occupy less than 5 per cent of the top positions in international organizations,[5] including the United Nations and the European Community.

- In April 1991, there were only seven female heads of State or Government: Corazon Aquino (Philippines), Gro Harlem Brundtland (Norway), Violeta Chamorro (Nicaragua), Mary Eugenia Charles (Dominica), Vigdis Finnbogadottir (Iceland), Mary Robinson (Ireland) and Begum Khaleda Zia (Bangladesh).
- In May 1991, France appointed Edith Cresson as the first female Prime Minister and Head of Government in its history; women in France only obtained the right to vote in 1946.[6]

Women's inferior social and political position, ascribed to the natural physical differences between the sexes, has been cited to justify their exclusion from many professions at least as far back as the Greeks and the Romans. "No vote can be given by lunatics, idiots, minors, aliens, females, persons convicted of perjury, subornation of perjury, bribery treating or undue influence, or by those tainted of felony or outlawed in a criminal suit," commented Sir William Blackstone in his treatise on eighteenth century English law. [7] Al-Bukhari, an Islamic text, ordained that "A nation will never attain success whose control has been entrusted to a woman.[8] Even in the twentieth century a British member of Parliament had the nerve to argue: "A woman in the House of Commons is a contradiction in terms."[9]

As the new French Prime Minister, Edith Cresson observed, "There are three places where women have always been excluded: the military, religion and politics. I would say that today, it is still in politics where they have the least access." [10] Here, perhaps more than any other profession, women have discovered that to reach the top, they often cannot just match men, but must outdo them. A proverb makes the point well: "Whereas a man can be made of silver, a woman must be made of gold". [11]

Milestones or Mirages?

The Inter-Parliamentary Union, an organization that tracks trends in legislative bodies worldwide, reported that 55 countries had increased their representation of women between 1975 and 1989, 15 had decreased it, and three had remained the same.[12] Taking a more specific indicator, female members of cabinets appeared to have risen in 23 countries, stayed the same in 18, and decreased in 21.[13] A United Nations study compared the representation of women in upper and lower houses of parliaments, by region:

	Upper House (percentage)	Lower House (percentage)
Europe	13.4	18.7
North/Central America	12.7	9.2
Africa	8.3	8.4
Asia and Pacific	6.8	7.2
South America	3.2	4.4 [14]

Analysis of data in the *World-Wide Government Directory*, shows that even the growing presence of women in parliament does not counteract the fact that they are invariably shut out of decision-making positions. In 1990, only three countries had more than 20 per cent women at the ministerial level—Bhutan, Dominica and Norway. [15] In fact, Norway distinguished itself by being the only country to exceed 20 per cent female representation at the ministerial level in four areas: social economic, law and justice, and political affairs.[16]

WOMEN AT THE TOP

Women have progressively been involved in social welfare, political consciousness-raising, campaigning and grass roots organizations, all of which have served as a springboard for reaching higher political office. In recent decades, many women have even been front runners in political races, yet few have been chosen to head governments; as previously mentioned, there were only eight female heads of State or Government as of May 1991.

Even where women are appointed to top government positions, they are predominantly assignment to selected areas such as education, health and social welfare. This has the effect of "ghettoization", prolonging women's ineligibility for traditionally male preserves. In 1991 there were only a handful of women serving as finance ministers (in Bhutan, Finland, New Zealand, San Marino and Taiwan); Malaysia had women in the two key cabinet posts of Public Enterprise and Trade and Industry. [17]

It is not unusual for women to be appointed as ministers without being given cabinet rank. Conversely, cabinet rank may be merely symbolic—Francoise Giround in France, who was put in charge of women's issues, made over a hundred proposals, only a few of which were actually implemented. [18] Success requires political support from largely male colleagues. For example, in Zimbabwe when the Minister for Women's Affairs, Joyce Mujuru, and her staff were entrusted with challenging the practice of *lobola*, or bride price, they faced enormous resistance and were subsequently accused of "cultural imperialism".[19]

Even when women succeed in occupying high positions in government, commitments to improving the lot of other women may or may not be part of the package. When a historic strike against male privilege was held by Icelandic women in 1985, female President Finnbogadottir stayed at home to show her support. [20] In the United Kingdom, Barbara Castle, former British Secretary of State for Social Services, supported equal pay policies; former French Health Minister Simone Veil fought for birth control and abortion legislation in France; Miet Smet, Belgium's Secretary of State for Environment and Social Emancipation, had a broad emancipation agenda that included political empowerment. [21]

On the other hand, although Benazir Bhutto appointed four women ministers of State and one woman of cabinet rank, [22] with the exception of the Nordic countries, the arrival of a female head of State or Government does not automatically have a "trickle down" effect. Former British Prime Minister Margaret Thatcher, whose cabinet after the 1987 elections did not include a single woman, [23] was known to believe that "a successful woman is the best advertisement for women's equality". [24]

PARLIAMENTS:

"Lost Weight to Gain Votes"

When the first female contender for the post of President of Colombia got major press coverage in 1974, the headlines read "Lost Weight to Gain Votes".[25] Media treatment of female politicians often makes a difficult battle even harder. Cultural, ethnic and religious barriers can be formidable obstacles in themselves without the additional burden of being a woman in what has been staked out as male territory.

In Kenya, Julia Ojiambo's election to Parliament was a daunting battle. In what she described as a tough test of her credentials, her family faced threats and intimidation from the five male contestants and their supporters, and her husband was nearly killed. Yet, her determination to prevail against such odds finally became her passport to political power.[26] While barriers to women's participation in politics are not always so blatant or brutal, there are always obstacles to overcome.

Today most of the 18 countries with the highest female parliamentary representation (in which women hold over 20 per cent of the seats) are in Western Europe, Scandinavian and Eastern Europe. Norway, Romania and the Soviet Union top list with 34 per cent, Cuba follows with 33.9 per cent, Finland and Sweden are not too far behind with 31.5 per cent, and Albania and Czechoslovakia record just under 30 per cent. [29] In other European legislatures, female representation has declined or grown sluggishly. Switzerland only gave women the vote in 1971; in two half-cantons they were deprived of their franchise in local affairs until quite recently. [28]

Women in Parliament

Although there was improvement between 1975 and 1987, women's parliamentary representation remains very low in most regions of the world. As a result of political changes in Eastern Europe and the USSR, women's parliamentary representation actually fell between 1987 and 1990

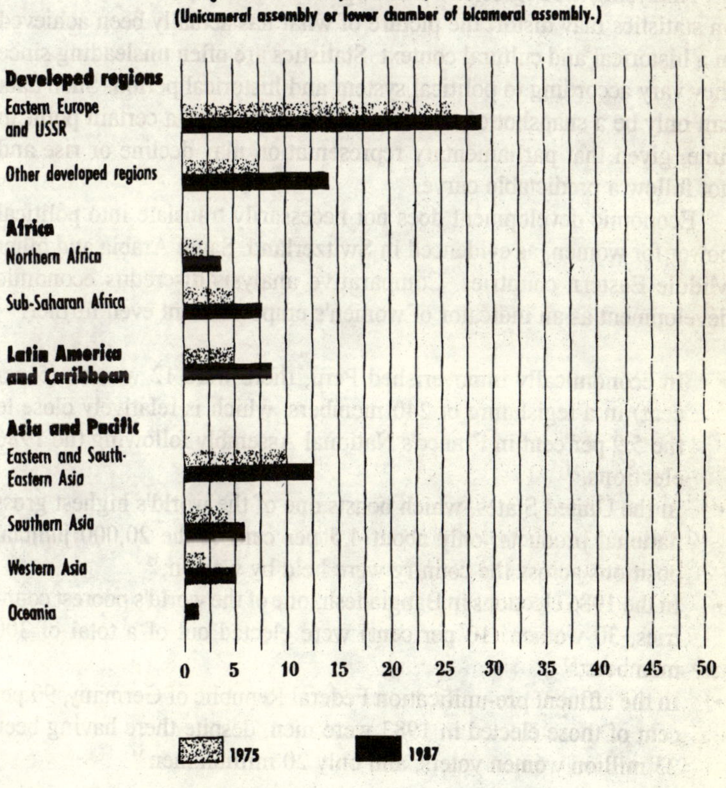

Source: The World's Women

In some developing countries, seats are set aside for women in parliament. One is Iran where 10 per cent of the seats are allocated to women although the candidates are nominated by men. [29] Some Islamic countries, such as Algeria, Egypt, Iraq and Turkey, have extended the franchise to women while others like Kuwait, continue to exclude them from voting or standing for election. [30] In the aftermath of the Persian Gulf conflict, however, Kuwaiti women are pressuring their Government for the right to vote along with other steps towards democratization.

Where North and South meet

Analysing the degree of women's political participation based purely on statistics may distort the picture of what has actually been achieved in a historical and cultural context. Statistics are often misleading since they vary according to political system and historical period. Such data can only be a snapshot of women's political status at a certain point in time, given that parliamentary representation may decline or rise and not follow a predictable curve.

Economic development does not necessarily translate into political power for women, as evidenced in Switzerland, Saudi Arabia and other Middle Eastern countries. Comparative analysis discredits economic development as an indicator of women's empowerment even further:

- In economically impoverished Peru, there were 12 women (5 per cent) in a legislature of 240 members, which is relatively close to the 5.9 per cent in France's National Assembly following the 1986 elections,[31]
- In the United States, which boasts one of the world's highest gross national products, only about 4.5 per cent of the 20,000 judicial positions across the country were held by women;[32]
- In the 1986 elections in Bangladesh, one of the world's poorest countries, 30 women (10 per cent) were elected out of a total of 300 members;[33]
- In the affluent pre-unification Federal Republic of Germany, 90 per cent of those elected in 1983 were men, despite there having been 23 million women voters, and only 20 million men[34]

POLITICAL PARTIES:

The Chrysalis of the Political Process

Around the world, women politicians have found that they often have to display a more impressive record of academic credentials and public service than men in order to compete effectively with them. Few women lawyers, university lecturers or journalists are selected, although these professions are often the training ground for potential male politicians. Nor are women frequently found in executive bodies of political parties, certainly a handicap if they aspire to political careers.

The Inter-Parliamentary Union, in a report for which 50 countries provided statistics, found that in only three (Austria, Israel and Luxembourg) had women ever been founders of political parties; in 21, women were leaders of parties, large and small; in 8, women were party vice-leaders. [35] Female membership in most European parties ranged between 20 and 40 per cent. In two cases, Norway and Sweden, membership in one of the parties was as high as 50 per cent, while in Great Britain female membership in the Conservative Party was 51 per cent. [36]

Even if more qualified women campaigned, however, it doest not automatically follow that a correspondingly larger number of women would be elected to office. A poll conducted in nine European countries for the Council of Europe revealed that 39 per cent of women felt that too few of their kind offered themselves as candidates, while 46 per cent of women preferred to vote for men; 36 per cent of the women polled also expressed the opinion that higher female representation in parliament would make no difference at all in public policy.[37]

Even where women's involvement in the party is significant, their election to positions of authority is not guaranteed. However, in cases where women have risen to influential positions in the party hierarchy, their subsequent ascent to parliamentary office was correspondingly smoother. Still, political parties are usually averse to taking risks and may not put women up for office. The evidence from European countries shows, on the contrary, that more women got elected than were presented as candidates by parties. For example, in Italy, 7.6 per cent were women candidates proposed by parties but almost double that figure (13.6 per cent) were elected.[38]

Very little global data analyses party activism by gender; what statistics do exist are restricted to Europe. Although information is scarce when it comes to political parties in developing countries, the pattern has generally been one of attempting to integrate women into the mainstream political process through support from a women's wing of the party. In Colombia, most of the 41 women party activities credited the women's branch with giving them a start in formal politics. [39] The women's section of India's Congress Party, which has a policy of fielding 20 per cent female candidates in state elections, was a stepping stone for Indira

Gandhi and other female politicians.[40] Unfortunately, too often women's sections reinforce gender distinctions.

Women get stuck in the lower echelons and do not even make it to party executive committees, or, if they do, may be token appointees with little real political leverage. In Malaysia, about half of the members of the United Malay National Organization are women-yet few are nominated for office or, if elected, chosen for the cabinet.[41] In Zambia, the Women's League of the ruling United National Independence Party concerns itself more with abstract, moral and ethical issues than with support for female candidates.[42]

Beyond the Pale of Institutional Politics

In 1965, Fatima Ahmed Ibrahim became the first female member of the Sudanese Parliament; she has since become something of a legend in her own lifetime. [43] Along with former schoolmates, she founded the Sudanese Women's Union, which demanded increased political rights for women. As a result, due to collaboration between the women's union, the worker's trade unions and intellectuals, a law was passed in 1968 guaranteeing women's social rights.

In many regions, the labour movement has been a hotbed of activism for women with political aspirations. Labour union in some countries, like Canada, Ireland and the United Kingdom, have designated a number of seats in their executive bodies to be filled by women.[44] In China, women represent 37 per cent of the workforce and there are 60,000 full time women representatives; 29 per cent of the Executive Committee of the All-China Federation of Trade Unions is female. [45]

Although women have contributed actively to many revolutionary and independence struggles that have occurred during this century, they have rarely been appointed to political office in the new government. One example is Nicaragua, where many women risked their lives during the struggle to remove President Anastasio Somoza, but in the government established after his overthrow only one woman was appointed to the cabinet, as Minister of Health; and even under the leadership of President Violeta Chamorro, the situation has not improved.

Examining Latin America as a region, the history of women in politics has often been a mixture of formal institutional participation and informal networking based on opposition to regimes and concern with human rights. Although Chilean women were enfranchised in 1949, an impressive growth in women's organizations was not noted until 1976, a few years after General Augusto Pinochet came to power. [46] In Argentina, the Madres de la Plaza de Mayo gained recognition for their singleminded demonstrations over a 10-year period for loved ones who had disappeared during military rule. [47] In the 1980s, another group in Argentina, the Housewives Organization, gained fame protesting cost-of-living increases. [48]

Some women prefer a path beyond the pale of institutional politics to forming women's parties or competing with men for political office. At a 1987 global gathering of women political leaders, most of the 62 women from 42 countries had their first brush with politics in non-governmental organizations and had arrived on the political scene through channels less often used by males.[49]

The Road to Political Empowerment

The political landscape of the twentieth century is dotted with gains made in the realm of women's political rights, especially in recent decades. Some major United Nations contributions to that political landscape include:

- *The Convention on the Political Rights of Women* (1952) and the International Covenant on Civil and Political Rights (1966), which urge States to put women's political rights on an equal footing with men's and to give women equal opportunity to serve in public life;
- *The Convention on the Elimination of All Forms of Discrimination against Women* (1979) with over 100 ratifications to date, which urges governments to ensure that women have the opportunity to hold public office, to participate in the formulation and implementation of government policy and to represent their governments at the international level;
- *The Nairobi Forward-looking Strategies for the Advancement of women*, adopted in 1985 at the end of the United Nations Decade for Women, which emphasized the fact that women were still inadequately represented in national and international political processes. It suggested that efforts be intensified to overcome prejudices, stereotyped thinking, obstacles to women joining the diplomatic service and denial of career prospects. It further declared that the role of women in national liberation struggles should be expanded to allow their equal participation in the national building process afterwards.

The United Nations Decade for Women also played a pivotal role in recasting the objective of bringing women to the political foreground as part and parcel of the process of development. In this sense, dialogue between women in developed and developing countries heightened the appreciation of the close linkage between gender issues and development. Thus, for women in developing countries, improving their status acquired its own legistimacy without a label reading "Made in the West".

One of the most beneficial outcomes of the Decade was the development of statistical and social information about women that was not available before. WISTAT, the United Nations Women's Indicators and Statistics database, which is a focal point for compilation of statistics on women throughout the world, became operational in 1988. Another sign of progress was that by the end of 1985 more than 90 per cent of United Nations Member States had official bodies for women's advancement. Although much remains to be done, a watershed has been reached and women are beginning to value political education and legal literacy.

A Helping Hand

The lament that "women cannot understand politics" or that "women and politics don't mix" has become something of a self-fulfilling prophecy. On the "demand" side, women have had to be spurred into exercising their voting rights independently, on the "supply" side, they have had to be encouraged to enter political life. To enter the political realm successfully, women need a helping hand to counter the subtle and not so subtle discrimination from male politicians. Besides building informal networks for women, steps need to be taken at the national and local levels to facilitate their institutional political participation. On the affirmative action front, more can be done to set targets or establish quotas for female representation, to ensure equal gender representation in all political bodies and to recruit females specifically into parties and unions.

In Austria, Ireland and Sweden, educational campaigns have encouraged female enrolment in branches of education that can lead to political life.[50] Other countries have pushed for the recruitment of women in public service so they may develop political skills. And some countries have seen the wisdom of narrowing the focus of the agenda by investing in education, health care and income generation as a complement to political empowerment.

To provide party systems with greater gender balance, quotas introduced for parliaments in some countries were subsequently adopted by political parties. Sweden was first to try out such a system, in 1972, with the result that female representation in the executive of the Liberal Party reached 40 per cent. Parties in Denmark, France and Norway have also introduced quotas.[51]

Vigorous attempts to introduce women to trade union politics and to give them access to decision-making positions are also under way. Whereas women constitute 30 per cent of the membership of the International Confederation of Free Trade Unions (ICFTU), their membership from individual countries varies.[52] Denmark, Finland and Sweden have over 50 per cent female members in the unions, as do Hungary, Mongolia and the Soviet Union.[53] Active recruitment of women to trade unions is being sought by ICFTU in Ecudor, Fiji, India, the Netherlands. Spain and the United Kingdom.[54]

Feminist parties exclusively for women have had difficulty in gaining credibility or translating it into political power. In Iceland, even with a woman as President, the women's party secures only 5 to 10 per cent of the vote. [55] The real value of women's parties in such instances may be to hold the balance of power, as many minority parties do when there is no outright winner.

And if inspiration is to be drawn, the Nordic countries provide a model of integration of women into political decision-making and public life, where high levels of education and involvement in women's organizations have been coupled with affirmative action by government .

Representation by women in Finland's Parliament registered a world record of 38.5 per cent as a result of the 1991 elections while an even higher percentage (41.2 per cent) was reached in the Finish Government, where seven of the 17 ministers are women.[56]

In Norway, over 34 per cent of parliamentary representatives, 31 per cent of municipal council members and 40 per cent of country council members were women in 1987, surpassing the 30 per cent "critical mass" that, according to experts, enables minorities to exert substantive influence. [57] Nearly half of Norway's cabinet is made up of women, and the media typically calls Prime Minister Brundtland's administration "a government of women".[58]

With women comprising one third of all ministers and parliamentary representatives, Sweden is also a pioneer in women's rights. As a result, public day-care and paternity leave have been transformed from "soft" to "hard" political issues, spurred by women's participation in political life.[59]

According to the United Nations Division for the Advancement of Women, there is evidence that a similar trend might be under way in Austria, Bangladesh, Germany and New Zealand where recent elections revealed that women appear to be voting differently from men, resulting in a marked increase of elected female representatives (up to 20 per cent).

Women and Democratization: Plight or Progress?

With the advent of *glasnost*, Soviet and Eastern European women began to protest that their legal equality and strong representation in State legislatures were merely "cosmetic rights" which masked a harsh reality—that is, a heavier workload but virtually no greater decision-making power than women without such prerogatives. Even women holding political office, it is argued, have had in effect no power than women without such prerogatives. Even women holding political office, it is argued, have had in effect no power other than that of endorsing decisions adopted by the State apparatus.[60]

Women's active role in the process of democratization has in some cases induced significant political and legal changes in their favour. In Romania, for example, one of the first acts of the new Government was to revoke the anti-contraception legislation which had resulted in dramatically increased maternal mortality rates over the past 20 years. In the Soviet Union, a Committee on Women, Family, Mother and Child Protection was recently organized in the Supreme Soviet—the first such committee to provide a legal basis for dealing with problems of women and the family. [61] In 1990, this Committee was instrumental in the adoption of a nation-wide programme of immediate action to improve the status of women and protect mothers and children. In other cases, however, democratization has not necessarily translated into political power for women: in Poland, for instance, the 1991 Government appointed only a token number of women. There are no women among the 49 local governors or among the Cabinet ministers, and there are fewer female deputy ministers than before. Despite the fact that women contributed to the Solidarity movement, only 4 to 96 National Solidarity Committee members are women.

Yet, despite such set-backs, there is a growing consensus on the part of Eastern European and Soviet women that, even though fewer of their kind are elected to office these days, the ones that make it have more decision-making power and are poised to play a more important role in the democratic restructuring of their societies.[62]

For the vast majority of women and particularly for poor women, however, democratization has often meant little more than increased hardship. As euphoria over the reforms in Eastern Europe and the USSR tapered off, dampened by the dramatic collapse of the centralized economies, women emerged as victims of the transition from State-run to free-market economies. New problems (e.g. unemployment and drastic cutbacks in social services, such as nursery schools) and new dangers (e.g. pressure to reinstate women's traditional social roles as dependent spouse, mother and housewife) are creating new obstacles to their advancement. Present developments appear to be reinforcing existing inequalities, but this need not be, argue many of the women concerned. The introduction of new political and economic system should, in fact, present a unique opportunity for the advancement of the status of women in all spheres of life by restructuring society to eliminate discrimination and foster equality.

In much of the developing world—from the Women's Movement for Amnesty in Brazil and the Women for Life in Chile, to the Black Sash and the African National Congress in South Africa—women are playing a prominent role in the democratization of their societies. Only seldom, however, do they reap the fruits of their labours. One notable exception is the case of Brazil, whose new constitution has incorporated most of the demands put forth by the National Council for Women's Rights.

Thus, the present wave of democratization does not mean that women's concerns will automatically be taken up by freely elected governments, nor will their participation in politics automatically be intensified. This should come as no surprise, for as author Rosalind Miles has observed, "All democratic experiments, all revolutions, all demands for equality have so far, in ever instance, stopped short of sexual equality" [63] And it seems facile to imagine that women can take on the mantle of political leadership unless basic needs are met and true gender balance is achieved in other areas of life.

The Turning Point

Even as unprecedented political change is sweeping the world, the silent revolutions that will propel women into the mainstream of political life are already under way; they need to be acknowledged and supported. Although the names that roll off our tongues when we recall women who have climbed the political ladder are often restricted to celebrities, the names of the vast majority of women in politics will not go down in the annals of history or become household words. Yet, theirs is a contribution that is inspirational because they are chipping away at resistance to women's political activity, slowly but surely penetrating the bastions of male power and blazing new trails. As Geraldine Ferraro, 1984 Vice-Presidential candidate in the United States, observed at the 1991 International Women's Day event staged by the United Nations in New York," What we need are not just a few women who make history, but many women who make policy".

With democratization as the catalyst, the 1990s are poised to be a critical decade that could either turn into a tragic era of missed opportunities or into a landmark in the advancement of women and civilization as a whole.

Political Challenges to the Year 2000

To boost women's political decision-making power, governments, non-governmental organizations, political parties, trade unions, the private sector, women's group and individuals should:

- Introduce special measures to increase the proportion of women involved in political decision-making
- Secure women's right to vote, stand for election and hold public or political office
- Encourage women to fully exercise the vote independently, according to their own individual preference.
- Generate support networks so that more women can campaign for public office, at the grass-roots, state national, regional and international levels
- Maintain rosters of qualified women for positions in government, political parties and trade unions
- Collect statistical data and publicize women's participation in high level decision-making bodies at the national, regional and international levels
- Promote qualified women to positions of power at every level within political, legislative and judicial bodies with the goal of achieving parity with men
- Encourage women in power to serve as mentors and otherwise support qualified women candidates in their career development
- Increase the number of women in leadership positions in public and private enterprise to at least 30 per cent by the year 2000, with a view to achieving future parity with men.

Notes

1 Rhoodie, *Discrimination Against Women,* op. cit., p. 17.

2 *The World's Women*: 1970-1990, op. cit., p. 31.

3 Ibid., p. 23

4 Ibid.

5 Ibid., p. 6.

6 *The New York Times*, 16 May 1991.

7 Sir William Blackstone, Commentaries on the Laws of England, cited in Morgan, *A Misogynist's Sourcebook*, op. cit., 216.

8 Al Bukhari, an Islamic text, cited in Miles, *The Women's History of the World*, op. cit., p. 67.

9 Enoch Powell, quoted in Morgan. *A Misogynist's Sourcebook,* op. cit., p. 66.

10 *The New York Times,* op. cit.

11 *Women in High-level Political Decision-making: A Global Analysis,* United Nations Expert Group Meeting (EGM/EPPDM/1989/WP.2), August 1989, p. 9.

12 Ibid.

13 Ibid.

14 *Women and Decision-making,* op. cit., p. 9.

15 *The World's Women:* 1970-1990, op. cit., p. 23.

16 *Women in High-level Political Decision-making,* op. cit., p. 11.

17 Ibid., p. 7.

18 Ibid., p. 11.

19 Ibid.

20 Rhoodie, op. cit., p. 178.

21 *Women in High-level Political Decision-making,* op. cit. cit., p. 13.

22 "Benazir Bhutto and the Future of Women in Pakistan", article in *Asian Survey;* May 1990, p. 435.

23 Rhoodie, op. cit., p. 34.

24 *Women in High-level Political Decision-making,* op. cit., p. 4.

25 Ibid., p. 6.

26 Perdita Huston, *Third World Women Sneak Out,* Praeger, (New York: 1979), p.106.

27 Praeger, *The World's Women*: 1970-1990, op. cit., pp. 31 and 32 using as source material the Inter-Parliamentary Union Reports and Document No. 14 (Geneva, 1987) "Distribution of Seats between Men and Women in National Assemblies".

28 Rhoodie, op. cit., p. 229.

29 Ibid., p. 347.

30 Ibid., p. 33.

31 Rhoodie, op. cit., p. 330.

32 Ibid., p. 32.

33 *Time Magazine, May* 19, 1986, as cited in Rhoodie, op. cit., p. 347.

34 Ibid., p. 27.

35 *Participation of Women in Political Life and in the Decision-making Process,* Inter-Parliamentary Union, Reports and Documents No. 15, International Centre for Parliamentary Documentation, 1988, pp. 30-34.

36 Ibid., 1988.

37 *The Situation of Women in the Political Process in Europe,* Council of Europe, Strasbourg, Vol. I, 1984, p. 70.

38 Ibid., p. 68.

39 "Peace: Full Participation of Women in the Construction of their Countries and in the Creation of Just Social and Political Systems", Report of the *Secretary-General to the Commission on the Status of Women* (E/CN.6/1989/7), Vienna, January 1989, p. 22.

40 "Women and Movement Politics in India", *Asian Survey,* October 1989, p. 943.

41 *Women in High-Level Political Decision-Making,* op. cit., p. 16.

42 Ibid. p. 17.

43 " So You Have to Fight", *Women of the Whole World,* Journal of the Women's International Democratic Federation, March-April 1989, pp. 54 and 55.

44 *Women in Politics: Still the Exception?* (UN Focus, DPI/1012), United Nations, Department of Public Information, November 1989.

45 Ibid.

46 Jane S. Jacquette (ed.), *The Women's Movement in Latin America:* Feminism and the Transition to Democracy, (Boston: Unwin Hyman, 1989), p. 150.

47 Ibid., p. 76.

48 Ibid., p. 78

49 *Women in Politics: Still the Exception?,* op. cit.

50 Ibid.

51 *The Situation of Women in the Political Process in Europe,* Council of Europe, Strasbourg, Vol. II, p. 113.

52 *Women at Work,* op. cit., Vol. I, pp. 29 and 38.

53 Testimony to the Committee on the Elimination of Discrimination against Women (CEDAW/C/5/Add. 1, p. 3, EDAW/C/5/Add.3, p. 5, EDAW/C/5/Add.20, p. 3 and EDAW/C/5/Add.12, p. 12), United Nations.

54 *Women at Work,* op. cit., Vol. II, p. 29.

55 Rhoodie, op. cit., p. 178.

56 "*Women in Politics*: *Finland Leads the Way*", United Nations Press Release (UNIS/WOM/358), 22 May 1991.

57 *Women in Norweigian Politics,* (Oslo: The Royal Ministry of Foreign Affairs in Cooperation with the Royal Ministry of Consumer Affairs and Government Administration, 1989), p. 9.

58 Ibid., p. 10.

59 *Women in Politics: Still the Exception?*, op. cit., 1989.

60 Lyudmila Gryaznova, *Social and Economic Status of Women in the Byelorussian Soviet Socialist Republic,* p. 6, and Zofia Kuratowska, *Present Situation of Women in Poland,* p. 10. Papers presented at the Regional Seminar on the Impact of Economic and Political Reform on the Status of Women in Eastern Europe and the USSR: The Role of National Machinery, Vienna, 8-12 April 1991.

61 Gryaznova, op. cit., p. 8.

62 Kuratowska, op. cit., p. 10.

63 Miles, *The Women's History of the World,* op. cit., p. 287.

WOMEN: VICTIMS OF VIOLENCE, ADVOCATES OF PEACE

Lysistrata's dilemma—that of being caught up in a war while powerless to influence its course through conventional means—is essentially the same dilemma in which most women find themselves in times of armed conflict. For, even though women have participated in and suffered from war for centuries, they have been virtually excluded from all stages of decision-making, from the commencement of hostilities to the conclusion of peace.

War is only one of many forms of violence to which women are subjected worldwide. There are other types of violence which affect most women at some point in their lifetime, regardless of their class, colour, religion or culture, and which can be equally devastating, even life-threatening. Every day, women are battered, sexually harassed, abused, raped and psychologically tortured in the home, the workplace and society.

Yet the problem of violence against women has only recently been recognized as a crime and major obstacle to equality, development and peace. In effect, peace—a fundamental human right—has been systematically denied to half the world's population for centuries, irrespective of the type of political and legal systems under which they lived. A woman's right to be free from danger and fear for her personal safety within the home, the workplace and society is likely to be the toughest battle women will wage in the 1990s.

What is Peace?

"Peace includes not only the absence of war, violence and hostilities and the national and international levels but also the enjoyment of economic and social justice, equality and the entire range of human rights and fundamental freedoms within society",[1] proclaimed the *Nairobi Forward-looking Strategies for the Advancement of Women in 1985*. This positive and comprehensive definition of peace brings into sharp focus the far-reaching implications of peace for women in that it highlights the absence of structural violence, [2] including "economic and sexual inequality, denial of basic human rights and fundamental freedoms, [and the] deliberate exploitation of large sectors of the population......"[3]

Even more importantly, the *Nairobi Forward-looking Strategies* were instrumental in creating a consensus: violence on the personal and international level are in fact inextricably linked. "The questions of women and peace and the meanings of peace for women cannot be separated from the broader question of relationships between women and men in all spheres of life and in the family," [4] it was argued.

WOMEN AS VICTIMS OF DOMESTIC VIOLENCE

> ".....the wife: however brutal a tyrant she may unfortunately be chained to —though she may know that he hates her, though it may be his daily pleasure to torture her, and though she may feel it impossible not to loathe him—[he] can claim from her and enforce the lowest degradation of a human being, that of being made the instrument of an animal function contrary to her inclinations." [5]
>
> —*John Stuart Mill*

It is a great tragedy that for most abused women violence begins at home with husbands, fathers, brothers and uncles. In developed and developing countries alike, physical, sexual and psychological abuse with the family affects an astounding number of women.

This bent towards brutality against women is reflected in popular culture the world over. The gist of a Spanish riddle is: "Question: What do mules and women have common? Answer: A good beating makes them both better". A Russian saying echoes the same refrain: "A wife may love a husband who never beats her, but she does not respect him:[6]

Owing to a paucity of research and the taboos surrounding admissions of violence against women in the family, and actual numbers of acts of violence will probably never be known. The fact that abuse is generally condoned by social custom and considered part and parcel of marital life, rather than a crime, is in itself a grim indication of its high incidence.

- In parts of Papua New Guinea, 67 per cent of women are victims of marital violence.[7]
- In Bangladesh, half of the 170 reported cases of women murdered between 1983 and 1985 took place within the confines of the family.[8]
- In the United States, a woman is beaten every 18 minutes; between 3 million and 4 million are battered each year, [9] but only 1 in 100 cases of domestic violence is ever reported.
- In Colombia, about 20 per cent of the patients in a Bogota hospital were victims of marital, violdence.[10]
- In India, five women are burned in dowry-related disputes each day, according to official figures, although the number estimated by activist group is much higher.[11]
- In the United Kingdom, one in three families is a victim of assault, according to a recent report by the Home Office.[12]
- In Austria, in 59 per cent of 1,500 divorce case, domestic violence was cited as cause in the marital breakdown.[13]
- Divorce petitions on grounds of violence in countries as diverse as Canada, Egypt, Greece and Jamaica are further evidence of the magnitude of the problem of domestic of the problem of domestic violence and of the fact that it is becoming one of the main grounds for divorce in many countries.

Despite these revealing findings, "the extent of violence against women in the home has been largely hidden and widely denied by communities that fear that an admission of its incidence will be an assault on the integrity of the family", [14] according to a recent United Nations study. Experts assert that domestic violence is not merely a social ill but a crime of equal stature with other crimes that urgently needs to be addressed as such. Without adequate legal protection and a social system responsive to domestic violence, women typically find themselves helpless before their spouses and before society as a whole.

In fact, it has been argued that marriage renders women even more vulnerable to violence, in this instance from their own husbands. Wife assault accounts of about 25 per cent of violent crimes in the United States, while one in seven wives in the United Kingdom has been raped by her spouse.[15] A United Nations study recently concluded that ' physical attack is often accompanied by sexual violence and rape, the psychological effects of which are perhaps more serious than rape by a stranger give the breach of trust that such conduct involves."[16] Yet, only a few countries, including Canada, Czechoslovakia, Denmark Poland, Scotland, the Soviet Union and Sweden have in corporated marital, rape as a crime in their legal systems. [17] Part of the reasons for the slow recognition of marital rape is that in many countries, marriage is perceived to give a man complete licence for sex, regardless of the wishes of his wife.

Violence does not occur as an isolated incident in the lives of abused married women and young girls. Physical brutality, as well as mental torture, usually occurs on a regular basis, causing incalculable suffering and inflicting deep scares on the victims, the victim's families and on society as a whole. Women's physical and mental health is often permanently danger or impaired, and in some cases violence can have fatal consequences. Pregnant women are particularly at risk. Not surprisingly, perhaps, abused women are 12 times more likely to attempt suicide than non-abused women. [18] For some battered women, alcohol and drug abuse become their escape, with disastrous effects on their health and well-being.

As a result, domestic violence has devastating repercussions on the family. Mothers are unable to care for their children properly. Often they transmit to them their own feelings of low self-esteem, helplessness and inadequacy. Children themselves may become victims of their father's abuse if they try to defend their mother. On the other hand, boys who witness their father beating their mother are likely to emulate this behaviour. In Canada, it has been found that sons of batterers are 1,000 per cent more likely to beat their own wives.[19]

The economic cost to society of dealing with this problem is enormous in terms of medical treatment and counselling for the victim, the abused woman's dependence on the welfare system, and the introduction of preventive measures. In Canada alone, wife battering cost the Government and taxpayers $32 million in 1980. [20] Yet, there is little guarantee that an abused woman will not be mistreated again. More ominously, domestic violence reinforces and perpetuates a status quo of political, social and economic discrimination against women.

Why are women Abused?

The reason why so many women "put up with" abuse in the home is primarily due to their unequal status in society and the fact that they have no viable alternatives available to them. Women are often caught in a vicious circle of economic dependence, fear for their children's lives as well as their own, repeated pregnancies, shame, ignorance of their rights before the law, lack of confidence in themselves and social pressures. Fear of harming a husband's career and apprehension about the attitude of the police also prevent women from reporting crimes of domestic violence. A recent British study revealed that even though 92 per cent of abused women sought the detention of their abusers, actual arrests materialized in only 24 per cent of the cases.[21]

VIOLENCE AGAINST WOMEN

Although domestic violence often goes unreported, many countries are now recognizing that there is significant violence against women both inside and outside the family. Some countries are providing immediate protective measures to assist abused women.

	Types of violence: Domestic violence	Incest	Homicide in family	Sexual assault and rape	Sexual harassment	Protective measures: Police	Shelters	Non-governmental organizations	Legal aid	Financial assistance	Housing assistance
Developed countries											
Austria	●		●			●	●				
Finland	●	●		●	●		●	●			
Greece	●		●	●			●	●	●		
United States	●	●	●	●	●	●	●	●			
Africa											
Kenya	●		●								
Nigeria	●								●		
Uganda	●							●			
Latin America/Carib.											
Brazil	●			●		●		●			
Chile	●	●	●								
Colombia	●	●		●		●		●			
Jamaica	●	●		●			●	●		●	
Asia and Pacific											
Bangladesh	●		●				●	●	●	●	●
China			●					●			
India	●		●	●	●	●			●		
Malaysia	●			●				●	●		●
Thailand	●		●			●	●		●	●	

Source: *The World's Women*

These factors effectively sentence abused women to a life of recurrent mistreatment from which they often do not have the means to escape. Social prejudice reinforces domestic violence against women. Particularly since wives are after considered as little more them their spouses' property, husbands assume that this subordinate role gives them the tacit right to abuse their wives in order to "keep them in their place"—the underlying notion being that women are at best naughty children in need of discipline.

Physical brutality and sexual abuse are widespread largely because they have been sanctioned for centuries by legal systems which grant women no protection or recourse. In nineteenth century England and North America, as well as in much of the developing world today, even when a wife died or was permanently injured as a result of domestic violence, the husband was often excused by the law under various pretexts and his sentence was remarkably light.[22] As recently as 1954, Scotland Yard Commander G. H. Hatherill boasted: "There are only about 20 murders a year in London and many not at all serious—some are just husbands killing their wives."[23] Indeed, in all cultures men have had the right to kill their wives on suspicious of adultery until very recently. [24] The same rules have not applied to male adultery.

According to a recent comparative study on the legislation of several Mediterranean and Arab countries (i.e.Egypt, France, Iraq, Jordan, Kuwait, Lebanon, the Libyan Arab Jamahiriya, Portugal, Spain, the Syrian Arab Republic, Tunisia and Turkey), crimes of honour continue to absolve husbands and other male relatives, partially or fully, from charges of homicide or severe bodily injury to this day. [25]

The sanctity of privacy within the family, which makes authorities reluctant to intervene, often leads women to deny they are being abused, despite obvious physical signs of brutality which they attribute to self-inflicted accidents. Thus, what are euphemistically called "domestic disputes", but which frequently involve broken ribs and disfiguring facial injuries, are dismissed as family matters, while rape within marriage is ignored or simply not acknowledged as a crime in the vast majority of countries.

Rape and physical assault also extend to the female children within the family. From the United States to Australia, Egypt, India and Israel, one in four families falls victim to incest. One report estimated that as many as 100 million girls, often under 10 years of age, are raped by adult men, very often their fathers.[26]

Yet these figures of domestic violence most probably represent only the tip of the iceberg, considering that only a fraction of all cases are ever reported. It is particularly ironic that, in spite of impressive economic, technological and social progress world-wide, million of women around the world are routinely abused within their own homes—a tragic crime which needs to be urgently addressed and vigorously tackled.

Penalizing Domestic Violence

Over the past 15 years, the United Nations has made a concerted effort to bring the problem of domestic violence into the open. It has requested its Member States to adopt short-and long-term strategies that will protect victims and to adopt preventive measures to eliminate its incidence. These recommendations were made at the 1986 expert group meeting on violence in the family organized by the Division for the Advancement of Women and the Crime Prevention and Criminal Justice Branch of the United Nations Centre for Social Development and Humanitarian Affairs.[27]

A number of countries have made the elimination of domestic violence against women a national priority. The challenge in the 1990s will be to make the penalization of domestic violence a priority in all United Nations Member States and place it at the top of the agenda of the international community.

Such a campaign would call for the adoption of legislation to protect women from violence and the enforcement of penalties for violence against women in the family, at work, and in society as a whole. It would also necessitate the creation of a network of support services for victims, including shelters or other similar crisis centres for battered women, free legal aid, welfare services and financial support. Training programmes on the dynamics of family violence for judiciary, health and social service personnel, as well as law enforcement officers, would help to ensure humane treatment of victims. Helping re-employ abused women and creating appropriate deterrent and corrective measures would also be required.

Longer term measures that would help curtail domestic violence include comprehensive legislative reforms and legal literacy programmes for women to protect them and ensure their rights; greater economic independence of women that would give them equal status within marriage; and a change in the education system so that it would condemn domestic violence outright, promote equality between spouses, and encourage peaceful approaches to conflict resolution. Below are some examples:

- In Argentina, the democratically elected Government which took power in 1983 began a campaign against domestic violence, supporting self-help groups for battered women which offer medical, legal and psychological assistance.[28]

- In Australia, major reforms in federal criminal law recently classified domestic violence as an assault, which, as such, is subject to police intervention. In addition, a nation-wide education programme has been launched and training is now offered to professional groups dealing with abused women. Some 43,000 Australian women and their children sought refuge in shelters in 1986-87.[29]
- In Costa Rica, the Government has made abuse of women illegal as a first step towards curtailing it.[30]
- In Zimbabwe, the Musasa Project, set up in 1988 in Harare, for the first time provides support and counselling to women who have been beaten or raped by their husbands or lovers and informs them of their legal rights and legal procedures.[31]

It is also essential to focus world attention on the urgency of community education to raise public awareness of the seriousness of the crime of domestic violence and to begin changing social attitudes towards it. In the United States, the incidence of violence dropped significantly between 1975 and 1985 as a result of changed attitudes and behaviour towards women which accompanied measures designed to curtail the incidence of domestic violence.[32]

The international community, led by the United Nations, could play a key role in monitoring domestic violence on a country-by-country basis, sponsoring research on the relationship between the portrayal of violence against women in the mass media and the actual incidence of violence against women in the family and society, and organizing conferences that would sensitize public opinion and regularly focus world attention on family violence.

VIOLENCE IN THE WORKPLACE AND SOCIETY

"A little bit of rape is good for man's soul"[33]

—*Norman Mailer, 1972*

If men find it so easy to abuse the women they are most intimate with—their wives, daughters, nieces or grand-daughters—it is only too clear how easy they must find it to abuse other women who are strangers to them.

Sexual harassment in the workplace affects millions of women around the world regardless of their profession, but legal systems offer them virtually no protection. Even when they do have legal recourse, the fear of begin fired, penalized or ridiculed, or else the promise of a much wantcd promotion, keeps many women silent. The tautology of the secretary/mistress might be a cliche, but when management has to choose between losing a highly qualified and competent male executive and a dispensable female secretary, the choice is obvious.

Sexual harassment in the workplace typically ranges from middley distasteful sexist comments and jokes, pornographic pin-up posters, provocative electronic mail and X-rated computer software all the way to outright assault and rape in extreme cases. Sexual favours rather than merit and hard work often remain the determinants of a woman's professional career in a male-dominated workplace. For example, in England sexual harassment affects one in seven women, and one in five professional women, according to a recent survey by the London School of Economics.[34] At Cambridge University, a 1989 study found that one in ten women undergraduate students reported unsolicited sexual harassment from dons and one in three students suffered similar unwanted sexual attention from male students.[35] No code of conduct or disciplinary framework exists, however, to deal with such complaints. Sexual harassment also affects domestic servants, factory workers, women in the informal sector, and virtually all professions throughout the world.

In the absence of a legal definition of sexual harassment in most countries, few mechanisms exist to combat it. Sexist language, leering, pinching, advances and an abusive working environment are not grounds for legal action. Only physical assault, a criminal offence, provides adequate cause for filing a legal suit and it is often difficult to prove in court.[36]

In the United States, sexual harassment was not recognized by law until the mid 1970s. It was only in 1980 that the Equal Employment Opportunity Commission published a set of guidelines identifying harassment and hostileenvironment harassment.[37] Six years later, the Supreme Court ruled for the first time that sexual harassment constituted a violation of the 1964 Civil Rights Act.[38] Now, as courts extend the definition of sexual harassment and penalize companies with punitive damages, some companies are being forced to listen to women's demands for dignity in the workplace.

After decades of inertia, Europe has begun making some headway in combatting sexual harassment. In July 1991, the European Community adopted a new Code of Practice of the Protection of the Dignity of Women and Men at Work which encourages employers and workers to draw up a company policy statement so as to ban sexual harassment, to appoint trained personnel to handle complaints and to agree on guidelines for disciplinary proceedings.

Spain, and more recently France, have made sexual harassment a criminal offense though, as the new laws are vague, it might prove difficult for women to exercise these newly granted rights. As of mid-1991 Britain and Ireland had recognized sexual harassment in judicial terms but had not yet adopted laws against it.

In addition to harassment in the workplace, women are also prime candidates as victims of violence. Few women walk the streets at night without genuine fear for their safety. There is growing evidence that crimes against women are rising the world over. For example, in Trinidad and Tobago, the number of men charged with rape increased by 134 per cent between 1970 and 1980, even though the population rate rose by under 30 per cent in that time.[39] In the United States, three out of four women will be victims of at least one violent attack in their lifetime, the Justice Department recently disclosed.[40]

Sexual assault is the single most under-reported crime in most societies. Virtually all sexual assaults are against women. In the United States, rape is increasing four times faster than other crimes, and at present one woman is raped every six minutes.[41] This chilling statistic becomes even more shocking considering that only one in ten cases are ever reported.

Popular culture reflects the leniency afforded to rapists and the contempt shown toward rape victims. For example, in 1983 a British parliamentarian replied to a question on paedophilia by relating that the maximum penalty for indecent assault on girls aged 13-16 was two years' imprisonment, while the penalty for assault on boys was 10 years.[42] In another example, Judge William Reinecke described a five-year-old girl who was sexually assaulted by her mother's boyfriend in Wisconsin, USA in 1982 as "an unusually sexually promiscuous young lady".[43]

Even though crimes against women are on the rise in many countries, little is being done to change the legal process that makes it virtually impossible for women to prove they have been raped. Many women prefer to keep silent rather than be twice victimized by a legal system that is insensitive to their plight. There is an urgent need for both sexual harassment and violence against women in society to be addressed at the national and international levels to expedite a strategy of action.

Women, War and the Peace Process

War, the most dramatic form of violence, exacts a heavy toll on women, rendering them among the most vulnerable social groups in time of conflict. Armed conflicts in Central America, the Middle East and

Africa are leaving behind a growing number of civilian casualties, an increasing proportion of which are women. Wars are also responsible for some 16 million refugees, the majority of whom are widowed or abandoned women and their dependent children. These women lead a life of permanent displacement, struggling to survive in overcrowded refugee camps, often with few prospects of resuming normal lives or returning to their countries of origin.

War victimizes men and women alike; however, it often serves as a catalyst for social and political change. For example, Kuwaiti women who remained inside their country during the Iraqi occupation daily risked their lives. "I have known what it is to suffer for my country," said one Kuwaiti woman. "No one can say I am not a true Kuwaiti. No one can say that I do not deserve the same rights as these men."44

Women in Arms

Women have contributed to war efforts for centuries, both directly and indirectly. In Latin America, a clandestine network of women significantly contributed to the Mexican War of Independence in the early nineteenth century.[45] In Zimbabwe, Mozambique and more recently in Namibia, women freedom fighters distinguished themselves in the struggle against colonialism.

During the Second World War, women in Germany, the Soviet Union and the United Kingdom played a critical role, running the armaments industries while the men fought in the front lines. Other women joined the resistance. After the war, women throughout Europe were instrumental in rebuilding their countries. This often meant working in mining, construction and other traditionally male occupations.

Today, women make up 11 per cent of the armed forces in the United States. During the Persian Gulf war, more than 27,000 women served in the armed forces, 6 per cent of the entire United States military in the region.[46] In Israel, women serve mandatory military service on the same basis as men.

Women in the Peace process

Not only has women's role in war gone unrecognized, underestimated or undervalued, women have been matter-of-factly excluded from all phases of the peace process. On the national level, government bodies dealing with defence and international relations have virtually no women representatives (only Finland and Canada have women at the ministerial level in defence), despite recognition of the necessity to increase their participation. In the developed world, fewer than one third of all countries have adopted measures to redress this problem.

On the international level, a recent United Nations report noted that from 1985 to 1988 women's representation in the Main Committee of the General Assembly dealing with disarmament and international security was under 8 per cent.[47] In fact, during the United Nations Decade for Women, the number of female representatives in parliamentary assemblies increased by less than 2 per cent.[48] Even within the United Nations, women rarely sit in the Security Council and are inadequately represented in disarmament, security and conflict resolution committees.

Low or no representation does not mean that women do not have a vested interest in peace. On the contrary, women have traditionally been among its most ardent advocates, In 1915, less than a year after the commencement of the First World War, women from all over the world met in The Hague, Netherlands, to establish the first international peace movement.[49] Since then, women have organized hundreds of demonstrations to protest against the neutron bomb and the nuclear arms race, and to support disarmament talks and the creation of peace camps. Women have also founded peace institutes to promote research into reducing the incidence of war and violence, including the Institute for Training in Non-Violence, founded by Beverly Woodward and World Priorities created by Ruth Sivard.

At all levels of society, women have a key role to play in peace education, which should promote racial and sexual equality, tolerance and cooperation. For, just as peace is not simply the absence of war, violence and hostilities, peace education is not merely about the causes of war and conflict resolution. According to Nancy Shelley, an Australian peace activist, "Peace education is concerned with: respect for persons, personal relationships.....social justice, sharing the world's resources, cooperation, and community. Peace education deals with oppression, sexism, racism, injustice and a recognition that violence has to do with power. Peace education involves a radical approach to curriculum, the structure of schools, and the personal relationship within schools. Peace education is concern for the planet, the environment and the connectedness of humans to other life....."[50]

Women as Advocates of Disarmament

The successful decolonization of Namibia through United Nations mediation and international negotiation and the ongoing dismantling of apartheid in South Africa amply demonstrate that conflict, however complex and deeply rooted, can be resolved by means other than force. Indeed, the Persian Gulf war has confirmed, yet again, that war does not necessarily resolve conflict. The complexity of Iraq's postwar internal crisis and the plight of millions of Kurds are ample evidence of the ineffectiveness of war in restoring peace.

MILITARY-FOR-SOCIAL-SPENDING SWAP

A more 5 per cent reduction in world military budgets would free an annual $ 50,000,000,000 for social services. Here's what that amount could buy in 1989 in terms of mass destruction or mass protection.

MILITARY	$ BILLION
20 Advanced tactical jet fighters	0.9
10 Vertical take-off combat aircraft	1.4
20 Stealth bombers	10.5
2 Sea-wolf attack submarines	2.3
10 Aegis cruisers	8.4
5 Nudear-powered aircraft carriers	15.9
243 Trident II submarine-launched missiles	7.9
1,700 Tomahawk long-range cruise missiles	2.7
TOTAL	$ 50.0

IS EQUAL TO:

SOCIAL SERVICE	$ BILLION
Maternal health and education	6.0
Community health centres	1.3
Child immunization	3.0
Supplomontary feeding programmes	20.0
Environmental clean-up of nuclear bomb plants	12.0
Safe water and sanitation	.8
Reliable technology	.2
Education and information	.2
Funding for World Health Organization	.7
Research	5.0
TOTAL	$ 50.0

Source: Ruth Sivard, World Military and Social Expenditures 1989.

National, regional and international conflict continue to recur in many parts of the world, and, as a result of technological advancement, acquire potentially more devastating dimensions for the security of the world as a whole. Thus, it is imperative that new ways be found to promote world security and peace.

The Forward-looking Strategies for the Advancement of Women made it clear that "women's equal role in decision-making with regard to peace and related issues should be seen as one of the basic human rights, and as such, should be enhanced and encouraged at the national, regional and international levels."

Yet another reason for the critical importance of the promotion of peace is that without it there can be no development. Military expenditures around the world since 1970 have increased by over 40 per cent in developed regions and almost 130 per cent in developing regions. [51]

The year 1987 alone witnessed a record number of wars (24) in which four fifths of the casualties were civilians.52 Some 27 developing countries spend more on defence than on health and education combined. Recently, peace scholars like Ruth Sivard pointed out that if military expenditures were reduced by 5 per cent, the $50 billion saved could go a long way towards eradicating poverty, malnutrition, illiteracy, disease, maternal mortality, morbidity and other obstacles to development.[53]

While women have supported military efforts in time of war and recognized the significance of national security, they have also realized that "security consists of not only military but also political, economic, social, humanitarian and human rights and ecological aspects. Enhanced security can, on the one hand, create conditions conducive to disarmament and, on the other, provide the enforcement and confidence for the successful pursuit of development."[54]

Though undercurrents in disarmament negotiations, women have been active at various levels of the disarmament process through non-governmental organizations, including petitioning and public awareness campaigns. Their activities contributed to the formulation of the Partial Test-Ban Treaty in 1963. Some years later, it was a woman, Randall Forsberg, founder of the Institute for Defense and Disarmament, who originated the concept of the nuclear freeze. Soviet cosmonaut Valentine Tereshkova, who was the first woman to go into space, has been at the forefront of disarmament and peace activities both in her country and abroad. [55] Alva Myrdal, a Nobel Peace Prize laureate, Swedish arms negotiator and economist, has made an important contribution to the public understanding of disarmament by exposing the underlying dynamics of conventional arms talks that make some weapons obsolete only to open the way for the development of more advanced wapons.[56]

Peace Challenges to the Year 2000

The issue of women and peace is, in fact, a two-edged word in that women are often helpless victims of violence—not only the violence inflicted by war, but also the insidious type of violence that pervades the family and then extends to the workplace and society. In order to eliminate this violence and ensure a safe society free of fear for women, governments must:

- Implement policies to prevent, control and reduce violence against women in the family, the workplace and society
- Make the elimination of domestic violence a national priority
- Institute comprehensive legislative reforms to protect women against domestic violence, sexual harassment and physical abuse in the home, the workplace and society, including strong deterrent and corrective measures
- Provide support services for female victims, including basic shelter, food and medical, legal and psychological assistance
- Provide employment support services to foster economic self-sufficiency amongst victims
- Institute training programmes for judiciary, health and social services personnel, as well as law enforcement officers, to ensure humane treatment of victims
- Promote legal literacy and peace education programmes in schools and in the media, underscoring women's plight as victims and women's potential as peacemakers
- Mount public awareness campaigns to curtail excessive violence and sex stereotyping in the media
- Revise educational curricula to shift the emphasis from war and violence to more peaceful aspects of civilization

War and Peace

Military conflict and diplomacy, which have traditionally been exclusively orchestrated by men, have failed to create a reliable system to safeguard peace. This makes the inclusion of women in all phases of the peace process at the decision-making level all the more imperative. To this effect, governments should:

- Establish a quota system to ensure the representation of women in delegations negotiating peace and disarmament at the decision-making level

- Promote the incorporation of women in peace education programmes in schools, conference and publicity campaigns to underscore their potentially significant role in mediation and negotiation
- Support peaceful methods of conflict resolution through mediation and negotiation rather than aggression.

NOTES

1 Nairobi forward-looking Strategies for the Advancement of Women, in *Report of the World Conference to Review and Appraise the Achievements of the (United Nations) Decade for Women*, op. cit., para. 13, p. 8.

2 The *1989 World Survey on the Role of Women in Development,* defines indirect violence as structural violence "because it refers to institutions and conditions that are based on, create or facilitate the social, economic, political or psychological degradation or exploitation of regions, States, groups or individuals," op. cit., p. 362. It adds: "Injustice and inequality underpin it and are maintained, if not furthered, by indirect violence. Racism, sexism and popularization are thus aspects of indirect violence. It breeds distrust and insecurity and helps to reinforce direct violence as a means of resolving conflict."

3 *Nairobi Forward-looking Strategies,* op. cit., para. 13. p. 8.

4 Ibid., para 257, p. 60. For a comprehensive analysis of the concept of peace in the Forward-looking Strategies, see I Hikka Pietila and Jeanne Vickers, *Making Women Matter: The Role of the United Nations* (London: Zed Books, 1990), pp. 61-65.

5 John Stuart Mill, *The Subjection of Women, quoted in Violence Against Women in the Family,* United Nations, V. 89-56940, October 1989, p. 11.

6 Both proverbs in Morgan, *A misogynist's Sourcebook,* op. cit., pp. 101-102.

7 *Violence against Women in the Family,* op. cit., p. 19.

8 Ibid., p. 18.

9 Newsweek, 16 July 1990.

10 *Violence against Women in the Family,* op. cit., p. 19.

11 " A Global Struggle against Violence against Women," cited in *Women's International Network News,* Vol. 15, No. 4, Autumn 1989, p. 35.

12 *The Times,* London, 15 April 1989.

13 *The World's Women,* 1970-1990, op., cit., p. 19.

14 *Violence Against Women in the Family,* op. cit., p. 17.

15 *Women: A World Report,* op. cit., p. 64.

16 *Violence against Women in the Family,* op. cit., p. 21

17 *Women: A World Report,* op. cit., p. 64.

18 *Violence Against Women in the Family,* op. cit., p. 21.

19 Canada: Wife Assault Fact Sheet, Justice Unit, Ontario Women's Directorate, cited in *Women's International Network News,* Autumn 1989, p. 37.

20 *Violence Against Women in the Family,* op. cit., p. 24.

21 *The Times,* 15 April 1989.

22 *Voilence Against Women in the Family,* op. cit., p. 11.

23 Morgan, op. cit., p. 105.

24 Miles, *The Women's History of the World,* op. cit., p. 14.

25 Rhoodie. *Discrimination Against Women,* op. cit., p. 91.

26 *Women: A World Report,* op. cit., p. 65.

27 *Domestic Violence against Women: The Hidden Crime* (UN Focus, DPI/1001), Department of Public Information, November 1989, pp. 1 and 2 and Annex: Increasing the Pace of Implementation of the Nairobia Forward looking Strategies for the Advancement of Women, No. 23, recommendaton XXII, in *Women 2000,* No. 2, 1990, p. 27. For a comprehensive in-depth analysis of measures to protect women against domestic violence see *Violence Against Women in the Family,* op. cit., p. 47-106.

28 "A Global Struggle against Violence against Women", cited in *Women's International Network News,* p. 35.

29 Ibid.

30 Ibid.

31 "Speak Out Taurai Khulumani" (April-June 1989), by The Women's Action Group, Harare, Zimbabwe, cited in *Women's International Network News,* Autumn 1989, p. 38.

32 *Violence Against Women in the Family,* op. cit., p. 98.

33 Norman Mailer speech at the University of California, Berkeley, 1972, cited in Morgan, op. cit., p. 94.

34 *The Sunday Times,* London, 23 April 1989.

35 *The Times, London,* 1 June 1989.

36 *The Sunday Times,* London, 23 April 1989.

37 *Business Week,* 18 March 1991.

38 Ibid.

39 *The World's Women: 1970-1990,* op. cit., p. 63.

40 *Newsweek,* 16 July 1990.

41 FBI statistics, *Newsweek,* 16 July 1990.

42 Morgan, *A Misogynist's Sourcebook,* op. cit., p. 78.

43 Ibid., p. 153

44 *The New York Times,* 3 December 1991.

45 Miles, *A Women's History of the World,* op. cit., p. 268.

46 *The New York Times,* 22 January 1991.

47 *Women 2000,* No. 2, 1990, pp. 9-10.

48 "The Participation of Women in Promoting International Peace and Cooperation", p. 4, *Women and Peace* kit, Joint United Nations Information Centre/non-governmental organization (JUNIC/NGO), Programme Group on Women.

49 *Women: A World Report,* op. cit., p. 88-89.

50 Nancy Shelley, conference paper for the Australian Women's Education Coalition, in "The Participation of Women in Promoting International Peace and Co-operation", Par II of the Women and Peace kit, p. 7.

51 *The World's Women: 1970-1990,* op. cit., p. 36.

52 *1989 World Survey on the Role of Women in Development,* op. cit., p. 368.

53 "Women and Disarmament", p. 3, from *Women and Peace* kit.

54 Final Document, International Conference on the Relationship between Disarmament and Development, para. 14 (A/Conf. 130/2), United Nations, in Introduction to the Subject, p. 5, *Women and Peace* kit.

55 "Women and Disarrangement", Part V, *Women and Peace* kit, p. 10.

56 Ibid., p. 11.

SITUATION OF WOMEN IN ASIA

Karen Oppenheim Mason
with the assistance of Amy Cardamone, Jill Holdren, and Leah Retherford

Observers disagree about the impact of economic development on women's situation under various historical conditions. One group argues that development enhances the status of women by improving their access to resources, increasing their autonomy and power, and benefiting their general well-being. An opposing viewpoint is that any apparent advances in women's situation under development are illusory or offset by a deterioration in other aspects of women's status. Proponents of this view cite women's lack of political power, legal barriers to full social and economic participation, differences between men and women in occupational status and pay levels, a loss of control over agricultural resources, and high levels of violence against women in economically advanced societies. Using several indicators of status, this Research Report assesses women's situation, especially in relation to men, in a variety of economic and cultural settings found in Asia. Where possible, it describes how their situation has changed during the last two to three decades and notes whether any tendency toward improvement or degradation can be observed according to a society's development level.

A major debate in the literature on the status of women concerns the impact of economic development on the autonomy, resources, and well-being of women as compared with men of their class or caste. One view regards our species's ancestral way of lifehunting and gathering—as an Eden for women. In that setting, women's economic and social contributions typically were as important for survival and as highly valued as men's, and the genders often lived harmoniously as equals (*e.g.*, Draper 1975;

Engels 1972, Friedl 1975; but compare with Collier and Rosaldo 1981). Those who view hunting and gathering as an idyllic existence for women often regard the invention of agriculture and the development of complex societies as women's downfall, a development in which they lost their traditional resource base and were reduced to dependency on men (Blumberg 1978; Boserup 1970). Only with advanced industrialization did they regain a modicum of autonomy.

A somewhat narrower version of the hypothesis that development has been bad for women takes early nineteenth-century agrarian societies in the West as its starting point, arguing that despite the legal and political liabilities married women faced in such societies, they wielded considerable domestic power because of their critical economic role as helpmates. Husband and wives, it is argued, were roughly equal because women's work—raising vegetables, keeping poultry, making clothing cooking, cleaning, and otherwise caring for family members—made them as critical to family survival as were men. According to this view, the rough balance between the sexes within the domestic sphere was undermined by the Industrial Revolution, which took men outside the home and allowed them to monopolize new and increasingly important market resources (*e.g.*, cash income) while leaving women labouring under preindustrial conditions (Engels {1884} 1972). Again, only with advanced industrialization and the mass movement of women into the paid work force has there been a reduction in gender inequality.

An alternative view argues that women in preindustrial agrarian societies in the West had little autonomy or domestic authority, that the movement of men into the "dirty" capitalist world outside the home actually enhanced women's moral authority in the domestic sphere, and that women subsequently increased their political power by gaining the vote and entering the work force in large numbers (Smith 1973). In this view, development is implicitly argued to have enhanced the status of women more or less from the start. There is no dark period of lost status followed by a recapturing of at least some of this status during the late stages of industrialization.

All of these viewpoints agree that development eventually gives women some degree of autonomy, resources, and power. In still other views, however, this assumption is questioned, especially in the context of contemporary Third World countries, where any apparent advances in women's situation are argued to be illusory or offset by a deterioration in other aspects of their position (Boserup 1990; Heyzer 1986; Joekes *et al.* 1994; Mies 1986; Vlassoff 1994). Proponents of this last viewpoint often mention the lack of political participation by women in most developing and developed countries, at least as political candidates and office holders, although perhaps not as voters, the legal barriers against women's full social and economic participation, large discrepancies between the sexes in occupations and pay levels; a loss of access to or control of agricultural resources under economic modernization; and high levels of violence against women in familial and other settings. This view holds that the progress that women are claimed to have made is illusory and that economic development tends to benefit men disproportionately, often degrading the position of women.

Whether these largely negative portrayals of the impact of development on the status of women apply equally to Asia as to other parts of the world is unclear. Writers on Asia (*e.g.*, Greenhalgh 1980), however, have joined those who decry the situation of women under development, despite the evidence that family systems and mortality regimes in much of South and East Asia historically disadvantaged women. Thus, for both Asia and elsewhere, there is extensive disagreement in the literature on women and development about the impact of development on women's status under various historical conditions. This disagreement sets the stage for the current review of women's situation in Asia.

We do not attempt a systematic test of alternative hypotheses about women and development. Rather, using several indicators, we ask whether the situation of women, especially in relation to that of men, appears to have improved or deteriorated during the last three to four decades in a variety of economic and cultural settings found within the region. Our aim is to describe the current situation of women in selected Asian countries, where possible, we also describe how their situation appears to be improving or worsening and note whether any systematic tendency toward improvement or degradation can be observed according to the development level of each country considered.

Asia's Subregions

It is common to subdivide Asia into several subregions that differ historically in culture and colonial experience, and that are currently at different average levels of economic and demographic development. Commonly distinguished are East Asia, which includes, among other countries and territories, China, Hong Kong, Japan, South Korea, and Taiwan; Southeast Asia, which includes Indonesia, Malaysia, the Philippines, Singapore, and Thailand; and South Asia, including Bangladesh, India, Nepal, Pakistan, and Sri Lanka. The countries of East Asia are heavily influenced by Confucian cultural traditions and have strong historical ties to one another. At present, East Asia is also the richest and demographically most advanced subregion of Asia. (In some classifications, Singapore is included in this group because of its largely Chinese population and high level of economic and demographic development, although its geographic location and political alliance place it within Southeast Asia.)

Characteristic of East Asian cultures are patriarchal family systems that emphasize the male line of decent and prescribe a multigenerational family household that includes at least two generations of men (father and adult son or sons) plus in-marrying women and dependent children. Such family systems have historically tended to give women little autonomy or power, especially during the prime childbearing years (Dyson Moore 1983). The wife of the senior male in the household may control the day-to-day lives of the household's younger wives, but her power does not extend beyond them, and she herself will have risen from a position of servitude as a young wife. Although many households have been unable to achieve the joint patrilineal ideal, the aspiration to do so has tended to disadvantage women, who are trained from an early age to play the role of obedient daughter-in-law.

To a remarkable extent, the family systems traditionally found in South Asia, especially in the northerly portion of that region, are like those found traditionally in East Asia, despite different religious and cultural traditions (mostly Hinduism and Islam, with some Buddhism). As in East Asia, continuation of the male family line is an important cultural value. Women marry into a household organized around two or more generations of closely related men and have little power or autonomy until after childbearing age, if then. In Pakistan, Bangladesh, Nepal, and northern India (but not in Sri Lanka), a woman tends to have few resources and little autonomy or power for much of her life unless her husband becomes the senior male in the household (Dyson and Moore 1983). Even then her power and autonomy are generally limited.

With the exception of Singapore, the countries of Southeast Asia have been dominated historically by Malay and Buddhist cultural traditions that, on the whole, are more benign to women during the prime adult years than are the cultural traditions found in either East or South Asia. Family systems in Southeast Asia tend to give equal emphasis to male and female lines of descent, or to emphasize female lines more heavily than male lines (see, *e.g.*, Geertz 1961; Geertz and Geertz 1975). They also tend to place more emphasis on the conjugal unit than do the patrilineally oriented family systems of East and South Asia. Thus, although women in Southeast Asia have not traditionally enjoyed equality with men, their situation has been on the whole less oppressed than in the surrounding subregions.

These cultural differences among Asia's subregions have combined with varying degrees of economic development to produce widely differing situations for women across the continent. To assess those differences, we examine five key indicators of women's situation in each subregion: education and literacy, employment, age at marriage, health and longevity, and sex preferences for children.

Indicators of Women's Situation

Conceptually, there are two types of indicators or women's status that can be examined (although the line between them is sometimes blurred): (1) indicators of the means to desirable outcomes or statuses in life, and (2) indicators of the desirable outcomes or statuses themselves. Commonly available indicators that fall under the category of means indicators include educational levels and literacy: employment status and occupation; and, because it indicates the material and psychological resources with which women enter marriage, women's age at marriage, both their absolute age and their age relative to that of their spouse. Outcome indicators include health and longevity and, as an overall indicator of the value of males versus females in the society, sex preferences for children.

Other indicators of both means and outcomes exist. For example, in addition to literacy and school enrollment rates, years or grades of schooling completed can be used to assess women's educational attainment. For the current review, however, because our interest is in assessing change, we avoid using indicators that are available for only a few countries of the region or for a single point in time (which is the case for years or grades of schooling completed). We also avoid using indicators known to be unreliable—for example, maternal mortality rates and most health measures. In what follows, we examine statistics for indicators that are widely available and reasonably reliable, beginning with the fundamental economic means to a better life: education and employment.

Education and Literacy

As *Table 1* shows for the years surrounding 1960, 1970, 1980, and 1990, both the level of female illiteracy and the size of the illiteracy gender gap vary enormously across countries. In South Asia, with the exception of Sri Lanka, female illiteracy is very high and the gender gap large. In contrast, in East Asia, with the exception of China and Taiwan (in the years for which data are available), the level of female illiteracy is low and the gender gap illiteracy is low and the gender gap small.

Table 1.
Percentage of Women Illiterate and Difference between Female and Male Illiteracy Rates, for Ages 20-24, by Year and Country: Asia, Recent Decades.

Subregion and Country	Circa 1960		Circa 1970		Circa 1980		1990 estimates (ages 15+)	
	% F	%F —%M	% F	%F —%M	% F	%F —%M	% F	%F/—%M
South Asia								
Bangladesh	u	u	81	27	75	22	78	25
India	82	32	67	29	63	29	66	28
Nepal	98	18	96	27	87	29	87	24
Pakistan	89	25	82	23	79	24	79	26
Sri Lanka	22	14	11	5	10	3	16	10
Southeast Asia								
Indonesia	59	30	26	12	21	10	32	16
Malaysia	u	25	u	u	20	9	30	16
Philippines	16	1	8	•	8	1	10	•
Thailand	21	9	9	4	4	2	10	6
East Asia								
China	u	u	u	u	23	18	38	22
Hong Kong	19	13	6	3	u	u	u	u
Japan	•	0	u	u	u	u	u	u
South Korea	15	9	2	1	u	u	6	6
Singapore	u	u	15	7	4	1	u	u
Taiwan	40	25	u	u	u	u	u	u

Sources: UNESCO, *Statistical Yearbook* (1965, table 5; 1970, table 1.4; 1978-79, table 1.3; 1986, table 1.3; 1991, table 1.3); United Nations, DESIPA (1994, series 2.1).

Note: Reference years and age ranges for individual countries may vary somewhat from those indicated, illiteracy may be defined as never having attended school, and data may not represent all areas of every country. Specific qualifications are available from the first author upon request. Percentages in this and subsequent tables have been rounded, which may have introduced small errors in some cases.

u data are unavailable. • Less than 1 per cent.

Data are unavailable for many East Asian countries because governments no longer consider it worth collecting statistics on a phenomenon that has become practically nonexistent. The Southeast Asian countries generally hold an intermediate position between the South and East Asian countries, although illiteracy among females in the Philippines and Thailand is quickly approaching the low level found in East Asia.

As the primary school enrollment statistics shown in *Table 2* indicate, the Southeast Asian countries are likely to erase the gender gap in illiteracy in the near future. In 1989-90, the female-to-male ratio of primary school pupils was well above .90 in all four major countries of Southeast Asia, a level similar to the ratios found in most East Asian countries. Levels were lower in most of South Asia, although even there female enrollments have been gaining over time. At the secondary school level, female-to-male enrollment ratios were also very high in East and Southeast Asia around 1990 (*Table 3*). Thus, female illiteracy is fast disappearing in Asia except in the northerly countries of South Asia. This suggests that economic development does not harm the schooling of girls (but cf. Greenhalgh 1985). To the contrary, the history of female education in the most rapidly developing countries of East and South-east Asia strongly suggests that an important accompaniment of development is improvement in female schooling, both in absolute terms and relative to the schooling of males

Although the gender gap in primary and secondary schooling has all but disappeared in most of East and Southeast Asia, it remains substantial at the tertiary level, where the number of females enrolled rarely reaches three-quarters of the number of males enrolled (*Table 4 and 5*). The Philippines constitutes an exception here: since the 1960s, the number of females enrolled in tertiary education in the Philippines has exceeded the number of males. As *Table 5* shows, the Philippines is also an exception in that almost as many females as males are enrolled in technical subjects (mathematics and physical sciences) and substantially more are enrolled in business, law, trades, and agriculture. In most countries for which statistics are available, female-to-male enrollment ratios are most favourable in the humanities, social sciences, and services. Although they are much less favourable in the technical, business, and professional fields, the situation has improved over time: female-to-male enrollment ratios have been rising in most countries. (We do not know precisely why the Philippines ratios in the "other and not specified" category has been falling; changes in definitions or statistical coverage may play a role.) Thus, even though women are unlikely to achieve parity with men at the tertiary level of schooling in the near future throughout most of Asia, some of the gender segregation by field that has characterized higher education may be easing.

In sum, with the notable exception of Sri Lanka, women's schooling is poorly developed in South Asia but is relatively well developed elsewhere in the region and promises to become even more so in the near future. The wealthier countries of East Asia and the rapidly developing countries of Southeast Asia have either achieved or are fast approaching gender parity in schooling at the primary and secondary levels. Although women continue to be underrepresented at the tertiary level of schooling (with the exception of the Philippines, where men are under represented), female-to-male enrollment ratios have risen recently in many countries and differences between men and women in fields of study have shrunk. Women's schooling therefore appears to improve rather than worsen as countries develop economically.

Table 2.
Female-to-Male Ratios of Pupils Enrolled at the Primary Level of Education, by Year and Country: Asia, Recent Decades

Subregion and Country	Circa 1960-61	Circa 1970	Circa 1980	1989-91
South Asia				
Bangladesh	u	0.47	0.59	0.79
India	0.47	0.60	0.64	0.71
Nepal	0.39	0.18	0.39	0.47
Pakistan	0.33	0.37	0.49	0.52
Sri Lanka	u	0.89	0.92	0.93
Southeast Asia				
Indonesia	0.75	0.85	0.85	0.93
Malaysia	0.74	0.88	0.94	0.95
Philippines	0.92	0.92	0.96	0.96
Thailand	0.89	0.89	0.92	0.96
East Asia				
China	u	u	0.82	0.86
Hong Kong	0.82	0.92	0.92	0.93
Japan	0.96	0.96	0.96	0.95
South Korea	0.82	0.92	0.96	0.94
Singapore	0.79	0.89	0.92	0.90
Taiwan	0.89	u	u	u

Sources: UNESCO, *Statistical Yearbook* (1966, table 2.10; 1975, table 4.2; 1985, table 3.4; 1991, table 3.4); United Nations, DESIPA (1994, series 2.3).
Note: Reference years for individual countries may vary somewhat from those indicated. Specific qualifications are available from the first author upon request.
u—data are unavailable.

EMPLOYMENT

Improved education for women is likely to translate fairly directly into an improved set of life chances because schooling is associated with improvements in the ability to understand social and legal conditions and to learn about services and practices important for health and survival. The relationship of employment to the status of women is more ambiguous. One reasons is that the relationship depends on the type of work. Employment as an unpaid family worker gives the worker less control of resources or rights to determine household or personal decisions than does independent, paid employment. Even employment that earns income may fail to give a worker control of resources or a say in

Table 3. Female-to-Male Ratios of Enrollments at the Secondary Level of Education, by Year and Country: Asia, Recent Decades.

Subregion and Country	Total 1960	Total 1970	Total 1980	Total 1990	General 1960	General 1970	General 1980	General 1990	Vocational and teacher training 1960	Vocational and teacher training 1970	Vocational and teacher training 1980	Vocational and teacher training 1990
South Asia												
Bangladesh	u	0.17	0.31	0.46	u	0.17	0.32	0.46	u	0.05	0.09	0.21
India	0.31	0.39	0.49	u	0.32	0.39	0.49	0.54	0.25	0.60	0.48	0.42
Nepal	0.19	u	0.25	0.37	0.17	0.16	u	u	0.40	u	u	u
Pakistan	0.19	0.25	0.35	0.39	0.19	0.25	0.35	0.39	0.43	0.41	0.20	0.34
Sri Lanka	u	u	1.04	u	u	0.97	1.04	1.06	u	0.52	0.92	u
Southeast Asia												
Indonesia	0.47	0.52	0.68	0.81	0.43	0.59	0.69	0.82	0.77	0.35	0.62	0.77
Malaysia	0.51	0.69	0.91	1.02	0.51	0.69	0.92	1.04	0.50	0.89	0.42	0.33
Philippines	0.84	u	1.14	0.99	0.89	u	u	u	0.61	u	u	u
Thailand	0.59	0.72	u	0.93	0.61	0.69	0.84	0.97	0.51	0.78	1.04	0.75
East Asia												
China	u	0.64	0.65	0.72	u	0.65	0.66	0.72	u	u	0.47	0.83
Hong Kong	0.65	0.72	0.97	0.97	0.67	0.74	1.02	1.04	0.45	0.50	0.47	0.46
Japan	0.91	0.98	0.98	0.97	0.96	1.03	1.00	0.99	0.64	0.79	0.88	0.87
South Korea	0.34	0.61	0.83	0.91	0.37	0.65	0.85	0.87	0.21	0.41	0.78	1.13
Singapore	0.64	0.91	1.00	u	0.67	1.03	1.06	1.00	0.69	0.14	0.29	u
Taiwan	0.52	u	u	u	0.79	u	u	u	0.45	u	u	u

Sources: UNESCO, *Statistical Yearbook* (1965, table 12-14; 1966, table 2.8; 1975, table 4.3; 1985, table 3.7; 1986, table 3.7; 1988, table 3.5; 1991, table 3.7); United Nations, DESIPA (1994, series 2.4).

Note: Reference years and education categories for individual countries may vary somewhat from those indicated, and data do not represent all areas of every country. Specific qualifications are available from the first author upon request.

u—data are unavailable.

important household decision if by tradition or employers' practices a woman's earnings are handed over to other family members or her work is seen as part of her duties as a wife or daughter (Jain 1970; Salaff 1981).

Unfortunately, although many national statistical accounts provide information on the type of work performed by women and men, more direct measures of control over earnings are rarely available. Our description of women's economic situation in Asia is therefore limited to the kind of formally recognized work they perform. Past studies (*e.g.*, Dixon-Mueller and Anker 1988) suggest that formally recognized work itself often constitutes only a fraction of all the productive or facilitative work done by women, especially married women. Official employment statistics are thus likely to underestimate women's economic contribution to households, communities, and the economy at large. Whether this implies that the extent of women's economic power or autonomy is also underestimated is less clear. Where women's labor receives little social recognition, it seems likely to yield them little power or autonomy, regardless of its objective characteristics.

We begin by examining the form of work that is least likely to yield power or control over resources to women—namely, employment as an unpaid family worker.[1] In most countries of the region, women are more likely than men to be unpaid family workers, as the female-to-male ratios shown in the right-hand portion of *Table 6* indicate (all but one ratio having a value over 1.00). In most Asian countries for which data are available over time, however, the percentage of female workers found in this employment category has declined, as has the female-to-male ratio. This trend undoubtedly reflects the decline of unpaid family work that tends to occur with industrialization and the proletarianization of the labour force.

Some societies in Asia have maintained a high level of family-run enterprises during the industrialization process; nonetheless, even in those countries the proportion of workers employed as unpaid family worker has declined with time. To the extent that unpaid family work does little to enhance women's status, the shift away from such work that occurs with development lends support to the thesis that development enhances rather than diminishes women's status.

1 An unpaid family worker is anyone who report herself as working but who is unpaid and works on a family farm or in some other kind of family-run enterprise (where "family" can be defined in a variety of ways).

Table 4.
Female-to-male ratios of enrollments at all tertiary-level institutions and in universities and equivalent institutions, by year: Asia, recent decades

Subregion and Country	All tertiary-level institutions				Universities and equivalent institutions			
	1960	1970	1980	1990	1960	1970	1980	1990
South Asia								
Bangladesh	u	0.11	0.16	0.19	u	0.16	0.22	0.28
India	0.20	0.31	0.35	0.43	u	u	0.39	u
Nepal	0.05	0.21	0.23	u	0.21	0.22	0.23	u
Pakistan	0.14	0.27	0.37	0.37	0.22	0.27	0.37	0.37
Sri Lanka	u	0.97	0.75	0.69	0.47	0.75	0.67	0.75
Southeast Asia								
Indonesia	0.33	0.34	0.45	0.47	u	0.38	0.43	0.47
Malaysia	0.30	0.42	0.63	0.85	0.30	0.41	0.53	0.72
Philippines	1.04	1.25	1.13	u	u	u	1.17	u
Thailand	0.43	0.72	0.67	u	u	0.72	0.67	u
East Asia								
China	u	0.48	0.30	0.49	u	u	u	u
Hong Kong	0.67	0.42	0.35	0.54	0.37	0.49	0.52	0.54
Japan	0.25	0.39	0.49	0.64	0.16	1.23	0.30	0.37
South Korea	0.20	0.32	0.32	0.47	0.19	0.28	0.28	0.41
Singapore	0.45	0.43	1.64	u	0.30	1.54	0.79	0.90
Taiwan	0.30	u	u	u	0.27	u	u	u

Sources: UNESCO, *Statistical Yearbook* (1965, table 15; 1970, table 2.13; 1972-79, table 4.2; 1975, table 5.1; 1985, 1986, table 3.11; 1987, table 2.13; 1991, table 3.11).
u—data are unavailable.

Whether this is the case, however, depends in part on whether women no longer working as unpaid family workers enter the paid labour force or are instead left unemployed. *Table 7* presents changes over time in the female-to-male ratio of percentages who are economically active. Although the economically active population includes individuals working as unpaid family employees, the table nevertheless gives an indication of women's potential access to earnings or income. Most of the countries in *Table 7* for which data are available do not show marked changes in the relative percentages of economically active women; but where change has occurred, more often than not it has been in the direction of increased labour force participation by women. Thus, over the period when unpaid family work has gradually declined as a proportion of all economic activity, the economic activity rates of females have

Table 5. Female-to-Male Ratios of Enrollments at the Tertiary Level, by Field of Study and Year: Asia, Recent Decades.

Subregion and Country	Field of study	1960	1970	1980	1990
South Asia					
Bangladesh	Total	u	0.11	0.16	0.19
	Humanities, social sciences, and services	u	0.12	0.18	0.22
	Mathematics and physical sciences	u	0.10	0.17	0.20
	Business, law, trades, and agricultre	u	0.01	0.10	0.12
	Other and not specified	u	u	0.28	u
India	Total	0.21	0.29	0.35	0.42
	Humanities, social sciences, and services	0.28	0.34	0.41	0.68
	Mathematics and physical sciences	0.13	0.28	0.36	0.31
	Business, law, trades, and agricultre	0.01	0.18	0.08	0.24
	Other and not specified	0.45	0.02	0.26	0.33
Nepal	Total	0.26	0.22	0.24	0.25
	Humanities, social sciences, and services	0.32	0.24	0.38	0.33
	Mathematics and physical sciences	0.16	0.16	0.25	0.28
	Business, law, trades, and agricultre	0.03	0.02	0.08	0.14
	Other and not specified	u	u	u	u
Pakistan	Total	0.14	0.23	0.37	0.22
	Humanities, social sciences, and services	0.19	0.36	0.92	0.68
	Mathematics and physical sciences	0.09	0.22	0.38	0.42
	Business, law, trades, and agricultre	0.01	0.01	0.03	0.07
	Other and not specified	u	0.23	0.23	0.20
Sri Lanka	Total	u	0.76	u	0.68
	Humanities, social sciences, and services	u	0.96	2.34	1.19
	Mathematics and physical sciences	u	0.53	u	0.74
	Business, law, trades, and agricultre	u	0.20	u	0.40
	Other and not specified	u	u	u	0.81

{Cont}

Southeast Asia					
Indonesia	Total	0.20	0.38	0.47	0.48
	Humanities, social sciences, and services	0.17	0.52	0.60	0.56
	Mathematics and physical sciences	0.35	0.48	0.62	0.48
	Business, law, trades, and agricultre	0.15	0.18	0.36	0.39
	Other and not specified	u	0.02	0.80	0.12
Malaysia	Total	0.48	0.42	0.63	0.90
	Humanities, social sciences, and services	0.59	0.63	0.93	0.25
	Mathematics and physical sciences	0.26	0.24	0.53	0.57
	Business, law, trades, and agricultre	0.04	0.10	0.34	0.02
	Other and not specified	u	0.40	2.16	0.43
Philippines	Total	1.06	1.22	1.15	1.43
	Humanities, social sciences, and services	1.46	1.63	3.38	2.57
	Mathematics and physical sciences	2.10	4.26	3.32	0.97
	Business, law, trades, and agricultre	0.11	0.08	0.84	1.63
	Other and not specified	0.92	1.23	0.58	0.35
Thailand	Total	0.40	0.72	u	u
	Humanities, social sciences, and services	0.59	1.10	u	u
	Mathematics and physical sciences	0.76	0.95	u	u
	Business, law, trades, and agricultre	0.07	0.16	u	u
	Other and not specified	u	u	u	u
East Asia					
China	Total	u	u	u	0.05
	Humanities, social sciences, and services	u	u	u	u
	Mathematics and physical sciences	u	u	u	u
	Business, law, trades, and agricultre	u	u	u	u
	Other and not specified	u	u	u	u

{Cont}

Hong Kong	Total	0.32	0.42	0.50	0.53
	Humanities, social sciences, and services	0.70	0.90	1.27	1.24
	Mathematics and physical sciences	0.28	0.25	0.33	0.36
	Business, law, trades, and agricultre	0.14	0.02	0.33	0.36
	Other and not specified	u	0.65	0.83	1.07
Japan	Total	0.30	0.39	0.49	0.63
	Humanities, social sciences, and services	0.35	0.57	0.75	0.93
	Mathematics and physical sciences	1.17	0.40	0.43	0.54
	Business, law, trades, and agricultre	0.02	0.02	0.03	0.07
	Other and not specified	0.05	0.47	0.33	0.75
South Korea	Total	0.24	0.32	0.35	0.32
	Humanities, social sciences, and services	0.35	0.48	0.91	1.47
	Mathematics and physical sciences	0.41	0.88	0.64	1.24
	Business, law, trades, and agricultre	0.03	0.02	0.06	0.20
	Other and not specified	0.23	u	0.35	0.64
Singapore	Total	0.31	0.43	0.64	0.72
	Humanities, social sciences, and services	0.41	0.92	2.78	2.75
	Mathematics and physical sciences	0.25	0.47	0.97	1.22
	Business, law, trades, and agricultre	0.18	0.08	0.35	0.42
	Other and not specified	0.00	0.00	0.21	0.26
Taiwan	Total	0.31	u	u	u
	Humanities, social sciences, and services	0.53	u	u	u
	Mathematics and physical sciences	0.26	u	u	u
	Business, law, trades, and agricultre	0.07	u	u	u
	Other and not specified	u	u	u	u

Sources: UNESCO, ***Statistical Yearbook*** (1965, table 16; 1973, table 4.3; 1985, table 3.12; 1991, table 3.12) United Nations, DESIPA (1994, series 2.5).
Note: UNESCO's definitions of the fields study listed in this table changed slightly in the latter two years from those in the first two. Reference years for individual countries may also vary somewhat from those indicated. Specific qualifications are available from the first author upon request.
u—data are unavailable.

increased, even in relation to those of males. This finding suggests that economic development has not simply shoved women, as a group, out of their traditional work without providing access to newer forms of employment. Of course, some individual women or particular subgroups, such as rural women with traditional use—rights to land, may have suffered a loss of economic opportunity (see, *e.g.*, Boserup 1970).

It should be noted that economic development is not the sole determinant of either female or male economic activity rates, as is indicated by the pattern of intercountry variation shown in Table 7 and also in the first two columns of Table 8, which presents the absolute activity rates of females and males over time. South Asia (with the exception, again, of Sri Lanka) shows the lowest female-to-male activity ratios (*Table 7*). Interestingly, the highest ratios are found in China and Thailand rather than in Singapore, Taiwan, Hong Kong, or South Korea, where income levels are, on average, far higher. Obviously, political and cultural traditions affect the extent to which women's economic activity rates approach those of men. China and Thailand also show some of the highest absolute levels of economic activity among women (*Table 8)*, those levels being the major reason that the female-to-male ratios are high there as well. The low female economic activity rates seen in most South Asian countries may therefore partly reflect cultural traditions that militate against female employment (for example, the practice of female seclusion, or *purdah*), rather than a low level of economic development per se.

In a volume published in 1989 that reviews data through the early-to-mid-1980, Shirley Nuss and two collaborators argue that women's economic participation rates have been falling in much of Asia and can be expected to recover only if exceptional efforts are made to create new employment opportunities for them. The data shown in the first two columns of *Table 8* suggest that this conclusion requires qualification in light of the experience since the mid-1980s. Although female economic activity rates rose only slightly in most of South Asia at the end of the 1980s, in Sri Lanka and many of the more prosperous countries of Southeast and East Asia these rates grew rapidly. Thus, economic growth again is associated with women's increased participation in the paid work force, rather than with declining opportunities for women. Although the causal processes that underlie this association are unclear—economic growth is likely to increase participation opportunities for women, but women's increased participation has also been argued to create economic growth—it appears that development is beneficial to women's participation in paid employment.

Table 6.
Percentage of the Labor force 15 Years Old and Older Classified as Unpaid Family Workers, by sex, and Female-to-Male Ratio of Percentages Classified as Unpaid Family Workers: Asia, Recent Decades.

Subregion and Country	Circa 1970		Circa 1980		Latest		Female/male ratio		
	Women	Men	Women	Men	Women	Men	ca. 1970	ca. 1990	Latest
South Asia									
Bangladesh	u	u	u	u	11	20	u	u	0.58
India	18	9	u	u	u	u	2.10	u	u
Nepal	6	2	4	2	u	u	2.67	2.51	u
Pakistan	56	23	28	15	34	14	2.47	1.92	2.37
Sri Lanka	11	4	6	3	u	u	3.15	2.39	u
Southeast Asia									
Indonesia	39	16	30	12	42	13	2.43	2.45	3.23
Malaysia	u	u	18	7	u	u	u	2.54	u
Philippines	30	16	18	15	23	11	1.89	1.18	2.14
Thailand	77	33	18	15	u	u	2.32	1.18	u
East Asia									
China	u	u	u	u	u	u	u	u	u
Hong Kong	4	1	3	1	u	u	2.91	4.11	u
South Korea	52	12	43	8	26	3	4.56	5.05	9.03
Singapore	6	3	4	2	2	1	2.23	2.07	1.31
Taiwan	40	10	u	u	u	u	4.04	u	u

Sources: Asia Development Bank (1993a, table 27).
Note: Reference years and age range for individual countries may vary somewhat from those indicated, and data do not represent all areas of every country. Specific qualifications are available from the first author upon request.
u—data are unavailable.

Does development also improve the types of work that women are able to find and the pay and work conditions likely to be associated with those types of work? The remainder of Table 8 answers this question with regard to class of employment—that is, whether women and men work as employers or own-account workers, as unpaid family workers, or as paid employees. (Not shown in the table is a residual category of unclassified workers.) In the right hand column, the index of dissimilarity between the employment-class distributions of females and males indicates the percentage of men (or women) who would have to change their employment class in order for the two class-of-employment distributions to be identical.

Of the dozen countries with data over time for both sexes, five show little change in the index of dissimilarity. Five others show a marked decline in its value, indicating that, over time, the employment-class distribution of female workers has become more similar to the employment-class distribution of male workers. In only two countries (Pakistan and Indonesia) has the index of dissimilarity increased markedly, in both cases because of a sharp rise in the percentage of females classified as unpaid family workers. We are unable to judge whether this increase in unpaid family workers is real or instead reflects improved enumeration of female workers in the wake of such studies as that by Anker, Khan, and Gupta (1988), showing that conventional methods of reporting female employment seriously underrepresent women's economic participation. Regardless, the predominant trend in the region appears to be decreasing concentration of female workers in unpaid family work and a concomitant increase in the similarity between men and women in their class-of-worker distributions.

In addition to information on classes of workers, information is widely available on the occupations of male and female workers. *Table9* shows changes in the occupational distributions of female and male workers and in the index of occupational dissimilarity between the sexes over time. It should be noted that the index of dissimilarity is sensitive to the level of detail with which occupations are classified. Generally, the finer the classification, the larger is the index of dissimilarity (see, *e.g.*, Presser and Kishor 1991). Because we use a broad classification of occupations, the index values we compute are likely to understate the true level of occupational segregation quite seriously.

If one compares Asian countries at different stages of development or examines changes in the same countries over time, the trends in the occupational distributions of male and female workers appear to parallel those seen historically in the West. With development, agricultural

Table 7.

Female -to-Male Ratio of the Percentage of Population Economically Active, by Age Group: Asia, Recent Decades

Subregion and Country	Circa 1970			Circa 1970			Circa 1970		
	15+	30-34	50-54	15+	30-34	50-54	15+	30-34	50-54
South Asia									
Bangladesh	0.04	0.03	0.04	0.05	0.05	0.05	0.11	0.14	0.11
India	0.22	0.22	0.21	0.26	0.26	0.23	u	u	u
Nepal	0.39	0.35	0.32	0.52	0.45	0.47	u	u	u
Pakistan	0:10	0.09	0.10	0.04	0.04	0.03	0.13	0.11	0.11
Sri Lanka	0.30	0.30	0.24	0.34	0.35	0.22	0.58	0.64	0.36
Southeast Asia									
Indonesia	0.45	0.42	0.48	0.46	0.42	0.49	0.53	0.49	0.57
Malaysia	0.47	0.43	0.44	0.49	0.42	0.41	u	u	u
Philippines	0.43	0.40	0.42	0.63	0.58	0.63	0.58	0.53	0.60
Thailand	0.84	0.82	0.79	0.80	0.78	0.76	0.81	0.82	0.75
East Asia									
China	u	u	u	0.81	0.90	0.56	0.86	0.92	0.66
Hong Kong	0.51	0.37	0.40	0.60	0.51	0.47	0.60	0.56	0.41
South Korea	0.51	0.38	0.49	0.53	0.34	0.54	0.63	0.50	0.65
Singapore	0.36	0.23	0.20	0.54	0.45	0.23	0.64	0.65	0.39
Taiwan	0.38	0.29	0.24	0.41	0.32	0.24	u	u	u

Sources: Asian Development Bank (1993a, table 24)

Note: Data do not represent all areas of every country. Documented exception are available from the first author upon request.

u—data are unavailable.

Table 8.

Economic Activity Rate and Class of Employment of the Economically Active Population, by Sex: Asia, Recent Periods

Subregion and Country	Economic activity rate (% of population)		% of economically active population, by class of employment						Index of dissimilarity for class of employment (%)
			Women			Men			
	Women	Men	Self employed	Family worker	Employoee	Self-employed	Family worker	Employee	
South Asia									
Bangladesh (10+)									
1961	11	56	u	u	u	u	u	u	u
1974	2	53	20	58	18	47	21	29	38
1983-84	5	54	16	11	69	40	16	42	30
1985-86	6	54	17	11	69	40	19	40	32
India									
1961	28	57	u	u	u	u	u	u	u
1971	12	52	u	u	u	u	u	u	u
1981	22	55	u	u	u	u	u	u	u
Nepal									
1961 (15+)	36	55	78	11	10	77	3	20	10
1971 (10+)	25	59	89	7	4	85	3	12	8
1981 (10+)	32	58	90	4	4	84	2	12	9

{*Cont*}									
Pakistan (10+)									
1961	6	55	u	u	u	u	u	u	u
1972	6	54	u	u	u	50	20	20	u
1981	2	51	32	26	35	57	14	26	25
1992-93	8	46	13	48	22	46	16	34	44
Sri Lanka (10+)									
1963	14	50	8	6	76	32	4	56	23
1971	19	51	8	8	53	28	3	54	22
1981	18	49	10	3	55	30	2	55	20
1992	27	55	12	19	49	30	7	53	21
Southeast Asia									
Indonesia (10+)									
1961	20	53	u	u	u	u	u	u	u
1971	23	47	29	40	28	45	18	35	23
1980	24	48	46	29	23	56	12	30	18
1989	34	51	29	47	21	51	16	30	31
Malaysia									
1957 (10+)	17	50	24	19	56	38	5	56	14
1970 (10+)	22	44	u	u	u	u	u	u	u
1980 (10+)	25	50	24	16	50	31	7	57	14
1988 (15-64)	26	47	17	22	60	30	7	63	16
Philippines									
1960 (10+)	16	46	26	32	31	49	20	26	23
1970 (10+)	21	46	23	27	41	43	15	39	19
1981	24	49	27	31	42	42	16	42	15
1992 (15+)	48	83	30	20	40	41	10	41	12

{Cont}									
Thailand									
1960 (11+)	51	54	11	82	6	47	35	17	47
1970 (11+)	46	52	12	76	10	45	33	20	44
1980 (11+)	49	53	14	68	15	44	28	24	40
1990 (13+)	53	60	18	54	25	41	26	30	29
East Asia									
China									
1982 (15+)	47	57	u	u	u	u	u	u	u
Hong Kong									
1961 (6+)	23	54	14	10	79	917	2		
1971 (10+)	29	55	6	4	86	13	1	82	7
1981 (15+)	37	62	4	3	89	12	1	83	8
1991 (15+)	39	62	5	2	89	14	•	82	9
Japan (15+)									
1960	36	58	14	44	42	27	11	61	34
1970	39	63	14	32	53	23	6	70	27
1980	36	62	11	24	63	20	4	74	20
1992	42	64	10	14	74	15	2	81	24
South Korea									
1961 (13+)	17	43	21	57	15	53	17	24	41
1971 (14+)	23	43	17	51	30	43	12	42	40
1981 (14+)	29	47	18	40	35	42	8	44	32
1991 (15+)	47	75	19	22	56	34	2	61	20

{Cont}

Singapore									
1957 (10+)	13	52	14	12	72	22	3	73	10
1970 (10+)	18	51	8	5	68	21	3	69	13
1980 (10+)	33	59	6	4	86	18	2	77	12
1992 (15+)	51	80	6	2	90	17	•	80	11

Sources: United Nations (1994, series 3.5), ILO, *Yearbook of Labour Statistics* (1945-89, 1983, 1988, 1992, 1993, tables 1abd 2A).

Note: The usual age span for the economically active population is 15-64, exceptions are noted in parentheses. Where percentages for women and men do not sum to 100, the residual consists of persons whose employment is not classifiable by status. Because of diverse data-collection methods, the data on which these percentages are based are not strictly comprable across countries, and some percentages are provisional. Data do not represent all areas of every country. Specific qualifications are available from the first author upon request.

u—data are unavailable. • Less than 1 per cent.

and other forms of extractive work occupy a decreasing percentage of the labour force, while white-collar and manufacturing employment occupies an increasing proportion. Agricultural work tends initially to employ a larger proportion of female than of male workers (note, for example, the 1961 figures for Bangladesh, India, and Pakistan) but with a decline in such employment comes an increasing participation of women in non agricultural employment. Especially during the later stages of development, female workers move rapidly into clerical and sales work (for example, in the Philippines, Hong Kong, Japan, South Korea, and Singapore), and to a lesser extent into professional, technical, and related work (in the East Asian countries). Insofar as these forms of white-collar work offer women salaries, prestige, and clean working conditions, the later stages of economic development appear to improve their occupational opportunities.

On the other hand, as the economies of Asia develop, production, transportation, and other forms of blue-collar employment become more heavily male dominated. This tendency, if parallel to the experience in the West, probably result in large wage discrepancies between the white-collar female employment sector and the blue-collar male sector. Moreover, as the index-of dissimilarity values shown in the right-hand column of *Table 9* suggest, development does not bring with it gender desegregation of the occupational sphere (as it does with class-of-worker distributions). Instead, development tends to exacerbate occupational segregation by gender. Thus, when changes in female versus male occupations are considered, the picture is mixed. Although development draws women into paid and relatively clean forms of work in the white-collar sector, it also segregates them out of the better-paid jobs in the manufacturing sector, thereby perpetuating gender inequality within the labour force. Whether, on balance, this leaves women better or worse off than under preindustrial, subsistence conditions is unknown.

Age At Marriage

Early marriage is thought to undermine women's power and autonomy within the household for at least three reasons. First, a very young age at marriage is typically associated with the bride's residence in an extended-family household, where she is likely to fall under the control of family elders. Especially where such households have a patrilineal structure, this puts young wives at a great disadvantage in acquiring political resources and allies (Dyson and Moore 1983). Second, regardless of household structure, women who marry early are likely to have fewer material and psychological resources at their command than are women who marry after acquiring more life experience (Presser 1971). Finally, women who marry young often marry men who are considerably older than themselves, and some scholars have suggested that this puts them at a great disadvantage or is indicative of a social system that does so (Cain 1993; Presser 1975). For all these reason, age at marriage and the age difference between husbands and wives are often treated as indicators of women's access to power and autonomy.

Table 10 shows trends in female age at marriage, as measured by the singulate mean age at marriage, or SMAM, a synthetic measure of age at first marriage calculated from the percentages never married at each age. The table also shows differences between the SMAMs for men and women and the percentages of women at ages 15-19 and 20-24 who have not yet married. The overwhelming trend throughout Asia suggested by these data is toward older ages at marriage for women and a declining age difference between the average married man and married women (see also Tsuya 1994).

The only exception to these trends occurs in countries where female age at marriage was already high by the end the 1950s and the age difference between married women and men already small (for example, the Philippines). Even in South Asia, where women traditionally were betrothed as children and married shortly after menarche, age at marriage has risen to late adolescence or the early 20s. And in most of East Asia, female age at marriage has risen to the late 20s—so late, in fact, that some governments in the region worry about the negative consequences for fertility and future population growth. Insofar as a higher age at marriage gives women greater resources and power after marrying, the trend toward delayed marriage in Asia suggests that the status of women is improving.

Table 9.
Economically Active Population (in percentages), by Sex and Major Occupation Group: Asia, Recent Decades

Subregion and Country and year	Professional, technical, and related workers		Administrative and managerial workers		Sales, clerical, and related workers		Service workers		Productionrelated workers, transport equipment operators and laborers		Agriculture, animal husbandy, and forestry workers; fishermen and hunters		Index dissimilaity
	Women	Men	Women	Men	Women	Men	Women	Men			Women	Men	(%)
South Asia													
Bangladesh (10+)													
1961	*	1	0	*	1	4	2	2	5	6	92	85	8
1974	2	2	*	*	2	6	10	2	12	11	70	78	12
1989	2	4	0	*	1	15	3	3	4	15	90	60	29
India													
1961	1	4	*	1	2	7	2	3	13	16	82	68	14
1971	2	3	*	1	2	3	3	8	14	83	70	15	
1981	2	3	*	1	2	9	2	3	6	16	76	63	20
Nepal													
1961 (15+)	*	1	0	1	*	2	*	2	1	3	97	92	5
1971 (10+)	*	1	0	0	1	0	*	1	1	3	98	93	5
1976	4	4	0	*	1	3	*	*	3	7	93	86	6
Pakistan (10+)													
1961	3	4	0	1	1	10	8	5	14	19	71	59	15
1972	5	4	*	1	2	11	4	4	4	19	31	51	45

	Col 1	Col 2	Col 3	Col 4	Col 5	Col 6	Col 7	Col 8	Col 9	Col 10	Col 11	Col 12	Col 13
1981	15	3	1	1	7	11	8	4	24	25	35	50	21
1991-93	6	4	*	1	3	18	4	5	15	26	55	42	27
Sri Lanka													
1963(10+)	8	7	*	1	3	11	9	7	12	20	57	45	17
1971 (10+)	6	3	*	*	3	13	4	5	12	24	42	39	22
1981(10+)	9	4	*	1	6	13	4	5	11	25	36	37	25
1985	7	3	*	1	8	14	5	4	17	27	42	40	16
Southeast Asia													
Indonesia(10+)													
1971	2	2	*	1	14	13	5	3	9	12	58	62	8
1980	3	3	0	*	20	14	7	3	15	21	52	56	10
1985	4	3	0	*	16	6	2	13	21	53	54	10	
Peninsular Malaysia (10+)													
1957	4	7	*	2	4	14	7	7	8	18	75	49	26
1970	5	4	*	1	8	15	8	8	10	23	54	42	20
Sabah													
1960(15+)	2	5	0	1	3	6	3	3	3	13	89	72	17
1970(10+)	4	5	0	1	7	9	4	7	3	20	64	53	23
Sarawak													
1960(15+)	2	5	0	*	2	8	2	3	1	10	94	74	20
1970(10+)	2	3	0	1	4	9	3	6	3	14	74	61	21
1980(10+)	7	6	*	1	15	15	7	8	14	27	38	32	14
Philippines													
1960(10+)	6	4	*	1	13	6	15	3	20	10	35	70	35
1970(10+)	10	3	1	1	15	7	15	4	19	21	31	60	31
1981	11	4	1	1	25	11	14	10	12	16	37	57	25
1991 (15+)	9	3	1	1	28	9	13	6	11	24	28	48	34
Thailand													
1960(11+)	1	4	0	=	6	6	2	2	4	8	86	78	8

1970(11+)	2	4	*	3	7	6	3	3	5	9	83	75	9
1980(11+)	3	3	*	3	10	7	3	3	8	14	73	67	10
1990(13+)	4	3	1	2	14	9	4	3	12	19	63	62	9
East Asia													
China													
1982(15+)	4	6	*	2	3	4	2	2	13	18	77	68	10
Hong Kong													
1961(6+)	6	4	1	4	12	23	24	11	45	43	9	6	17
1971(10+)	6	4	1	3	14	20	15	14	54	50	4	4	8
1981(15+)	6	6	1	3	26	20	15	16	51	51	2	2	6
1991(15+)	10	8	2	6	46	24	22	16	17	42	*	1	30
Japan(15+)													
1970	6	10	*	4	21	21	10	4	20	35	43	26	23
1960	6	7	*	6	30	22	11	5	25	43	26	15	25
1980	10	8	1	7	38	26	12	6	24	42	13	9	25
1992	12	11	1	6	42	27	12	7	25	41	77	6	21
South Korea													
1960(13+)	2	7	1	1	10	10	9	4	6	10	65	60	11
1970(14+)	2	4	*	1	12	17	11	4	14	25	59	45	21
1980(14+)	3	5	0	2	19	21	9	5	19	31	43	30	17
1992(15+)	9	7	*	3	31	27	17	7	22	40	18	14	18
Singapore													
1957(10+)	10	13	*	2	16	31	35	11	24	32	12	7	29
1970(10+)	12	6	*	2	23	27	19	10	25	38	3	4	21
1980(10+)	10	8	2	6	36	22	13	8	33	42	1	2	21
1992(15+)	19	19	4	14	26	6	14	13	35	39	*	*	22

Sources: ILO, *Yearbook of Labour Statistics* (1945-89, 1982, 1983, 1988, 1993, tables 1 and 2B4).

Notes Because of changes made after 1970 in the ILO's International Standard Classification of Occupations, the data on which the percentages in this table are based are not strictly comparable for all periods. The usual age span for the economically active population is 15-64, exceptions are noted in parentheses. Data do not represent all areas of every country. Specific qualification are available from the first author upon request.

*Less than 1 percent.

Table 10.

Singulate Mean Age at Marriage (SMAM) for Women, Differences in SMAM between Men and Women, and Percentages Never Married Among Young Women, by Country and year: Asia: Recent Decades

Subregion, country, and year	Female SMAM	SMAM difference between men and women	% of women never married Ages 15-19	Ages 20-24
South Asia				
Bangladesh				
1961	13.9	9.0	8	1
1974	15.9	8.1	24	3
1981	16.4	7.5	31	5
India				
1961	15.8	5.8	29	6
1971	17.2	5.2	44	10
1981	18.13.	2	56	10
1991	20.1	4.1	68	24
Nepal				
1961	15.4	4.1	26	5
1971	16.8	4.0	39	8
1981	17.2	3.5	49	13
1991	18.1	3.3	54	13
Pakistan				
1961	17.6	5.9	47	12
1973	20.0	5.8	72	25
1981	19.7	5.4	68	21
1990	20.6	4.4	75	28
Sri Lanka				
1963	22.1	5.9	85	41
1971	23.5	4.2	89	53
1981	24.4	2.8	90	55
1987	24.8	u	93	57
Southeast Asia				
Indonesia				
1964	18.6	u	60	14
1971	19.2	4.5	63	18
1980	20.0	4.0	70	22
1991	21.5	u	80	36
Malaysia				
1960	19.4	5.0	65	21
1970	21.8	3.5	82	41
1980	23.5	2.8	90	51
Philippines				
1960	22.2	2.7	87	33
1970	22.8	2.6	89	41
1980	22.4	2.4	86	51
Thailand				
1960	21.6	2.9	83	35
1970	22.0	2.7	81	38

{Cont..........}

1980	22.7	2.2	84	44
1987	23.4	1.9	83	48
East Asia				
China				
1960	19.8	u	76	18
1970	20.7	u	87	27
1980	22.8	u	97	54
1990	22.1	1.7	95	41
Hong Kong				
1961	21.9	6.8	94	49
1971	23.8	6.4	97	68
1981	25.3	3.4	97	71
1991	28.2	2.3	98	83
Japan				
1960	25.0	2.4	99	68
1970	24.5	2.9	98	72
1980	25.1	3.6	99	78
1990	26.7	3.5	98	85
South Korea				
1960	21.5	4.9	98	49
1970	23.3	3.9	97	57
1980	24.1	3.2	98	66
1990	25.4	3.1	100	80
Singapore				
1957	20.3	5.7	80	33
1970	24.2	3.6	95	65
1980	26.2	2.2	98	74
1990	27.1	2.8	99	79
Taiwan				
1956	21.1	3.7	88	29
1966	21.9	4.2	91	40
1970	22.6	2.7	93	50
1980	23.8	1.5	95	58
1990	25.9	2.8	98	77

Health and Longevity

One of the most basic indicators of health and longevity is life expectancy at birth, a synthetic measure of survival that summarizes the age-specific mortality rates found in a population at a given time. Although this measure does not capture all aspects of health (particularly aspects that are not life threatening but may nevertheless degrade the quality of life), it is widely available and conveniently summarizes the risks of dying at various ages. As *Table 11* indicates,, life expectancies for both females and males vary widely across the region, with survival generally being lowest in South Asia and highest in East Asia, particularly in the wealthier countries of that subregion. Life expectancy has been rising in virtually all the countries examined, indeed, in the period covered in *Table 11,* life expectancy increased by an average of 2.8-4.7 years per decade among females and 2.7-4.4 years per decade among males.

Table 11.

Years of Life Expectancy at Birth for Females and Males, and Female-to-Male Ratio of Life Expectancy, by Year and Country: Asia, Recent Decades

Subregion and country	Females 1970	Females 1980	Females 1992	Males 1970	Males 1980	Males 1992	Female/male ratio 1970	Female/male ratio 1980	Female/male ratio 1992
South Asia									
Bangladesh	47	50	54	50	52	55	0.95	0.96	0.99
India	47	52	58	48	53	57	0.97	0.98	1.01
Nepal	38	44	51	41	46	51	0.93	0.96	0.99
Pakistan	49	52	58	50	52	56	0.97	1.00	1.02
Sri Lanka	65	71	74	62	67	69	1.04	1.06	1.08
Southeast Asia									
Indonesia	45	55	62	42	52	58	1.06	1.06	1.07
Malaysia	62	67	71	59	62	66	1.06	1.08	1.09
Philippines	62	65	68	56	60	62	1.11	1.08	1.09
Thailand	62	66	72	55	61	65	1,12	1.08	1.10
East Asia									
China	63	67	69	60	65	67	1.05	1.03	1.03
Hong Kong	76	78	84	68	72	76	1.11	1.09	1.09
Japan	77	79	81	72	73	76	1.07	1.07	1.08
South Korea	68	69	73	62	63	67	1.10	1.10	1.10
Singapore	72	74	78	66	69	73	1.10	1.08	1.07
Taiwan	71	74	78	66	69	72	1.08	1.07	1.09

Sources: Asian Development Bank (1993a,table 1); for Japan: United Nations (1992,104).
Note: Reference years for individual countries may vary slightly from those indicated. Specific qualifications are available from the first author upon request.

More important from the standpoint of assessing the changing status of women is that gains in life expectancy were greater for females than for males in most countries. This is indicated by the rising female-to-male ratios shown in the righthand panel of Table 11, especially in South and Southeast Asia. It can also be seen in the average per-decade increase in years of life expectancy at birth for the three subregions:

	Female	Males	Female/Male ratio
South Asia	4.4	3.2	1.4
Southeast Asia	4.7	4.4	1.1
East Asia	2.8	2.7	1.0

Table 12.

Percentage of Total Population, Ages 65 and Over, and Female-to-Male Ratio of Population, Ages 65 and Over, by Year and Country: Asia, Recent Decades

Subregion Country	%of total population 65+ 1960	1970	1980	1992	F/M ratio of population 65+ 1960	1970	1980	1992
South Asia								
Bangladesh	4	4	3	3	0.8	0.9	0.9	0.9
India	3	4	4	4	1.0	1.2	1.0	1.1
Nepal	4	3	3	3	1.1	1.0	1.0	1.0
Pakistan	4	3	3	4	0.8	0.9	1.0	1.0
Sri Lanka	4	4	4	5	0.8	0.8	0.9	1.0
Southeast Asia								
Indonesia	3	3	3	3	1.1	1.3	1.3	1.2
Malaysia	3	3	4	4	0.9	1.0	1.1	1.2
Philippines	3	3	3	4	1.6	1.1	1.3	1.1
Thailand	3	3	4	4	1.2	1.2	1.3	1.3
East Asia								
China	5	4	5	6	1.2	0.9	0.8	1.2
Hong Kong	3	4	6	10	2.3	2.3	1.6	1.3
Japan	6	7	9	12	1.3	1.3	1.4	1.5
South Korea	3	3	4	5	1.8	1.4	1.7	1.7
Singapore	2	3	5	6	1.4	1.3	1.3	1.2
Taiwan	u	5	6	7	u	1.2	0.6	0.9

Sources: ESCAP (1992, 187), Asian Development Bank (1993 a, 118-119) United Nations (1993) u-data are unavailable.

In East Asia, the greater gain in life expectancy for females than for males may reflect the greater inherent frailty of males. In this region, where the risks of dying in infancy and childhood have been low for some time, it is the aging of populations that produces the widening female survival advantage. In contrast, in South Asia, female-to male ratios below 1.0 prior to 1980 or 1992 suggest that the greater gain in female than in male survival represents improved nutrition or medical care for women and girls. Either there has been a lessening of traditional forms of nutritional and medical discrimination against girls (see, *e.g.*, Chen, Huq, and D'Souza 1981) or maternal mortality has declined—or both. The data in Table 11 thus suggest that in South Asia especially and in parts of Southeast Asia as well, the health status of women and their survival prospects have improved during the past two decades.

Although development may enhance the health and survival of women, both in absolute terms and relative to men, it brings with it new problems for women. One such problem is suggested by *Table 12*, which shows the percentage of the total population aged 65 and over along with the ratio of women to men in this age group. As can be seen for many of the South and East Asian countries, as longevity increases, the ratio of older women to older men rises. In modern, low-fertility, low-mortality populations, this shift eventually results in a large proportion of older women without spouses.

Thus, whereas the enhanced survival of females relative to males in South Asia represents an improvement in the status of women, the enhanced survival of women in East Asia may mean the loss of support or companionship for them in old age. Given the choice of longevity and widowhood or death at an early age, however, most women would probably choose the former. Greater awareness that they are likely to end their days as widows may cause women to strive for greater economic independence. It may also, however, strengthen their preference for sons, the topic to which we turn next.

Sex Preferences for Children

A strong preference for sons has characterized much of South and East Asia in the past and is associated with excess female mortality during childhood (Klasen 1994). Even where son preference does not lead to the neglect or outright killing of infant girls, it serves as a general indicator of the value placed on males versus females, a value that typically is correlated with the resources and power enjoyed by each gender. Women's sex preferences for children, which fertility surveys frequently measure, thus form a general indicator of the extent of gender inequality in a society. For this reason, we end our review of the changing status of women in Asia with an examination of sex-[reference data collected in the mid-to-late 1970s.

Table 13 shows one measure of such preferences, namely, the sex of the next child that women would prefer. (This measure is shown only for women who were married and biologically capable of having more children and who said they would like to have another child). The ratio of the percentages saying they wanted the next child to be a boy to the percentages saying they wanted the next child to be a girl are shown in the righthand column of the table. In all but one of the countries for which data are available (the Philippines being the exception), the ratio is above 1.0, indicating a preference for sons. As has been noted in other sources, the ratios are generally higher in South and East Asia than in Southeast Asia, where most of the ratios are fairly close to 1.0. Sri Lanka, however, has a ratio more in line with the ratios found in Southeast Asia than with those found in South and East Asia.

Table 13.

Preferences for the Sex of the Next Child and Ratio of Preferences for Sons Versus Daughters Among Currently Married, Fecund Women Wanting Another Child, by Country: Asia, 1970s (Word Fertility Survey data)

Subregion and Country	Preference (%)			Preference ratio[a]
	Boy	Girl	Undecided	
South Asia				
Bangladesh	60	8	32	3.3
India	u	u	u	u
Nepal	67	8	25	4.0
Pakistan	72	5	23	4.9
Sri Lanka	52	31	17	1.5
Southeast Asia				
Indonesia	34	29	36	1.1
Malaysia	36	28	35	1.2
Philippines	34	37	29	0.9
Thailand	49	34	16	1.4
East Asia				
China	u	u	u	u
Hong Kong	u	u	u	u
Japan	u	u	u	u
Korea, South	67	14	19	3.3
Singapore	u	u	u	u
Taiwan	u	u	u	u

Source: United Nations (1987, table 36, p. 6).
u—data are unavailable.
a. Ratio of women preferring a son to women preferring a daughter, with those undecided allocated equally.

We do not know whether these ratios have changed over time, nor do we know the extent to which they are affected by development or by demographic change. The strong preference for sons found in South Korea however, suggests that neither development nor a decline of fertility to modern levels necessarily weakens a society's preference for sons. Couples in Korea have small families *despite* their strong preference for sons, rather than having weakened son p4reference because of their desire to have small families (part and Cho 1995). Son preference appears to reflect a country's sociocultural landscape rather than its economic level. Thus, although development in Asia may have improved the lot of women in several key respects, in South and East Asia women still face considerable disadvantages accruing from the mere fact that they were born female.

Conclusions

This report has taken a selective approach to assessing the situation of women in Asia. We have focused on only a few of the many possible facets of women's status that might be considered and have examined them for selected countries rather than for the entire region. Moreover, primarily because of data limitations, we have been able to examine change for only a restricted period of time and, in the case of sex preferences for children, at only a single point in time. Despite these limitations, the data examined suggest two conclusion about the underlying causes of women's situation. First, the sociocultural traditions of a particular region or country can have a strong and enduring impact on women's situation, regardless of economic or political conditions. And second, economic development clearly improves the situation of women in certain respects, even if not in others.

The first of these conclusions is illustrated on one hand by the case of South Korea, where sons preference persists despite rapid economic development, and on the other by the case of Sri Lanka, which stands out among South Asian countries by virtue of the advanced position of women on several of the indicators examined here. Sri Lanka's level of economic development is close to that found in the other South Asian countries. In 1991, for example, the World Bank estimated that per capita income in Sri Lanka, in US dollars, was $500, as compared with $ 400 in Pakistan and $330 in India (Asian Development Bank 1993b, 15). These levels contrasted with far higher levels in many Southeast and East Asian countries — for example, $2,490 in Malaysia, $1,580 in Thailand, $13,200 in Hong Kong, and $6,340 in South Korea. Sheer development or wealth therefore cannot explain the far lower level of illiteracy, far higher female-to-male ratio of school enrollment, older age at marriage, greater life expectancy at birth, and weaker son preferences of women in Sri Lanka compared with those of women in other South Asian countries. Women in Sri Lanka are better off, both in absolute terms and relative to men in their country, because of sociocultural traditions that accord them a more equal position than is given to women in the northerly portions of South Asia.

Economic development, however, does appear to affect the situation of women in many Asian countries, or at least is contemporaneous with changes in their status. For example, the enormous disparities in education and employment between the northerly countries of South Asia and the other countries examined here can be attributed at least in part to the disparity in incomes between subregions. A majority of the changes in women's status associated with development reviewed here have been positive. Both in comparisons between richer and poorer countries within the region and in comparisons over time within a single country, development goes along with an improved educational status for women, both absolutely and relative to men; with a movement of women out of unpaid family employment into remunerative work; with an older age at marriage for women and a narrowing age difference between spouses; and with improvements in women's health and longevity-improvements that in some instances are suggestive of decreasing nutritional or medical discrimination against girls.

Development, however, especially during its early stages, is no guarantee that women's position will improve. This review has noted much slower improvements in female education and employment in most of South Asia than in most of Southeast and East Asia, where incomes have risen more substantially.

It should also be kept in mind that as societies become wealthy and demographically modern, new problems for women arise to replace the old ones, For example, when fertility declines, although population growth slows, the proportion of the population that is old also grows and eventually becomes quite large (one-fifth or more of the total population). Because of men's greater biological frailty, this aging of the population normally involves an increasing feminization of the aged. Therefore, as economic development proceeds, problems of illiteracy and lack of earning power may abate for younger women, but problems of support for older women are likely to grow.

Nevertheless, development appears to have several salutary effects on the situation of women, even if it fails to guarantee them equality with men or improvements in all spheres of life. In most parts of Asia except the most backward, women today appear to be better off than their counterparts of 20-30 years ago and also better off in relation to men. One can only hope that as Bangladesh, India, Pakistan, and other relatively poor South Asian countries with strong patriarchal traditions experience further economic growth and demographic modernization, the women in those countries will increasingly enjoy improved education, employment opportunities, and health.

Acknowledgments

We thank Shireen J. Jejeebhoy, Valerie Kincade Oppenheimer, and Harriet B. Presser for helpful comments on an earlier draft, Joann Vanek of the United Nations for supplying us with the WISTAT data files from which several of the tables in this paper were constructed, Sandra Ward for her superb editing, Connie Kawamoto for her editorial assistance,

Russell Fujita for his production assistance, and the William and Flora Hewlett Foundation for partial support of the work reported herein. The conclusions reached in this report represent the opinions of the senior author alone, neither the United Nations nor any other organization bears any responsibility for them.

References

Anker, Richard, M.E. Khan, and R.B. Gupta. 1988. *Women's participation in the labour force: A methods test in India for improving its measurement.* Women, Work and Development, 16. Geneva: International Labour Office.

Asian Development Bank. 1993a. *Gender indicators of developing Asian and Pacific countries.* Manila.

—1993b. *Key indicators of developing Asian and Pacific countries.* Oxford: Oxford University Press for the Asian Development Bank.

Blumberg, Rae lesser. 1978. Stratification: Socioeconomic and sexual inequality. Dubuque, Iowa: Wm. C. Brown.

Boserup, Ester. 1970. *Woman's role in economic development.* New York: St, Martin's press.

1990. Population, the status of women and rural development. In Geoffrey McNicoll and Mead Cain, eds, *Rural development and population: Institutions and policy,* pp. 45-60. New York: Population Council.

Cain, Mead T. 1993. Patriarchal structure and demographic change. In Nora Federici, Karen Oppenheim Mason, and Solvi Sogner, eds. *Women's position and demographic change,* pp. 43-60. Oxford: Clarendon Press.

Chen, Lincoln C. Emdadul Huq, and Stan D'Souza. 1981. Sex bias in the family allocation of food and health care in rural Bangladesh. *Population and Development Review* 7(1)55-70.

Collier, Jane F, and Michelle Z. Rosaldo. 1981. Politics and gender in simple societies. In Sherry B. Ortner and Harriet Whitehead, eds. *Sexual meanings: The cultural construction of gender and sexuality.* pp 275-329. Cambridge: Cambridge University Press.

Dixon-Mueller, Ruth, and Richard Anker. 1988. Assessing women's economic contributions to development. Background Papers for Training in Population, Human Resources and Development Planning, No.6. Geneva: International Labour Office, World Employment Programme.

Draper, Patricia. 1975. Kung women: Contrasts in sexual egalitarianism in foraging and sedentary contexts. In Rayna R, Reiter, ed. *Toward an anthropology of women,* pp. 77-109. New York: Monthly Review Press.

Dyson, Tim, and Mick Moore. 1983. On Kinship structure, female autonomy, and demographic behavior in India. *Population and Development Review* 9(1):35-60

ESCAP (Economic Commission for Asia and the Pacific). 1992. *Statistical Yearbook for Asia and the Pacific.* Bangkok.

Engels, Frederick.(1884) 1972, *The origin of the family, private property, and the state.* New York: Pathfinder Press.

Friedl, Ernestine. 1975. *Women and men: An anthropologist's view,* New York: Holt, Rinehart and Winston.

Geertz, Hildred. 1961. *The Javanese family: A study of kinship and socialization.* Prospect heights, Illinois: Waveland Press.

Geertz, Hildred, and Clifford Geertz. 1975. *Kinship in Bali.* Chicago: University of Chicago Press.

Greenhalgh, Susan. 1985. Sexual stratification: The other side of "growth with equity" in

East Asia. *Population and Development Review* 11(2): 265-314.

Heyzer, Noeleen. 1986. *Women farmers and rural change in Asia:Towards equal access and participation.* London: Milton Keynes Open University Press.

ILO (International Labour Office). Various years. *Yearbook of labour statistics*. Geneva.

Jain, Ravindra K. 1970. *South Indian in the plantation frontier in Malaya.* New Haven: Yale University Press.

Joekes, Susan, with Noeleen Heyzer, Ruth Oniang'o and Vania Salles. 1994. Gender, environment and population. *Development and Change* 25(1)137-65.

Klasen, Stephan. 1994. "Missing women" reconsidered. *World Development* 22(7): 1061-71.

Mies, Maria. 1986. *Patriarchy and accumulation on a world scale: Women in the international division of labour.*

London: Zed Books

Nuss Shirley, in collaboration with Ettore Denti and David Viry. 1989. *Women in the world of work: Statistical analysis and projections to the year 2000.* Geneva: International Labour Office.

Park, Chai Bin, and Nam-Hoon Cho. 1995. Consequences of son preference in a low-fertility society: Imbalance of the sex ratio at birth in Korea. *Population and Development Review* 21(1)59-84.

Presser, Harriet B. 1971. The timing of the first birth, female roles and black fertility. *Milbank Memorial Fund Quarterly* 49 (3, part 1): 329-59.

———. 1975. Age differences between spouses: Trends, patterns, and social implications. *American Behavioral Scientist* 19:217-26.

Presser, Harriet B, and Sunitha Kishor. 1991. Economic development and occupational sex segregation in Puerto Rico: 1950-80. *Population and Development Review* 17(1): 53-85.

Salaff, Janet W. 1981. *Working daughters of Hong Kong: Filial piety or power in the family* Cambridge: Cambridge University Press.

Smith, Daniel Scott. 1973. Family limitation, sexual control, and domestic feminism in victorian America. *Feminist Studies* 1:150-66.

Tsuya, Noriko O. 1994. Nuptiality change in Asia: Patterns, causes, and prospects. Lecture presented i a Distinguished Lecturer Series to celebrate the 25th anniversary of the Summer Seminar of Population, East-West Center, Honolulu, Hawaii, 20 June.

UNESCO (United Nations Economic and Social Commission). Various dates. *Statistical yearbook.* Paris.

United Nations. 1987. *Fertility behaviour in the context of development: Evidence from the World Fertility Survey.* New York.

———.1992. *World population monitoring* 1991. New York.

———. 1993. *Sex and age distribution of the world's populations: The 1992 revision.* New York.

United Nations, DESIPA (Department for Economic and Social Information and Policy Analysis). 1994. *Women's indicators and statistics database, Version 3.* [Electronic database.] New York.

Vlassoff, Carol. 1994. From rags to riches: The impact of rural development on women's status in an Indian village. *World Development* 22(5): 707-19

MEASURING WOMEN'S UNPAID WORK

United Nations and INSTRAW

It is still before sunrise, about 6.30 a.m., when the researcher arrives at the family's doorstep. For the next hour, as unobtrusively as possible, she records what each household member is doing, at that hour probably washing and getting dressed, preparing breakfast, feeding livestock, gathering materials for school or market. Each separate activity is timed, and all interactions within the household recorded — a mother helping a child or elderly parent with shoes or hair, for instance. For the rest of the day the researcher will alternate visits at this and another nearby household, observing all activities and interviewing household members on their activities during her absence. To minimize intrusion, no more than four hours are spent with either family in a given day.

The researcher is taking the first painstaking steps in the process of gathering gender statistics. The technique is an old one, a time-use study. The results will be new: When compiled, the data will capture many activities not captured before. Up to now, these activities have been statistically invisible. They are usually not included in conventional data collection, and are therefore largely unvalued—and are mostly undertaken by women. A few examples tell the story: the women who works as a dressmaker in her spare time who is paid in cash or in kind by her customers, the income unrecorded and the final product uncounted; the older women who cares for her grandchildren while her daughter is away at work; the farmer's wife who helps plant and harvest the commercial crops, tends the poultry and the kitchen garden completely unassisted and is unpaid. Her role as a housewife, difficult and time consuming, is not valued in conventional economic terms—and she herself probably thinks of being a housewife as "doing nothing".

The Challenge: Correcting the Database

That informal, unpaid and household production needs to be measured and valued was recognized in principle two decades ago, at the first world conference on women in Mexico City. Despite an avalanche of other computer-generated statistics, there was and still is almost no evailable data, especially in the developing countries,on the extent and value of what women do. This statistical gap is more than a gender issue: it goes to the heart of effective economic and social policy planning. Statistics, which may appear mind-numbing to many, are, in fact, the engines that drive the decision-making process. It begins with gross domestic product (GDP). If this base figure is wrong or inadequate, so will be all the government functions which follow, such as social services, urban planning, transportation, education etc.

GDP, a nation's total output of goods and services, tends to omit as much as it includes. In sub -Saharan Africa, for example, women are estimated to be responsible for more than 80 per cent of food production for home consumption, and over half of all agricultural production. Official GDP figures for the region, however, generally count only the produce actually brought to market or exported— the cash crops grown largely by men.

The System of National Accounts (SNA), which determines GDP, was revised to include all goods produced in the household and, by extension, production-related activities like water-carrying. All of the dressmaker's output, part of the so-called informal sector, became recognized economic production. Although unpaid domestic and personal services (cooking, mending, child care etc.) are still not included, the 1993 SNA suggests that alternate concepts of GDP be devised for use in satellite accounts.

Eliminating Gender Bias

Clearly, part of the problem lies behind the statistics, in methods that are either gender-biased or at best gender-neutral. In censuses and surveys, for example, a resident male is assumed to be the head of household and is usually the one interviewed. Any bias in his response will be recorded as fact, which, in combination with other similar facts, will ultimately be used to determine government policies.

The challenge for the statistician is to develop and implement new concepts and methods of collecting data that will reflect reality and document changes in the situations of both men and women. This can also mean accounting for factors impacting on gender to reveal some of the causes of inequalities. A tally of schools, for example, should include the number of female students who "drop out". these statistics can indicate where school schedules might be tailored to fit seasonal work patterns in various geographic areas, to encourage more girls to attend and stay in school. Perhaps most important, accurate baseline data will also help Governments set realistic goals —and more effective policies with which to achieve them.

Development of valid gender statistics must be a two-pronged process: eliminating gender bias in conventional data collection and filling in the glaring statistical gap in calculating national productivity, i.e., the contribution of women's — and men's —unpaid and household work. Eliminating gender bias in conventional statistics means reviewing and questioning past assumptions and adapting old techniques accordingly. Age and sex are important variables, and the same questions asked of men and women may elicit very different responses. Routinely interviewing only male heads of household, for instance, may not indicate the true division of responsibilities among family members or reflect the priorities of the whole family. Similarly, policies designed for heads of household do not necessarily mean improvements for the rest of the family. Gender specific information should therefore be carefully integrated into all conventional censuses and surveys.

REDEFINING A DAY'S WORK

Currently, there is only one comprehensive technique for measuring unpaid work: systematic time-use surveys to demonstrate how a person uses his or her time, provide accurate estimates of unpaid household activities and show the daily, weekly and seasonal patterns of such activities and their relationship to economic and non-economic activities,. Such detailed accountings of how days are spent, whether at work, play, eating or sleeping, have been widely used in the industrialized countries, but in only a handful of developing nations. The techniques usually required— distribution of diaries and interviews by specially trained personnel-are frequently inappropriate to developing countries, particularly in remote rural areas, where literacy rates tend to be low.

It is precisely in these areas that the need for basic data is greatest, however. In Nepal, for example, although more than two thirds of family income is generated by household-level enterprises, including subsistence agriculture, 1993 GDP figures indicate that much of the post-harvest or later food processing, done primarily by women, is left out;

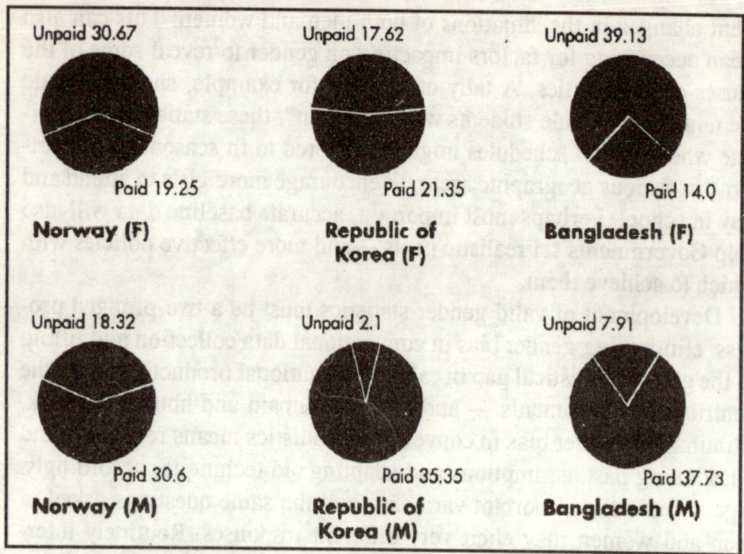

Time Allocations Between Paid and Unpaid Work by Sex, 1990-1991

only the production of cottage and other industries is included. This means that GDP omits many minor crops grown—mainly by women—for household consumption.

New techniques being developed by researchers are designed to capture uncounted work as well as the potentially far greater economic contribution of domestic services. All data is separated by gender to reflect the true impact of these activities on both the household's welfare and the national economy as a whole. Statisticians in several countries are currently working to develop a new satellite accounts system to help document and further define the dimensions and productivity of the household economy.

Separate categories would be established to include all unpaid activities done for others, such as cleaning, laundry, handling family finances etc. The new satellite accounts system would also include "personal development" activities, such as education and skills training, which have important investment value. These would be calculated as part of an extended concept of GDP. Other personal activities, such as eating, sleeping and recreation, which clearly cannot benefit or be performed by anyone else, would be categorized as either personal maintenance (*e.g.* washing one's own hair as opposed to giving someone else a shampoo) or personal consumption (*e.g.*, reading, watching TV). These would be excluded from the actual accounting of production, but the time spent on them might be measured as a component of the quality of life.

Potential Pitfalls

Of course there are some problems in the time-use approach. For example, practically no one engages in any activity in isolation or in strict sequence. Many different tasks and the time spent on them tend to be simultaneous or to overlap. Simultaneous activities are frequent in a household environment, particularly where child care is involved. Rarely does a mother do anything, whether cooking a meal or travelling to visit a friend, that doesn't coincide with some other activity related to child care. These some overlapping activities can cross into the economic area as well, *e.g.* mother tending a cash crop with a child at her side.

Next Steps

Despite these problems, collection of time-use data remains the only valid method for capturing normally overlooked activities. Development of general methodological guidelines, a combination of conventional statistical theory and field observation, is the necessary next step.

One survey, which included the pre-dawn visit described earlier, used conventional time diaries which were completed using a combination of direct observation and a listing of activities recalled by the subjects during face-to-face interviews. It was designed to document all productive activities undertaken by the men, women and children in 100 households. Five different communities were selected to represent a cross section of the society at all income levels, in both urban and rural settings. The results were encouraging; the time-use data did in fact reveal many activities not before included in statistics.

The establishment of a system of satellite accounts to include unpaid domestic services would estimate the quantity and value of all these statistically "new" activities. In one approach, this means estimating the market value of the labour inputs, which in turn requires carefully measuring the time used. There is a broad range of possible methods to be used to value non-market production—for example, by determining the number of shirts or dresses a woman could make and sell in the time she spends on child care every day. The time use study would indicate the amount of time spent, the market price of the hypothetical garments would equal the value of that time.

The impact of a system of satellite accounts could be enormous, helping to provide an accurate accounting of essentially very private matters for crucial public purposes. While development policies are generally geared to increasing productivity, increases in productivity are not necessarily reflected in increases or improvements in standards of living. In the industrialized countries, for instance, there are questions about the real benefits of full-time employment for mothers in the absence of adequate child-care arrangements or more sharing of household responsibilities by fathers. In the developing countries, living standards may actually deteriorate while GDP rises. Preliminary studies in Nepal show that as a result of increased commercialization of farm produce, household members tend to work longer hours, travel farther, spend more on superfluous consumer goods and sometimes even eat less, as more and more home production is sent to market. Economic development, in this case, is an illusion.

Inclusion of time-use data and the establishment of a satellite system of national accounting will dispel the illusions and make clear the magnitude and value of unpaid household work. Perhaps more important, it will show that the burden is carried disproportionately by women, beginning with the fact that they almost invariably work longer hours. In the case of Nepal, time-use data show that women not only match men hour for hour in paid work, but in non-marketable activities they outwork men by two to one.

Equally significant, placing a recognized value on unpaid work will demonstrate a women's social as well as economic contribution as a provider of a wide range of vital services. This is particularly true in many rural areas, where there may be no services available and women have generally provided them without recognition or assistance. With statistical visibility and value, women would be entitled to access to the same services— education, health care, sanitation etc.— as the rest of the society.

The next steps will inevitably be a process of trial and error. Any new techniques will require testing, refinement and, to the extent possible, standardization. Finding a statistically valid formula for measuring and evaluating the data collected will require accounting for wide variations in local and national conditions. The procedure will be exacting and tedious, but ultimately will bring the long-range goal set at Mexico City into reach: the heretofore invisible contributions of women will become visible—accepted, evaluated and integrated into the world's economies.

REFUGEE WOMEN

UN AND UNHCR

The need to cross military lines or regions affected by lawlessness or civil war puts women and girls at particular risk.

The explosion of ethnic conflicts in the 1990s, as the end of the cold war unfroze long-dormant disputes, has created humanitarian crises whose number and magnitude seem to increase dramatically every year. In 1994, the scale and geographical spread of such violent upheavals reached proportions that have few parallels in recent history. In tiny Rwanda, in the space of less than four months, between half and two thirds of the country's population were killed, died from epidemic diseases, or fled. It was the largest and most catastrophic exodus the Office of the United Nations High Commissioner for Refugees ((UNHCR) has ever witnessed. Among the hardest hit by the violence and uncertainty of displacement were young girls, elderly widows, single mothers— women.

Protection is at the heart of the responsibility that the world bears towards refugees. Protection means freedom from assault. Deprived of the protection of their State, detached from their families and communities of origin, and considered helpless foreigners in an alien land, refugees are, by definition, in any culture, vulnerable to violence. Refugee women and their children are the most vulnerable of all. Despite the strength and courage that have carried them out of their homelands, refugee women have special needs in terms of shelter, supplies and health care. They also require measures to protect them from sexual violence and exploitation in all phases of their lives as refugees.

The problem is vast, though a complete picture is not available. Statistics on refugees and asylum seekers are, even today, rarely broken down by gender. UNHCR estimates that 23 million refugees and 26 million internally displaced people have been forced to leave their homes because of conflict, massive human rights abuse, or the direct effects of conflict, such as famine and lawlessness. As a rule of thumb, more than three quarters of those destitute displaced people are women and their dependent children. That proportion of women and children may rise to 90 per cent in some refugee populations, when husbands or fathers are killed, or taken prisoner, or drafted as combatants. Most take refuge in remote, poorly developed areas where there is little security. Many have already been attacked— exactly how many is simply not known. "Sexual violence against women is widespread", says UN High Commissioner for Refugees Sadako Ogata. She call the phenomenon "a global outrage"

Sexual Violence and Exploitation

Rape is a common element in the pattern of persecution or terror or "ethnic cleansing" that drives refugee families from their homes, and civilians increasingly become the intentional targets-rather than the accidental victims— of warfare. From Myanmar to Somalia and Bosnia, refugee families frequently cite rape or the fear of rape as a key factor in their decision to leave.

Subsequently, the road to asylum is itself paved with threats of sexual violence and exploitation. The perpetrators may be bandits, smugglers, border guards, police, military and irregular forces on both sides of the border, or elements of local populations taking advantage of defenceless arriving refugees. The need to cross military lines or regions affected by lawlessness or civil war to reach safety puts women and girls at particular risk.

Once in exile, women and girls are still vulnerable to sexual violence or exploitation, by camp officials or other refugees. Some countries automatically incarcerate people who enter without visas in detention centres, often alongside hardened criminals. In some cases they detain women or young children together with adult men. The potential for abuse in such circumstances is obvious. In camps, refugee women may be forced into sex in exchange for material assistance for themselves or their children—particularly if the distribution of basic supplies is left to all-male camp committees. Officials, too, sometimes use rations or identity papers in order to sexually coerce women. Domestic violence often escalates with the pressures, disruptions, confinement or enforced idleness of refugee life. Later, victims of sexual violence may be further assaulted because of the shame they are alleged to have brought on their society.

In 1993, the incidence of rape was reported to be alarmingly high at camps for Somali refugees in Kenya, which were located in isolated areas plagued by bandits and Somali militia. Hundreds of women refugees were raped in night raids, or while foraging for firewood. UNHCR set up a pilot project to improve protection. The camps were fenced with thorn-bushes and protected by expanded patrols. Vulnerable women were relocated to safer areas. Community outreach was expanded. A number of victims of violence, who were suffering from acute forms of ostracism, were relocated to other refugee camps or given more rapid opportunities for resettlement abroad.

How to Protect Refugees from Sexual Violence

UNHCR has developed formal guidelines on preventing and responding to sexual violence, based on detailed recommendations by fieldworkers experienced with the rapes of and piracy attacks on Vietnamese boat people, the rapes of Somali women in Kenya, or the barbarous "ethnic cleansing" rapes of Bosnian women. The guidelines aim to provide field workers with practical, non-specialist advice on the medical, psychological and legal ramifications of sexual violence. They are also intended to dispel the discomfort of many refugee workers with such acts — or any tendency to dismiss them as an inevitable by-product of social breakdown. Ann Howarth-Wiles, UNHCR'S Senior Coordinator for Refugee Women, calls the guidelines "a fundamental primer" that should "immeasurably improve the sensitivity and skills of people who work with refugees, whether for UNHCR or our implementing partners."

UNHCR has also developed gender training, known as People Oriented Planning (POP), to encourage staff to focus on the protection and assistance needs of refugee women. A key element is encouraging women to participate in camp decision-making and the distribution of basic supplies. When men claim that women have no traditional role in decision-making, UNHCR staff encourage women to form separate committees. The alternative—leaving key decisions and distribution in the hands of all-male groups-has in the past led to the theft or misuse of key supplies, sexual exploitation, and the failure to supply key basics to very vulnerable families, especially those headed by women.

Not every group of refugees can easily accept the empowerment of women. The problem is compounded when refugees come from very conservative societies, which may react to exposure to a foreign environment by even more extreme practices. UNHCR staff report that among Afghan refugees in Pakistan, the practice of purdah has actually intensified during exile. Women who had previously worked in fields alongside male members of their family are no longer even permitted to leave their compounds, because of the mixing of various tribes and communities in the camps. To ensure proper health care for such women, and a modicum of skills, literacy and nutrition training, UNHCR has taken steps to increase the number of its female staff officers —who must often focus their initial, confidence-building efforts on elderly women (less socially restricted) and young children.

In an emergency situation, a proper focus on women's particular needs may, in practice, be close to impossible to maintain. Faced with an overwhelming inflow, such as the quarter of a million panicked and dying people who daily flooded out of Rwanda in the first few days of August 1994, field staff can often do little more than identify a few members of the most vulnerable groups, and perhaps sketch the basic foundations of intelligent camp design. In emergency situations, refugee families may be obliged to share tents. Hastily constructed latrines and washing facilities may offer little privacy, or be located too far from living areas. In extreme circumstances, sufficient food may not be getting to the most vulnerable members of a social group, such as widows with children, or elderly women on their own. Such circumstances are not acceptable, and are never tolerated for long. UNHCR field staff are, without exception, committed to maintaining proper assistance to all refugees.

Redefining Women's Refugee Status

Many women have trouble substantiating their claims to refugee status, especially if those claims are based on sexual persecution. Though no gender restriction was intended, the 1951 Convention Relating to the Status of Refugees that is the bedrock of UNHCR's work was written using male pronouns. It defines a refugee in terms of a well-founded fear of persecution based on race, religion, nationality, political opinion or "membership of a particular social group." UNHCR has issued policy statements encouraging countries to consider that when rape or other forms of sexual violence are committed for reasons of race or political opinion, for example— and particularly when this is condoned by the authorities concerned—then they should be grounds for refugee status.

Some countries have recognized this, and in addition have ruled that women who face inhumane treatment because of perceived transgressions of social mores should be eligible for refugee status, as members of a "particular social group". Canada, for example, has recognized that a women should be considered a refugee if she fears that she may be persecuted in her home country because of her refusal to inflict genital

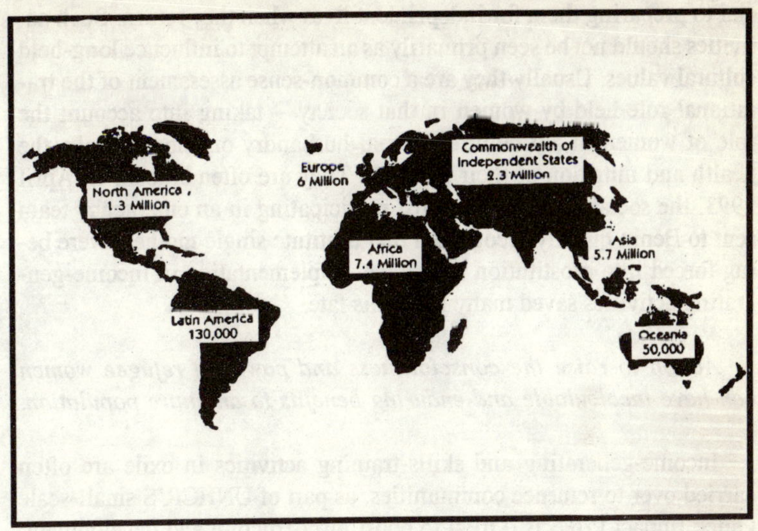

Where are all the refugees?

mutilation on her baby daughter, or to wear heavy, restrictive clothing. There has been similar progress on issues of gender-based persecution in Germany, the Netherlands and Switzerland. In 1984, the European parliament determined that women facing cruel or inhuman treatment because they seemed to transgress social mores should be considered a particular social group for the purposes of determining refugee status. UNHCR has encouraged the parliament's members States (as well as all other countries) to formally adopt this interpretation.

Still, very few countries employ women staff in their refugee status determination procedures. despite the quite obvious reluctance of most refugee women to discuss sexual persecution with men. Many States dismiss allegations of sexual violence as irrelevant to refugee status. Indeed, many countries rarely consider the asylum claim of a married women separately from her husband. Only sustained and active lobbying by UNHCR and other refugee groups can hope to change this situation.

Preparing Refugees for Independent Life

The goal of most refugees is, ultimately, to return home, once conditions of peace and stability have been re-established. Women are no different—and of course should have their own say in such fundamental decisions as repatriation. Because refugee women are often single heads of households, with limited education or income-generating skills, well-designed and well-targeted development-oriented activities can be crucial to preparing them for independent lives when they return. Such activities should not be seen primarily as an attempt to influence long-held cultural values. Usually they are a common-sense assessment of the traditional role held by women in that society— taking into account the role of women in agriculture, animal husbandry or, more simply, the health and nutrition of their children. They are often crucial. In April 1993, the social services specialist participating in an emergency team sent to Benin quickly recognized that destitute single mothers were being forced into prostitution to survive. Implementation in income-generating activities saved many from this fate.

Action to raise the consciousness and power of refugee women can have incalculable and enduring benefits to an entire population.

Income-generating and skills-training activities in exile are often carried over to returnee communities, as part of UNHCR'S small-scale Quick Impact Projects (QIPs) to boost infrastructure and development. In Nicaragua, "QIPFEMs" were designed specifically for returnee women, concentrating on non-traditional skills such as been-keeping, agriculture, and reforestation, and on the construction of hand-pumps, threshing mills and day-care centres to reduce women's domestic workload. Returnee women were also given loans to enable them to set up cooperatives and businesses. Contracts with UNHCR's implementing partners in Nicaragua commonly stipulated that women must benefit from at least 50 per cent of wage-earning, income-generating and training opportunities provided by QIPs, and should receive equal pay. As a result, the income, skills, expectations and confidence of returnee women rose dramatically, and traditional communities became familiar with the concept of women as economic actors.

The Cairo International Conference on Population and Development in September 1994 recognized that "reproductive health care and family planning are vital human rights". Those vital rights are still absent from many refugee camps. UNHCR and the United Nations Population Fund (UNFPA) have embarked on a series of joint activities to promote reproductive health for as many refugees as possible. A practical guidance manual for reproductive health is being developed, using the experience of dozen of field officers. The aim is to provide refugee health services with guidelines to deal with gynaecological diseases as well as with broken legs and cholera. Better health facilities will be able to treat complications resulting from the genital mutilation of baby girls, and the resulting tearing during rape or marital sex. They will provide female examiners and counselling on nutritional advice, AIDS and sexually transmitted diseases, as well as access to family-planning information.

Sustaining a Culture

Women are the life-sustaining force of any refugee community. Together with their dependent children, they often from the numerical majority of a refugee population. They also play a central economic and social role. They have the power to nurture future generations, re-establishing the family and culture in exile, and re-creating it again on return to their homeland.

Although UNHCR has always intended that female refugees should receive equal, adequate and appropriate benefits, UNHCR activities have not always been planned with full regard to the needs, abilities and aspirations of refugee women. Neglect of their particular needs has at times meant that programmes, from health clinics to skills training have benefited male refugees disproportionately. The result, in every case, has been an unnecessary and wasteful degree of dependency—weakening not only women, but the community as a whole.

Action to raise the consciousness and power of refugee women can have incalculable and enduring benefits to an entire population. "In exile, we women became very united, of necessity, although we did not know each other", says Maria Eugenia, who returned to El Salvador in 1988 after many years of exile in Honduras. "We were 11,000 refugees all together, most of us women. It was up to us to organize and promote our needs. We stated our problems and sought solutions in every area. We received training in areas like health and education and agriculture, people started to learn skills. We had chicken farms and different types of workshops, making clothes and shoes. When we returned, we had changed. Here, outside in the countryside, peasant women used to be ignored. We did not vote, we had no voice. Now, thanks to UNHCR, and to our organization while we were refugees, that has changed. We have a voice. We make it heard".

MAHILA SAMAKHYA : WOMEN'S EMPOWERMENT

The Mahila Samakhya Programmes is launched by Government of India to empower women through education

I. THE MAHILA SAMAKHYA EXPERIENCE

Twenty years ago serious policy discourse hardly admitted the argument that women's educational needs required a different focus as distinct from men. The literacy classes and condensed courses offered had not takers. Mahila Samakhya Programme 1988 was responsible for a radical policy departure as it shifted the focus from delivery design to conditions that make education possible for poor rural women. The assumption was that gender stereotypes should first be questioned seriously by women and accepted by the community. That alone would counter the reason for women's non-access to the world of education. Facilitating access through questioning was the first step. Mahila Sanghasas forums for such a questioning emerged as a strategic choice in the programme.

The present study addresses this basic assumption. Has the programme succeeded in the formation of genuine groups distinct from mere aggregates of rural women eligible as 'beneficiaries' of a scheme? How do groups form? What happens when a group starts coalescing? What kind of priorities emerge? Does this process lead to essential education? How does it alter gender equations in society? And does the second generation get a better deal in life? Must access to resources, political participation and other spin-offs precede the inevitable impact on gender violence? How do Sanghas approach this?

Other questions needing deeper reflection and debate are: is the Sangha a medium or the final empowerment answer? What Next? A Federation? Can the Sangha acquire enough flexibility and maturity to accommodate the needs of increasing and differential levels/types of individual empowerment of its members? These and many other related questions hang together around the vision of the 'Future' in Mahila Samakhya.

This report is woven broadly around five major concerns:

1. The issue of Sangha Formation. What has been the range of processes in this specific programme? How do they fit into the announced Government polity of 'collaborative development' efforts?
2. The issue of understanding empowerment—what are its multiple dimensions? Education: its broader and narrower definitions?
3. Women's access to political and economic resources through Mahila Samakhya processes.
4. Careful examination of vulnerable areas, future possibilities and cautions.

Attempts are made throughout this exercise to distill certain general propositions from a large set of specific experiences. One hopes that it would inform policy on women.

A: Mahila Sangha

"Only when we all get together can we achieve something; when ten people walk, a path is formed."

Background

Department of Education (Ministry of Human Resource Development) initiated the Mahila Samakhya Programme. Its objectives were delineated by NPE and POA; and initiated under the banner of "Education for Women's Equality".(Mahila Samakhya 1988). The narrow sense of literacy was emphasised as the possible means of allowing women to participate as equal citizens. In fact women were encouraged to "plan and monitor their own education, to reach out to a new body of knowledge "(Mahila Samakhya 1988). One hoped that an experience of equality would impart the necessary confidence required for women to reach out towards previously inaccessible knowledge. The reality of gender subordination was reiterated; an attempt made to address and alter those mechanisms through which subordination is legitimized, taken for granted and internalized as 'personal destiny' —therefore, unchngeable.

Patriarchal structures of power reward 'good' women who conform to a narrow definition of their identities: obediently and faithfully fulfilling roles while confined among family, community and social requirements. Simultaneously the 'bad' women are punished: because they dared to step out of stereotyped roles.

Understanding Powerlessness

Women have been shut out historically from the closed triangle of knowledge, power, economic power and political power. The triangle gives access only to a limited and privileged control-group. Poor rural women live in permanent fear and paralysis due to their powerlessness in the face of events daily, monthly or merely as games played by adversaries. They lack initiative to change the given variables of a situation. Individuals have failed to break through territorial monopolies. To counter powerlessness women need to collectively alter their self-image and therefore social-image. This can happen when women come together as an organic unit, discover strength of commonality and bonds of solidarity, and initiate joint action, thereby discovering and experiencing their inner power.

Mahila Samakhya viewed sanghas as the means of countering powerlessness. Sanghas were the instruments that would enable women to plan, implement and direct their own empowerment. The role of the outsider was to facilitate the coming together of women, allowing them 'time and space' to determine direction and pace of social change. 'Delivery' of skills or education was outdated, education could not be thrust upon women. Once the Sanghas were established, it would come about naturally within the collective reflection of its format.

Unlike most other development plans, the original plan document (October 1988) of Mahila Samakhya was kept deliberately amorphous and open-ended. It had to be consonant with the flexibility and philosophy of the programme, which was not centered around predetermined targets and 'timelines' but as a plan that allowed women to plan. It was hoped that experiential learning would help fill in the gaps left open by the plan.

Since the original plan document, which dubbed Mahila Samakhya as women's education for equality, the programme has come full circle: viewing the struggle for equality as a necessary condition for women's education. The demand for information, knowledge and education is seen as the natural outcome of collective reflection and resistance against gender subordination. This revised theme can be termed as 'Women's equality for Education'.

Sangha Formation

Mahila Samakhya was initially operationalised in the following 10 districts from 3 states in India.

Baroda, Rajkot and Sabarkantha from Gujarat;

Bidar, Mysore and Bijapur from Karnataka;

Varanasi, Banda, Sharanpur and Tehri from Uttar Pradesh.

Each district had its specific socio-economic-political scenario, neccessitating a contextually relevant process for initiating the project.

* The first approach consisted of taking an identified group of women created through NGO intervention attempting to weave in the agenda for empowerment of women through Mahila Samakhya.
* The second approach was to initiate group formation through specially designed processes independently of existing structures. These comprised principally of attempts at establishing emotional rapport and creating a forum for women's issues.

The strategy of initiating the programme through wellestablished local voluntary organisations, was crucial to the smooth fast and effective launch of Mahila Samakhya especially as it was an amorphous and an openended programme. This method showed quick results; proved that MS is possible, thus increasing visibility of the programme.

Problems

Despite this smooth and efficient entry problems arose along the way. The strategy of NGOs as a point of entry did not function as originally envisioned; it ran into several problems in all three states. Womens equality and struggle against gender subordination was not necessarily an NGO priority. Most of them had been working on creating women's collectives for rural development, so the specific agenda of empowerment of Mahila Samakhya was seen as 'too vague' by them.

Although some NGO leaders were also able to comprehend the power of women's collectives, they were unable to relinquish control over decision, making to these women's groups. Essentially, the NGOs were in total control. This kind of leadership was inimical to changing gender subordination pattern.

Competition, not collaboration became the NGO motto; instead of coming together to formulate a common agenda based on MS philosophy, the NGOs indulged in territorial struggles to gain control over MS women (Sahayoginis, Sakhis or Sangha Women) towards furthering their own organisation specific agendas. For example, some NGOs were unwilling to release "their" women for district level or state level Mahila Samakhya melas. Despite multiple efforts made in several districts (U.P, Karnataka, Gujarat) to federate local NGOs, the Mahila Samakhya programme failed to became a thread of commonality between these NGOs. One of the possible reasons for this could be basic distrust of government programmes; this has been internalized and Mahila Samakhya viewed as just another government programme.

The net result of this and other constraints was a gradual move away from NGOs to initiating processes, through Sahayoginis for facilitating and collection of rural women.

Direct Intervention by Mahila Samakhya

The alternative route to sangha formation has been through sahayoginis. The broad pattern emerging in all Mahila Samakhya states is, that District Implementation Units (DIU's) select and train a team of sahayoginis taking help from trainers either from nongovernment, professional groups or from existing human resources within the state. These sahayoginis are specially trained in building rapport with village women, understanding them and facilitating them to understand themselves. In some states U.P. and Gujarat) the sahayogini helps identifying sakhis who act as women leaders. While the shahyoginis role is broadly the same in all states of MS the role of sakhis and their position in the Mahila Samakhya structure shows a wide range of difference. On the whole, the shift has been from grafting the Mahila Samakhya programme on existing groups to forming fresh autonomous groups for initiating Mahila Samakhya programme.

The varied approaches to sangha formation include:

* Door to door visits so as to initiate personal contact.
* Getting involved, in and assisting with the daily chores of women.
* Participating in family and community functions like marriages, deaths, births, and festivals; and sharing in the joys and the suffering of women.
* Organizing special meets/meals and celebrating occasions such as Women's Day, Independence Day, and Environment Day.
* Organizing and taking part in women's activities at the village level where talk of sanghas is initiated by people who are respected in the community and whose opinion matters.
* Getting women together to indulge in creative activities like singing songs and bhajans, dancing, and putting up plays.
* Organizing alternative modes of information dissemination such as puppet shows and street theater, which foster a sense of fun and collective enjoyment.

PROBLEMS

Even this reformulated process of establishing sanghas as autonomous bodies, independently of NGOs, has not been without its problems. The process of establishing the credibility of MS as a government programme, and of initiating the sangha formation process has met with several hurdles at the village community and family levels, besides running into conflictual situations with outside agencies working in the region.

There have also been cases of resistance to sangha formation in different states.

There was a case in Bijapur district in Karnataka where MS functionaries were deemed thieves. The villagers were under the impression that the Sangha people observe in the morning and steal things at night. They also held the blind belief that these people take girl children and sacrifice them. The villagers thought that these people take Devadasis on the pretext of arranging their marriage but sell them instead. For all these reasons the villagers put up a strong resistance against sangha formation. (August 1996)

The Keri people who live in another part of Bijapur district were also opposed to sanghas. When some DIU functionaries visited a village, they were looked upon as thieves and locked up in a nurse's house. No amount of coaxing and convincing worked. The villagers even called the police. The police did not believe the MS functionaries either because they were unable to provide identity cards when asked to do so. MS women showed a letter from the Samakhya to the police instead but the villagers believed that the Samakhya women had found and picked it up from the street. Fortunately a teacher in the village knew one of the Sahayoginis and he was able to convince the police that MS is a government body and not a gang of thieves. The head policeman was convinced. He had been on duty for three months only and apologized for being unaware of this particular government programme. The MS women were released. After this episode, photo-identity cards with the MS seal were issued to all the Sahayoginis so as to avoid similar situations from arising again. (*Source*: Mahila Samakhya Bijapur, August 1996).

FAMILY PRESSURES

People did not view MS as delivering immediate, tangible benefits. Daughters, sisters, and daughter-in-laws were prevented from joining sanghas for all kinds of other reasons as well. In some cases there was mistrust of MS women who were considered outsiders. The intentions of these outsiders where thus questioned at both the community and the family levels. There was also the issue of house work not getting done if the women of the house joined sanghas.

Other Issues

Issues of caste and even gender membership of sanghas have come up repeatedly in all four states during implementation. Village women have raised questions regarding the inclusion of Scheduled Caste women in sanghas. There have also been instances where lower caste women have absolutely opposed the inclusion of upper caste (and therefore "Privileged") women in sanghas. In some cases villagers have objected to the notion of all female sanghas and have insisted that both men and women be included and that all meetings be held in public. Men have expressed the suspicion that allowing their wives to join sanghas would alter the male-female (husband-wife) relationship in a manner that would be detrimental to the present gender relations, and thus destabilize marriages. There was a case in Bidar district, Karnataka where men actually hid behind screens and spied on the initial sangha formation meetings held in their village. They asked all sorts of questions and ridiculed even the possibility of women coming together and achieving something concrete.

Disbelief in Linkages

In one particular example from Bidar district in Karnataka, villagers argued that if Mahila Samakhya had been a State-sponsored government programme, it would have come through the offices of the BDO or the Tehsildaar. Since this was not the case, the Mahila Samakhya programme must be from another country! Responses of this kind came in many quarters. They demonstrate the ambivalent attitude towards the government system. At one level, a common response from the people is that "nothing can happen in this system". At another levels they also feel that anything outside this system cannot have lasting qualities. It cannot be strong enough to allow people to hope!

This response in a way validates the MS design which is fully supported and 'owned' by Government but promotes an alternative style of management. (*Source:* MS Karnataka, 1996)

Revised MS-NGO Relationship

Using NGO as implementors of the Mahila Samakhya programme allowed for a quick and effective initiation but problems arose along the way that needed to be addressed and the strategy of initiation changed accordingly. With the shift to independent launching of sanghas, without assistance from NGOs, problems and resistances are being faced at the initial stages of the programme itself. But once the MS functionaries persevere through this initial phase and a sangha gets established, the later sanghas are generally more sustainable in the long run. This is not to say that MS does not view NGos as partners in the programme anymore. On the contrary,, NGOs at the national level continue to provide MS with invaluable insight and assistance. At this level NGOs as initiators and trainers help weave in sensitively, flexibility, critical questioning of the system, and assist in establishing country-wide support networks of women's organizations. Even at the state level NGOs continue to play a critical role in capacities other than implementors of the programme as is evident from the following observation.

"At present we have many individuals from various NGOs helping us at different levels from village level activities to state level trainings and workshops. They contribute on the basis of requirements of the programme as and when required. Some work with us on a part-time basis regularly, some occasionally giving specialized inputs in various components".

(Source: U.P. Mahila Samakhya report, 1996)

It is through the non-government linkage that MS has able to get its niche in the national women's networks—women's studies groups as well as the autonomous women's groups.

Sakhi, Sahayogini and Sangha

Despite a fresh nomenclature in Mahila Samakhya, its basic linkage to WDP concept is most apparent in the Sakhi, Sahayogini roles. They are a revised, redesigned version of Sathin and Pracheta of WDP, Rajasthan. The WDP concept of Sathin as a village women leader who could act as catalyst in forming village level forums for women, which in due time could emerge as strong pressure groups for raising genuine demands, fighting injustice and creating an environment for 'equal' treatment of women, was initially accepted in Mahila Samakhya with appropriate modification. The change was towards making it more broad based,with flexible planning for smoother and effective expansion of the process of group formation. The honorarium for sakhis was also a reminder of sathin-heritage, though the exact amount and number of women taken as sakhis in a particular block/taluk varied greatly. The variations were from a single paid sakhi to two paid sakhis two rotating sakhis, three rotating sakhis and sometimes (in Gujarat) even four sakhis sharing the honorarium. Sahayogini, as a Taluk level worker, was similar to a Pracheta, seen in a supportive role as also a link to the District Implementation Unit.

Paid Sakhis

- They shoulder the burden of being leaders by virtue of being paid by the programme.
- They are spokespersons (at times) for the sanghas.
- They are the yardstick of empowered women at village level, according to the sanghas.
- The paid sakhis are a convenient link in the structure for operationalising the programme in the beginning.
- Sanghas still feel very dependent on the sakhi-in fact they look up to her for guidance.

Sanghas Without Sakhis

- Sahayoginis develop relationships with sangha women directly-not through an individual.
- The whole process of collective formation takes longer to crystallise.
- The sangha interacts more directly with sahayoginis, and DIU to access information.
- Decision-making processes within some sanghas are more active when there is no dependency on a sakhi
- Where sakhis are absent, more women come forward to take up leadership roles.

This model was accompained by another, freshly evolved concept in mahila Samakhya, *i.e.* that of sangha formation as a direct step supported by sahayogini, trainers and DIUs resource persons and finding to be given to the collective rather than to individuals. This model avoids the problems created by single or few dominating leaders and works on a more democratic functioning of a group with the possibility of emergence of multiple leadership for different kinds of skills.

The above excerpt from one of the workshops conducted for this study records the pros and cons of the two broad models existing in Mahila Samakhya as perceived by the sangha women and sahayoginis:

It is noteworthy that the major trend is towards a model of sangha which dos not rely on specific leadership roles. Karnataka and Andhra Pradesh have totally opted out of the paid sakhi model. These examples illustrate the flexibility of the programme plan which has allowed for continuous modifications of the proposed models. It highlights the fact that the initial plan had been a set of open-ended guidelines which needed to be (and were) reinterpreted according to the demands of the local setting. This has allowed for a plurality of approaches that are contextually relevant and situation specific.

The regular functioning and vitality of certain sanghas has altered the heretofore accepted wisdom that even if women were provided a space to come together they would not be able to do so because they do not have any time given their heavy work schedules. Experience from sanghas in all four states shows that women make time for issues and activities that are of importance to them. Most sanghas meet at least once in two weeks, and there are cases where sangha women are meeting once or even twice a week, usually after 10 p.m. when all the other work is done.

Processes of Sangha Spread

In one of the important processes, Sanghas are spreading to new areas on their own initiative through alternative systems of communication like word of mouth, without the involvement of ''official' motivators like Sahyoginis. New sanghas are being initiated by women who have kinship network in MS villages through which they receive information about the Programme. In some sense existing sanghas are playing the role of Sahyoginis in disseminating information and encouraging the formation of new sanghas. Kinship networks are a crucial mode through which women in non-MS villages and taluks/blocks become aware of MS. The other important channel of information on MS is migrant labour. This spread through kinship networks and migrant labor is not only happening within states but across state boundaries as well. For example, there was a case in Andhra Pradesh where labour migrants to Gujarat learnt about the MS Gujarat programme and brought the information back to their village in Andhra Pradesh. They also learnt about the rotational paid Sakhi strategy being followed in Gujarat and questioned the alternative process of common sangha fund in their state.

Sangha: from an Aggregate to a Group

Collecting women together for a specific purpose, an outsiders objective—is not synonymous with the notion of a group. A group to have an identity must experience and act as a unit with an inner momentum. How does this happen? or, when can it happen? MS experience clearly demonstrates that in the final analysis, a group emerges only under certain conditions. What are the specific steps that help such an emergence of a group? The response from MS groups is as follows:

* *Training*: At the basic level, women must discover their commonality not merely at a verbal level but as a live experience. To realise that they are a unit in some respect women have to fed a unit. For

women who have internalised their role and status as a subordinate member in the society, this experience arises in a very authentic way, if and when they can distance themselves from their personal context and look at their shared situation. An in house, residential training situation helps this experience to emerge. And this,initially facilitates a core leadership for a sangha.

* *Support*: Emotional and Institutional. With an altered perception of women's identity, their world view goes through turmoil. What appeared straightforward, God decreed 'destiny' to them, alters into a human cultural situation which needs to be changed. This newly acquired state, which is an inevitable outcome of sensitive training, needs strong support at an emotional level. This is the most critical first step in empowerment which Ms strictly adhered to. It is this which constituted the major departure from bureaucratically managed interventions (Government or Non-government). Strong sanghas In MS vividly recall their experiences of internalising the supportive gestures by Sahayoginis and DIUs. Also, absence of this can be seen as a crucial factor responsible for the break-up of Sanghas.
* *Strong and Sensitive Sahayogini*: The position and role of the Sahyogini is crucial to the successful emergence of a sangha. She should be a fulltime functionary, trained in the MS philosophy and approach, and devoted to not more than the villages. The three major facets of her position are a Mahila Samakhya functionary, a group organizer, and a trainer (*Source*: Mahila Samakhya, U.P.1996). The women in this position should be able to culturally relate to the village women and serve as a rolemodel for them. She should be able to establish emotional rapport, solidarity and a relationship with sangha women which requires going beyond the traditional confines of the "government official"(sarkari) label that comes with her position. She should avoid potentially conflictual situations and monitor the pace of change closely so as to keep it within 'acceptable' limits. She must always view accountability to the village women as a priority. The Sahyogini needs constant capacity building through on-going training and educational upgradation. She should have easy access to a contextually relevant information system which will assist her in her role as a facilitator/motivator of local women.
* *Flexible, Responsive and Supportive MS organizational structure*: The Ms structure should motivate and not stifle emergence and operation of sanghas. In addition, timely and appropriate intervention is required by all functionaries to solve problems as and when they arise. The MS structure should creatively facilitate situations that bring

women together, encourage them to do this collectively and discover their commonalities as women.

* *Transparency of functioning*: Transparency in the functioning of the Ms structure, information sharing, and decentralization of decision making are crucial elements that contribute to the processes of successful sangha formation.
* *Collective activities*: Besides the role of the Sahyoginis and a supportive, facilitative MS structure, the sanghas must go through the rites of passage, the necessary steps, and indulge in collective activities before they can build a sense of solidarity. It has been observed that struggle plays a central role in the emergence of sanghas. A sangha that does not go through a history of struggle over issues will remain a loose aggregate (or break apart) and not emerge as a collective in the real sense of the word. This also implies that a sangha needs sufficient time to formulate its priorities and engage in the necessary struggle to achieve success. A sangha formed in a quick manner is generally unstable and unsustainable.
* *Caste and class*: Some interesting common trends have emerged with respect to the caste and class composition of sanghas in all the states included in this study. It has been observed that organically strong sanghas generally tend to be case-specific and most sangha members hail from lower castes. In addition to one-caste sanghas there are many instances of mixed sanghas where members come from several lower-caste groups. For example, in Bidar district (Karnataka) there are 44 mixed caste sanghas out of a total of 202 sanghas in the whole district, and in Bijapur there are 66 mixed sanghas out of a total of 210 (Refer to Table 1). Mixed sanghas have also formed across caste lines as long as there is a commonality of class affiliation. In other words, women belonging to different castes will come together in one sangha as long as they belong to the lower class. There are no instances of purely upper class sanghas or sanghas where there is an intermixing of upper and lower class women. That is to say that while caste boundaries can and are transgressed during the process of sangha formation, class boundaries are hard to collapse.

BREAK-UP OF SANGHAS

Based on the afore-mentioned preconditions for emergence of sanghas, the following configurations lead to disintegration of sanghas:

* Overpowering leadership at all levels of the MS structure has emerged

as one of the leading causes of the weakening and dissociation of sanghas. Leadership that suffocates rather than enables—be it at the sangh level, Sakhi level, Sahyogini level. DIU level or the state office level is not conducive to the strengthening of sanghas. Sangha women, Sakhis, and Sahyoginis need to work collaboratively rather than competitively with each other.

* Sanghas also disband when Sahyoginis and the DIU/state office functionaries do not respond to sangha needs in a timely and appropriate manner. Apathy on the part of programme functionaries kills the sangha spirit. This includes lack of regular visits to the villages and systematic reviews of sangha activities and progress. Another important factor contributing to the decline and sanghas is restriction on smooth information flow both vertically and horizontally through the various levels of the MS structure. This becomes especially problematic where money is involved because it flouts the very basic principle of accountability.
* Situations in which sangha activities take on a sense of ritualism leads to the stagnation of sanghas. In addition, making personal grudges into sangha issues is detrimental to the growth of sanghas because it accords precedence to the individual over the collective.
* Intervention from outside agencies — whether governmental or non-governmental which follow a philosophy that is antithetical to the basic premises and processes of Mahila Samakhya leads to a decline and eventual break up of sanghas. Conflicts with NGOs have been discussed previously in this report. It has been observed that government schemes for women's economic development (like DWCRA) that impose aggregation of women from without rather than building collectivism from within result in the disbanding of sanghas. This has been the experience of all four states particularly where governmental (or non-governmental) loan schemes are concerned.

B. Education

Mahila Samakhya understands 'education' in the broadest sense of the term. To draw-out; to lead forth to realise potential; to discover ones inner resources. Education in the MS context spells out as:

* Acquiring self-confidence and esteem.
* Becoming able to deal with authority in the home, in the community, in Government offices.

INDICATORS FOR STRONG SANGHAS

Based on discussions on the preconditions for the emergence of sanghas and the factors contributing to their break up, the following indicators for strong sanghas have emerged, the absence of which in turn gives indictors for sangha weakness also. These indicators refer principally to the processes of Sangha functioning and not to the initial investments. In other words, the first few steps taken in any Sangha are the choices made by them out of a whole set "Possible" ways of doing things. What emerges as the outcome from them can be estimated through the following indicators:

A strong sangha is one which:

* takes initiative in identifying a common cause
* responds with sensitivity to issues of exploitation/violence on women
* integrates community concerns in its agenda
* takes a decision without guidance from Sahyogini
* builds an image of "a power to reckon with" at the community level
* Pressurises the existing system for greater accountability to people.
* attracts and sustains participation from different sets of women and men over varied issues.
* holds regular meetings in which women take active interest and part, and indulage in creative, open-minded problem solving.
* encourages alternative forms of learning.
* Provides leadership opportunities to greater numbers of women.

* Knowing about ones own body, about health problems and remedies; and being able to apply this knowledge in daily life.
* Learning of vocational skills.
* Knowing about the law and being able to articulate with the legal system to redress wrongs.
* And again, reading and writing: literacy as a part of education.

Losing one's feelings of helplessness; becoming empowered to say " I can change", "I can bring about change" is the result of education. Finally, becoming a human being among other human beings, treating others likewise and expecting the right to be treated the same: this is what Mahila Samakhya education is all about.

Education, viewed in this light, permeates all of the MS programmes: Its energy, empowerment not only of immediate members, but in widening circles all those associated with the MS at the district, state and national level.

In the context of the Sangha members these related aspects of education are operative. This section examines three different but related aspects of education: Education as life skills; education as information/knowledge and education as literacy.

In case after case in every area of their expanding lives, women have taken action, fully armed with information and supported by other women. They have not always been successful nor always balanced blind justice with understanding but there has been enough success to make women confident of their action methodologies.

Mahila Shiksha Kendras (MSKs) are a truly exciting an innovation of MS. It has taken time for the idea to catch fire, but at present demand far exceeds supply. The MSK's are residential schools for girls and women. The very fact that they are residential (necessitating being away from home at least three months at a time and spending each day with ones peers), is half the battle won.

The NEF Centres and especially the MSKs are Sangha-replicas in so far as they provide that environment on non-fear and togetherness which foster "empowerment" in this case for children and young girls.

C. Access to Resources

"All this (Sangha activities) is not our work—it is our right"

For women who have internalized a subordinate status in society over centuries, the notion of 'access to resources' unfolds itself through a long circuitous journey. Money and property are obvious, tangible resources over which they have never had direct control. The possibility of accessing them, therefore rests on a basic ability to understanding the larger context and confidence to reject the structure which has justified and perpetuated it. Such an ability stems from an Inner Resource the Power Within. It is this pre-condition which allows for access to more visible and tangible forms of material resources. the previous section 'Education' explored this precondition.

In this section we deal with the tangible/material resources of basic amenities, resources for health, and economic resources.

Basic Amenities

Water is one, if not the main issue addressed by Sangha women in all MS areas. Many of the cases are about unequal availability of water on a caste and class basis.

Authorities are pursued relentlessly for seeing that justice is done, rather than taking the law into their own hands.

Negotiation is part of the MS strategy as also to make the administration responsible and accountable to the people.

Other basic amenities that Sangha women have organised themselves for (usually successfully) are street lights, roads drains, electricity, ration shops, increase in the number and frequency of bus routes, handpumps, latrines, safe school buildings. This has happened in almost all villages were there are strong Sanghas. Also by implication, these activities are missing where the Sanghas are weak or have fallen apart for some reason or the other.

Health

Trainings in health have been a major pre-occupation in all MS States: information about how the body functions; what causes illness and how to prevent disease; the importance of personal and environmental hygiene. In addition to practical value, this demystification helps women feel more in control'.

Surveys

Participatory Surveys have also been a means to getting information about local illnesses and subsequent workshops are related to findings *e.g.* health workshop : women specific ailments, malaria, T.B. etc. have tied in outside information to existing local situations.

Camps

Gujarat (as also districts of other States) has held training camps regularly for young girls, regarding the functioning of their own bodies. Worries about ailments and little known facts about one's body are discussed openly, which has been a very empowering experience for participants.

Traditional Medicine

An equally empowering experience has been the collecting of information about and putting into practice traditional medical practices. In the absence of allopathic medical facilities in view of their higher cost, traditional medical practices become doubly important. That known usages are being affirmed adds to the process of empowerment. Karnataka has published a book on local traditional medical practices and this is being translated into different languages. 30 types of medicinal herbs have been identified and some women are growing them for their own use as wall as for sale. About 10 of these herb varieties are for treating women's ailments. But the growing and selling of herbal medicine has not yet been systematised or taken off in a big way.

Allopathic Medical Facilities

Though allopathic medical facilities are hard and costly to come by, networking is done for better collaboration with the system.

Holistic Health

Not only are health and medical matters demystified and firmly related to the practical, but the relationship of health of nutrition, social taboos, women's status in the home, etc. makes for a holistic understanding of the entire area of health and its maintenance.

Economic Resources

Access to economic resources can be discerned under three categories:

1. Fair/higher wages;
2. Government schemes;
3. Savings and thrift;

1. Wages

Next to water, wages is perhaps the most common issue around which women have organised themselves. While the struggle is on, other women in the village help out with food. Hearing of successful cases from other areas acts to keep spirits from flagging.

At places there have been struggles for equal wages with men. Where successful, often men subsequently demand a rise in their wages.

2. Government Schemes —(including credit from National Banks)

Unlike the struggle for wages, where Government schemes like DWCRA, IRDP, SC/ST housing etc. have been accessed, it is only some women who are selected for schemes on a quota basis; the majority of Sangha women do not benefit. At times this has threatened to break up the sangha and at times women have refused schemes/loans because all the women could not benefit. It is a very delicate balance, between the individual and the group. There are no ready answers, especially in the situation of deprivation in which most Sangha women live.

Banks by and large are not unwilling to give loans to women, as women have a long-standing reputation of 100% and on-time returns.

To rationalise government rules to be user-friendly to poor people is part of the mandatc of MS. Not knowing about the immutable reputation of monolithic government rules, perhaps makes them less formidable and therefore easier to change.

Savings and Thrift

Savings and thrift are not the most important activities of these self-help group:

This is perhaps because the central tenet of MS philosophy and practice is the collective strength of Sangha members for fighting against the inequality and oppression which is contained in 'n' number of areas of daily life.

The general experience in MS regarding savings and thrift is that it is detrimental to sangha coherence, especially if such activities is introduced in the early days of Sangha formation.

Savings have been used in different ways: Crisis loans for emergencies, loaning out to other women at lower rates of interest than money lenders charge, for group activities, like generation of forest and grass cover, for running literacy centres, etc.

Women borrow money from the Sanghas to start income-generating projects. There is an impressive array of these from fruit and vegetable vending, mat weaving, cattle rearing, rope making and even sericulture.

Everywhere women have formed their own rules, interest rate, schedule of returning loans etc., according to local needs and convenience.

Sanghas have two types of funds

* From the personal saving of Sangha members
* From the MS programme. In Karnataka and Andhra Pradesh, individual sakhis are not paid —the amount is deemed to be the Sangha fund from which women draw to a limited extent for Sangha work. In Uttar Pradesh too, there is one paid sakhi per Sangha (in place of 2 sanctioned posts) and the additional money becomes the Sangha fund.

A big question for the Sangha is —after MS what? A federation of Sanghas? A women's bank? Money saved suggests the feasibility of some such alternatives. Some of the options being explored will be discussed in the section on the future.

By accessing resources especially tangible/material resources,women actually enlist the community on their side—water, roads, loans, are shared assets. Facing violence and resisting it is threatening— men via social mores are quick to blame women for attempting to break up the family, a prospect which touches deep insecurities among both men and women. The next section is about how, despite this, women have started dealing with the issue of violence.

D. Women and Violence

" We have made a bundle of all our fears and thrown it in the river"

Violence against women emerges as a truely universal issue in Mahila Samakhya. From the very outset, it was recognised as a non-negotiable point around which Sangha women thought it necessary to reflect and act. While it is a recorded fact that women's groups in every Taluka/block of all MS district have, at some point or other, demonstrated strongly against violence on women and on many occassions managed a 'success story' in as much as the culprints have been punished, it is equally true that no intrinsic barrier for committing violence against women has been created. The Intricacies and delays of the legal system are proverbial. And for poor rural women, the route to legal justice is even more exhausting and impoverishing. Cases of rape, murder and battering continue to occur despite all resistance. This appears to be the hardest ground to break. However, what this study indicates is a steady, positive shift at two levels, which can be taken as serious indicators for maturity of understanding and responses of Sangha women to issues of violence.

Moving towards a deeper understanding of what 'hurts' and humiliates a women, Sangha women have also responded to 'violence' at the basic human level *i.e.* humiliation and injury to the personhood of all subordinated groups. This has included reacting to caste discrimination as violating the dignity of persons.

Naming

A significant-change that can be clearly discerned across the Mahila Samakhya canvas is with respect to what is named as violence. The aggregated list emerging from meetings held with sangha women and sahayoginis is as follows:

* Wife beating
* Rape
* Mental Torture: forcing women to obey and accept in an unquestioning manner.
* Humiliating treatment of infertile women and calling them "barren"
* The devadasi tradition

* In-human treatment of widows : isolation and segregation
* Labelling defiant, non-conforming women as "Dayan"
* Eve-teasing
* Forced abortions and female infanticide
* Humiliation of wives when they don't please their husbands.

Recalling earlier experience in Mahila Samakhya trainings and meetings, the Sahyoginis now find a major shift in the manner in which women perceive violence' During the initial Mahila Samakhya training situations women almost always shared personal agonising experiences by describing them "dukh" or suffering. The group interpretation of personal suffering was generally" what women have to go through " or "how women are treated in society" Physical vulnerability and emotional vulnerability were intimately connected aspects of what was termed "the tragedy of womanhood. "This suffering, pain, and sense of vulnerability was invariably seen as the common bond between women that cuts across caste, class, rural and urban divides. Now the change in the self-image of women, leading to a sensitive interpretation of what constitutes basic dignity of a person, these and similar experiences are renamed as violence' on women.

The case on family violence on is apparently a "failure" case in as much as the last minute decision of the girl to "back out" left the sangha women very disappointed. However, the case clearly demonstrates the following:

* The desire on the part of rural women to reject the old habit of "accepting" what is done within a family, particularly by the head of the family.
* The public image of the sangha as a forum where girls and oppressed women can find support and redress.
* The enormity of the battle which continues to be fought.

Establishing New Forums for Justice

"The process of justice in formal systems is long and troublesome for women. It needs much time and money, so we have created this system which is our own arrangement.

"Who will believe in our verdict of justice?"

"We are giving the judgement and the people will surely believe in it."

"People say that women have framed law for themselves!"

"It is always said that women do not have any sense which is why lawyers treat us badly. They stretch out our cases for any length of time"

In Gujarat, the main aim of Nari Adalats was to provide justice to women. It was a dream come true for women who were suffering from injustice within the society but not able to respond to it due to the self image of "Bechaari Aurat". Now it is not limited to Padara and Waghodia Taluka only but is being extended to other places.

Mahila Samakhya Baroda has organised a legal course for women to strengthen the 'Nari Adalat' concept. This had two broad objectives:

* Facilitating women to develop their power for analysis and think seriously before coming to a judgement.
* Acquire an understanding of the relationship between feminist ideology and alternate legal system (Nari Adalat).

This course extended over a period of two and half months in which 25 women participated. They interacted with experts confidently. Since all the women were "Dalits", so the major thrust of the course was to link women's issues with Dalit movement.

After completing this training, these women disseminated informaison about 'Nari Adalat' to as many women as possible. Now Nari Adalat as dealing with not just issues of violence but also trying to make Government programmes more accessible to women. It is emerging as an alternative forum of justice where women can talk fearlessly about themselves and seek justice as a 'right'.

Main Features

* Women sitting in a open place and talking about themselves, it itself a matter of significance and a cause for astonishment within the village community. Now, women have acquired this public space for themselves. Because the venue of Nari Adalat is the office of the block panchayat, it has caused a lot of impact on Government workers too.
* In the past, this group has dealt with a wider range of issues, *viz.* Stree-Dhan (an asset which women acquire at the time of marriage), divorce, wife beating, right of child, harassment by police, problems (liquor related and scholarship for PDS), issues pertaining to property, sale of daughters and livelihood for women. The number of cases is anywhere between 5 to 30 on each issue.

DPC Report, Baroda, August, 1996

Similar forums are coming up in almost all districts of MS. They are not exactly well defined but functionally operative whenever a noteworthy case comes. They very fact that such forums function publicly with an ever growing number of cases points to:

* Families making public that which was strictly kept under covers be-

fore. Which means the woman is no longer considered solely to be blamed for rape, harassment, etc. That there is perpetrator of violence is recognised— who can then be apportioned blame for the misdeed.

* The community by way of the gram panchayat, elders, etc. by the very act of taking part in judging the misdeed, are acknowledging that the many ways of harassing women are indeed wrong, calling for punishment of the perpetrator of this violence. This is a stronger indicator of change than settling a case in court, for law is often ahead of existing social mores and does not reflect real social change as much as actual community action does.

The overall pattern emerging through hundreds of small stories from various Sanghas in MS is that now Sangha women do not take insults quietly. It is apparent that:

* They have a judgement of their own which rests on a sensitive understanding of justice.
* They have a self image to maintain which is one of resisting all forms of injustice, in which personal violence is one sub-set.

E. Empowerment: Multiple Dimensions

In previous sections we have looked at how 'empowerment' has been operative in the daily lives of women. What is the texture of this empowerment and how does it operate in the different areas of womens' lives?

How do women handle power? Differently from men? If so in what ways? Do women, singly or in small numbers in a man's world, follow given patterns of power-play? And does a critical mass of women behave differently? What has empowerment' meant to Sangha women? How does the age-old internalized self-image of the sacrificing, nurturing, do not know anything woman articulate with the newly acquired ability to "make things happen"?

There are not new questions for which there is one clean, easy answer. MS experience has been that the sangha women have acted in myriad ways— all along the scale, from continuing to stay oppressed to taking on the attitudes of power they see around them. There however, appears to be a pattern for the majority bunched in the middle. By and large, the women who have felt some power within, have acted in practical ways— give a little, take a little, two steps forward, one step back. They have negotiated rather than confronted; maintained relationships rather than acted in terms of ultimate and abstract 'truths'. And this is visible in their encounter with the community and now, increasingly, in panchayats.Their immediate political arena, the home, is possibly the last one for demonstrated change.

It is possible to discern a pattern in the 'Empowerment' of sangha women, which cuts across the specificity of their environment. The experience from all four states broadly demonstrates three stages in the process of shedding off 'powerlessness'. These are demarcated more at a conceptual level rather than seen as a chronological ladder. More often than not, the three layers are intertwined through continuous struggle for change in women's position at home, in the community and in society as a whole.

The first stage of empowerment is visible when they can distance themselves from a given situation and recognise the structures of power, decode the symbols and look into them straight without fear. This may not alter the situation at all, but it alters the chemistry of the encounter. Women learn to analyse the situation and in the process, the 'fear' gradually turns into an 'understanding'. This can only happen when they discover that their personal suffering is a 'kind' of systematic phenomenon, a chronic situation, which need not cripple their morale.

The next stage in this process is when women can experience the change of not only being able to 'name' the injustice but also by resisting it: what is not 'right' need not be accepted. Hence, the courage to protest is experienced. And this is possible in the 'togetherness' of the collective.

At the third stage a more mature state of realisation emerges: *viz.* that we need to know more, learn more, find out more—before making simplistic judgements. Basic confidence in oneself generated by predictable support from a group nurtures the learning spirit and humility in one's own stand.

Moving away from this broad pattern, and as a clean contrast, one can discern multiple cases of these very Sangha women who take family violence as a quiet suffering. What they do with ease in a public forum becomes the most difficult battle at home individually. The important message here is that empowerment processes exhibit their impact, to begin with in the public situation where the collective can visibly be together. Whether it is wage or caste or other struggles. Women have tempered justice with their conditioned reflexes of nurturance. Also, in most community level action, perhaps because women become a critical mass, they are more easily able to act in deviant (from the traditional) ways, unlike at home, where they battle the very roots of power, ultimately, alone.

THE PANCHAYAT

A freshly discovered arena for struggle to shake off domination is the panchayat. This being a very recently entered area, patterns are barely discernible. A women by herself is often squashed or, if sufficiently ambitious, follows (or is urged to follow by those at home supporting her), power patterns that are all around her. However, where there are more than two or three women in the panchayat and receiving support from women outside (in this case the Sangha), there is an attempt to use this newly acquired power for doing good to more than just oneself. This, a more readily recognizable pattern in the longer existing community level action, is only a glimmering in the context of action in panchayats.

IN THE FAMILY

Changes in the power structure within the family are the most difficult to achieve, to record or even to observe. In public spheres of the community and panchayat, visible actions reflect changing empowerment. In the private world of the family, this is much more difficult.

"We confront men outside but it is a no-win situation with our own family members at times".

Women who are towers of strength in public, appear willing to put up with beating and being cowed down at home. Women choose their spaces an it is easier to effect changes outside the home. However, many report to more respect being shown to them in their homes and also of their insistence that their daughters go to school. The change in image outside the home does have its repercussions in the home, but the exact texture of this impact has not been captured.

Apart from the Sanghas, there are in many of the MS Districts, forums for hearing cases of violence against women, including violence in the home. Here again, we do not know what effect this discussion of family violence in public, is having on the power relationship in the home. Widows in many of the MS districts now wear bindi, jewellery, bright clothes —what effect this has had on their status in the home— we do not know.

How does empowerment in the home happen? This needs to be further researched: so that we begin to understand how women are negotiating for more 'space' in decision-making at home and how actions in the family and outside interact in enhancing a women's status. Such that we have a more complete picture of how empowerment works in different arenas.

F. Areas of Vulnerability

Future

There is no available experience of large scale programmes for women's empowerment and therefore no precedence to fall back on for weighing alternatives about 'what next? or will 'X' produce the required 'Y'?

Is empowerment measurable? Is there such a thing as being 'fully empowered? And is there a point in the process of empowerment when it becomes self-perpetuating? Does the means, to empowerment differ according to class, status, circumstance? *e.g.* The sahayogini is less dependent on collective action for enhancing her self-image than the sangha women is. And at the District, State and National Level, MS associates have recourse to choice of several forums (groups) to meet the needs of self-growth.

The above and related questions are of immediate concern in the context of plotting activitites for the future. Given that MS is a programme for social change and that empowerment is not a package deal, with a neat beginning and end (like digging a well or building a house), future action is not as clearly visualisable as is habitually expected of planned developmental programmes.

II. MAHILA SAMAKHYA : A COLLECTIVE ACTION ON COMMON PROBLEMS

The empowerment of poor rural women through knowledge, organisation building and collective action being the main objective of Mahila Samakhya (MS), the success of the programme can be gauged from the extent to which the sanghas operating the villages have been able to articulate their demands and to take independent actions. MS has often been faced with the issue of how to capture conceptually the process of development a sangha goes through till it can be called a 'successful' unit. Discussions on this have led to the understanding that though empowerment is an ongoing process and has to be defined by the sanghas themselves, the programme could be deemed to have played its professed role when the sanghas become vibrant and self-reliant in dealing with issues they consider important. In tracing the process till a sangha reaches this stage, the Andhra Pradesh team identified four stages of Sanghas formation : the rapport building stage when the Sahayogini meets the women and has casual talks with individuals and groups of women, the formative stage when a structure takes shape with more regular meetings, regular members and perhaps attaching a name to the group; then the consolidation stage when more controversial issues start coming up, days of meetings are fixed, and agendas set and attempts are made to change circumstances through collective action. Leaders emerge, too at this stage. The last stage is that of independent sanghas which can mobilize their own support and actively influence the social, cultural, political and economic environment around them. But the path of Sangha growth is not linear or vertical, but a series of 'crests and troughs', where they spurt forward in certain directions and slip backwards at other times, only to team up and regroup for regroup sustained action.

The Focal Point. The Mahila Sangha

* Strong Sanghas
* Groups with social space
* Where women gain strength from the collective
* Where women have developed a perspective on their status concerning them
* Have a common goal and understanding
* A recognized status at social, and legal forums
* They take initiatives
* Have created alternatives
* Have created alternative$
* They have an active social identity

Weak Sanghas

* Do not fully understand MS values and philosophy
* Have Sakhis who are over active or dominate
* Self-interest of Sakhi
* Ineffective Sahayogini who does not pick up the right issue
* Insufficient inflow of information
* Binding factor is missing, so is leadership, merely issue based
* Sahayogini preoccupied with DIU work
* Lack of acceptance by village
* Apathy and self-contentment
* Too many leaders

UP MS

Other than this, the team also collectively defined a strong sangha as one which comprises of a group of 20 women or more that meets at regular intervals, has a name and leaders, seeks information and is willing to participate in cluster meetings, takes initiative in decision making, addressing issues that concern it, raises funds for travel expenses for meetings or for visiting officials, and maintains it own accounts. The group concluded that one cannot assume that sanghas which were willing participants in the beginning will remain so or that not much achievement could be expected of groups that were initially hostile. The opposite may well be the case.

On the basis of its observations over the years, the Andhra Pradesh MS intends to extend the amount earmarked for Sakhi honorarium to 'strong' sanghas in order to ensure that sanghas are adequately prepared for this, it does not break their unity and that the amount is invested in the right direction. The funds are to be used for collective purposes such as literacy, child care, kitchen gardens, sangha huts, to meet travel expenses for group purposes or for emergencies, and not for child marriages, festivals and religious purposes. Other conditions have been added, such as a minimum of ten women should be functionally literate.

Uttar Pradesh, where the sangha process was not too visible three years ago, today boasts of 264 strong sanghas. There are 251 sanghas which are strong in some respects and weak in others, and 330 (130 in old areas and 200 in the new areas) which are categorized as 'weak'. This opinion was expressed in a workshop in mid-1995 which was organised to analyse the sangha process in the State, before any further concrete input is made. Recognizing that until two years ago the focus was on indirect strengthening of the sanghas through the Sakhis, a conscious decision was made to focus on the sanghas directly. As a first step there has been clarification of perspectives and concepts at all levels. Sangha women have been encouraged to attend Sakhi meetings. This issue of strength or weakness among sanghas in Gujarat came up in 1996 when the question of sanghas autonomy in terms of continuation of work and financial self-reliance was raised. Strong sanghas gather regularly and take collective decisions, share information and experiences, learn from each other, are identified as a collective by outsiders and are sensitive to and prepared to address which gradually brings in financial independence: the amount is split between Sakhi honorarium and collective fund; or the sanghas decides on retaining the Sakhi rotation model.

Karnataka has similarly categorized 713 of its 914 sanghas under' active sanghas'.

These exercises have been carried forward to the sangha level across the country and have thrown up questions and initiated decisions on the part of the Sanghas. Accordingly, in some areas sanghas have decided to take things in their hands beginning with finances. For instance, some sanghas in Gujarat decided to fully or partially bear their travel costs for celebrations, and women from sanghas in Andhra Pradesh attend meetings on their own expenses.

Many of the successful or strong sanghas initiated by MS are from 'old' areas where the MS process began early. But their strength or weakness foes not entirely correspond to the number of years invested in them. Some of the 'old areas' sanghas have fallen into 'troughs' and some new sanghas have risen to relative self-reliance under their own momentum. The strengthening of the sanghas has become an issue of major focus in MS over the past three years, especially after the National Evaluation, 1993 brought this up as a major area requiring focus.

Issues Addressed in MS

Over the past two years, the sanghas, with the assistance of the support units and functionaries have been able to take up several issues that relate to dignified survival in the villages, especially of women and girls. Since life is perceived as one single process in the world view of the villagers and each action taken by the sanghas impinges on this in different ways, it is difficult to articulate the totality of achievements of MS in concrete terms. We nevertheless try here to bring out our more tangible achievements in articulating the needs and demands of women, in the form of specific issues that were addressed over the past two years. The fact that the sangha women are able to address these issues is indicative of the latent and more qualitative achievements of the programme in empowering women.

Literacy and Learning

MS has recognized right from the beginning that literacy, once a demand for it has been created, becomes an important element in the empowerment of women. This belief has been further reinforced during the last three years, which have witnessed a much greater focus on literacy within MS. This is mainly because of the tremendous demand for literacy that has emerged over the years.

The literacy programme of MS is part and parcel of the sangha building and strengthening process mainly because it is seen as a vehicle of empowerment and not an end in itself. "Creating an environment for learning has been taken seriously in MS. As this environment emerges and the sangha becomes stronger on action components, a prominent demand is literacy, either as an action in itself or as part of the struggle for better access to existing government programmes. Since the sangha process is also one of gender sensitization, the demand for girls education gets crystallized. Very often this demand comes up when the women feel inadequate in dealing with larger forces such as the market, Panchayats, Block offices and courts because of their illiteracy. Here adult literacy gets articulated. These processes also bring out issues such as workload and availability of women and girls for literacy, and in the process are evolved a series of activities around creating the conditions and the environment for literacy.

In the MS states, various patterns have emerged in children's and adult women's literacy.

Adult Literacy

There are several local structures and processes linked to adult literacy (particularly of women). The most visible one is the Adult Education Programme or Non-Formal Education, which comprises of centres with regular literacy sessions in village. These may be linked or independent of the total Literacy Campaign. As MS emphasizes the full participation of sanghas women in the planning and management of these centres, women are involved in the production of literacy materials, deciding upon the time and place as well as managing and in some places, even arranging the finances. This further encourages interest in literacy, by the logic of learning by doing. Then, MS is fully involved in literacy camps which creates a wider constituency in the literacy mission.

Reports from the States show the various paths that the MS adult literacy programme takes. Gujarat has over the years observed that there are a number of motivating factors in literacy, other than the sheer desire to read and write. For instance, the inability to write applications, the need to maintain child care centre records or write the minutes of the sangha meetings, the urge to read newsletters, the necessity to get information through interactions with government offices, or just the urge to reach out to the outside world through the written word compel sangha women to venture into literacy. The team encourages this by various means. MS has now a regular link with the government Total Literacy Campaign (TLC), to a lesser extent in Sabarkantha and more in Baroda and Rajkot. In Rajkot sangha women decided to prepare lists of illiterate persons in the village and for this there were cultural programmes that generated a lot of enthusiasm. Women also prepared literacy manuals and other materials. In 1994-95, the campaign ended in Rajkot and Baroda and the Post Literacy Campaign was launched. In many areas the demand for literacy has led to pressure building for the efficient running of government literacy structures, thus addressing at the same time the vital issue of accountability of the government to its people. The celebration of the Literacy Day, as in the case of the Women's Day has now become an annual affair. These in turn increase the demand for literacy Today the volunteers drawn even from among school-going children, hold regular classes in the vilalges, but the demand for volunteers far exceeds their supply. The demand for literacy is such that when a teacher is difficult to find, women go to other villages to learn. The women are encouraged to write to the DIUs and the State Offices. Apni vat, a women's newsletter launched by the State office is sent directly to those women who are able to write their names and addresses. The adult literacy programme has thus taken its own momentum in Gujarat.

In Uttar Pradesh, literacy for adult women received a thrust mainly through literacy camps, which in turn created even greater demand for women's literacy. These have region specific curricula. For instance in Saharanpur, where physical violence is a growing concern, literacy was organised around this, while the focus in Varanasi was panchayat raj and the wage issue. In Tehri, eco-regereration found focus and in Banda, the problem of water and wages. A total of 16 literacy camps were organised in 1995-96 itself. U.P. is a case where the need for literacy was first articulated through issue based action where the women felt inadequate without the knowledge of reading and writing. From here there was a progression to regular literacy centres where gender sensitive literacy was imparted through specially trained instructors. Available gender sensitive primers were used, and new ones developed through the participation of the newly literacte women. The mahila dakiya is now popular and women have even gone in for training in block printing and drawing to make their efforts self -reliant and successful. Today there are a total of 133 literacy centres in four Districts. Some sanghas have their own simple library with reading materials, audio records, discussion groups, ecology-club etc. In Banda, adult women, alongwith young girls, receive literacy also through the newly opened Mahila Shikshan Kendra (MSK) which is a residential programme lasting six months (in two sessions of three months each). The curriculum is learner centered, holistic (rather than subject-area oriented), encourages learning and develops a critical understanding. Innovative methods of learning are women into the method. So far, 80 women and girls have passed through the MSK.

In areas of Karnataka where literacy is popular and accepted by women, the sanghas have books and materials for the non-formal education (NFE) and adult education (AE) centres, which are the main village level education centres. Up to mid-1995, there were 119 NFE and 120 AE centres. The sanghas have awarded the title of 'Ghana Gelathiyaru' (guiding light) to women who have learnt to read and write and are now teaching others. This has added to the status of 'literate'. In general literacy is in great demand, but in some areas such as parts of Mysore where migration is high, progress in literacy is slower despite the demand. Temporary migrants are unable to catch up with learning. An exercise with the village women of this area showed that illiteracy is perpetuated through parental illiteracy , poverty and the consequent pre-occupation with livelihood, the lack of opportunities, bad learning environment in schools and the great distances to schools.

In Andhra Pradesh the demand for literacy became more persistent since 1993-94. It is now a regular issue at sangha meetings. In many cases, the savings scheme of the sangha has led to the demand for literacy. There have also been attempts to mobilise the literate to teach the illiterate and the sanghas have been able to press upon this. Attempts are also on to train village women to teach the illiterate. The women have demanded states and materials from the TLC. The teaching methods are innovative, as in other States. Literacy kits created by the TLC and the Adult Education scheme too are used, with supplements. The DIU teams have held regular workshop as well as training programmes on literacy and its methodology. In 1996, a total of 373 women from 27 villages in Mehbubnagar and 373 from 29 villages in Medak were at various stages of learning to read and write. But analysis of the demand and extension of literacy showed that it remains of problematic issue.

In Medak where the women find it easier to learn to read, the focus has been on strengthening this component, at the same time ensuring that 2 or 3 women from each sangha can write as well. In Mehbubangar, MS is actively participating in the TLC.

Literacy Among Children and Adolescent Girls

In view of the feeling that literacy among children and adolescent girls has not picked up the momentum it deserves; this was a special focus area for 1994-95 and 1995-96 in U.P. As a result girl child education has been stepped up and dropout reenrollment has increased. The 'udankhatolas' in Varanasi, the hindolas' in Saharanpur and buranshs' in Tehri have gain tremendous popularity over the past three years. In some cases children have attached names even to various grades within the literacy centres. The anudeshikas or teachers in these centres, who are selected by the sanghas, are given special training. In places, Sakhis too have become anudeshikas. Over the past three years in some areas students have been able to organise and run their centres. Saharanpur saw an increase in bal sabhas (children's meeting) and bal meals (camps with games, nature walk etc.) have increased the potential of children to learn from each other and from their surroundings, as well as display their talents. In Tehri, during 1995-96, 'hilansh' was launched to increase environmental knowledge. The method of imparting literacy skills in all areas is innovative with painting, singing, dancing, poetry and games are being used. Street plays come in handy, too.

Sanghas negotiate for resources with MS, which extends such support. The responsibility of discussing the logistics of the support lies with the Sahayogini, who also analyses the needs articulated by the women, the dynamics, and strengths of the group as wells as existing problems and their solution.

The last year, 1995-96, saw a greater demand for units set up exclusively for the education of the adolescent girl child, *i.e.* Kishori sanghas in U.P. as girl child education requires an approach that is different from the education of children of a smaller age group. Health education, law, environmental education and vocational training were decided as the priority areas.

In 1996, a workshop was organised in the State where the scope for the literacy centres to become formalized, the upgradation of anudeshika training, better materials and methods, scope of the bal kendras, areas requiring DIU support as well as the conceptual issues in literacy, were discussed. On the issues of pedagogy, the workshop concluded that an 'eclectic' method that combines the alphabet, word and language methods is the best course of action for literacy. It was decided that in the coming year, anudeshika and children's training camps will be increased, there will more literacy campaigns for girl children, the curriculum for girl child education will be improved, a magazine will be launched at the State level for articulating of opinion on literacy and that there will be two major workshops on the issue. Decentralization of literacy efforts will be given further impetus and there will be more linkages and exchanges with other literacy programme. A general decision was taken to broaden the literacy programme. In 1996, one MSK was introduced in the State.

In Andhra Pradesh the literacy programme for girl children so far has not been different from those of adult women. The general experience has been that while literacy among adult women is less problematic, girl child literacy is more difficult. Initially, the camp method was the main venue of addressing this. In 1994, there were specific focus camps with a view to increase enrollment of girls in formal schools. With this also rose the demand for anganwadis and girls hostels from the government and in some areas in Medak, the sanghas have managed to get the anganwadis shifted to the SC localities. As part of the Mehbubnagar District administration's drive for Universalisation of Elementary Education, surveys were conducted on the situation of children' education which led to the formation of Village Education Committees. Sangha women began taking interest in these Committees, leading to an increase in enrollment of children in schools. The women also expressed the desire to have educational activity for older girls. NFEs were envisaged. In 1995-96, it was decided that an approach different from the camp method has to be adopted and hence the Bal Mitra Kendras (BMKs) were introduced, although larger issues in this such as child labour have not yet been addressed. The BMKs are non-formal centres that encourage enrollment of girls in the 9-plus age group. These are Sanghainitiated and the sanghas select the teachers, too. Every month there is a review meeting-cum-training programme for the teachers. The issue of financial support for the kendra teachers was solved with the decision that the sangha, the parents of the child and the APMSS will contribute Re.1, Rs.3 and Rs. 6 respectively towards each child. Of the Rs. 6 from the MSS side, Rs. 3 will be earmarked for ensuring minimum literacy for the child. In June 1995, 18 BMKs in Mehbubnagar and 1 in Medak (where the response was lukewarm) were started.

An MSK was also started in each of the two Districts in 1995-96, in which the young girls (12 to 18 years) learn about social, political, legal and current affairs in addition to receiving literacy and vocational training.

As part of the long-term plan, APMSS has decided to press for enrollment and retention of children in the 5-7 age category in class 1, to create a model village with 100 per cent access to literacy, to expand the Bal Mitra Kendras for girls, to create MSKs at cluster levels and to generally strengthen literacy efforts. The sangha-school linkage will also be strengthened through parent teacher committees.

In Gujarat, there have been spontaneous girl child literacy efforts. An indicator of the interest of the sanghas in girl child education is that in 1995-96, six sanghas in Khedbrahma Taluk in Sabarkantha managed to persuade three girls associated with MS to hold regular classes in their villages for girl children. Young girls in the State have become more enthusiastic towards literacy and many sanghas in the District plan to hold literacy camps to help their illiterate sisters. Literacy camps in general were stepped up during the past three years and camps for young girls were increased. A MSk was started in Sabarkantha District during the past year.

In Karnataka, the Adult Education Centres and the NFEs encourage the sangha women to send their girl children to school. There is a conscious effort to establish NFE centres to cater to girl children and in several cases, as in Raichur, the sanghas have been successful in locating literate women and persuading them to teach in the centres. By mid-

1996, Bijapur recorded 81 centres with 2250 children, Gulbarga 41 with 534 children, Mysore 21 with 600 children and Raichur 46 with 400 children. There has therefore been considerable expansion over the past three years. Besides, the close link between the sangha and the centres and the ability of the sanghas to run these centres smoothly are becoming apparent. The sanghas in Bijapur are reported to be taking full charge of supervision, motivation of parents, selection of teachers, resolving problematic issues, mediating between MS and the centre and encouraging teachers to participate in sangha activities. Indications are that the sanghas understand their financial responsibilities towards the centres, too. The direct impact on the students is encouraging: there is more interest in further education and the children identify with socially progressive norms between MS and the centre and encouraging teachers to participate in Sangha activities. Indications are that the sanghas understand their financial responsibilities towards the centres, too. The direct impact on the students is encouraging: there is more interest in further education and the children identify with socially progressive norms.

The MSK too is a very popular mode of education of girl children in the State. There are three MSKs to date, which contribute to pre-formal education for young girls and towards the education of adolescent girls.

Child Care Centres

Child care centres have proven to be a crucial factor in promoting literacy both among children and adult women. Most often as it appeared in Gujarat, basic care of children is itself a problem for women who work the whole day. In such a situation, their education is a possibility that they have not even considered. Hence child care emerged as a problem right from the beginning even when the issue of attending sangha meetings was raised. The support units took this up in earnest, by analysing the problem with the women and making a list of women with these problems. A study in Baroda in collaboration with the Department of Human Development and Family Studies and the Women and Household Development Research and Information Centre analyzed the life situation in the villages and the kind of child care support that was desirable under the circumstances. It also evolved participatory, process-oriented training strategies for the functionaries as well as the village women and documented the same. Child care centres emerged as a major requirement, as nine out of ten villages had no child care facilities. The women were too preoccupied with earning a living. When the centres were subsequently introduced, balsakhia ('friends of children)' were selected by the sanghas. They received special training on child care, pre-school education, child development, health and nutrition, educational opportunities, gender sensitivity, strategies for obtaining support from other MS components, etc.

Over the years, Gujarat MS has evolved an organised system of initiating child care centres. The process begins at the sangha level with awareness generation on women's situation, their work and roles, after which collective decisions are taken on the nature and type of child care, choice of time and place, selection of a balsakhi, management of the centre, follow-up, and its longtime goals. Committees are formed comprising of senior members, anganwadi workers, the Sahayogini and the Sakhi. internal resources are mobilized as much as possible, *e.g.* space for the centre, provision of snacks for the children and payment for the worker. Mahila kutirs are used as much as possible and in this process of demanding for a space for the centre, women also learn to exert their right over public places. The pattern is different in different villages : where sanghas are strong food may be paid for by the sangha or by each parent or women may purchase the materials and maintain accounts themselves. In some villages, mothers drop and pick up their children. As the sangha gets stronger, it may be able to bring the ICDS programme into the village. In parts of Sabarkantha, women are now able to keep records of their child care centres as well as maintain regular accounts of the sanghas.

In the selection of balsakhis the sangha ensures that she is local, willing and available, has sufficient free time, has the consent of her family, is acceptable and good with children. Sometimes, Sakhis volunteer to become balsakhis.

At present Gujarat has a total of 58 child care centres which cater to the age group of 0-6 years. In Baroda, the sanghas evaluate each other's centres and taken action for improvement of the centres.

Analyses have shown that as a result of these efforts, the tensions of women and their families in general have reduced, that the women are able to meet each other and share problems and that even family income has increased because women no longer have to bear the burden of child care through the day. On the part of the children they receive social and moral education, are able to perform better in formal schools and are in general more disciplined. They learn to keep their village clean, plant trees and keep personal hygiene. Girl children particularly are released of work burden.

In U.P., an analysis of the combined effort in child care between UPMS and Nirantar in Banda showed that the effort has been rather different from the other efforts in the State in that the programme is need based, flexible, managed by the village women, caters to a wide age group using different models and that the child care worker is selected from among the same community, by the sangha.

Karnataka is another State which has porgressed substantially where child care centres are concerned. In Bijapur, where more attention has been paid to villages without anganwadi centres, there are today 12 creches. In some villages where there is shortage of funds, the women have begun to provide food for the children. The success of the creches corresponds to the extent of interest taken by the sangha. Gulbarga had 22 centres by mid-96, an increase of 9 during the year. Raichur has 11 creches. The children in these child care centres in the State receive medical help in addition to food and personal care. The centres have also contributed significantly to girl child education by relieving young girls of the burden of looking after their younger siblings.

MSKs and child care are also emerging issues in the new MS States, Bihar has 7 MSKs as well as informal jagjagi centres for children, adolescent girls and women. These are complementary to the DPEP programme. The focus in these is on gender sensitive education, especially for girls. There are awareness campaigns and enrollment drives. Training of Shiksha karmis is now on in full swing. Leadership is emerging. The issue of social violence is being addressed as well.

In conclusion, one of the main contributions of MS in literacy has been encouraging literacy among girls and adult women and in creating an environment for gender sensitive education as such. Acknowledging the need to strengthen this further, there is greater emphasis today on internalizing issues of pedagogy and establishing more effective linkages in literacy.

Women in the Political Process

the 73rd Amendment to the Constitution that ushers in decentralization of the political process through the Panchayat Raj is eliciting response all over rural India. MS has gone full fledged into this with the view that translating the MS non-negotiables into action needs linkages with the political process as much as with other processes. Political process is an important point of address in order to tackle the issue of women's subordination. But it is recognized that the results will be diluted if women were to merely join the existing structure without critical understanding of the political process.

A study by Srilata Batliwala in 1995 on the participation of sangha women in the panchayat Raj elections in Karnataka has observed that so far women have either been co-opted or pushed out of the process because of the lack of a critical mass of women in politics, the lack of strategic linkages between the women's movement and the women in politics and because of women not having experienced power in the public domain. So far power has been held over and not on behalf of larger social good. Karnataka has provision for 25 per cent reservation for women in the sill (district) parotid and manual (village) panchayat. As the women became more active in the sangha porcess, they realized that they were mere fronts in the political arena, and not active women representing women's issues. This led to a demand for training on the political process. Workshops were organised for men and women at the manual level. Soon it was realized that training has to be introduced before elections.

The discussions also threw up several logistical issues such as what would be the relationship of the active parotid members with their sanghas and what will be their accountability to the sanghas. The women in many sanghas came to the consensus that the candidates could stand for election in their own name but have to formally relinquish their sangha roles, so that the sangha does not become another political party. They can make use of the sangha learning process. The successful candidates will not be able to use corrupt means to influence the voting pattern but can use the integrity and respect that the sanghas hold. They will also have the responsibilities of fighting for women's rights and development and giving feedback on panchayat decisions to the sanghas. Sanghas have also evolved systems of pressuring ineffective panchayat members to step down, beginning with a warning, going on to termination from the sangha and as a last resort, organised protests and challenges. The sanghas have therefore emerged as watchdogs as well as supporters and guides of the Panchayats.

The State reports that against 199 women who contested the panchayat elections, 135 have won in the five Districts.

Similar processes have preceded panchayat election in other States In U.P. 27 women in Banda and 93 in Varanasi were elected at various levels in 1995. Gujarat has gone into this issue actively in the past years and cases of women's participation in elections are coming up. Sahayoginis have filed nominations too and in one case, a Sahaogini is reported to have preferred to opt out of politics rather than relinquish her position in MS. In Andhra, 54 women were elected as Ward Members (out of 63 who had contested) and 6 as Sarpanch. Attention was focused on the issue of political participation of women during 1995-96 through workshops and discussions. Politically active women and potential political leaders also receive special attention in literacy through camps because very often illiterate women and men are promoted as 'fronts' by the powerful.

Activating the sanghas on the political participation issue is now a regular process in MS. In UP the traditional method of story-telling called the Phad has been very successful in this, as much as mock elections.

Women Fight for Dignity and Justice

Physical Violence and the Dignity of Women

As awareness of gender issues increases, sangha women spontaneously take action against women's oppression and exploitation. Physical violence is a basic issue in this context, to which women are exposed frequently. The MS empowerment process has made it evident that what has been assumed to be a personal problem of women' is in actuality a social issue. In all the States there have been combined actions against physical violence that targets women. In Saharanpur in U.P. where the crime against women is high, this has become a virtual movement where women gather together to protest and demand legal action. In most places community pressure exerted by women is sufficient and the sangha women actively take up action and negotiation with offenders, as well as bring the problem to public fora. Another issue that has come up prominently in the State is alcoholism among men and its impact on women. In parts of Tehri in U.P., women have managed to take up a two pronged action against this by preventing men from drinking and at the same time breaking the bhattis or the local liquor breweries. The women also launched a handout called 'sharab ka dancha'(structure of alcoholism) showing the larger issues around alcoholism including state incomes through this and vested interests in its maintenance. Similar fights against alcoholism are also reported from Karnataka during the past years. The women now approach courts, police and government offices and when noting works, they take it upon themselves to demolish the local breweries. The women here have also managed to mobilise women liquor traders against the trade.

The Gujarat group reports that in cases of physical and social violence, where law fails, group pressure succeeds. Some sanghas here have been able to declare a total ban on wife-beating. The nari adalats that emerged out of legal committees in the villages are a good example of women establishing their own systems for effecting the provision of justice.

III. MAHILA SAMAKHYA IN ANDHRA PRADESH

During the past year, many more sanghams have actively accessed various resources and schemes. It must be emphasised that the role of APMSS has been to provide information and initial guidance. All the follow-up of applications has been done by the sanghams themselves.

Housing

Since 1994-95, housing has been an important activity of sanghams. During 1995, 216 houses in Medak, and 338 in Mahabubnagar were sanctioned.

These sanctions were the result of one and a half years of persistent hard work, repeated visits to various offices and being constantly heckled in the village. The beginning of construction activities has built up a strong image for the sangham in the village.

Several problems arose in Mahabubnagar. Peddajatram sangham which was one of the first to actively pursue this matter, has yet to start construction because of problems with the identified land. Though the RDO has been very supportive of the sangham, this problem is yet to be resolved. Consequently, the image of the sangham has suffered in the village.

In other village, where construction has started, different problems surfaced. The sanghams of Chityala and Karne decided to find their own mason for construction. When the sangham of Pulimamidi decided on a similar course, the Housing Inspector objected and insisted that they accept the mason he suggests. The sangham refused and there was a sangham's grit compelled the Inspector to accept their terms.

Toilets

As a result of the continuous discussions with the sangham women on the importance of hygiene for good health, we gave information on the scheme for construction individual toilets which required 'shramdaan' worth of about Rs: 400, as part of the labour component. In Medak, 838 women from 30 sanghams have been sanctioned toilets. The construction activity has started. This has led to some sanghams asking for masonary training.

Roads

In Oblapur, Utkook Mandal, Mahabubnagar district under the employment Assurance Scheme, the sangham has been sanctioned the contract for the construction of a road.

DWCRA

During the course of the year, the stronger sanghams have applied for DWCRA loans. The sangham of Lingampally village, Makthal Mandal, Mahabubnagar, consisting mainly of stone cutters, is planning of apply for a sanction of a lorry or a tractor from the DRDA to market stone in the Narayanapet division. Some sanghams in both districts are also seriously considering applying for PDS dealerships.

48 in Medak groups and 35 in Mahabubnagar have been identified for DWCRA loans and are awaiting disbursal of money.

In Medal, negotiations are on with the SC corporation to provide loans to 9 sanghams on an experimental basis for a land-lease activity.

School Buildings

In Kondareddypalli and Potureddypalli villages in Medak, the construction of school buildings has started. The sangham of these villages must be given full credit for having pursued the matter with the authorities and getting a defunct project restarted.

Land-Lease for Agricultural Purposes

6 Villages (Devnoor, Lakshmisagar, Aksanpalli, Chautkur, Taddanpalli and Watpalli in Medak) have leased land by pooling their sangham funds and thrift money. They have opted for dry-irrigated crop production like jowar, ragi and ground-nut. Two of these groups suffered a loss because of heavy rains. In the coming year many more sanghams plan to engage in land lease and negotiations have started for this at village levels.

Watershed

During 1995, 10 villages in Utkur/Makthal mandals, Mahabubnagar district, have been identified by DPAP,(based on A.P. Remote Sensing Agency Surveys) for watershed programmes. As APMSS was already working in this area since June 1993, we were approached by the district administration to participate in the DPAP programme.

People's involvement and participation, and transfer of funds directly to the village watershed associations were key elements of the revised DPAP guidelines. Since mobilising and organising of women resulted in strong sanghams in some of the identified DPAP villages, it was felt that DPAP would provide an opportunity for the sanghams to actively interact in larger fora. With their new found articulation and enhanced self-esteem they would be able to influence the community on their problems and priorities. The women may be able to steer the association towards more sustainable development.

This would also enable them to access natural and financial resources. The increased access to fuel and fodder may also lead to other collective economic development programmes. Many of the sangham members are below the poverty line, and they frequently migrate to cities in search of work. The physical component of project would provide wages under EAS for the next four years. This would enable women to stay in the village and play an active role on a continual basis to motivate parents for enrollment of children, immunisation, literacy, etc.

Another major factor which clinched our decision was that funds would be transferred directly into the village watershed association accounts and APMSS would be only facilitators. The capacity of the community specifically sangham women, in organisational, administrative, technical and financial skills would be increased. The watershed development team consisting of a Civil Engineer, Agriculture, Forestry and Social mobiliser was formed. These member were trained at APARD Rajendranagar. This was the first time that four men were taken to work with APMSS.

PRA was used for preparation of a four year abstract and action plan for first year. Watershed Association Committees were formed, registered and bank accounts opened. We tried to ensure that at least two sangham women, who are not sangham leaders, become members of the committee.

Watershed Association Committee members and the DIU team have been taken to PIDOW, Myrada Gulburga for exposure visits. This visit has helped us in breaking barriers and established stronger rapport with them.

By the time action plans were prepared and sanctioned it was April, 1996. The bunding work could not be executed because the soil was hard, and the labour were finding it difficult in adhering to SSR specifications.

Out of 8 villages, work was started in 6 villages. In each village, works of 2 lakhs have been undertaken. In the first year we have planned only bundings and plantation of bunds. Hence the entire 2 lakhs would be used under the wage component. Except in Jaklair and Peddajatram, sangham women are also working on these bunds. In each village 150 acres of bunding has been completed.

The process of grounding and operationalisation of the programme has been highly appreciated by the Mahabubnagar DPAP. There are, however, many problems.

In grounding the programme, in one village of Utkur, PRA itself was not taken up because people refused to participate for two reasons: (i) their previous experience with DPAP (ii) Utkoor being mandal headquarters,has all the political leaders stationed there, and each faction responds only when their leader intervenes: APMSS has not been able to get all the leaders onto one platform to discuss the programme.

In another village, manthangoud, Makthal mandal, the local MLA was not satisfied with the committee formed. A stalemate ensued and the programme has not moved forward.

The participation of sanghams at all levels has not been to our expectations. The DIU, State Office and WDT has continuous discussions on this problem. One of our major efforts was to sharpen the team's and sangham women's understanding on why APMSS has taken DPAP, its link to programme objectives and importance of women participating in decision-making committees. Slowly, women are coming forward in a few villages to take an active part in the programme.

However, on the more positive side, in villages where sangham were weak and formation of sangham has been difficult, the grounding of the watershed programme and frequent visits by WDT members evoked a strong response.

In Anugonda, Makthal mandal, during the course of forming the Watershed Association, it was emphasised that the committee should also focus on village development and take special interest in children's education, literacy, health and immunisation. Many people responded positively, including women, who were not very cooperative when the Karyakartha first visited the village. A significant outcome was the active participation of the Sarpanch who took the responsibility in public to support the sangham and Watershed Association in their activities.

Though initially we had reservations about taking men into the programme, we have been fortunate that they have integrated with team. They actively support the DIU in various activities. The Civil Engineer is taking active interest in the construction of sangham kutirams, the agriculture and forestry members are helping in training and disseminating information on these subjects.

IV. MAHILA SAMAKHYA IN KARNATAKA

Problems of women are discussed at taluk level sangha meetings. At this meeting, sanghas that have problems seek help from the more successful and active sanghas. Quite often, sangha women and sahayoginis from other sanghas visit the troubled areas and help them solve their problems.

For example women in Kustagi taluk have taken a united stand to address the problem of land. Together they have able to receive DWCRA loans. Women of Yelburga taluk could not locate an appropriate place for the taluk meeting. They went in a group to tehshildar's office, arranged for a place and obtained a possession certificate for it. Women of Yediyapur village have been able to start nurseries and women of Gaddigera, Siddhapura and Marakote village have become part of DWCRA groups. Many of these achievements are a consequence of regular taluk level meetings.

The taluk level meetings in Karnataka also play an important role in legitimising women's problems with social evils like alcoholism and the 'Devadasi' tradition. No longer do these remain isolated instances of individual misery. Once these problems are discussed at the taluk level, the women as victims of these practices and those who are perpetrators of the social evils, both realise that the situation can and must change. This goes a long way in achieving changes in attitudes towards the problems faced by women. The changes are brought about by involvement in the Samakhya programme, both at the individual and the collective level.

Women and Health

Amongst the main achievements in the fields of health is the growing realisation among sangha women about their own health and the need to inform other women about good health-practices. They have realised that several of their health problems are aviodable or easily curable. Women have themselves met the medical officer and arranged for health workshops in their villages. These workshops cover a range of subjects including nutrition, immunisation, basic health care for mother and child, hygiene, sanitation and the importance of a clean environment.

Samakhya has also conducted several workshops on the uses of herbal medicines. Several women are not just using herbal medicines for themselves but are preparing and selling them in other villages. They are treating common ailments like white discharge, bleeding, stomach ache during menstruation, ear discharge, asthma, fevers, piles and eczema. One of the sangha women in Marakote village has prepared a herbal oil with the help of government facilities. Women have also tried to locate suitable land and water sources for herbal gardens. Once in two months the women of the sanghas bring their children to the creches for medical check ups.

The programme keeps responding to the needs of the women and to new dimensions of current problems. In keeping with this philosophy, several workshops have been held on AIDS. The women who attended these workshops have been very active in spreading basic information about the dangerous nature of AIDS infection. Thus women are learning to give priority to health issues over and above beliefs that such sensitive issues should not be publicly debated.

Women realised that there were few trained dais and maternity nurses in their areas and a training for dais was conducted at the district level. Table 1 gives the no. of persons trained and cases handled by them.

Table 1

Details of Dais Conducting Delivery Cases

Taluk	No.of Dais trained	No, of delivery cases handled
Yelburga	36	75
Devadurga	10	15
Kustagi	15	15
Raichur	4	15
	65	135

Kits are supplied to the dais and these are being used as and when required. Awareness is also being created about the importance of breast feeding immediately after child birth and allaying women's blind belief that this is not good for the child. Care is also taken to register births and have periodic check-ups for pregnant women. This has been achieved by building up good relations with the ANM and nurses and collecting the required medicines from them. This has happened in Balagere and Thonasihalla Thanda. Information is given to pregnant women on the importance of their own health. After delivery, women who have problems are advised to take certain herbal medicine for the complete removal of the placenta.

Literacy Initiatives

The sangha activities develop a keen desire for knowledge and literacy among the women. When it was found that not literate women was available, a workshop on literacy was conducted for 10 women each from 10 villages. The outcome of this workshops is that at least a few women have learnt to write their names and the name of the sanghas. Realising the importance of literacy for girls under 14, sangha women discussed this issue and located a teacher who had an Senior Secondary Level Schooling (SSLS). SHE was appointed by the sangha and this was later confirmed by Samakhya. Subsequently a selection workshop was held. The matter was discussed in the gram sabha and with the cooperation of the villagers, a Non-Formal Education (NFE) centre was opened. This pattern has been followed in several areas. In 1994-95 there were 12

NFE centres. An additional 34 centres have been opened in the past year taking the total to 46. The talukwise distribution is as follows— Yelburga —36, Kustagi —7, Raichur—1, devadurga—2

Table 2
Literacy Status of Children

Phases	No. of Children	Alphabetical Knowledge	Numerical Knowledge
I Stage	47	46	45
II Stage	57	57	49
III Stage	56	56	49
Iv Stage	25	25	25
Total No. of Children in Centres		=	400
Attendance		=	350

V. MAHILA SAMAKHYA IN UTTAR PRADESH

Violence and Atrocities

In 494 villages, the issues of violence has had preponderance over all other issues. We have yet to compile profiles of cases handled to categories them. Perhaps a study would prove valuable.

At some time or the other over the year, in each of the villages there was some case regarding violence on women. As the sanghas have become more conscious and alert about the issue, any matter of family discord, ill-treatment of the women/ girl child, harassment, beating, rape, or any other form of violence is a magnet for their attention. The other aspect is that many such cases are also 'referred' to sanghas for resolution.

The strategies they evolve from case to case are specific but one fact is certain: that no incident escapes the notice of the sakhi, sangha or sahyogini. "Sanghas, like women have the same needs: the commonality of joy sorrow, hope and fear".

The Strategies that have evolved in sanghas are:

* Holding private meetings with the victim and her family
* Holding talks with the opposite party.
* discussing the case in the sangha.
* Discussing the case in the public forum of the village (if the above fails).
* seeking social justice for the victim and acceptance at village level.
* Involving the law enforcement machinery as and when required.
* maintaining public pressure to resolve the issue

* following up the issue or the case from time to time.

Besides these, there are many other ways of dealing with the issues as there is no set formula, like there are no set cases.

Para-legal Training

Taking up issues of violence is a conscious decision of sanghas. Certainly all sanghas did not decide to take up issues of violence at the same time. But as and when the issues were raised, the case were taken up. The kind of cases handled by the sangha and its success or failure in dealing with it is definitely a barometer for measuring its solidarity and strenth. Sahyoginis and sangha women have received para-legal trainings in several phases last year. This year too there were several rounds of trainings of sangha women in three districts pertaining to law and legal procedures. In time they will require further orientation and 'refreshing'.

Wages

"The procedures are so cumbersome that village women feel they lose a lot of time and wages while running to obtain justice."

This is a perennial recurring issue which has troubled women constantly since they have to struggle on several fronts:

* Demand equal wages as given to men.
* demand wages as per standardised rates.
* resist paying commission in the case where they do wage labour for government schemes.

In most of the villages where MS is in operation, the knowledge about wage rates is extensive not only within sanghas but also outside them. This is a phenomenon in about 250+ wages. The women are extremely alert regarding rates of wages and demand wages as per rates. In both Varansi and Banda they have continually struggled for raise in daily wages from two and a half kg. (cereal) to six kg. and one and a half kg. (cereal) to two and a half kg. per day.

This was not achieved in a day but happened over five to six years of hardship, constant struggle, and persistent effort. Earlier when the struggle started there were constant tensions between daily wage earners and upper caste landlords who threatened dire consequences if women did not come for harvesting, transplanting paddy or weeding. But as groups and then masses of women protested they relented and paid the wages as per demand. In Saharanpur women took contracts for on farm jobs such as planting, transplanting, harvesting cane, processing grains etc. For the season. Much of the earlier resistance of landlords has diminished. They often say that these women are a force to reckon with so they succumb to their demands. Some sangha women in Banda say "They call us saheb, now we can talk to them eye to eye".

The increase in wages has gone a long way in strengthening the strategic needs of women with long term effects on family incomes. (Men too have got raised wags with agitation taken up by women). This has also resulted in a change in gender relations and roles of men and women in many ways.

The women also receive admiration from men because they started something which was not even thought about five years ago. People in these areas had never dreamt that they would ever have access to the wages that they can take home today.

However, much still needs to be done. The whole issue of wages has yet to become a movement. It cannot remain confined to small pockets where MS is an operation.

There needs to be a lot more clarity at around level so that many more can join the movement. Definitely, the sangha women if equipped with the right information, adequate planning and concrete strategies, more consistent organisation can mobilise a movement together with men not only in their areas but in adjoining and other areas too. They can even develop a network with other such organisations and movements.

Accessing Government Schemes

Through sahyoginis and sakhis, sangha women have become much more aware of the various government schemes and programmes for village development and women. Earlier their position was "We were not able to obtain ration card forms costing 50 p. as the Pardhan issued them for Rs. 5.00." The sangha and the sakhi, felt defeated despite all their Jaankari and 'strength'.

In over 431 villages sanghas have accessed:

* hand pumps for the backward communities in their localities.
* organised camps for health check ups an dimmunization.
* housing for women and families under the Indira Awas Yojana.
* contracts for village level work under Jawahar Rozgar Yojana.
* Medical care facilities through ANMs/PHCs.
* enrollment/scholarships for SC/ST children in government schools.
* many other facilities through heir initiatives..

This phenomenon came through a great deal of preparedness, dialogue, negotiation and goodwill on the part of all sangha. At times the confrontationist strategy was adopted but only in extreme circumstances. The women knew very well that making too much noise would be detri mental to their interests. On thc part of the sanghas it was an exercise of gathering complete information, being sure of what they were doing following up the matter consistently, presenting a common front and voicing their claims and opinions justly with transparency. While on the other hand at the level of the government functionaries too there was and is a change in attitude, acknowledgment and respect for them. Hence today, it has become quite a common sight (in MS areas) to see group of women at the block office, panchayat office the PHC, the pradhan's house, village level forums and banks, to speak out, to air their grievances and tell that they mean business. It is surprising that the inputs of four to five years now appear somewhat fruitful. What is often heard in many intelligent forums about integration and convergence of services has actually started to happen. Of course the direction in this case is not from the top but from the sanghas at village level to the top. The sanghaas are demanding accountability of what they receive in the villages for development, for whom and whether they are getting it or not. They are the ones who are raising the questions and eliciting answers to get things moving at village level. Certainly there are varied opinions of people who think that:

* women have become too smart.
* they get a lot of information in their meetings.
* their information is correct.
* They are becoming educated.
* they move from village to village.
* they are able to dialogue with men openly.
* they are fearless.

VI. MAHILA SAMAKHYA IN GUJARAT

Impact of Nari Adalats in Vaghodia and Padara Clocks

Nari Adalats consists of completely voluntary action of rural poor women evolving out of a government sponsored programme. It represents women's collective attempt to look for an alternative system where women have space for expression while seeking justice. Women who have issues and approach Nari Adalat feel confident when presenting their side of these issues. Women in the Adalat provide a lot of moral support in the empowering process of self-expression. It has also led to visibility of women in public spaces- theatre, compound or block office compound where otherwise no woman would normally' be there without males accompanying her. Men also get used to the presence of women in such places, wondering at the way issues are handled and resolved, appreciating such less costly methods of resolving disputes and the attitude of helping whenever approached. People from villages other then those covered by Mahila Samakhya also come to the Nari Adalat with their concerns. Government officials who now believe in the potential of these women, after looking at the resolved disputes,extend their helping hand. The point that has been made out loud and out is that women no more are only seekers of justice; they also can pass judgements about family matters in public. This gives many other struggling women courage to come out and voice their oppression.

Considering the needs of Nari Adalats and to strengthen and make them more autonomous, posibilities of starting a para-legal courses were explored. In February 1996 orientation training for women wanting to join legal courses was conducted. Fifty women attended the day long course where primary concepts were discussed. A three months course is planned to begin from April 1996. The district team worked hard to evolve the course design, contacting legal experts and consultants, creating material required for the course. The women are preparing themselves for the forthcoming course.

Rajkot Procesesses

Mahila Samakhya Rajkot continued with their legal aid guidance processes this year. Cases of maintenance or divorce are most visible where Sangha, Sahayoginis and district support the women in difficulty. Wherever the case is complicated linkages have been made with Morbi Vikas Vidyalaya. Contacts and coordination was established with the district judge and attempts were made to appoint Sahayoginis on the block level legal guidance committee. The Civil Judge of each block was also approached. There is a legal committee in the district which meets every month to discuss cases and strategies to solve them. In a number of maintenance cases alimony money has been paid to women. There have been awareness workshops by block legal aid committees which were attended by Sahayoginis and Sangha women. These workshops arranged by the district judge provided new set of information to Mahila Samakhya women. This year Mahila Samakhya Rajkot also became active in taking their cases to the Lok Adalat of their areas.

Sabarkantha

In Mahila Samakhya Sabarkantha this year the legal consultant of the district organised a number of village-based legal awareness meetings. The meetings made their impact in terms of action. In Jaswantpura village of Meghraj block, Sangha women and their husbands were victims of attrocities of their own family members. After attending the legal awareness meeting the women felt confident of taking the step of submitting a complaint to the police. There was follow-up action and the family members were jailed. Mahila Samakhya Gujarat has succeeded in creating collective and moral support to women for taking such a step. and undoubtedly the process to gain courage and in turn provide support to other women invariably continues.

Women in Politics

The 73rd amendment regarding 33 per cent reservation for women in Panchayati Raj institution got implemented with State Assembly elections in June 1995. At Mahila Samakhya Gujarat discussions and information sharing on the role of women in Panchayati Raj had already started by the end of last year. There was lots of confidence and enthusiasm among Sangha women who were getting the change to show their "empowerment" at the public forum. The enthusiasm was to be channelised and supported by Mahila Samakhya, a facilitator to the process.

Baroda District

Mahila Samakhya Baroda approached Unnati, an Ahmedabad based NGO for a Panchayati Raj workshop. In april 1996 a two-day workshop for Sahayoginis was conducted which was attended by representatives from other two districts.

Panchayati Raj

Baroda district vaghodia Block and Chotta Udaipur Block

In Baroda district on 8th September 1995 'world Literacy Day was celebrated by Vaghodia block. Women who stood for the elections shared their experiences of difficulties they faced as women, their struggles, and support they received in the process. This also helped in discussing such issues in public which were never talked over before. In March 1996 women filled up forms for remaining panchayati elections. In Voghodia, Drishti —an Ahmedabad based NGO made a film of Panchayati Raj titled "Swaraj" in which Sangha women and village men played roles and participated in the film-making process.

Rajkot District

In Rajkot district after the information sharing about reserved seats and general seats, processes took momentum for filling up the forms. In many villages women stood for the general seats also with the objectives of getting an exposure and learning new things, even in the enventuality of loosing the election. The Sahayoginis and district team members supported the women by providing necessary guidance in filling up the form. When they were to choose symbols it was realised that wherever Sangha was in existence, women came to the office while from other villages only men came. Interesting discussions took place on selecting the symbols at the Sangha meeting. One women selected rising sun saying "33% women reservation is a new sun and an opportunity to work and do new things". The other women who selected an Aeroplane said: " Now women have started moving out and getting new information. If Aeroplane wins, women will get more and better opportunities to go out". Government officials and other people at the block and district level were also amazed by the enthusiasm of Sangha women. Another experience was that wherever Sangha was active in canvassing for the women candidate, political parties were ready to give money to support but women through collective decision-making did not want to be part of such a process.

Rajkot District Kotdasangani Block Mota Mandva Village

Trainee Sakhi Labhuben of Harijan Caste stood for the election for Sarpanch Post. The women contesting against her was a Patel. Other women and Sakhis of surrounding villages canvassed for Labhuben. On the night before the voting day she was contacted by Patel caste people and told to declare her support in favour of Patel women. She was offered Rs. 10,000. Labhuben was firm in her conviction that she stood for learing, knowing,and winning and not for buying others or selling herself. Sangha women immediately called a meeting. Men of Harijan caste parted in favour of Patels and afterwards Labhuben came to know that voters were bought for Rs. 100 each and she was the victim of an unfair and undemocratic process. While the counting took place Sangha women were not allowed and only Labhuben along with her husband could go inside. She expressed that she felt lonely there being women. 30-40 sangha women consistently supported her in a struggle for change. Labhuben related her learnings of the sakhi trainings to her real life experiences on politics of subordination

Sabarkantha District

Mahila Samakhya, Sabarkantha district, officials were invited for information sharing in Sahayogini meetings. Sahayoginis conducted Sangha meetings and women on their own created support systems from surrounding villages. After election Sahayoginis organised Sarpanch meetings for their cluster of villages.

Jetpur Village Bhiloda Block Sabarkantha District

Navalben wanted to stand for the elections but she was not getting the form to fill up her candidature. Sangha women got together and decided to help her in accessing her right to stand for the elections. Members of the sangha approached taluka/block level office and got the form for Navalben. Though she lost the election, the processes helped the members of the group to realise how women are marginalised in the process of political participation.

In April 1995 representatives from all the districts participated in capacity building sub-regional workshop for Panchayati Raj insitutions organised by Unnati in collaboration with Rajiv Gandhi Foundation. It gives MSG an opportunity to network, know others and share their experiences for preparations for the forthcoming elections.

Panchayati elections provided opportunities for discussing issues that otherwise would not have been brought out by Sangha women. Their experiences of entering into political sphere led to realisations and learning about how women are 'not heard' and sidelined in public sphere and how they can assert themselves. It also led to experimentation space for women in creating their place in an otherwise male-dominated field of politics. It was also a test for women's collectives to keep their solidarity intact against outside forces.

And we women at Mahila Samakhya can say that we succeeded in this new area as individuals and as a programme. We became visible and learnt to handle ourselves against external pressures while realising internal strengths and feelings of togetherness.

THE ADVANCEMENT OF WOMEN: AN OVERVIEW

The struggle for women's rights, and the task of creating a new United Nations, able to promote peace and the values which nurture and sustain it, are one and the same. Today—more than ever—the causes of women is the cauase of all humanity.

—Secretary-General Boutros Boutros-Ghali, message for International Women's Day, 8 March 1993

In a century punctuated by unprecedented change, revolution and innovation, perhaps the most pervasive and lasting transformation has been the emergence of women as a major presence and force in public life the world over.

Women are assuming positions of influence in steadily accelerating numbers in our communities, schools, workplaces, governments, media, and in virtually every long-held bastion of male privilege and power.

This transformation, albeit erratic and uneven, is the result of the complex interaction of human development. The improved status of women could not have occurred on the present scale without the ceaseless work of hundreds of millions of women — and men-to overcome women's second-class status, powerlessness, marginalization and indignity.

Women have always contributed to all areas of economic and social life-as farmers, entrepreneurs, traders, workers, home-makers and mothers. Yet women share unequally in the fruits of their labour because of persistent discrimination. They constitute a majority of the world's poor and continue to suffer disadvantages in education, health and employment.

The emergence of women into the public arena from the circumscribed world of the home and family has essentially been a battle for human rights-the essential values that promote the fullest development of individuals and societies. Moreover, the struggle for equal status with men and full participation in society has also led to the recognition of broader rights of women as wives, mothers, daughters and as home-makers.

Long-standing forms of discrimination— from certain divorce laws to physical abuse—are no longer considered private matters. The right to family-planning methods, education and other family-related services are increasingly considered to be as important as the right to vote or hold a job.

And while women have advanced more rapidly in some societies than others, almost everywhere women's concerns are still accorded second priority, and women continually face discrimination, both subtle and flagrant.

Even in areas where progress has been achieved, there is fear today of a backlash that may reverse the gains that women have so painstakingly accumulated. Civil, religious and ethnic strife, underdevelopment and economic reversals are continuing threats to women's advancement.

The struggle for women's rights—reflecting an ever-deepening interplay between individuals, national women's movements and the international women's movement— has found a staunch ally in the United Nations over the past fifty years.

The expanding influence of the women's movement since the first **world conference on women** in 1975 is especially encouraging. Under UN auspices, the advancement of women has received sustained attention and review, ensuring that women's issues remain on the international agenda until effective action is taken.

Today, the enormous diversity of women around the world and even within any given society is better appreciated, a sensitivity that has been enhanced by the international meetings among women's advocates within the UN, among Non-governmental Organizations (NGOs) and Governments.

The need to forge an equal partnership with men continues to gain support and is a central theme of the **Fourth World Conference on Women**, to be held in Beijing from 4 to 15 September 1995. Consensus is growing that:

* Overcoming discrimination is intrinsically linked with the issue of power;
* Women will remain second-class citizens in the absence of access to the economic, political and social resources and levels of deci-

sion-making enjoyed by men;

* Women are central to development, particularly in developing regions; the wider objectives of human development and peace cannot be achieved without eliminating discrimination against women.

An important step in reversing past inequalities is recognition by policy-makers that their decisions affect women and men differently. Introducing gender analysis into policies on development, the environment, nutrition and health will accentuate the impact of these policies.

Women must be engaged at all levels in efforts to eradicate poverty, promote peace and achieve sustainable development. Female perspectives are crucial to understanding the full dimensions of human society and facilitating constructive change.

An Equal Partnership

Women will change the world when they lead it, but they will change it with men as their partners.

—Gertrude Mongella, Secretary-General of the Fourth World Conference on Women

Proponents of women's rights increasingly see a partnership between men and women based on equality as a crucial way to foster development, overcome discrimination and construct more prosperous, equitable and harmonious societies. Such a partnership implies mutual respect for the inalienable right to the same privileges, responsibilities and opportunities.

There is increasing consensus that for true equality to take root, profound revisions are required in the roles of both men and women.

No fundamental change in favour of women is possible without a massive change in male attitudes. This is more than a philosophical point: men control the legal, administrative and financial systems which effectively deny a vast number of women the right to own land, inherit property, establish credit, enter the professions or rise in business.

—Dr. Nafis Sadik, Executive Director of the United Nations Population Fund

A majority of UN Member States recognize international agreements, such as the **1979 Convention on the Elimination of All Forms of Discrimination Against Women (CEDAW),** that promote equality between the sexes and women's rights. Support for legislation against discrimination continues to increase worldwide. However, there remains a serious gap between *de jure* and de facto recognition of women's rights. Women often do not enjoy the rights, protections and freedoms guaranteed to them by law.

Discrimination against women will not be abolished by modifying laws alone. Lasting progress requires the commitment by the State and civil society to truly implement the law.

- The attainment of an equal partnership will depend on the legal and financial commitment of societies to the advancement of women. Little doubt remains that investing in women's health, education and work skills is perhaps the most rewarding contribution that society can make. Initiatives that improve women's status pay large returns in terms of family well-being, social integration, economic growth and quality of life.
- Research demonstrates that countries that targeted, for example, women's education and health early in their development, have become the most successful economically. Investment by society in women offers a high rate of return.[1]
- "Gender blindness", or ignoring the special needs and roles of women, is now recognized as a serious obstacle to meeting the wider targets of development programmes.

Persistent sex stereotypes at home, in school, on the job and in virtually all social institutions, slow efforts to broaden perceptions of both men and women's roles in society.

- Studies show that girls educational and occupational choices are influenced by stereotypes of women promoted by their families, communities, schools, religious institutions, mass media and advertising.
- Boys are equally vulnerable to internalizing notions about their dominant place at home and in society, often adopting attitudes that hinder the realization of their potential as husbands, fathers and colleagues.

Given the breadth of the objective, much more needs to be done to eliminate discriminatory practices and encourage men and women to share equally the responsibilities and rights in the family and society at large.

Women's Rights as Human Rights

Everyone is entitled to all the rights and freedoms set forth in this Declaration, without distinction of any kind, such as race, colour, sex, language, religion, political or other opinion, national or social origin, property, birth or other status.

—Universal Declaration of Human Rights, Article 2

Establishing universal agreement on a body of human rights standards and principles is one of the UN's greatest achievements. Internationally, equal rights for women are being viewed as fundamental human rights.

The Convention on the Elimination of All Forms of Discrimination **Against Women (CWDAW) see**: UN Milestones in the Advancement of Women, page viii), which covers measures to be taken by States to eliminate discrimination against women, obliges States to:

- Pursue a policy of eliminating discrimination against women by all appropriate means and without delay;
- Reaffirm the equality of human rights for women in society and the family;
- Take action against the social causes of women's inequality;
- Remove laws, stereotypes, practices and prejudices that impair women's well being.

Since the UN General Assembly adopted CEDAW in 1979, 139 countries have ratified its provisions. However, 29 ratifying States have issued substantive reservations concerning some articles.

The **World Conference on Human Rights** in Vienna in 1993 further reaffirmed that "the human rights of women and of the girl child are an inalienable, integral and indivisible part of universal human rights."

Women and Decision-Making

In tandem with women's movements around the world, the United Nations and its family of organizations are placing greater emphasis on initiatives that propel women into all levels of decision-making.

Women must enter the halls of power—in government bodies, political parties, labour unions and community organizations— in order to make known their preferences, concerns and interests.

Locally, strategies must encompass women's practical needs and cultural values to ensure that their political participation becomes a reality.

There is growing pressure on Governments to secure the effective participation of women in the decision-making process at the national, state and local levels by adopting appropriate laws and administrative measures.

However, most countries are far from achieving the target of 30 per cent women in decisionmaking levels by 1995 as set by the United Nations Economic and Social Council. A level of at least 30 to 35 per cent in decision-making bodies is generally considered the "critical mass" necessary for qualitative change in a decision-making body.[2]

Few women reach top levels of political participation and even fewer reach major decision making positions. This, despite the facts that:

- Most countries now democratically elect political leaders;

- Women make up at least half the electorate.

Women are increasingly being elected heads of State, notably in developing countries, Channels currently available for raising awareness about women's political rights include formal and informal education, political education, NGOs, trade unions, the media and business organizations. Governments can lead the way, but all sectors of society must work together actively to bring about the advancement of women.

Violence against Women

For millions of women, acts of violence are a part of everyday life and a denial of the rights to "life, liberty and security of person." (Universal Declaration of Human Rights, Article 3)

Popular attitudes towards violence against women are undergoing profound change. The issue has risen to the top of UN conference agendas. Increasingly, violence against women is no longer considered a family affair or tacitly condoned. But the incidence of violence persists and may be one the rise, afflicting all regions of the world, in all economic and educational strata.

The growing concern about violence against women was highlighted at the World Conference on Human Rights. The Conference called for the "elimination of violence against women in public and private life" and identified full human rights for women as a priority for Governments and the United Nations. This includes action against:

- "All forms of sexual harassment, exploitation and trafficking in women";
- "Harmful effects of certain traditional or customary practices, cultural prejudices and religious extremism,"; and
- "Situations of armed conflict" in which violations include "murder, systematic rape, sexual slavery and forced pregnancy".

In 1993, the General Assembly adopted the **Declaration on the Elimi nation of Violence Against Women,** which:

- Condemns any act causing "physical, sexual or psychological harm or suffering to women," in the family or the general community or by the State;
- Warns States against " invoking any custom, tradition or religious consideration to avoid their obligations" of basic protections for women;
- Urges officials to prevent, investigate and punish acts of violence. It recommends establishing support mechanisms for victims and their children, and educational measures, including training of public officials, to raise awareness;

- Suggests intensified efforts in gender-based statistics-gathering, organizing women's advocacy groups and in United Nations system-wide activities.

Many States are heeding the calls for action. In the case of the traditional practice of female genital mutilation (FMG), some countries have taken concrete steps to curb the practice. For example, Kenya banned female genital mutilation in 1990 and Burkina Faso has incorporated into its draft constitution a prohibition of female circumcision.

The Diversity of Women

There is just one..... global agenda. But women will put different..... priorities on the issues based on where they come from and where they want to go. The result will be that societies will be different, but built equally on the visions of men and women.

—Gertrude Mongella, Secretary-General of the Fourth World Conference on Women

Today, international women's organizations are addressing a wide variety of situations and finding common ground that reflects the concerns of all women.

Respecting women's diversity is a prerequisite for international and intercultural dialogue among women's organizations. Priorities vary from region to region to but the world's women share a common feature: discrimination.

The regional meetings held in preparation for the Beijing conference identified different priorities in this regard. Trafficking in women has been a major concern voiced by women's movements in Asia. For African women, environmental management and food provision are still urgent needs. Women from some parts of the developing world stress literacy campaigns, while those from developed countries have focused on political and economic equality.[3]

The heterogeneity of women as a "group" was illustrated in a case study undertaken in the Philippines.[4] The study highlights ideological differences between educated middle—and upper-middle-class women in politics, and organizations of poor, uneducated women with urgent survival needs.

The report concludes that it is important for any agenda for women to reflect the prevailing conditions of women in all strata of society and respond to their needs and demands. Otherwise, it continues, "career feminism will liberate merely a tiny sector of the female population while perpetuating the socio-economic order that oppresses and exploits the majority of women".

The need for sensitivity to the broader socio-economic needs of all women as opposed to those of a relatively privileged elite is complicated by the broad range of differing priority concerns that characterize different regions of the world. For example:

- In the industrialized countries, the task is to eliminate more subtle forms of discrimination and "glass ceilings" that limit opportunities and advancement in the high echelons of the private and public sector;
- In developing regions, traditional practices and low levels of education are priority concerns.

Role in Development

The slow pace of development, particularly in rural areas, has underscored the long-standing neglect of women as a key element in development policy. Governments and the international development community are reformulating policies and reallocating resources in the understanding that the low social and economic status of women translates into slower rates of economic growth.

Previously, development policy-makers linked women's needs almost exclusively with public health and population issues such as nutrition, child-rearing and family planning. Women are now recognized as central agents of change and development, acting as an economic force. Programmes to advance women increasingly emphasize economic growth through productive employment and increased participation in decision-making.[5]

The majority of poor people in the world are women. In many developing countries, many structural adjustment programmes—characterized by market-oriented measures, privatization, cuts in social services, conditionality of loans from the World Bank and the International Monetary Fund—place a disproportionate burden on women by demanding greater productivity, while reducing services in education, health and child care. Still, there are encouraging signs. In Africa, a region with high illiteracy rates, countries such as Cameroon, Congo, Senegal, Swaziland and Tanzania have achieved a parity between girls and boys in primary school enrolment.

Globally, the feminization of poverty is evident in the growing number of women, and women with dependent children, in the ranks of low-paid workers; or, as in Greece, Austria, Denmark and Eastern Europe in particular, women are increasing among the long-term unemployed.

Poverty among rural women is growing faster than among rural men, and an increasing number of households are headed by women; women often share unequally in household income and have little control over their earnings.

In times of crisis, hardship falls mainly on women as their food and other consumption tends to be reduced first; they take on additional responsibilities as the single heads of household if the male wage-earner leaves or abandons the family in search of livelihood elsewhere.

Women and Democratization

All democratic experiments, all revolutions, all demands for equality have so far, in every instance, stopped short of sexual equality.

—Rosalind Miles, writer

In much of the developing world—from Brazil's Women's Movement for Amnesty and Chile's Women for Life to South Africa's Black Sash— women play prominent roles in democratizing their societies.

During the 1970s and early 1980s, authoritarian regimes in Latin America restricted parliamentary action and popular organizations. But organizations such as the Mothers of the Plaza de Mayo in Argentina and the Women's Group in Uruguay were among many that struggled to re-establish democracy.[6]

The present wave of democratization in the world, however, does not mean that women's concerns are automatically taken up by freely elected governments, nor does women's participation in politics automatically achieve the desired results.

The sudden transformation of the East European economies and political systems has caused major changes in people's lives including many freedoms and the promise of new opportunities. Under the former system, women were represented at middle and lower levels of decision-making and management. Now they are challenged by loss of work and social safety nets— and political marginalization, at least in the short-term.

Slavenka Drakulic, an outspoken women's advocate and journalist from former Yugoslavia, asserts that there is a concerted drive "to put women 'back where they belong' into the house with children recognizing them only in their maternal function."[7]

Natalia Kraminova, a Russian journalist wrote in the *Moscow News*: "We're concerned about the way new social organizations are turning into male strongholds. The woman question is not a question of minor socio-economic discrepancies, but part of the general question of human rights in our countries."[8]

Women in East European countries have experienced serious setbacks:

- They are more likely than men to lose their jobs and status;

- Health-care and child-care facilities, widely available before to women, now have been largely dismantled.

Privatization has had a differing impact on women and men. Growing evidence shows the exclusion of women from the process of acquiring state assets made available to private buyers.

Many women are left without opportunities with elimination of the quota system, whereby women were reserved a minimum number of positions in the ruling party, government and in industry, engineering and science.

In some other countries, by comparison, women's active role in the process of democratization has induced significant political and legal changes in their favour. Where access to contraception was limited and in some cases illegal, in Romania for example, family-planning programmes have been introduced following legislative reform.

There are clear signs of progress elsewhere as well: Sudan, for example, has established a 10 per cent minimum quota level for women's representation in all positions of local, municipal and state government; and Argentina has implemented a law establishing quotas in the lists of political parties to guarantee a minimum of 30 per cent participation by women.

Role of National Women's Movements

Although the world's women's movements have multiplied in the last two decades, equal rights for women is hardly a new idea. Women's emancipation in modern times became a movement in the mid-19th century, mostly among the educated women in countries undergoing the industrial revolution.

- The first women's movements in the United States evolved from the abolitionist campaigns against slavery.
- The Industrial Revolution in Europe and North America, which saw the transfer of work from home to factory, also gave birth to labour and social movements, including women's organizations.

War helped determine the advancement of women in this century. During the two World Wars, women replaced men on farms and in factories of the industrialized world. As result, the right to vote, education and fair employment achieved recognition in many countries. After World War II, women achieved suffrage in France and Japan, largely as a result of their war efforts.

- The non-industrialized countries were largely occupied with fighting colonialism and women's suffrage occurred in many cases soon after national independence was won.

- The socialist bloc countries officially promoted women's rights from their very inception. Although women played leading roles in government and the economy, they were usually excluded from policy- and decision-making at the highest levels.

In response to national women's movements, most UN Member States have governmental bodies to tackle women's issues. Many, however, still rely on NGOs to address the concerns of women.

The process of establishing national mechanisms for women at the governmental level began only in the late 1970s. Efforts have been increased to strengthen their programmes, to create instruments at the national, regional and local levels and to enhance their functions.

Nearly all countries in Western Europe have governmental mechanisms, sometimes ministries, devoted to women's affairs (an exception is the United Kingdom, which has a mixed governmental and non-governmental body).

The same is true in Africa and Latin America, where most mechanisms are governmental with the exceptions of Cuba, Bolivia and Panama. There are fewer governmental bodies in Asia and the Pacific.

National women's movements and governmental bodies play a strategic role in monitoring and improving the status of women. National organizations also disseminate information to women on their rights and entitlements.

Since they were called for by the World Conference on Women in Nairobi in 1985, several UN Member States have created national mechanisms for women for the first time. The number of instruments at the local, regional and national levels increased notably where a strong governmental mechanism was already in place.

The Nairobi Conference also established goals—called **Forward-looking Strategies**-to achieve by the year 2000. The Review and Appraisal of the Nairobi Forward-looking Strategies observes:

- National machinery, despite resource limitations, has been significant in keeping the Strategies alive in individual countries;
- The effectiveness of national bodies depends on the political commitment of Governments, reflected in appropriate resource levels, institutional status, competence in technical fields and ability to use information. Improving these factors is essential to eliminate other obstacles.

The United Nations has increased support for national efforts by providing advisory, training and information services, and by coordinating exchanges among national organizations. Some UN organizations seek out partnerships with women's organizations and networks, directly supporting them, for example, to take part in national and international conferences.

Role of NGOs

A recent international development of great importance and interest is the emergence of NGOs as advocates, arbiters and activists for the spectrum of issues from human rights to the environment, from political and economic accountability to media monitoring and consumer protection.

For the women's movement, NGOs are vitally important. Less hampered by the bureaucratic and political constraints of official bodies, they have access to information and local sources unavailable to Governments.

In the last two decades, the diversity and breadth of women's NGOs have increased rapidly. They span a range of interests and fields but their unifying force is the advancement of women and their rights.

In developing countries, working with local communities, these NGOs provide credit and marketing schemes, income-generating activities, health care, family-planning and education—including training in all fields.

NGOs are at the forefront of efforts to advance the status and conditions of women—from the Women's Networking Association in Cameroon to the Self-employed Women's Association (SEWA) of Ahmedabad, India.

The links between national and international efforts to advance women are direct, vital and increasingly effective. The Women's Tribunal, a parallel NGO event at the Conference on Human Rights in Vienna (1993), presented evidence and speakers from around the world on human rights violations especially violence, against women.

Such NGO events can be highly effective at drawing public attention to issues by pooling resources through their highly developed networks.

- Collective campaigns, especially by NGOs, helped to pressure Governments to adopt the Declaration on the Elimination of Violence Against Women (1992).[9]
- Women's NGOs networks bring effective international pressure to bear, for example, in exposing the systematic violence and rape now used as weapons of warfare.
- International collaboration among women's groups has been crucial for spotlighting such issues as female genital mutilation, trafficking of women and AIDS.

Obstacles, Trends and Goals

The three themes of the United Nations Decade for Women were "Equality, Development and Peace". They are also the central themes of the Fourth World Conference on Women. These three themes are increasingly seen as mutually reinforcing and indivisible.

Women are vital to peace efforts. They are the silent majority-the mother's farmers workers and vendors— whose voices and needs have been ignored, but whose participation is essential for peace to exist at the local, regional or global level.

In the "global village", societies have more access to information about other cultures, values and ways of governing. Women also have unprecedented opportunities to become more unified, more tolerant, more creative in strategies for advancement.

Women are taking action. They are no longer spectators in the events of our times. The Fourth World Conference on Women provides an occasion for Governments, NGOs, grassroots organizations and the mass media to take the pulse of the burgeoning international women's movement. Delegates will explore ways to promote equality and the empowerment of women and all that it implies: access to all levels of decision-making, from the individual to village councils to government cabinets.

Among the principles and concerns contained in the Draft Platform for Action that will be finalized in Beijing are these:

- Empowerment starts in the family through respect for the independence and dignity of women as bread winners or bread makers, and demands for their entitlement to the rights and responsibilities of the household;
- Violence against women-cloaked in traditional practices like female genital mutilation (FGM), dowry deaths or female infanticide—requires universal condemnation and decisive action to eradicate;
- Systematic assaults on women during war and armed conflict—*e.g.* murder, rape, torture and forced prostitution- require special attention. Although war itself can be considered a violation of human rights, the specific injustices suffered by women flagrantly depart from all internationally recognized norms;
- The feminization of poverty is a worldwide phenomenon. Poverty eradication programmes must continue to focus on improving the incomes, health and education of women to release them from the downward economic spiral;
- Although more women are joining the work force, they are usually in lower-ranking, low-paying jobs with few opportunities for improving skills or promotion. Equal pay for equal work, access to child

care and freedom from sexual harassment require redoubled efforts to confront and solve;

- Health-care services, including maternal health, family-planning and reproductive rights, are still unavailable to many women. The Vienna Declaration of Human Rights includes women's right to "the highest standard of physical and mental health throughout their lives" as a human right.

MANY CURRENT TRENDS ARE HOPEFUL:

- More women now enter non-traditional fields: medicine, law, engineering and science. Women have joined the ranks of electricians, biologists and truck drivers, shattering stereotypes and expanding the job market for half of humanity;
- The number of female university graduates continues to swell, despite high illiteracy rates among women and low school attendance rates for girls in some areas. The next generation will furnish the world economy with a growing supply of female professionals and managers;
- Women's participation in the political arena has improved dramatically in recent years. There are more female prime ministers, members of parliament and policy makers than ever before— though far from the 30 per cent representation level considered to be the "critical mass" for real influence;
- In the information age, public awareness about women's issue has intensified. The messages—to stop violence and discrimination, to combat sex stereotypes and promote positive, accurate images of women—are spreading.

The future is bright despite the immensity of the challenge. With the increased participation of women in politics, and the widespread adoption and enforcement of more equitable and gender-sensitive laws, the international community can more effectively undertake the task of creating a more sustainable, prosperous and healthy world order.

UN World Conferences on Women and other UN Events

The first world conference on women, the World Conference of the International Women's Year, was held in Mexico City in 1975 and marked the starting point for achieving international consensus on women's rights. The conference determined that women's roles are closely linked to the political, economic, social and cultural conditions that constrain them from advancement and that factors determining the economic exploitation, marginalization and oppression of women stem from chronic inequalities, injustices and exploitative conditions at all levels.

Deliberations were hampered by cultural and regional misunderstandings, especially by differences in perception between North and South. The greatest accomplishment was opening the channels for communication for establishing an international network of players involved in women's issues, a network including the United Nations, /Governments and NGOs that has grown stronger and expanded in the ensuing years.

The **United Nations Decade for Women** (1976-85), whose themes were "equality, Development and Peace" highlighted global issues of women's rights and women's role in development and inspired a wide range of activities throughout the world, especially the establishment and reinforcement of national bodies to monitor and promote the advancement of women. The Decade was instrumental in bringing to light the diversified needs of women and in publicizing the role of women in development and the need to promote a perspective in policy making and planning.

In 1980, the UN held the **second world conference on women** in Copenhagen. The Conference declared that equality entails not only legal recognition and elimination of de *jure* discrimination, but de facto equality of responsibilities and opportunities for the participation of women in development, both as beneficiaries and as active agents of change. Dialogue was characterized by political controversy, particularly the demands for including the situation of women under apartheid and Zionism on the agenda. Nevertheless, the grounds for consensus were growing with common support for progress in the fields of education, health and employment.

A breakthrough occurred in 1985, at the end of the UN Decade for Women, in Nairobi at the **Third World Conference on Women**. Many referred to this meeting as no less than the "birth of global feminism." Dialogue was aided by a flood of information gathered during the Decade and by heightened understanding and mutual respect particularly among advocates for the advancement of women that had been fostered in the years between conferences. The major issues at Nairobi were still closely linked to women's basic survival strategies, with emphasis on poverty and education.

At the third world conference on women, participants adopted by consensus the **Nairobi Forward-looking Strategies to the year 2000** (NFLS). The comprehensive Strategies call for the participation of women as equal partners with men in all fields of work, equal opportunity for education and training, protection of women at work and recognition of women's needs to become effective producers or managers of political, economic and social affairs. The document called for efforts to overcome prejudices, stereotyped thinking and obstacles to women joining previously male-dominated professions including promotion to decision-making positions. It further declared that the role of women in national liberation struggles should be recognized and their equal participation in the nationbuilding process afterwards be encouraged.

The **World Summit for Children** (New York, 1990) emphasized disadvantages faced by girls compared to boys in its review of the global status of children. It issued a **World Declaration on the Survival, Protection and Development of Children** that called for "strengthening the role of women in general and ensuring their equal rights will be to the advantage of the world's children." Girls must be given equal treatment from birth.

The Declaration stressed the importance of maternal health and family planning as fundamental rights of women that are also connected to the well-being children. It also stated that "equal opportunity should be provided for the girl child to benefit from the health, nutrition, education and other basic services to enable her to grow to her full potential".

The **United Nations Conference on Environment and Development** (Rio de Janeiro, 1992) recognized the pervasive role of women in sustainable development and in environmental protection. Since women constitute a large number of the world's agricultural producers and in many cultures are responsible for securing water and fuel supplies for their families, they are vital in any efforts to safeguard the environment. The **Plan of Action forSustainable Development, Agenda 21**, called for the involvement of women in the management and protection of natural resources, particularly in rural areas.

The **World Conference on Human Rights** (Vienna, 1993) reaffirmed that all human rights are universal, indivisible, interdependent and interrelated and that the human rights of women are an inalienable, integral and indivisible part of universal human rights. It also recognized violence against women as a violation of their human rights as well as the systematic violation of those rights in situations of war or armed conflict. The Vienna Declaration and Programme of Action was adopted by the consensus of 171 Member States of the United Nations. The Conference recommendation to Establish a special Rapporteur on Violence Against Women and to adopt the Declaration on Violence Against Women were subsequently agreed to by the 48th General Assembly later that year.

The **International Conference on population and Development** (Cairo, 1994) emphasized that the empowerment and autonomy of women are bases for development. It reviewed the status of women worldwide, especially in light of their access to adequate health, maternal care and family planning facilities. The final conference document reinforced women's right of choice in child-bearing, and underlined the critical importance to society as a whole of education for girls and women.

The **World Summit for Social Development** (Copenhagen, 1995) called attention to the pivotal role of women in development. It also focused attention on women's social issues and the discriminatory practices that prevent their full participation is society.

Notes

1. Kristen Timothy, Deputy Director of the Division for the Advancement of Women and Coordinator of the Fourth World Conference on Women, from presentation to preparatory meeting to the Fourth World Conference on Women, New York, October 1994.
2. *Second Review and Appraisal of the Nairobi Forward-Looking Strategies for the Advancement of Women,* January 1995 draft.
3. *UN Chronicle*. "Perspective UN Decade for Women", Volume 7, 1985, p. xii
4. Socorro L. Reyes, *Asia Pacific Women's Studies* Journal 1992, Institute of Women's Studies Manila.
5. *Review and Appraisal of the Implementation of the Nairobi Forward-looking Strategies for the Advancement of Women,* Report of the Secretary-General, A/C.167, 31 October 1994, p. 11.
6. Brazilin writer Jacqueline Pitanguy, IPU Symposium,"Women and Government." p. 49.
7. *Women and Government: New Ways to Political Power* edited by Mim Kelber, Women USA Fund Study, 1994.
8. *Ibid.*
9. See note 5, p.149.

WOMEN AND WORK

Women, of course, have always worked. Today, in addition to the traditional unpaid labour required to maintain a household, which often involves growing food and securing water and fuel supplies, women increasingly take on paid work outside the home to augment personal and family income.

The world over, these dual responsibilities—respectively termed "reproductive" and "productive" by social scientists—have always played a vital role in human economic activity. Although women as workers have traditionally been regarded as dependent adjuncts of their husbands, partners or closest male kin, the rapid influx of women into labour markets worldwide over the past three decades has become a key factor in the growing independence of women, economically, socially and legally.

Increasingly, too, their "household" work, long taken for granted, is being acknowledged as a central contribution to society's wealth.

Similarly, their right to equality with working men is finally being recognized. Equally important, the new-found economic independence of millions of women has inevitably caused dramatic transformation of women's self-image, their growing sense of independence as well as mounting responsibilities and expectations at home and in their communities.[1]

Towards Equality

Although women now constitute 30 per cent of the global industrial force, legal hurdles and traditional barriers still hinder the vast majority of women in their efforts to achieve parity with men.

The pioneering efforts of the International Labour Organization (ILO) led the way for increased world attention on the concerns of working women. Many ILO principles and standards were integrated much later into the **Convention on the Elimination of All Forms of Discrimination Against Women (CEDAW),** which was adopted by the UN in 1979. CEDAW clearly spells out the fundamental rights of women in the work force:

- The right to work as an inalienable human right;
- Equal employment opportunities, including the application of the same criteria for hiring;
- The rights to promotion, job security and vocational training and retraining;
- The right to equal pay for equal work—still far from a reality in nearly all countries.

CEDAW also outlines the rights of rural women to help overcome the special problems they face in their vital—usually unpaid—roles in agriculture:

- Participation in development planning at all levels;
- Access to extension services;
- Organization of self-help groups and cooperatives;
- Access to credit and loans, marketing facilities; appropriate technology and equal access to land and other property.

In addition, building upon ILO's 1952 **Convention on Maternity Protection**, CEDAW includes provisions for the recognition of maternity as a social function. It calls for the establishment of services, notably child-care facilities, "to enable parents to combine family obligations with work."

Above and beyond these basic rights, women need more access to economic resources and control over them. Land, capital, technology and, increasingly, information. The work of many UN organizations has sought to support advancement in these areas. Some example:

- **Land**: Since its 1979 World Conference on Agrarian Reform and Rural Development, the Food and Agriculture Organization (FAO) has encouraged Governments to focus on land use within a household unit—notably the plot on which the women of the house grows food, rather than cash crops, which tend to be produced by men- and to design programmes of land redistribution in response to women's needs;
- **Capital**: Since the 1980s, UNICEF, like many other members of the UN family—notably the World Bank and the International Fund for Agricultural Development— has worked to expand women's access

to credit. In Cartagena, Colombia, for example, it has helped form "solidarity groups" of three to five women who operate the same kind of business in the informal sector and who need small sums to expand their enterprises. Peer pressure to repay, in addition to the incentives of further and larger loans, as well as technical assistance in management and marketing, has resulted in a repayment rate of nearly 100 per cent;[2]

- **Technology**: The United Nations Development Fund for Women (UNIFEM) has funded workshops for women farmers in Indonesia Malaysia and Thailand on the use of locally produced, environmentally sound pesticides, rather than costly, hazardous, imported chemicals;[3]
- **Information**: the United Nations Development Programme (UNDP) has funded projects on data gathering and media production to give rural women access to information technology.

UNDP and other agencies place a great deal of emphasis on the design of projects that further the integration of women in development. As UNDP Administrator James Gustave Speth explains:"........ sustainable human development is people-centred, participatory, pro-poor and therefore pro-women."[4]

Paid Work

Many forces are channelling women increasingly into the world of paid work. These include:

- Widespread decreases in male income;
- Impoverished rural homesteads;
- Changing family structures, notably the emergence of female-headed households;
- Heightened expectations, especially for children;
- Urbanization;
- Expanded educational and career opportunities;
- Reach of telecommunications into remote areas;
- Industrialization;
- Consumerism.

Women's participation in the labour market, both formal and informal, during the last decade has frown an average of 10 per cent in all regions of the world-twice the rate of men.[5]

In developing countries, the per centage of women in the paid labour force force increased from 28 per ccnt in 1950 to 41 per cent in 1993.[6] The average ratio of women to men in the economically active population-according to ILO, all who provide labour for the production of economic goods and services- doubled worldwide between 1970 and 1990:

- In **Africa**, from 39 to 71 women for each 100 men;
- In **Latin America and the Caribbean**, from 35 to 62;
- In **Western Europe and North America**, from 45 to 72;
- In **Asia and the Pacific,** from 28 to 48, most markedly from 1970 to 1980;
- In **Eastern Europe,** from 79 to 85.[7]

The Wage Gap

On average, women the world over receive 30 to 40 per cent less than men for work of comparable value—whether in cash or kind, in benefits or food. In cash terms alone, women's earnings continue to fall short of men's:

- In the United Kingdom, women earn on average 70 per cent of men's wages;
- In Kenya, 74 per cent;
- In Brazil,51 per cent;
- In the Republic of Korea, 51 per cent;
- In Japan, 43 per cent.[8,9]

Nor has national legislation succeeded in bridging the pervasive wage gap. Where it has begun to narrow, as in many developed countries, it is due not only to increased paychecks for women, but shrinking salaries for men.[10]

Higher Unemployment

Women also represent a disproportionate share of the unemployed in every age group and in every region:

- In some **Latin American and Caribbean** countries, women account for more than two thirds of total unemployment; their unemployment rate is double that of men;
- In **Eastern and Central Europe**, female unemployment has risen to an alarming 60 per cent since the collapse of Communist regimes beginning in 1988;
- Even in **Asia**, where women have moved rapidly into export manufacturing in the newly industrialized countries (NICs), available data indicate higher unemployment rates for women than for men in China, Indonesia, Malaysia, Pakistan, Philippines, Thailand and Sri Lanka. In Indonesia, the unemployment rate for women who have finished secondary school is almost twice as high as for their male counterparts.[11]

The Formal Sector— New Opportunities, New Problems

Since the early days of the Industrial Revolution in the Western world and now the world over, women have tended to find work in the formal sector only in low-wage, low-status jobs, whether in manufacturing or services:

- Manufacturing work often reflects traditional female household tasks, such as processing and serving food and producing textiles and clothing;
- Office work usually entails women serving men. Clerical and secretarial work, both in the private and public sectors, has been feminized almost universally.[12]

In today's world of work, in both developed countries and the NICs, women are moving rapidly into the areas of highest growth:

- Light industry—women, who for centuries performed skilled tasks of sewing, basket-making and handicrafts, now produce precision instruments and electronic parts;
- Informatics—women perform data-entry tasks rather than programming or repair;
- Modern services, such as finance or communications- in which, women are more likely to staff the switchboard than to occupy the boardroom.[13]

According to the united Nations Industrial Development Organization (UNIDO), women in industry in the mid-1990s find themselves in a world very different from the previous decade. The globalization of industrial production, the structural adjustment programmes in many developing countries, and the transformation of centrally planned economies have also had fundamental effects on the industrialization process. Production has shifted from labour-intensive, assembly-line oriented systems to become skill-and technology-intensive, and from import-substitution to export-led growth and trade.

The competitive advantage enjoyed by developing countries, often based on plentiful and cheap labour, is gradually being eroded by increasing technological innovations and competition from other labour markets. The introduction of computerized technologies and automation has reduced the importance of labour-intensive production significantly, rendering predominantly "typically female" occupations redundant, *i.e.,* low-skilled assembly jobs in industrialized as well as industrializing countries.

Within this context, women have borne the brunt of technological redundancy and unemployment brought about by industrial restructuring, technological changes and relocation patterns. Insofar as one can speak of global cultural biases as pertains to gender, this is a remaining vestige: women tend to have less technological training then men. Women at all levels are losing ground because technologies are playing an increasing role in all services.

- According to UNIDO, in general, when technologies are introduced to a sector, women with few or no skills are displaced by men.
- Educated women in transition economies are finding that their specific skills have become obsolete.
- Men have been targeted almost exclusively for retraining. Women need to build on the skills they already possess through upgrading or retraining, to make them competitive in the very markets which have now rendered them unemployed.

Women in management also need t acquire new skills in order to maintain their positions. Women entrepreneurs and managers need to adjust to new structures, which require a combination of skills in technology, reading markets, product design and adaptation, quality control, pricing, marketing, personnel management, leadership.

In the NICs, women constitute some 80 per cent for the workforce of export-oriented manufacturing-not only because of their manual dexterity, according to Lin Lean Lim, an ILo Senior Specialist, but perhaps even more important because of "their greater docility.. deference to command, willingness to subject themselves to the rigid discipline and tedious monotony of the assembly line and their lower likelihood to form or join unions".[14]

Yet as one Asian labour expert has remarked, "With industrialization, women in the Asian NICs have for the first time in history been able to earn incomes instead of playing the centuries old role of unpaid mother-wife-labourer."[15]

The increasing flexibility of today's markets -changes in regulations, contracts, and practices that make it easier both to hire and fire workers- has laos opened new pathways for women to enter the formal sector.

- Part time work is increasingly a female phenomenon; in almost all developed economies, the majority of those employed part-time are women.[16]

While many labour leaders fear that this trend may undermine hard-won rights, reduce career prospects and weaken both job protection and social security, women's groups since the 1960s have argued that greater flexibility in working hours as well as part-time arrangements can benefit workers and their families.

- "There is a danger of judging.. the operation of the labour market according to standards which see full-time, life-long jobs... as the desirable 'norm' to which all workers aspire......", said labour expert Diane Elson.[17] "This is a male norm that most women have never enjoyed and many women do not want".

- "As long as the rights of workers are safeguarded," said Susan Bullock, "the disintegration on traditional forms of "regular work' may create the basis for progressive social transformation."

By contrast, others feel that this kind of employment for women may represent a trade-off of quantity for quality and may eventually lead to paring down benefits such as health care, maternity leave and unemployment insurance.

Women as Business Owners and Managers

The results of women entrepreneurs...... may be misjudged if compared to men's. The mystique of entrepreneurship, often male-centred, needs to be understood so as to make room for both men's and women's entrepreneurial styles. Men and women become entrepreneurs for different reasons. At the risk of oversimplification, it could be said that while men go into business to make a killing, women go into business hoping to make a living.[18]

—Claire L. Bangasser, *Women Entrepreneurs*

Women are increasingly turning to self-employment and establishing their own enterprises.

- In the United States and Canada, women own 30 per cent of all businesses. In the US, women are forming small businesses at almost twice the rate of men and employ one worker out of every ten—more people than all the Fortune 500 companies combined.
- In **Latin America**, women represent 15 to 20 per cent of all employers, concentrated largely in the commercial and service sectors. [19]

Women go into business for themselves for all sorts of reasons, ranging from limited opportunities elsewhere to entrepreneurial drive.

- The fact that she was nine months pregnant did not deter 35-year-old Jane Royston from convincing a group of senior Swiss managers that they needed the services and products of the small software company she had founded in 1987; she had grown tired of hitting her head on the "glass ceiling" of the multinational for which she worked. In 1993, she was named Swiss businesswoman of the year.[20]
- Half a world away in an Indian slum, 30 year-old Elvasrasi cooks savoury breakfast rice for customers on a tiny stove outside her mud hut. Her decision to become an entrepreneur stemmed from despair at watching her husband drink himself unconscious as her children starved.[21]

Women on The Land

The women of Africa with very poor technology have managed to feed that continent. They are empowering those Governments that would have collapsed had there been a food crisis. And the women of Asia are empowering their male Governments by their informal activities that now compose the breakthrough in Asian trade balances.

- Gertrude Mongella, Secretary-General of the Fourth World Conference on Women, Informal remarks, 8 March 1994

Subsistence agriculture still dominates the working lives of more than half the world's women. The true value of their labour, says the International Fund for Agricultural Development (IFAD), is difficult to measure because so few of their activities are monetized.

- In **Asia** alone, some 375 million landless female labourers— more then Western Europe's entire population - perform exhausting menial chores like weeding, hoeing and milling, while living with the concern that the increasing mechanization of agriculture will deprive them of the seasonal work to which they still have access.[22]
- In **Africa**, women produce 78 per cent of the continent's food-meat as well as staple grains—on subsistence plots to which the vast majority hold no title. They receive only 2 to 13 per cent of the technical assistance and training provided by extension services.[23] Lack of ownership often bars them from loans that could improve their small and often marginal lands.
- Although statistics for **Latin America** are sparse—in large measure because women are seen primarily as housewives—it is estimated that almost half of family income in the overcrowded and poor small-farm sector is generated by women and that on many such holdings, women are replacing men as the mainstay of farm labour.[24]

The Informal Sector

The data on women working in the informal sector reveal a mix of positive and negative trends. Flexible, precarious and now far more dynamic than the formal sector in many regions, the informal sector has always absorbed female labour and continues to do so.

Between 70 and 90 per cent of women in developing countries now work in businesses that are unregistered and largely unregulated—and under conditions that frequently threaten health and are sometimes tantamount to slavery.[25]

The good news is that the changes-the opening of markets, the trend toward privatization, the encouragement of entrepreneurship —are also opportunities.

Governments in developing countries seeking new sources for promoting economic growth will find hitherto untapped potential in many small-scale, informal activities traditionally conducted by women. In the majority of developing countries, women make a substantial contribution to output and value added of the manufacturing sector. Small-scale industries constitute one of the areas where women's role is most pronounced. Because of the lack of opportunities for them in the formal sector, they take up or take part in activities in the informal production sector out of necessity, and now dominate that sector.

Yet, the entrepreneurial potential that exists in these activities is rarely realized beyond the basic level required to sustain the family. According to UNIDO, despite the importance of the informal sector for overall economic growth, and women's dominant position in it, they do not receive support. The large number of women in small-scale and micro-industries often lack access to resources to fulfill their production and profit potential, and to alternatives to technologies and production methods detrimental to themselves and to the environment.

Micro-enterprises

Women today own and operate approximately half of the world's micro-enterprises according to UN estimates. At a time when the formal job market is failing to provide employment for the 43 million job seekers who now enter the workforce each year, these micro-enterprises furnish between 40 and 66 per cent of urban employment:[26]

- Many are extensions of agricultural activities, such as the processing and marketing of home-grown produce and fishing catches;
- Other comprise cottage crafts such as basketry, weaving, the crafting of clay utensils for cooking and storing food and other handmade products;
- Still others are flourishing services such as trading used goods, dressmaking operations and curbside beauty salons.

The case of entry to such work makes it a natural option for women who face obstacles in the formal labour market. According to the ILO, the other major characteristics of these informal enterprises are:

- Reliance on local resources;
- Family ownership;
- Small-scale operations;
- Labour-intensive work, using low-cost technology;
- The use of skills acquired outside schooling;
- An irregular and competitive market.[27]

Such micro-businesses have been hailed as evidence of women's resourcefulness and entrepreneurial skill, vital counterparts to failed efforts at industrialization or rural development.

Homeworking

A contemporary form of the piecework system in which pay is based on the units produced and which has faded in most affluent societies, "homeworking" provides income—usually at a pittance—to millions of women throughout the developing world who are tied to domestic chores, especially child care, throughout the working day.

It incudes, for example, the production of lacework and embroidery and the rolling of "beedis", the poor man's cigarette on the Indian subcontinent. Often it is the last stage in a sub-contracting chain that assembles or produces goods for Western markets: toys, garments, shoes, lampshades—and components for high-tech industries.[28]

Child Labour

To secure family survival, many parents throughout the developing world indenture their children, particularly their daughters, as domestics and slave-like semi-skilled labour in under ground enterprises that evade regulations of minimum wages and maximum hours:

- In India's match factories, girls below the age of 15 work for up to 10 hours a day.[29]
- In Peru alone, 1.5 million girls are live-in maids, whose education is often neglected and they are frequently subject to sexual abuse.[30]

Child labour is also flourishing a new in economies in transition: petty criminals use minors to evade law enforcement in the former Soviet Union and girls sweatshops are cropping up elsewhere in Eastern Europe.

Migrant Labour

While not strictly a characteristic of the informal sector, migrant work often fits in this category. In their search for livelihoods, women are moving not only from the countryside to cities, but from one country to another:

- In **Latin America and the Caribbean**, women's migration has reached the same levels as men's;
- According to Lin Lean Lim's paper "Women at Work in Asia and the Pacific: Recent Trends and Future Challenges," for the UN/ILO International Forum on Equality for Women in the World of Work, the demand for male guest workers is slackening because of a slowdown

in construction in the Middle East. Instead it is women who give up hearth and family for work overseas, mainly as housemaids, entertainers (including prostitutes), nurses and helpers in retail shops and restaurants. Many Asian countries, he says, "have come to rely increasingly on 'the comparative advantage of women's disadvantages'."[31]

Because of their relative lack of information and security, women are far more likely than men:

- To be charged exorbitant fees for finding work abroad;
- To find that these jobs involve prostitution or domestic service;
- To be promised wages that are never paid.

Another reason why female migrant workers tend to be more vulnerable, explains Lim, is that they go into individualized situations, such as domestics in households, where there is greater isolation and lower likelihood of establishing networks of information and support compared to men working in groups, such as on construction sites.[32]

Organizing Women

When we are isolated, we are weak. How can there be a noise from a single hand? But if we form a group and then clap, a loud noise can be made.

— Working Women's Forum/UNICEF film

Much of the upsurge in grass-roots efforts to fulfill basic needs and to win human rights in both reproductive and productive work has resulted from the action of women's organizations.

- In Ahmedabad, India, since 1972, the Self-Employed Women's Association (SEWA) -which also means "service" in Hindi) has organized home-workers, hawkers and small vendors into savings and credit cooperatives to provide working capital to its members, as well as better prices for their goods. It also offers training in traditional male skills such as carpentry, plumbing, radio repair, accounting and management. It has also secured legal recognition for women in the informal sector as workers and access to the rights embodied in labour legislation.[33]
- In Sierra Leone in 1976, the women farmers who joined the Kassasi Women's Agricultural Organization (KWADA) drained and cultivated a communal swampland to increase food supplies and income. The sale of the first harvest subsidized the next larger one. Accorded a respect they had never known previously, the women became involved in the decision-making of their village.[34]

The Feminization of Poverty

The workforce for the most precarious and least-rewarding work in the informal sector remain the most poorly paid. Extreme poverty, which is distinguished by the inability to obtain adequate nutrition and essential non-food requirements, shackles more than 1.3 billion people the world over, roughly one-fifth of the global population, according to UNDP. Many of those who fall into this category are women. Some put the figure as high as 70 per cent.

Although largely a phenomenon of developing countries, extreme poverty is no stranger to affluent societies. There, too, the brunt is borne by women:

- By the end of the 1980s, approximately 75 per cent of all poverty in the United States was concentrated among women, particularly single mothers and older African-American women, many of whom head households of grandchildren. The number of families headed by poor women is rising by some 100,000 each year;
- Without welfare payments, 70 per cent of all single mothers with dependent children in the Netherlands would slip below the poverty line.[35]

Throughout the developing world, notably is its rural areas, it is not uncommon to find households in which women's and children's malnutrition coexist with male spending on such comparative luxuries as digital watches and transistor radios:[36]

- When family income sinks, poor women—and often their working daughters— make sacrifices to maintain the welfare of their husbands, sons and brothers.
- In Bangladesh, women wage-earners in poor households have only 1.3 meals a day as compared to 2.4 eaten by men.[37]
- When poverty threatens or strikes, women's assets are often sold before those of men.[38]
- Once poverty reaches a point perceived as desperate in many societies, men sometimes abandon their families, leaving the mothers with impossible responsibilities.[39]
- The privatization of traditional common properties—woodlands, meadows, springs, ponds and streams—affects poor rural women severely, especially where they still perform the traditional tasks of gathering fuel, fodder and water for their households.[40]

Economies in Transition

The transition from Communism to market economies in Central and Eastern Europe has radically lowered living standards and impoverished many women—among them the highly skilled and educated:

- In a gender backlash, male mangers are recruiting men even in previously femaledominated sectors.[41]
- In its report to the UN's Division for the Advancement of Women in 1993, the Government of Kyrgyzstan concluded that "the feminization of poverty has become the distinctive feature of the post-Soviet period." Three quarters of that country's unemployed are women. In Poland, women accounted for almost 60 per cent of the school graduates registered as unemployed. Only in the Czech Republic has women's unemployment remained unchanged in the shift to market economies.[42]
- A 1991 survey in the Russian Federation revealed that a growing number of men feel that a women's place is in the home. In the media, many social problems, including increases in petty crime, have been blamed on "the emancipation of women"[43]

Nonetheless, in many of these countries, women are taking on entrepreneurial roles in small businesses that they could not have assumed under Communism. Women retain a dominant position in the less remunerative services of several Central European countries— education, health and social care— and their share in these occupations is increasing.[44]

The Impact of Structural Adjustment

"Women have been at the centre of the (economic crisis of the 1980s) and have home the brunt of adjustment efforts," declared the Commonwealth Expert Group on Structural Adjustment.[45]

Although apparently gender-neutral, structural adjustment programmes (SAPs) have demanded more of women than of men in both the formal and informal sectors of the economy. They reduced services essential to family welfare and, in many cases, reversed female economic gains achieved during the three prior decades.

Everywhere, government cuts in social services, including food subsidies, have increased the burden of poor working women, especially for those who head households. Many have resorted to bare survival strategies, among these:

- Reducing family consumption of fundamental necessities, including food;
- Withdrawing their children, particularly daughters, from school;
- Sending their children— even bonding them—into demeaning and often dangerous work, including prostitution and foraging in dumps.

"Women's health has been adversely affected by increased hours of work and by reduced availability of food and health care facilities," the Commonwealth Expert Group on Structural Adjustment reported." Less healthy women are less efficient and this reduces their productivity in each of their roles, thereby diminishing national health and welfare." Others have pointed out related problems:

- Malnutrition rates among children rose by 50 per cent in both Ghana and Peru during the first half of the 1980s. Nutrition deficiency—related deaths increased by 20 per cent in Zaire between 1981 and 1987;[46]
- Of the poorest countries implementing structural adjustment policies, 37 halved their health budgets, shifting health care costs almost entirely onto poor mothers, just as prices of essential medicines soared to prohibitive heights;[47]
- Female school enrolments dropped by as much as 50 per cent in many rural areas of Africa as school fees were introduced and families withdrew their girls from class to help grow food, perform other household chores and earn money outside the home;
- In post-Communist Central and Eastern Europe, the closure of childcare facilities formerly paid for by Governments has forced women to reduce their dwindling incomes by paying for such services or to reduce their paid working hours.

Strategies for Reducing Female Poverty

"The feminization of poverty raises complex questions as to the role of the welfare state in the reduction of poverty,"states the UN Division for the Advancement of Women (DAW). "It has become apparent that the simple redistribution of income by means of government transfers does not always work towards a solution to the problem of poverty, let alone the reversal of the feminization trend, and that it often leads to the perpetuation of both."[48]

At present, there are three major approaches to reducing female poverty that move away from traditional State-controlled safety nets:

- Emphasis on the role of the market in creating income-generating opportunities for women. An important aspect of this approach is recognition that the sustainable basis for economic growth—rather than the rate of growth—determines whether it will benefit or marginalize women.
- Emphasis on expanding the rights of the poor, notably through education, training, credit, information, and participation in development planning. The challenge is to maximize the potential of the market, minimize its hostile influences and provide public assistance in the

least distortive way.

- A third approach to the eradication of female poverty" requires the recognition of women's economic potential and should aim at enhancing women's capabilities," concludes DAW." Conversely, the agenda for development should begin with targeting women in poverty, because time and again experience shows that any approach to poverty reduction that leaves the economic status of women unchanged tends not to achieve its goal."[49]

Revaluing Women's Work

Within traditional GDP and GNP categories [the measure of Gross Domestic and Gross National Products], the whole spectrum of social productivity from the reproduction of human beings in the household to the maintenance of relationships that promote the cohesion of the community are ignored. The devaluing of this work runs parallel to the subordinate status of women, since it is women who do most of this 'caring and sustaining'. To link productivity only with paid employment continues to render invisible the enormous amount of unpaid work that women do that undergirds and subsidizes all other kinds of work.

—Juan Somavia, summation of the exchange of views of the first session of the Preparatory Committee for the World Summit for Social Development, 1993

The world over, women's dual responsibilities, even in affluent societies, translate into longer working hours than those of men, many unpaid.

Some experts hold that if women's unpaid work were factored into national accounting systems, GDP would increase by 30 to 40 per cent:

- Argentina has calculated the value of the domestic activity carried on by its women and estimates that it amounts to between 28 per cent and 49 per cent of its GDP.

In its report submitted to CEDAW, Argentina has stressed the need for domestic production to be included among the indicators of national production.

- In certain provinces of Argentina, local legislation has provided for retirement pensions for housewives. A Housewives' Union has been organized, with more than 80,000 members in 30 branches throughout the country, that provides medical services to its members. It has submitted a bill which envisages a wage for housewives, pension rights and their own social security:

The United Nations International Research and Traning Institute for the Advancement of Women (INSTRAW), in collaboration with UN Statistical Division, has developed a framework for counting and valuing the unpaid and usually invisible economic contributions of women by measuring their use of time:

- In one developing country, a typical women's day was 30 hours long, after housework and child care (some of these tasks performed simultaneously) were calculated and added to the task of growing the family's food.[50]

Although women's tasks in household management differ from rural to urban areas, from region to region, and from class to class, their responsibilities in family care *vis-a-vis* men remains largely predominant. For this reason the equal sharing of household responsibilities with male partners is an improvement that would have immediate and widespread impact on the quality of women's lives.

- Mothers and mother-surrogates are responsible not only for the physical well being of children, but their cognitive development as well. Since children "process" more information during the first two years of life than in all the years to come, their mothers are their most important educators.
- Women's traditional roles also encompass the care of the elderly' given increasing life expectancy the world over, women will be responsible for extended care of their relatives.
- The line between family and community of often thin. Women not only organize the parent-teacher association in affluent North American suburbs, but communal kitchens in the slums of South American cities.

During the last 20 years, the issue of home-making as a fulfilling career for women has received growing attention:

- A 1992 ILO survey carried out in the Czech and Slovak republic revealed that only 28 per cent of married working women would willingly give up their jobs if their husbands salaries increased sufficiently. By contrast, 43 per cent of the men interviewed stated they would prefer their wives to stay at home if the household could afford it .

Obstacles, Trends and goals

According to Lin Lean Lim, author of a paper entitled "Women at Work in Asia and the Pacific: Recent Trends and Future Challenges," appropriate policies and programmes for women's productive employment would offer a window of opportunity for countries to get out of the poverty trap and would also promote the social integration of currently excluded groups. [51]

The planning of productive employment options for women should include:

- Finding innovative and effective alternatives (beyond social safety nets) for the protection and organization of women workers in various types of vulnerable situations;
- Promoting female entrepreneurship and encouraging and supporting the successful setting up of micron-enterprises by women, especially those in the informal sector;
- Helping women cope with the impact of new technologies, which will necessitate:
  - — Providing appropriate skills training and retraining programmes;
  - — Strengthening labour relations so that employers and workers together can establish procedural rules for the introduction of technology changes and related problems;
  - — Improving the advertising of job opportunities in the labour market;
  - — Providing social protection and retraining for those suffering technological unemployment.

Some trends are the focus of growing concern, such as:

- Government negligence in bringing laws into conformity with CEDAW and ILO conventions;
- Practices and attitudes, notably sexual harassment, that tend to perpetuate occupational segregation;
- The danger of marginalizing female labour in tight job markets;
- Emergence of the "glass ceiling" the world over in which female executives are stalled in middle-management jobs.

Nonetheless, other emerging trends are promoting gender equality in the working world. The growing need and /or preference of women to work outside the household is liberalizing traditional male and female attitudes towards paid work, even in countries where women have been secluded.

Partly as result of these changing attitudes, new opportunities and career paths are opening up for women the world over— from construction and metal-working trades in Latin America, East Africa and North America to engineering, urban planning, finance and international law among university-educated women.

To assure that these advances of women in the area of work continue, the priority goals of guaranteeing women equal access to employment opportunities and equal pay for work of equal value are likely to remain at the top of the women's agenda.

Notes

1. Preliminary Version of the 1994 *World Survey on the Role of Women in Development*, E/1994/86, para. 18
2. Wignaraja, Ponna, *Women, Poverty and Access to Credit*, UNICEF, New York, 1988, p. 90.
3. Bullock, Susan, *Women and Work*, published by Atlantic Highlands, New Jersey, and Zed Books, London, 1994, p. 51.
4. *Heading for Change*, UNDP 1993 Annual Report, p.1.
5. *Review and Appraisal of the Nairobi Forward-looking Strategies for the Advancement of Women*, Report of the Secretary-General, Draft A/C.167, 31 October 1994, p. 92.
6. *Ibid.*, p.93.
7. *Ibid.*, p.92.
8. *Women: Challenges to the Year* 2000, United Nations, New York, 1991, p. 44.
9. Lim, Lin Lean, "Women at Work in Asia and the Pacific: Recent Trends and Future Challenges", paper for the International Forum on Equality for Women in the World of Work: Challenges for the Future, Geneva, June 1994, p.1.
10. See note 1, para. 26.
11. See note 9, p. 2.
12. See note 5, p. 96
13. See note 5, p. 21; also see note 3, pp. 70-86.
14. See note 9, pp. 2-3.
15. See note 3, p.72.
16. See note 5, p. 19.
17. See note 3, p. 33.
18. Bangasser, Claire L., *Women Entrepreneurs*, UN Expert Group Meeting on Women and Decision-making, 1994.
19. *Ibid.*, p.1.
20. *Ibid.*, p.1.
21. *Ibid.*, p.9.
22. IfAD, "Banking on Women: Facts and Figures", press release for the publication of *The State of World Rural Poverty*, New York, 1992.
23. See note 5, p.112.
24. IFAD, *Report on Rural Women Living in Poverty*, Geneva, 1992, p. 29.
25. See note 3, pp. 56-59.
26. *Ibid.*, p. 59
27. *Ibid.*, p. 56.
28. *Ibid.*, pp. 63-65.
29. UNICEF, unpublished manuscript, *Children in Especially Difficult Circumstances* (CEDC) p. 11.
30. *Ibid.*, p. 31.
31. See note 9, p. 3.
32. *Ibid.*, p. 8.
33. UNDP *Human Development Report* 1993, p. 87.
34. See note 3, p.126.
35. See note 5, p.30.
36. Jacobson, Jodi L., "Closing the Gender Gap in Development" in *State of the World 1993: A Worldwatch Institute Report on Progress towards a Sustainable Society*, New York, 1993, p. 68.
37. See note 5, p. 32.
38. See note 5, pp. 31-32
39. *Ibid.*

40. *Ibid.*, p.108
41. *Ibid.*, p.13.
42. *Ibid.*, pp. 29 and 13.
43. *Ibid.*, p.15.
44. *Ibid.*, p.13.
45. *Engendering Adjustment for the 1990s; Report of a Commonwealth Expert Group on Women and Structural Adjustment*, London, 1989, P. 18.
46. *Ibid.*, p.70
47. Dr. Sadik, Nafis, *Investing in Women: The focus of the '90s*, UNFPA, pp. 9-10.
48. See note 5, p.30.
49. See note 5, p.32.
50. "Time as a Tool: Bridging the Gender Gap", *INSTRAW News* 21, second semester 1994, p. 10.
51. See note 9, p. 6.

WOMEN AND HEALTH

The health status of women and the disparties in health between the sexes are often critical indicators of equity in a society.

—*Intersectoral Action for Health,* WHO 1986

Women throughout their lives have unequal access to health-care systems and services relative to men a fact that has received serious attention only since the 1985 Nairobi Conference on Women. In recent years, health-care services have expanded globally reaching out to both men and women in larger numbers. However, the special needs of women are often overlooked by health-care professionals and planners.

This is as true in the developed world as in developing regions, and especially so in the case of poor women.

Since the situation has not improved in any dramatic way in recent decades, women's health is now a central concern reflected in the Draft Platform for Action of the Fourth World Conference on Women in September 1995. The Draft Platform proposes several measures- from providing universal family-planning services to non-formal health education for women and girls— that can be implemented at the local, national and international levels in order to increase women's access, throughout their lives, to appropriate, affordable and quality health care and related services.

The **Global Commission on Women's Health,** [1] established by the World Health Assembly in 1992 to advance the cause of women's health, considers it imperative to look at women's health within a life-cycle perspective; in other words, throughout the evolving stages of a women's life. The health conditions in one phase of a women's life not only affect subsequent phases of her own life, but also have an impact on future generations. This intergenerational link is a characteristic unique to women.

In this chapter, we follow the life-cycle approach to explain some of the more important health concerns of women.

Girl Child

The health of women is a telling window on female inequality, and it is most telling at the most vulnerable time of life: infancy and early childhood.

—*Girls and Women: A UNICEF Development Priority, 1993*

The girl child, as UNICEF categorizes the female child up to the age of 15, has become the focus of attention in recent years. Several areas, such as education, work and health, are being re-examined with the specific needs of the girl child in mind.

As today's girl is tomorrow's women and will bear the responsibility for a new generation, it is imperative that the health needs of girls are met.

In many societies and families, **early childhood** can be a severe test of survival for the girl child.

Although female children enjoy the biological advantage of being more resistant to infection and malnutrition, the mortality rate of the girl child in the two-to-five age group is higher than that of the boy child in the same age group in a number of developing countries:[2]

- In Bangladesh, the under-five mortality rate for girls was recorded as 175 per 1,000 live births, as against 160 for boys and in Nepal, 187 for girls as against 173 for boys. In India, there are 957 females aged four years or less for every 1,000 males in the population:[3]

Why this discrepancy? Several studies suggest that the existing higher mortality rates of the girl child in many developing countries are not due to poverty or biological reasons, but because of a preference for boys that can lead to discriminatory treatment of girls in terms of food, basic health provision and even parental care. This male preference has complex historical roots that vary from culture to culture. In many traditional societies, the preference for boys stems on the reliance on males as primary bread-winners and providers of security in the parents' old age,while females are accorded secondary support roles.

Although breast-feeding is a traditional practice in developing regions, some traditions negatively affect the girl child. One such tradition, practised particularly in Africa, Asia and the Middle East, is early weaning of a female infant—usually intended to enable early conception of another child, preferably a male.

Curtailing breast-feeding deprives a baby girl not only of nutrients and antibodies in her mothers milk but also of maternal interaction and bonding that is essential for latercognitive and psychological development.

UNICEF and WHO have consistently and vigorously promoted **breast-feeding** in their safe-motherhood programmes and they have also identified another reason for a decline in breast-feeding, especially in the industrial world: the promotion of infant-food formulas by the baby-food industry as a substitute for mother's milk.

The early 1970s thus saw the beginning of an international campaign to stop the inappropriate promotion of breast-milk substitutes, particularly where poverty, unavailability of potable water and illiteracy prevail. UN agencies have joined with NGOs in a worldwide effort to encourage breast-feeding of both girls and boys:

- In 1981, the World Health Assembly adopted the International Code of Marketing of Breast-milk Substitutes—the code calls for broad restrictions on certain practices, including a ban on advertising of breast-milk substitutes to the public and their promotion in health-care systems.
- In 1991, UNICEF and WHO launched the "baby-friendly hospital initiative", which encourages hospitals to adopt practices that support breast-feeding. To date, this is supported by 144 nations.[4]

Women and girls often have a secondary place in the nutritional priorities of families, especially in developing countries and in areas of extreme poverty.

Through nutritional equality between boys and girls was recognized as a critical concern at the **International Conference on Nutrition** in Rome in 1992 girls often suffer disproportionately from malnutrition, especially when prevailing customs or beliefs sanction preference for boys.

In some countries, a bias in favour of males determines nutritional intake. In areas where a preference for sons is strong, girls get a smaller percentage of their food needs satisfied than do boys. Boys also tend to get the more nutritious food:

- The typical girl in these countries, according to UNICEF's 1989 **Annual Report**, receives 20 per cent fewer calories than her brother and is more likely to be malnourished.
- In one region of India, girls were four times more likely than boys to suffer from acute malnutrition, and 40 times less likely to be taken to hospital.[5]

Malnutrition of female children under the age of five often contributes to their morbidity and mortality from a variety of infections and chronic diseases. Stunted growth caused by protein-energy deficiency in girls is responsible for subsequent problems in childbirth. Malnourished mothers tend to give birth to underweight babies, who, malnourished in the womb, are likely to remain so in the crucial years of early childhood development. (See also Chapter Five, sections on female infanticide and gender-selective abortion.)

Basic Health Care and Immunization

The expansion of primary health care has greatly benefited female children and women. Basic health-care and immunization are now increasingly available to them. However, boys still enjoy an advantage.

Boys are taken more often for medical care when they are sick, and more money is spent on doctors' fees and medicine for them.

Health workers in several developing countries have also noticed that when immunizations are offered free, parents get both boys and girls immunized. When a cash fee is charged, then more boys than girls are brought to the clinics to be immunized:

- In the Kanghura Community Health Project in the Republic of Korea, only half as many girls as boys were brought for measles immunization after a small fee was introduced.[6]

Adolescence

There are many health concerns specific to adolescent girls. Like every growing child, the teenage girl has increased nutritional and health needs. In many cases, these are not adequately met:

- An adolescent girl requires, but rarely gets, 18 per cent more iron per kilogram of body weight then male adolescents. Many adolescent girls suffer from iron deficiency.
- At least 25 per cent of adolescent girls in developing countries are also affected by iodine deficiency. This seriously affects the next generation as iodine deficiency can cause mental retardation and goitre and affects a woman's reproductive functioning, causing brain damage in foetus and in infant.

Teenage Pregnancy

The passage from girlhood to womanhood marks the beginning of concerns connected to a women's biological role in reproduction. Sexual maturity in females has always provoked greater concern than that of males because of the possibility of pregnancy, and, in many cultures, because of the value attached to virginity as a bridal asset.[7]

In many developing countries, women marry at a very young age-around 50 per cent of African women, 40 per cent of Asian women and 30 per cent of Latin American women are married by the age of 18, according to the **World Fertility Survey.** Child-bearing for them also starts early.[8]

Teenage pregnancy is not limited to the developing world. In fact, early child-bearing is a growing trend in several developed countries. It is cause for great concern in industrialized countries because it is increasingly taking place outside of the institution of marriage. These teenage parents are often unable to establish an equal partnership and stable:, relationship, with negative consequences for them and their children:

- In the United States. for example, more than two-thirds of births to adolescent mothers now occur outside of marriage, compared to one-third in 1970[9]; and 30 per cent of all teenage pregnancies end in abortion, while in Norway, a staggering 87.5 per cent of pregnancies of girls under 18 are aborted.[10]
- Aside from the medical and health problems, pregnancy outside marriage puts increased pressure on the young girl who has few, if any, social systems to help her cope with the pregnancy and, later on, with the child. As a result, many choose the option of abortion.
- At least one million and as many as 4.4 million adolescent women have abortions in developing countries each year — most performed illegally and under unsafe conditions.[11]
- Worldwide, nearly 15 million teenage women give birth each year, accounting for up to 10 per cent of all births globally.
- More than 80 per cent of teenage mothers are in developing countries.
- In **Africa,** 50 per cent of women have given birth by age 20, compared to 35 per cent in **Latin America and the Caribbean** and 30 per cent in **Asia,**[12]
- While in **North America,** almost 15 per cent of all births occur to women under the age of 20, in **Europe** it varies with more than seven per cent for northern Europe, 12 per cent for eastern Europe, six per cent for southern Europe and nearly four per cent for western Europe.[13]
- In general the annual number of births per 1.000 women aged 15 to 19 in the more developed regions is 32, the less developed regions is 65 and the least developed countries is 140.[14]

These "children having children" the physically and emotionally immature for child-bearing and rearing. Medical evidence confirms that women who give birth before the age of 20 suffer more complications during birth than women aged 20 to 35 and thus have higher maternal mortality and morbidity rates:

- One quarter of the 500,000 women who die every year from causes related to pregnancy and childbirth are teenagers.[15]
- Teenage mothers suffer more pregnancy and delivery complications including toxemia, iron-deficiency anaemia, premature delivery, prolonged and obstructed labour, hypertensive disorders of pregnancy and even death.

Similarly, the children born to young mothers are at increased risk of mortality and morbidity—often suffering low birth weight that leads to infant death and conditions such as cerebral palsy, autism and learning disabilities.

Current research demonstrates that if adequate prenatal and postnatal care are given to these young mothers and social support, the health risk to them and their children is reduced. There is also evidence that teenage pregnancy often repeats itself in generational cycles, Daughters of teenage mothers are more likely to be teenage mothers themselves:

- In the Philippines, interviews with 108 teenage mothers found that 60 per cent of their mothers were under age 20 at their first birth. [16]
- Similarly in the United States, daughters of teenage mothers are between one-third and two times more likely to be adolescent mothers than are daughters of older mothers.[17]

There are also social consequences of early childbearing. Teenage pregnant girls may face expulsion from school, a lack of career opportunities, low wages, increased welfare dependency and social ostracism.

Some countries in Africa, however, have reversed their policy of expelling pregnant schoolgirls and teenage mothers. In Kenya, for example, the Government reversed its expulsion policy in 1994 and launched a new programme for girls who drop out of school because of pregnancy and early motherhood.

Even where not mandatory, most girls drop out to work to support their children because they lack support services that would enable them to stay in school and take care of their children.

The **programme of Action** adopted at the **International Conference on Population and Development** in Cairo in September 1994 acknowledges that the reproductive health needs of adolescents as a group have been largely ignored to date. The programme thus specifies one of its objectives as being:

To address adolescent sexual and reproductive health issues, including unwanted pregnancy, unsafe abortion, sexually transmitted diseases and HIV/AIDS through the promotion of responsible and healthy reproductive and sexual behaviour, including voluntary abstinence, and the provision of appropriate services and counselling specifically suitable for that age group.

The **Cairo Programme of Action** asks Governments and NGOs to establish educational programmes and health services to address adolescent reproductive needs. Among successful adolescent outreach programmes are:

- **Gente Joven** (Young People), an adolescent programme in urban areas if Mexico. Launched in 1986 by MEXFAM, Mexico's largest private family-planning provider, the programme uses a decentralized, community-based approach, and youth promoters for outreach activities. It has services in 42 cities and towns, reaching a population of 350,000 teenagers. Since its inception, the programme, which was developed to improve sex education and family-planning service delivery for teens, has distributed two million condoms and conducted several educational programmes using radio and a soap-opera format video series;
- The **Health Agents Programme** operates in the slums of Recife in Brazil. One of the programmes of Casa de Passagem, an NGO in Brazil is the Health Agents Programme begun in 1989 training young girls in the slums to become "community health agents", who counsel their peers on a variety of health issues,including family planning, early pregnancy, AIDS education and their basic rights as women. The chief activities include individual and group peer counselling, condom distribution, health prevention presentations and health theatre.

Adult Women

The health of women in the years from 15 to 45 is predominantly influenced by their reproductive and maternal roles.

This is also the period when women are more likely to suffer from illnesses related to their reproductive roles such as sexually transmitted diseases, anaemia, and complications resulting from childbearing.

Globally, 51 per cent of pregnant women and a third of women of reproductive age who are not pregnant are anaemic. This causes fatigue, reduces productivity and lowers their resistance to disease. In pregnancy and childbirth, it means greater risk for the life and health of both mother and child.

The United Nations Decade for Women (1975-1985), the Nairobi Conference on Women in 1985, the Mexico Population Conference in 1984 and the Cairo Population Conference in 1994, all brought the world's attention to the issue of women's reproductive health problems.

The **Global Commission on Women's Health** considers reproductive health as referring to all aspects of well-being related to the reproductive system throughout the life cycle. It encompasses fertility, infertility and the enjoyment of sexual health without fear of disease or unwanted pregnancy.

Women's reproductive health was one of the central themes at the **1994 Cairo World Conference on Population and Development.** Its Programme of Action clearly states that all countries should strive to make reproductive health care—including family-planning counselling, information, education, services for prenatal care, safe delivery and post-natal care—accessible to all through the primary health-care system.

Reproductive health-care programmes must involve women in the leadership, planning, decision-making, management, implementation, organization and evaluation of services. Community participation in reproductive health-care services should also be promoted by decentralizing the management of public-health programmes.

Reproductive Rights

The **The Cairo Programme of Action,** adopted in 1994, affirms that reproductive rights are basic rights for all couples and individuals:

- To decide freely and responsibly the number, spacing and timing of their children;
- To have the information and means to do so;
- To be able to attain the highest standard of sexual and reproductive health;
- To make decisions concerning reproduction free of discrimination, coercion and violence.

For a long time, health and development planners have tended to see women primarily in context of their reproductive role. Thus solutions to women's health needs has by and large been restricted to expansion and improvement of maternal and child systems. Even that has often not been adequate.

Women are increasingly seen today as people possessing reproductive rights, among other human rights. These include:

- The right to safe motherhood;
- The right to plan one's family and have access to full and timely knowl-

edge about all aspects of reproductive health and sexuality.

SAFE MOTHERHOOD

The fact that 1,500 women are being allowed to die each and every year from 'maternal causes' is one of the least-protested scandals of the late 20th century.

—UNICEF, The State of the World's Children 1995

- Every year, approximately half a million women die from causes related to pregnancy, abortions and childbirth.
- According to UNICEF estimates, at least 70,000 of those women die as a result of illegal and unsafe abortions.
- The gap in maternal mortality between developed and developing regions is extremely wide. For at least 99 per cent of maternal mortality cases are in developing countries. Here, maternal mortality is responsible for one-fourth to one-third of all deaths of women of child-bearing age.
- Besides these, there are several thousand more women who survive pregnancy and child birth but remain scarred from the experience with injuries, diseases and disabilities.

The death of a mother has dramatic consequences on the family, especially the young children she leaves behind. When a mother dies, it doubles the death rate of her surviving sons and quadruples that of her daughters.

In contrast to the dramatic decline in infant mortality rates in recent years, there has been no significant reduction in maternal mortality rates in the past two decades.

—Dr. A. Petros-Barvazian, Report to a Workshop on Women's Health, at the meeting of the Task Force on Child Survival, March 1990[18]

As Sue Armstrong and Erica Royston write in the introduction to their book, **Preventing Maternal Deaths**:

....maternal death and injury in developing countries...., is a tragedy that has been largely ignored by those who set national and international health priorities, because those who suffer generally live in remote places, are poor, illiterate and politically powerless.[19]

The great majority of those deaths can be prevented by a combination of:

- Improved family -planning services;
- A wider awareness of the need for immediate hospitalization of problems arise; and
- More traning of district-level hospital staff to provide emergency obstetric care (including Caesarean section).

To respond to the high rates of maternal mortality, the **Safe Motherhood Initiative** was launched in February 1987 at conference in Nairobi co-sponsored by WHO, the World Bank and UNFPA, with support from UNICEF and UNDP. These agencies are now partners in the initiative along with many NGOs and bilateral aid agencies.

The Initiative identified the underlying causes of women's death in childbirth as the lack of proper prenatal care, having too many children, fear of going to the hospital or using contraception, illicit and unsafe abortions, and malnourishment among others

Maternal care can save lives. Sri Lanka, for example, has the same per capita GNP as Pakistan, but a maternal mortality rate taht is one fifth of Pakistan's. WHO attributes this to the fact that almost all births in Sri Lanka are attended by trained personnel, the availability of good family-planning services and high female literacy.[20]

At its inception, the Safe Motherhood Initiative called for political commitment to reallocate priorities and resources to implement the available strategies that can reduce maternal mortality. The need for a comprehensive, multisectoral approach was stressed.

On the most successful strategies used to reduce maternal mortality has been the involvement of **traditional birth attendants (TBSs)** in the process:

- In southern Ethiopia, the Government and an NGO are working together in a district with TBAs, training them in primary health care and visiting them once a month. TBAs are given the responsibility of identifying all the pregnant women in their village and deciding which those are at risk of a complicated delivery and at what stage should be transported to a hospital. For emergencies, a system of village messenger is used to alert the local primary-health-care clinic.[21]

Family Planning

Family planning involves an array of services to help couples have the number of children they want, when they want them. It includes helping infertile couples as well.

Access to contraception is essential. Globally, 57 per cent of couples, where the wife is of reproductive age, use contraception— **nearly a fivefold increase in contraceptive use since the 1960s.**

Much of the decline in average fertility rates for developing countries can be attributed to national family-planning programmes.

Government backing for family-planning programmes has increased in recent years. Between 1976 and 19884, the number of Governments providing direct support for family planing rose from 97 to 125, Governments limiting access to family planning fell from 15 to seven.[22]

Survey data shows that about 120 million women in the developing world who are currently not using family planning say they want to avoid pregnancy and would use a family-planing method if information and services were available and their family and community were supportive.[23]

In developed countries, most women have access to a variety of contraceptive methods. According to recent surveys, in France three per cent of married women were at risk of an undesired pregnancy because they were not using contraception; in the United Kingdom three to five per cent; and the United States four per cent. The level was higher in the countries in transition—in the Czech Republic 13-15 per cent, Hungary 10 per cent and Romania 10-12 per cent. It is, however, important to note that such figures tend to understate the number of women with an"unmet need" for family planning, because they only take account of married women and not of women who are sexually active but not married.[24]

When there is no access to effective methods of contraception, women frequently resort to dangerous, illegal abortions in order to control their fertility. Illegal abortion kills up to 100,000 women a year in developing countries and permanently injures the health of countless more.[25]

Thus the Cairo Programme of Action saw the need for effective and safe family-planning programmes:

All countries should take steps to meet the family-planning needs of their populations as soon as possible and should, in all cases by the year 2015, seek to provide universal access to a full range of safe and reliable family-planning methods.

The Programme of Action also emphasizes men sharing responsibility and actively involving themselves in responsible parenthood, sexual and reproductive behaviour, including family planning; prenatal, maternal and child health.

An example of a successful family-planning programme is **PROFAMILIA** in Colombia, which is responsible for approximately 65 per cent of all family-planning activity in that country. It not only offers family-planning services, but assistance in reproductive health and women's empowerment issues. It has developed innovative programmes that include legal services for women and gender-training workshops as part of the family-planning service delivery. It also conducts workshops on gender issues and analysis for physicians and health personnel.

Contraceptive Choices

The key to improving the quality of family-planning services is a broadening of contraceptive choices. Several modern methods have some undesirable side-effects. There is thus need for more research into better contraceptive technology.

The proper use of many techniques such as Norplant and IUDs requires a good health-care infrastructure, which simply does not exist in many developing countries, particularly in rural areas.

According to Dr. Mahmoud F. Fathalla, Professor of Obstetrics and Gynaecology at the Assuit University in Egypt, contraceptives are meant to empower women and to enable them to maximize their choices, to control their fertility, their sexuality, their health and their lives.

The modern contraceptive revolution was driven largely by policies aimed at lowering the fertility rates and though women benefited, they were not at the centre of the process. This has led to women's concerns about the use of technology to control rather than empower them; about safety issues of contraception and the greater burden of family planning on women as compared with men.[26]

Dr. Fathalla suggests that there is a need for a second contraceptive technology revolution for the 21st century, what he terms, **"contraception-21 initiative",** driven by women's needs and perspectives. In both industrialized and developing regions, the greater burden of responsibility for contraception on women is a concern that needs to be addressed.

Cancer

Cancer is one of the leading causes of mortality in women both in the developed and developing countries especially for those aged 35-55. However, early detection and screening can reduce cancer risks.

The malignant tumours affecting adult women most frequently are breast, cervical, colorectal and stomach cancer. While cancer of the cervix is the most common cancer in developing countries, breast cancer is most frequent in women in industrialized countries:[27]

- At present there are half a million new cases of cervical cancer a year.[28]
- Breast cancer takes the lives of at least 300,000 women each year and it is estimated that 700,000 or more new cases occur each year. This cancer is predominantly found in North America and northern Europe. The probability of developing breast cancer between birth and the age of 75 varies from 1 to 12 per cent depending on the country of residence. The lowest rates are observed in Africa and the highest are among Caucasian women in the US.[29]

SUBSTANCE ABUSE

Smoking currently kills over half a million women each year in the industrialized world. Not only does making cause an increase in lung cancer and cardiovascular diseases, it also affects women's health in ways that are specific to women alone, putting them at added risk:

- Women smokers have higher rates of cervical cancer.
- Those who smoke and use the oral contraceptive pill are several times more likely to develop cardiovascular diseases than those who use neither.
- Smoking also affects women's reproductive health, increasing the risks of earlier menopause, miscarriage and low birthweight babies.[30]

Unfortunately, among young women in many countries, the proportion of smokers is rising most rapidly, even as it is decreasing among young men.[31]

Alcohol use among women has also risen:

- Research shows that women are more sensitive than men to alcohol. A woman absorbs more of the alcohol she drinks into her bloodstream due to a biochemical difference in the stomach lining.
- In the US, where alcohol abuse is a serious public health problem, studies have shown that the average alcohol-dependent women had her life-span shortened by more than 15 years.[32]
- In general, women who drink heavily are more likely than men to develop cirrhosis of the liver.
- Socially, women alcoholics tend to become totally isolated.

Women and girls in fairly large numbers are also users of **psychotropic drugs** such as marijuana, hashish, cocaine, crack-cocaine, heroin and LSD. In addition to all the well-known health risks associated with them, women have further risks associated with drugs:

- Those who use drugs during pregnancy, especially crack-cocaine, run the risk of producing infants with serious birth defects. "Crack babies" suffer withdrawal symptoms after birth, and a high per centage are victims of permanent damage, including physical and sensory problems, learning disabilities and personality disorders.

Increasingly, women's health networks, largely in developed countries, are now expressing concern over the use of legally prescribed psychotropic drugs-minor tranquillizers and other benzodiazepines that have a sedative effect on the brain—among women. Doctors tend to prescribe such drugs more for women than men, even when both report similar psychological symptoms.[33]

STDs AND AIDS

Sexually transmitted diseases (STDs) and reproductive-tract infestions affect women in all walks of life, and they often suffer unnecessarily due to lack of access to appropriate care, poor nutrition and adverse living conditions.

The impact of STDs are severe on young women, since infections have few symptoms and may go untreated.

- An estimated 250 million sexually transmitted infections occur each year with complications including pelvic inflammatory disease, infertility, pelvic pain and life-threatening ectopic pregnancy.

Acquired Immunodeficiency Syndrome (AIDS) has emerged as a major health problem since the mid-1980s for women. A decade ago, women seemed to be on the periphery of the AIDS epidemic, but today almost half of the newly infected adults are women.[34]

According to the Global Commission of Women's Health:

- Every minute worldwide, two women become infected by HIV;
- Every two minutes a woman dies from AIDS;
- More than one million women were infected by HIV in 1993 alone;
- AIDS has become the main cause of death among women as well as men aged 20-40 years in some major cities of the Americas, Europe and sub-Saharan Africa;[35]
- By the year 2000, WHO estimates that over 13 million women will have been infected with HIV and about four million of them will have died;
- Women appear biologically more vulnerable to the HIV infection. Transmission of HIV from men to women is as much as two to ten times more likely than from women to men.

AIDS has serious and often painful implications for women in their role as actual or potential mothers:

- A woman with AIDS will be hindered by ill health in looking after her children;
- As infections among women rise, so do infections in the infants born to them. A woman infected with HIV runs the risk of passing on the infection to her infant. Evidence suggests that between 25 and 40 per cent of infants born to HIV-infected mothers will be infected. Most of these children will die before they are five.

AIDS also presents problems for women who are not HIV-infected themselves but have to care for someone in their family—a spouse, child or sibling-who is infected. As care —providers for long periods of time, these women have to suffer physical, mental and emotional stress from watching a loved one, often in the prime of life, weaken and die.[36]

Violence and Health

The consequence of violence against women has been increasingly recognized as a health -related issue. (Report to Chapter Five for the presentation on violence against women.)

Violence against women leads to psychological trauma, depression, substance abuse, injuries, STDs, HIV infection, suicide and murder.

Based on limited data, the World Bank estimates that in the industrialized countries, rape and domestic violence account for almost one in every five healthy years of life lost to women aged 15 to 44.[37]

There is also the inter-generational effect. Some experts claim that children who have been physically or sexually abused or grown up in families where they have witnessed domestic violence are more likely to be abusive themselves as adults.

NGOs have played an important role in informing women about their human rights (which include the right to be protected from violence); in providing them refuge from such violence, and in supporting them in their claims before the courts.

Elderly Women

As life expectancy increases around the globe, it is estimated that **the number of women over 65 will increase from 330 million in 1990 to 600 million in 2015,** a trend that requires greater attention by policy makers and governments in both developed and developing countries.

Many of these elderly women would have faced poor nutrition, reproductive ill-health, dangerous working conditions, violence and lifestyle-related diseases (heart disease and obesity, for example,) all of which exacerbate the post-menopausal phenomenon of increased likelihood of breast and cervical cancers and osteoporosis.

In urbanized and industrialized societies, older women also have to face neglect, poverty, loneliness and alienation from their families:

- Only two per cent of those aged 60 and over in Fiji, Korea and the Philippines live apart from their families. Nearly a third of elderly Americans, however, live alone and nearly half of those aged 75 and over do so. In the United Kingdom 80 per cent of elderly people living alone are women.[38]

However, in many parts of the world, older women are organizing themselves:

- The **Women's Initiative** within the **American Association of Retired Persons** sponsors the Women's Health Advocacy Project, which publishes information that encourages older women to maintain healthy lifestyles and attitudes.

- **Help Age International,** a federation of national organizations of the elderly, supports projects for older women in developing countries and publishes a newsletter with practical tips for the elderly on how to preserve their health and make everyday life easier for themselves.

Obstacles, Trends and Goals

The World Health Organization's goal of **Health for All by the Year 2000** has helped promote a reorientation of global health strategies by drawing attention to fundamental issues of access to and equity in health.

In the two decades since the first women's conference in Mexico City, some strides have been made in ensuring that women get equal benefits from health systems.

- Women have benefited from primary health care with its emphasis on improving health through intersectoral activities in areas such as nutrition, water, sanitation and education, in addition to basic health services.
- More informations is now available on women's health issues and concerns.

However, the data on women worldwide shows clearly the disparities that still exist in health. Not just disparities between women and men, but between regions, between countries, and between different socio-economic, ethnic and age groups within a country.

Providing women easy accessibility to health care—whether it is in locating a primary health-care centre closer to a women's home, having transport available to reach that centre when the need arises, keeping the cost of the health care low or staffing medical centres with female health workers—is one of the keys to bridging those disparities.

Increasing economic pressures and implementation of structural adjustment policies are, however, forcing many countries to cut public health spending. This has detrimental effects particularly on marginal populations, although more recent programmes are attempting to safeguard spending on social services such as health.

National and international health policies have to take into account the specific needs of women.

The **Cairo Population Conference,** where reproductive rights and women's health issues took centre stage, was a major step forward. It underscored the fact that women are critical to success of population programmes and favoured the approach of looking at them as active participants of family-planning programmes. There seemed to be a consensus that the population issue revolves around women having greater control of their own lives, including their own fertility.

However, setting an agenda for women's health must firstly begin with a recognition that not only are women's health needs different than men's but also that the systems that identify and determine that health need are fashioned by gender-biased models. Gender discrimination tends to be hidden within the general issue of poverty and underdevelopment.[39]

Lack of Research on Women's Health

Women's illnesses—or conditions like menopause that affect only women—have often been neglected by medical research. Some, like breast cancer, only recently have begun to receive attention after women's groups and the women's media raised the question again and again.

While the positive side is that a feminization of medicine is taking place—more women are taking up roles of scientific researchers, doctors and medical staff—this by itself is no guarantee that they will advance women's health concerns. It does, however, set the stage for a better and broader understanding of such issues.

Experts recognize the need for gender-specific drug testing as well as the need to foster research on women's health—especially on prevention, treatment and health-care systems for diseases and conditions that affect women and girls differently.

Health Consequences of Violence

In conclusion, it is essential to view women's health in a holistic way within the social, economic and political context of their lives.

There has also been a tendency to deal with women's health-care needs through separate programmes related to particular health issues. Here too, a holistic view is necessary as the well being of a woman in each stage of her life is dependent on her past wellbeing. Similarly, the fate of future healthy generations also depends on the women of today.

Women will only enjoy the right to health once progress is finally made in overcoming barriers to equality and choice. The **Global Commission on Women's Health** uses the term **"heath security"** to describe this right. Health security traces the entire life cycle of a woman from *in utero* through to old age and encompasses all aspects of the basic human right to health.

NOTES

1. Global Commission on Women's health (GCWH). The Commission was set up in response to a world Health Assembly resolution, WHA 45.25.
2. From the WHO presentation to the seminar on "Women in Extreme Poverty", Vienna, November 1992: "Experiences and lessons learnt by the UN System".
3. *Second Review and Appraisal of the Nairobi Forward-looking Strategies for the Advancement of Women,* UN Division for the Advancement of Women (DAW), draft copy, February 1995.
4. UNICEF, *Facts and Figures, 1994-1995.*
5. Sadik, Dr. Nafis, *Investing in Women: The focus of the '90s,* United Nations Population Fund (UNFPA) 1989.
6. UNICEF, *Safe Motherhood Newsletter,* Issue 1, November 1989— February 1990.
7. *Girls and Women: A UNICEF DEVELOPMENT Priority,* 1993.
8. See note 5.
9. Study by Simons, J., Final B.,and Yang, A., 1992, "The Adolescent and Young Adult Fact Book", Children's Defense Fund, Washington, D.C.
10. See note 5.
11. Study by a United States-based NGO, the Center for Population Options, Hirsch &Barker, 1992.
12. Fertility Behaviour in the Context of Development, *United Nations, 1986, p.99; 1985-* 1992 Demographic and Health Surveys Comparative Studies, *NO.10,p.28,*
13. Age Patterns of Fertility *1990-1995 (1994 revision) UNFPA publication.*
14. *Ibid.*
15. See note 3.
16. Study by Palattao-Corpus L.,1991, "Situation of Adolescent Filipinos 1991: Focus on Teenage Mothers", prepared for UNICEF International Child Development Centre, Florence, italy.
17. Study by Kahn, J., and Anderson, K., 1992, "Intergenerational Patterns of Teenage Fertility", *Demography,* 29, No. 1.
18. *World Immunization News* MAY -jUNE 1990.
19. Armstrong, Sue, and Royston, Erica, *Preventing Maternal Deaths.*
20. WHO, *Safe Motherhood Information Kit, 1989.*
21. Ibid.
22. *The State of World Population* 1990, United nations Population Fund (UNFPA)
23. Ibid.
24. From draft of *UN: Levels and Trends of Contraceptive Use as Assessed in 1994, Population Division, UN.*
25. See note 4.
26. In his paper on "Contraceptive Research and Development: A Women-Centred Approach" at the Roundtable on Women's Perspectives on Family Planning, Reproductive Health and Reproductive Rights, Ottawa, Canada, August 1993.
27. Stanley Stjernsward and Koroltchouk, *Women and Cancer.*
28. *Women's Health: Towards a Better World, Global,* Commission on Women's health, World Health Organization, Geneva, April 1994. p.21.
29. Ibid., p. 22.
30. Drs. Amos, Amanda, and Chollat-Traquest, Claire, in *World Health,* April- May 1990.
31. Smyke, Patricia, *Women & Health,* Women & Development Series, Zed Books, London, 1991.
32. *Women and Substance Abuse: A gender Analysis and Review of Health and Policy Implications,* World Health Organization, WHO/PSA/93.12

33. *Women's Health Journal*, 1987, publication of ISIS International, Latin American and Caribben Women's Health Network.
34. See note 3.
35. See note 7, Issue 2, March-June 1990.
36. "Women & AIDS," Dr. Renee Danziger, in *World Health*, October 1989.
37. Davies, A.M., "Older Populations, Aging Individuals and Health for All", *World Health*, Forum, vol. 10, -1989.
38. See note 3.
39. See note 28, p.15.

WOMEN AND EDUCATION

The past 30 years have witnessed dramatic advances in education worldwide. Overall, student enrolment has increased, spending on basic education has grown, national and international actions have been taken to raise literacy levels. In most developed regions and in a growing number of developing countries near universal literacy for young people has been achieved.

Women have benefited from this so-called "quiet revolution". Today, more girls and women are entering school. In some countries, such as Qator, Dominica and Lesotho, there are more women than men enrolled in higher education.

Despite this progress, years of neglect have left very high illiteracy rates among adult, especially rural, women in many developing countries. Huge gaps also exist in women's educational achievements, as in science and technology, for example.

Women and girls in both developed and developing countries still do not have equal access to education and training resources.

It is clear that education:

- Has a major impact on social change; and
- Is an investment that pays significant dividends in economic growth, improved health and quality of life for Women and men alike.

As citizens, community leaders and mothers, women have emerged as major agents of social progress; their education is critical to sustain this momentum.

In most parts of the world, girls and boys now have the same access to schooling; in some regions, equality in enrolment is being achieved in tertiary education. Yet some imbalances persist:

- Of the world's nearly one billion illiterates, two thirds are women.
- Of the 130 million children without access to primary education, more than 80 million are girls:
- On average, by the age 18, girls have received 4.4 years less education than boys.[1]

Economic crises and government budget cuts hurt girls more than boys. Faced with hardship, families in some societies keep sons rather than daughters in school- because of the male's expected role as breadwinner—no matter which child has shown greater aptitude or achievement. This raises new challenges:

- **For girls entering school:** How to keep them there and insure quality education that prepares them to enter any field, exposes them to science and technology, stimulates their creativity and fosters their self-esteem;
- **For adult women:** Providing education and training to help them overcome the consequences of past discrimination that leave them lacking in essential skills.

Education as a Human Right

The right of every individual to education is one of the first provisions of the Universal Declaration on Human Rights. But education is often neglected in societies struggling to meet the many needs of their people. Only recently has education received greater priority as planers finally recognized it is a key factor in determining the pace of development.[2]

Creating educational opportunities for girls and women is strongly emphasized in the work of the UN. Supplementing the 1960 UNESCO **Convention Against Discrimination,** Article 10 of the **Convention on the Elimination of All Forms of Discrimination Against Women (CEDAW),** in 1979, outlined a comprchensive agenda for promoting gender equality in education. Its provisions require that societies:

- Provide women access to the same curricula, examinations, and quality teaching staff as boys;
- Eliminate any stereotyped concept of the roles of men and women, by revising textbooks and school programmes and adapting teaching methods to the needs of girls;
- Offer the same opportunities for career and vocational guidance and for scholarships and study grants;
- Promote the active participation of girls in sports and physical education.

The Convention, which is aimed at narrowing the gender gap in education, recommends:

- Making available the same opportunities in programmes of continuing education, including adult and functional literacy programmes;
- Reducing female drop-out rates, and organizing programmes for girls and women who have left school prematurely.

Echoing principles from the 1968 Teheran Declaration on Human Rights produced by the First World Conference on Human Rights, CEDAW includes a provision that sparked controversy at the 1994 **World Conference on Population and Development** in Cairo:

- Access to specific educational information to help ensure the health and well being of families, including information and advice on family planning.

Early marriage and child-bearing are major factors cutting short the education of girls and women. Thus,UNICEF's 1989 **Convention on the Rights of the Child** called for national legislation that sets 18 as the minimum age for marriage.

Towards Education for All

The **World Conference on Education for All,** sponsored by UNESCO, UNICEF, the World Bank and the UNDP and held in Jomtien, Thailand, in 1990, took stock of the persistence and dimensions of the gender gap. Looking to the year 2000, its Final Declaration stated:

- "The most urgent priority" is guaranteeing access to, and improving the quality of, education for girls and women. This means eliminating all obstacles to their active participation. Specifically, "all gender stereotyping in education should be eliminated" (Article 1);
- Focusing on skills that are actually learned rather than years of schooling completed, the Declaration recommends "active and participatory approaches", such as problem-solving and learning by doing, to counter the image of passivity to which girls are often expected to conform (Article 4);
- Drawing attention to poor environments experienced by hundreds of millions of girls, it calls for ensuring "that all learners receive the nutrition, health care, and general physical and emotional support they need"(Article 6).

The Gender Gap by Region

The recession of the 1980s led to cuts in education budgets worldwide, particularly in developing countries where economic recession and structural adjustment programmes constricted social spending. However, generally this did not affect rates of female school enrolment which increased worldwide at all levels. But gross enrolment rates mask certain vital measurements of genuine progress:

- The number of students who stay in school;
- The number promoted to the next grade;
- The number who complete each school cycle.

Rarely are these factors measured systematically:

- In **Africa**, the average percentage of girls to boys in primary education rose to 79 per cent in 1990 from 65 per cent in 1970; in secondary education to 69 per cent from 46 per cent; and in higher education to 32 per cent from 20 per cent—the largest gains of any region.[3]
- **However, in places where girls'primary enrolment reached parity with those of boys—such as in Cameroon, Congo, Senegal, Swaziland and Tanzania— or surpassed the rates of boys (as in Botswana and Lesotho), high drop-out rates in secondary schools tend to offset the gains. In many countries of the region, early marriage and pregnancy keep 80 to 90 per cent of adolescent girls out of high school.[4]**
- In **Asia and the Pacific,** the average percentage of girls to boys in primary education increased to 84 per cent in 1990 from 66 per cent in 1970; in secondary education to 77 per cent from 58 per cent; and in higher education to 84 per cent from 46 per cent.[5]
- In **South Asia,** where dowry traditions keep many girls from furthering their education beyond the primary level, some bridegrooms' parents are beginning to accept the higher educational levels of prospective daughters-in-law as an important element of dowry, in part because of education's increasing prestige, and because it may translate into higher earning power for the household.[6]
- Throughout most of **South Asia,** however, in 1990, girls spent on average only 1.26 years in school, an increase of only 0.10 per cent over a decade.[7]
- In **Latin America and the Caribbean,** the average ratio of girls to boys in primary education rose only to 95 per cent in 1990 from 94 per cent in 1970. The average ratio of girls to boys in secondary education rose to 109 per cent in 1990 from 98 per cent in 1970 and in higher education, it rose to 106 per cent from 72.[8]
- Drop-out rates for girls in rural areas are often twice as high as in towns and cities, especially in the poorest countries of the region. In Haiti, only two per cent of rural girls complete high school, compared to 25 per cent in urban areas.[9]

- Adolescent pregnancy, a major cause of school drop-out, is rising steeply; in Venezuela, pregnancies among under-15 girls increased 32 per cent during the 1980s; in the Caribbean, 60 per cent of first babies were born to teenagers.[10]
- In **Eastern Europe,** thc average ratio of girls to boys in primary education rose to 96 per cent in 1990 from 94 per cent in 1970; in secondary education, however, it decreased from 97 per cent in 1970 to 94 per cent in 1990, while in higher education it rose to104 per cent from 78 per cent in the same period.[11]
- In **Western Europe and North America,** the average ratio of girls to boys in primary education remained at a steady 95 per cent from 1970 to 1990. It rose in secondary education to 98 per cent in 1990 from 90 per cent in 1970 and, at the tertiary level, to 94 per cent from 53 per cent, largely because the job market increasingly requires higher academic credentials.[12]

REDRESSING ILLITERACYSD

Literacy properly understood is not only an initiation in the three R's, but also an apprenticeship in coping with the modern world.

—Colin power, Assistant Director-General for Education.
UNESCO, January 1990 speech launching International Literacy Year.

High drop-out rates in the early primary school years are a major cause of illiteracy among women. Although the gender literacy gap has narrowed since 1970, female illiteracy still constitutes a servere barrier to national and personal development in many countries.

The data collected in the 1990 census rounds revealed that.[13]

- In **Africa,** 61 per cent of the women are illiterate, compared to 45 per cent of the men.
- In **Asia and the Pacific,** 34 per cent of women are illiterate, compared 22 per cent of the male population.
- In **Latin America and the Caribbean** 16 per cent of the female population are illiterate, as compared to 14 per cent of the male population.
- **Eastern Europe** showed the lowest illiteracy rates: 2.3 per cent of women and 0.9 per cent of men.
- In **Western Europe and North America**, 10 per cent of women and 9 per cent of men are illiterate.

Investing in literacy campaigns for women pays off. Even where rudimentary literacy facilities are available, girls and women tend to make greate: use of them than do men, often making time for learning despite work pressures.

- In Senegal, adolescent girls attend literacy classes after working 13-hour days.
- In Guatemala, working girls and women attend literacy classes on Sundays after working a six-day week.[14]
- In Egypt, overall Illiteracy in urban areas remained constant for men between 1976 and 1986, while it dropped by 9.5 per cent for women during the same period.[15]
- In Cuba, where mass literacy campaigns have been carried out since the 1960s, less than two per cent of girls and women over the age of 10 are unable to read and write.[16]

The most successful literacy programmes for women combine income-generating skills and reading materials relevant to the students' lives.

- In Togo, 520 centres set up with help from UNESCO combined literacy instruction in local languages with the manufacture of soap and palm oil, and vital agricultural training. The project also trained local writers, including some of the students, to establish newspapers or contribute to existing ones with articles on the concerns of women from different linguistic areas.[17]
- In Indonesia, newly literate women are eligible for government loans of approximately $240 to set up their own small businesses.[18]

Returns on Female Education

> *If you are to plan for one year, you plant rice; if you are planning for five years, you plant trees, if you planning for a generation and the future, you educate your children.*

Had this old Chinese proverb substituted "girls" for "children", it would have anticipated a 1993 World Bank study, which demonstrated that education of girls is one of the most rewarding investments a nation can make.[19] Not only does it contribute to overall development, it also raises income, promotes health and increases productivity.

Among the many high returns of female education are:

Higher Productivity

> *Few will dispute that educating women has great social benefits. But it has enormous economic advantages as well.. The wages of female workers rise by 10 to 20 per cent for each additional year of schooling. Returns of this magnitude are impressive by the standard of other available investments, but they are just the beginning...*
>
> —Laurence Summers, 1992, as Chief Economist at the World Bank[20]

Educated women are more productive both at home and in the workplace. A World Bank global study showed the nations that had invested heavily in female primary education benefited through higher economic productivity.

Smaller Families

Over the long term, the single most effective and enduring way of reducing population growth,even more than by the diffusion of contraception, is by giving women more and better education.

—The Economist, 3 September 1994

Educated women tend to have fewer children, slowing population growth. A woman with at least seven years of education has 2.2 fewer children than a woman with not schooling.[21]

Uneducated mothers in Brazil have on average 6.5 children, those who have completed high school 2.5.[22]

Better Family Nutrition and Health

Mothers education may be even more important to her children's health than flush toilets or piped water.

—Dr. Nafis Sadik, Executive Director of the UN Population Fund

An educated mother can raise a healthier family. She not only knows about nutrition, but may have learned how to respond to health-related emergencies.

Every year of a mother's schooling leads to a decrease of up to nine per cent in the mortality rate of under-five children.[23]'

Enhanced Learning for Children

The family is "the world's smallest school".. Most [pre-adolescent] children in developing countries spend more time....... with their mothers than with any other educational "medium", including school.

—UNESCO's 1993 World Education Survey

In fact it has been noticed that when women are educated, they tend to encourage their children to become educated as well.

Enhanced Social Status for Women

An educated women almost always has more value and status in the eyes of her husband, her family and her community. She is more likely to share in family decisions about how many children to have, how to bring them up, how to spend money, how to organize domestic life.

—Gertrude Mongella, Secretary-General of the Fourth World Conference on Women.

Educated women tend to make more independent decisions and stand up for themselves. But for poor families the costs of girls' education can be high. They include:

Direct expenses— tuition, books, clothing, shoes, transportation;

Opportunity costs— lost work by daughters in the household or the market place, as well as lost time for training them in traditional crafts and skills that add to household income or contribute to the duties expected of a wife and mother.

Cultural costs— of defying society's standards of acceptable female behaviour. In several societies, women's education is equated with women becoming independent-minded. This is considered unacceptable behaviour for women. As an African male educator at a UNICEF conference said, "Women who talk back to men stay unmarried."[24]

Old Obstacles, New Approaches

Many countries striving to increase and improve the education of girls have been able to counter traditional barriers with innovative programmes.

Educating Parents to the Benefits of Educating Daughters

Because of cultural and labour market restrictions on women's work..... the private benefits to the family that pays for a daughter's education are often not large enough to offset the costs. Unless parents see and appreciate the benefits of educating daughters, they will not be willing to pay the economic costs or the costs of defying cultural norms.

—Elizabeth M. King, Education Girls and Women: Investing in Development

- In Mali since 1989, media campaigns have been the crux of a "social marketing" effort to promote the education of girls as an investment.[25]
- Morocco launched a successful programme in 1989 in which extension workers visit rural communities to encourage local participation in building and maintaining schools; and distribute materials that illustrate the benefits of educating daughters.[26]
- Throughout **South Asia,** a UNICEF— initiated, multi-media campaign projects an empowering view of a little girl named Meena as a problem-solver in health and nutrition. She even resists parental pressure to drop out of school and marry early. Through television programmes, video cassettes and comic books, the Meena initiative targets both parents and children in an effort to change the image of girls as passive, dependent victims of prejudice and poverty.[27]

ENHANCING THE EARLY LEARNING ENVIRONMENT

By the time they have reached school age, girls and boys have usually internalized knowledge consistent with social expectations of their gender roles. Pre-school educational programmes can significantly reduce such differences:

- During the 1980s, China established sibling-care facilities at primary schools to release girls from babysitting duties that interfered with their education. The facilities also provide equal preschool learning opportunities for their younger sisters and brothers.[28]
- In Colombia, the PROMESA programme was launched in four poor coastal villages. Educators worked with mothers in the home to enhance their educational relationships with their children, designing games and other devices to spur learning. These mothers then trained others in 10 more villages to give all their children a head start for school. The programme also improved malaria control and other health conditions in the area.[29]

BROADENING SCHOOL ACCESS

- Throughout **Africa** and **Asia**, girls shoulder adult responsibilities, notably sibling care, as early as the age of six.
- In India rural girls work an average nine hours a day, 315 days a year.[30]
- In Peru, seven to 14-year-old girls work more than twice as many hours as their brothers.[31]

In rural areas of virtually all developing countries—and a few developed ones as well—girls are often barred from education, either because schools are few and far between and their families cannot afford their transport and/or fear for their safety, or because their labour is vitally needed in the houschold and on the farmstead.

To encourage school attendance for girls, a number of countries have developed innovative programmes that reduce both the direct and the opportunity costs, often by offering informal education.

USING COMMUNITY RESOURCES

- The **Bangladesh Rural Advancement Committee** (BRAC) pioneered a widely replicated scheme in 1985 in which local houses and storerooms serve as classrooms staffed by teachers recruited and trained locally. The parents, largely landless peasants, "invest" in the system by attending monthly meetings to chart progress and discuss improvements. The vast majority of each school's 30 students—60 to 70 per cent of whom are girls—complete a three-year primary cycle and then move into the formal school system.[32]

Designing Flexible School Schedules

- Colombia launched its *Escuelas Nuevas* (new schools) in 1976 to provide a fiveyear primary education cycle in poor rural communities where girls labour in the home and on farmsteads is essential and precludes them from spending six hours in school each day. Girls come when they can to one of more than 15,000 rural schools to study at their own pace with the aid of a teacher assisted by selected student leaders.[33]

Providing Incentives

- A project in Ghana, offering a mid-day meal and take-home rations, found significant increases in enrolment and attendance rates for girls. In addition to their incentive value, such programmes help redress nutritional deficiencies, notably of iodine and iron, common among girls.[34]
- In Guatemala, a project launched in 1987 gave small scholarships to primary school girls and partially compensated parents for the loss of their daughters' work ; textbooks were issued free of charge. The programme also sought to discourage early marriage and childbearing: families of girls who had not become pregnant and attended 75 per cent of classes received and additional monthly payment.[35]

Single-sex Schools

The issue of "separate but equal" all-girls schools and other same-sex facilities generates considerable controversy:

CEDAW suggests "encouraging coeducation" as one way of eliminating the stereotyping of women. Many educators feel that coeducation prepares girls for the obstacles they will face in the working world.

However, evidence from widely different countries shows that girls achieve more in singlesex than coeducational schools, especially in such traditionally male subjects as mathematics and science.[36] Other studies reveal that in mixed classes, teachers devote more time to boys than girls.[37]

Some educators, such as Judith R. Shapiro, President of Barnard College in New York, claim that girls' schools and colleges "are places where girls and women get more attention, more respect and more room to be individuals."[38]

In some cultures in which girls and women are traditionally secluded, parents allow girls to attend only single-sex schools with female teachers or else withdraw their daughters from coed schools at the onset of puberty.

- In Sudan, Ahfad University, a women's college, sends students into villages as extension workers and literacy instructors. There they identify gifted girls and try to persuade parents that education at a similar institution will not endanger traditional morality.[39]
- In Bangladesh, Kenya, Mail and Pakistan, primary education for girls is conducted in neighbourhood mosques; the presence of the Imam as co-teacher allays parental fears about their daughters' safety.[40]
- Because of solid preparation in single-sex secondary schools, women in several North African and Middle Eastern countries are better represented in both science and engineering studies than in some Western nations: 40 per cent in Egypt; 45 per cent in Turkey; 46 per cent in Jordan.[41]

Recruiting Female Teachers

Increasing the number of female teachers contributes to raising female enrolment. It reduces parental anxiety, and provides role models that encourage students to continue their education.

- Despite numerous studies indicating that women teachers tend to be more sensitive to their girl students, only one third of primary school teachers in developing countries are women, less than one-fourth at the secondary level and only a tenth of those in higher education.[42]
- A programme in Nepal, which trains girls with secondary education as primary school teachers, increased girls' enrolment by 11 per cent.[43]
- Throughout **Africa** and other parts of the developing world, efforts to increase the number of female teachers face numerous difficulties.
- Most women cannot met the minimum requirement—eight years of education —for teacher training.
- Most training institutes are situated in cities to which rural girls, those most likely to staff rural schools, cannot afford to come.
- Salaries of female teachers are often lower than wages available to semi-skilled labour in growing industries.[44]

Course Offerings

The world over, schools usually respond to social pressure for coursework that reinforces traditional roles of women:[45]

- In most **Western** countries, courses in "home economics" or "domestic science" are still offered to girls rather than boys; rarely do both sexes study household management in school.

- In Mali, instruction in child care is an essential part of female education.
- In Jordan, vocational training for girls is largely limited to areas such as nursing and dressmaking, with traditionally high female employment rates.

A balance must be struck between providing courses that help women fulfill traditional roles and at the same time not allowing curricula to lock women out of wider educational opportunities.

—Elizabeth M. King, Educating Girls and Women: Investing in Development, World Bank, 1990, p.12

Overcoming Stereotypes

Schooling for girls and women must overcome stereotypes and equip students with not only the "three Rs", but with knowledge about their legal rights, as well as training appropriate for entering new or traditionally male fields:

- To counter traditional portrayals of women as submissive and dependent within and outside the home, Mexico has made sweeping changes in textbooks and other instructional materials.[46]
- In Nepal's remote mountainous regions, a programme for girls uses course materials based on a female character who confidently overcomes the hardships of rural life.[47]
- An interactive video porgramme developed by the US Department of Education encourages high school girls to explore traditionally male fields ranging from the construction trade to industrial chemistry.
- The Dutch, French and German Federations of University Women promote the entry of women students in such areas as computer technology and engineering.[48]

Training in Traditionally Male Fields

One major obstacle to increasing the number of women in fields dominated by men is the prevalence of male-only training facilities. Recent experience demonstrates the effectiveness of opening up technical fields to women:

- In Pakistan, as recently as 1990, 72 per cent of secondary vocational schools barred women; similarly, in the Dominican Republic, girls could not enrol in three of the major public institutes for middle-level technology.[49]
- By contrast, Morocco's Inudstrial and Commercial Job Training Programme for Women, launched in 1979, recruited young women with nine years of education— no diploma required—to train to drafting and electronics and placed them in apprenticeships. Many em-

ployers continue to request new students.[50]

- Since 1987, vocational schools in Ghana have opened courses in welding, carpentry, masonry and technical drawing to girls, who have earned prizes in these subjects. Conversely, courses in sewing and cooking under such titles as "tailoring" and "food services" cater to increasing numbers of boy. [51]

Providing Family-Planning and Sex Education

- "Family Life Education" curricula, pioneered in India, Nigeria and the United States, includes information on sexuality and contraception as part of broader teaching in responsible parenthood.[52]
- The Canadian-produced animated cartoon and wordless comic book, *Karate Kids*, is used by Brazilian, Kenyan, Filipino and North American community centeres for school drop-outs and street children of both sexes to teach AIDS prevention and other aspects of sexual health.[53]

Giving Teenage Mothers a Second Change

- In Barbados, the PAREDOS (Parental Education for Development) Programme reaches 20 per cent of teenage mothers in Bridgetown, offering remedial instruction, vocational training and counselling.[54]
- Throughout Europe, North America and many Latin American and Caribbean countries, millions of women attend night classes or enrol in correspondence courses after their child-bearing years. They pursue higher education, often in fields closed to females when they were adolescents.

Obstacles, Trends and Goals

It is increasingly understood that education must be combined with other opportunities to overcome the cultural and economic barriers that still relegate women to inferior status in virtually all countries and communities.

Education may allow a woman to take the first steps towards self-determination and security. But her society may forbid her from developing her new-found confidence.... It is as though women are allowed to see the possibilities, but not to translate what they have learned into improvements in their lives.

— "Literacy: a Key to Empowerment", UN/DPI feature No. 1567 (1994)

Affirmative Action —Positive steps to eliminate existing, remedy past, and prevent future discrimination—in support of expanding education for girls and women can greatly increase their empowerment.

- In northern Ghana, villages offer primary-school scholarships to girls. Community involvement has educated parents to the importance of educating girls, thus their enrolment and retention rates have increased by one third.[55]
- Malawi has reserved one-third of its secondary school places for girls.
- Australia links funding to its colleges and universities with their success in increasing the number of women in traditionally male courses and fields of graduate study.
- Sweden aims to achieve attendance of a minimum of 40 per cent of either sex in all educational programmes.[56]

Women Studying Science

Beatrix Potter, the creator of the Peter Rabbit children's books, was the first botanist to catalogue the fungi of the British Isles, but was excluded from all the English scientific societies of her day.[57] Today, male dominance in science and technology is slowly, if grudgingly, giving way to increasing numbers of women graduates.

- During the 1980s, young women constituted 17.4 per cent of Singapore's engineering students and 10.3 per cent of its natural science students at the university level.[58]
- More than one third of French students preparing for entry into leading schools in science and technology are women.[59]
- Today 50 per cent of Hungary's physics professors are women, while 32 per cent of Argentina's astronomy faculties are made up of women. Both are fields that were long dominated by males.[60]
- In 1989 women in the United States received 27.8 per cent of the doctorates awarded in science and engineering, an increase of almost 20 per cent since 1966. This increase is modest in light of strenuous efforts to attract women into science since the 1970s. "We have to look deeply into the culture of science", comments a prominent historian of science,"and see what is turning women off."[61]

Women's Studies

The problem of low self-esteem is endemic to many women in all societies..... especially where women's position is legally and economically as a permanent juvenile and dependent..... As a girl or women abandons the stereotypes, she also abandons what she knows best, the sense of self with which she and many generations before her were raised.

—NGO Committee on UNICEF, report on 1992 Conference on Education for All Girls: A Human Right, a Social Gain

Programmes of women's studies have attempted to dismantle stereotypes and build up women's self-esteem. Special studies reveal both:

- The extent to which women have been deprived and oppressed, and
- Elements in the traditions of all civilizaions that promote positive images and ease the conflicts experienced by many women in pursuit of their advancement and new roles in society.

Goals to the Year 2000 and Beyond

Two goals are envisioned by the Fourth World Conference on Women for raising the educational status of women:

- Reduction of adult illiteracy to half its 1990 level with sufficient emphasis on female literacy to significantly reduce the current male/female disparity.
- Universal female access to and completion of primary education. The two most important measures are:
- Lowering the direct and indirect costs for girls' education;
- Raising public awareness of the need and benefits of educating girls.

What is needed is not a separate and discrete plan of action for girls'education, but an engendering of the current plans, programmes, policies and strategies in ways that improve the prospect of attaining the goal of universal primary education.

—Khadija Haq, World Bank/UNICEF Seminar on Girls'Education, Guilin, China, 1994

Reflecting the emphasis the entire UN organization is placing on the Advancement of Women, UNESCO states in *Women in a Changing Global Economy,* 1994 World Survey on the Role of Women in Development:

The success of development efforts depends upon making women full partners.... To be certain, education, by itself, is not a panacea, but it is a necessary, if often insufficient, condition for the advancement of women and girls. It is in schools and adult education programmes that the journey out of poverty and towards employment and decision-making power begins.

Notes

1. Black, Maggie, *Girls and Women: A UNICEF Development Priority,* New York, 1994, p. 23.
2. *Review and Appraisal of the Nairobi Forward-looking Strategies,* Report of the Secretary-General, A/C.167,31 October 1994, p.33.
3. Division for the Advancement of Women, UN Secretariat, based on information in *Women's Indicators and Statistics Data Base* (WISTAT), version 3, 1994.

4. UNICEF document E/ICEF/1992/L. 5. para. 52.
5. See note 3.
6. king, Elizabeth M., *Educating Girls and Women: Investing in Developing,* World Bank, 1990, p. 11
7. ESCAP report for the Review and Appraisal of Implementation of the Nairobi Forward Looking Strategies for the Advancement of Women, Regional Priority Issues and Proposals for Action, E/ESCAP/RUD/MCWD(2)/1, 30 May 1994.
8. See note 3.
9. King, Elizabeth M. and Hill, Anne M., Editors, *Women's Education in Developing Countries: Barriers, Benefits and Policies,* World Bank, 1993, p.184.
10. See note 4, para. 47.
11. See note 3,
12. *Ibid.*
13. See note 3.
14. Unpublished UNICEF manuscript on *Children in Especially Difficult Circumstances* (CEDC), p. 51.
15. See note 3.
16. See note 14.
17. Chlebowska, Krystina, *Literacy for Rural Women in the Third World,* UNESCO, 1989, pp.110-111.
18. See note 17, p. 47.
19. See note 9.
20. From *People and the Planet*, joint publication of the International Planned Parenthood Federation (IPPS,) UNFPA and the World Conservation Union, published by IPPS, London, vol. 2, no .1, 1993, p. 17.
21. *The State of World Population* 1990, p. 15.
22. UN/DPI feature 1567: "*Literacy*: A *Key to Empowerment*", 1994.
23. Sadik, Dr. Nafis, *Investing in Women: The Focus of the 90s,* UNEPA, New York, 1989, p. 22.
24. See note 22.
25. See note 9, p. 308.
26. Ibid.
27. Mayo, John K., and Chieuw, Juliet S.F., *The Third Channel: Broadening Learning Horizons,* UNICEF, New York, 1993, pp. 51-54.
28. Hill, Anne M., *Closing the Gender Gap in Education,*EDUC/1994/WP4, p. 27.
29. *Education for All Girls: A Human Right, A Social Gain,* UNICEF, New York, 1994, p. 17.
30. *The New Internationalist,* No. 240, "Girls and girlhood", February 1993, p. 19.
31. See note 6, p. 25.
32. *Primary Education for All: Learning from the BRAC Experience,* ABEL, Washington, D.C., 1993.
33. See note 9, p. 305.
34. Kurz, Kathleen and Parher, Cynthia, *Sharing the vision: Strategies to Improve the Quality of Life for the Girl Child,* UNICEF, New York, 1994, p.16
35. See note 9, p. 300
36. See note 30, p. 17
37. Bullock, Susan, *Women and Work,* London, 1994, p. 90.
38. *The New York Times,* article, 28 November 1994.
39. See note 35, p. 22.
40. *Education Girls and Women: A Moral Imperative,* UNICEF, New York, 1992, p. 30.
41. See note 9, p. 146.
42. See note 6, p. 12.

43. See note 9, p. 296.
44. *Ibid.*, p. 295.
45. See note 6, p. 16.
46. See note 9, p.194
47. See note 42.
48. See note 39, p. 96.
49. See note 6, p. 11.
50. See note 6, p.11.
51. Yeboah-Afari, Ajoa, "Chalking Up Victories", *The New Internationalist,* No. 240, February 1993, p. 24.
52. See note 34, p. 2.
53. See note 27, pp. 47-48.
54. Cameron, Sara, see note 51.
55. See note 51.
56. See note 2, p. 50.
57. Holloway, Margaret, "A Lab of Her Own", *Scientific American,* November 1993.
58. See note 9, p. 259.
59. French national report to the CEDAW.
60. See note 57.
61. See note 57.

VIOLENCE AGAINST WOMEN

He strangles me and takes me into the garage and tell me, "Now you're going to die." He has one hand on my throat and pulls back the other one to slap me in the face; with is fist in the air, he looks me straight in the eye and says, "You want to die?..

This is just one of the many testimonies presented to the Canadian Panel on Violence against Women, whose report on the subject appeared in 1993. It could be the voice of a women any where in the world.

Violence against women is a global problem that occurs in both public and private domains, instilling fear and insecurity in many women's lives. It is pervasive, and yet it is often invisible. Though some types of violence against women, such as rape, have long been considered criminal acts, it is only recently that violence against women has been recognized as a violation of basic human rights.

Evolution of the Issue

Violence against women is as old as human civilization. However, it became a matter of international concern in 1975 when the UN held the first world conference on women in Mexico City. Gender-based violence was given prominence during the UN Decade for Women (1976-1985) and became a matter of priority in the second half of the 1980s. The increasing concern over the victims of violence and the need for change were voiced both by bodies within the UN and by NGOs.

At the second and third UN conferences on women, the issue gained further momentum with calls for national and international measures to curb the incidence of such violence.

In 1979, the UN General Assembly adopted the historic **Convention on the Elimination of All Forms of Discrimination against Women (CEDAW).** More than 130 Member States have to date agreed to abide by most the Convention's provisions. They have committed themselves to modifying their laws customs and practices to promote women's equality and rights. Although the Convention's focus is comprehensive, it never specifically singles out violence against women, although Article Six condemns "all forms of traffic in women and the exploitation of prostitution of women".

The **Nairobi Forward-looking Strategies,** adopted in 1985, recognized gender-specific violence as a serious form of abuse. The Strategies provided a framework for action at the national, regional and international levels. Legal measures to prevent violence were outlined, as well as the requirements for setting up national mechanisms to deal with the problem.

A later review of progress in the implementation of these Strategies found that violence is often linked to and reinforces the social, economic and political inequality that women experience as part of their daily lives.

In 1992, the Committee on the Elimination of Discrimination against Women formulated General Recommendation 19, which specifically categorized gender-based violence as violence that is directed against a woman because she is a women or violence that effects women disproportionately and is discriminatory.

The **Vienna Declaration of Human Rights** in 1993 (paras. 18 and 38) deemed violence against women as a violation of human rights. It recognized the egregious nature of violence against women and its human rights dimensions, paving the way of international recognition of the issue.

The **Declaration on the Elimination of Violence against Women** was adopted by the UN General Assembly in late 1993, on the recommendation of the Commission on the Status of Women. It emphasizes violence against women as a violation of human rights and recommends strategies to be employed by Member States and the specialized agencies of the UN to eliminate it.

- **Article One** of the Declaration defines for the first time what constitutes an act of violence against women. The term "violence against women" implies any act of gender-based violence that results in, or is likely to result in, physical, sexual or psychological harm or suffering to women, as well as threats of such acts, coercion or arbitrary deprivation of liberty, whether occurring in public or private life.

- **Article Two** of the Declaration specifies the types of violence to which women are subjected both within and outside the family as well as violence perpetrated or condoned by States.

Focus on the issue further intensified in March 1994 when the UN Commission on Human Rights condemned all acts of gender-based violence and appointed a **Special Rapporteur on Violence against Women.**

The Special Rapporteur will seek and receive information on such violence, its causes and consequences; recommend measures at the national, regional and international levels for its elimination; and work closely with the Commission on Human Rights and the Commission on the Status of Women.

Though much action has taken place on the issue, the draft Platform for Action of the **Fourth World Conference on Women** goes further by observing that violence against women derives essentially from the lower status accorded to women in the family and in society. Physical, psychological or sexual violence, whether occurring in the home or in society, is linked to male power, privilege and control.

Violence against women is seen to be abetted by ignorance, lack of laws to prohibit violence, inadequate efforts by public authorities to enforce existing laws, and absence of educational and other means to address its causes. The lack of adequate statistics about violence thwarts efforts to elaborate programmes and monitor its prevalence.

Responsibility of the State

In the past decade, efforts at the international level have forced national policy makers to address the issue of violence against women. The signing of international declarations and charters is just one step in a long-term effort. Unless individual Member States of the United Nations take action in their respective countries and accord violence against women the serious attention it deserves, progress will remain slow.

The Declaration on the Elimination of Violence against Women identifies the kinds of violence perpetrated or condoned by the State.

Article Four spells out in detail the role and responsibility of the State in condemning violence against women and in taking action to abolish it. **States "should condemn violence against women and should not invoke any custom, tradition or religious consideration to avoid their obligations with respect to its elimination".**

Several Governments have responded and taken action to enact and strengthen legislation and establish support systems for women who are victims of such violence.

States also have the responsibility to ensure that women feel protected sufficiently to report complaints of violence. Some positive steps have taken place in the regard:

- In Pakistan, for example, the Government is currently establishing women-only police stations, an experiment which has already met with success in Brazil, Colombia (where by end of 1992, 60 special stations has been set up), Uruguay and Peru. The reporting of crimes against women has substantially increased in these countries;
- In the Philippines, since 1993, all police stations have been obliged to establish women's desks staffed by specially trained female officers who investigate crimes of violence against women.

Before these desks existed, few statistics were available to assess the dimensions of the problem. A 1993 police study in the Philippines found that 80 per cent of rape reports and data on other forms of violence against women, such as battering, harassment or verbal abuse, were omitted from police records and crime-index tables. To date, more than 160 women's desks have been established in police stations in the Philippines, staffed by over 275 policewomen. As a result, the police now take the issue of violence against women more seriously.

The draft Platform for Action of the Fourth World Conference on Women expects Governments to take several measures to eliminate or at least limit violence against women. These include:

- Reviewing existing legislation on violence;
- Providing training and orientation to police and judicial personnel, doctors, nurses and social workers to recognize abuses perpetrated against women;
- Supporting shelters that offer protection to women from abuse.

Domestic Violence

Violence against women cuts across all racial, social, cultural, economic, political and religious spectrums. Often it is perpetrated by those whom they have been encouraged to trust and respect, and those whom they love.[1]

The most endemic form of violence against women is spousal abuse, or, more accurately, abuse of women by intimate male partners. While forms of abuse range from humiliation and economic coercion to physical brutality, the abuse itself is universal, occurring in developed, industrialized countries with the same frequency as in the developing world.

Studies have shown that in many countries, one quarter to more than half of women report having been physically abused by a current or former partner. An even larger percentage have been subjected to continuous emotional and psychological abuse.[2]

Given the low status of women in many societies, the following statistics should come as no shock:

- Reports from France indicate that 95 per cent of its victims of violence are women, 51 per cent of these at the hands of their husbands. In Denmark, 25 per cent of women cite violence as the reason for divorce.[3]
- A historical analysis of murders at the end of the nineteenth century in England and Wales showed that abut 50 per cent of the victims were murdered by their husbands, lovers or boyfriends. The comparison with official figures in the United Kingdom today shows that his pattern has not changed.[4]
- In the US, more women are injured in domestic violence incidents than in car accidents, rapes and muggings put together. Thus, for the past four years, US Surgeons General have warned hat domestic violence—not heart attacks or cancer or strokes—poses the single largest threat of injury to adult women in the US.[5]
- In a study of 80 battered women in San Jose, Costa Rica, 49 per cent reported being beaten during pregnancy.[6]
- In Canada, 62 per cent of women murdered in 1987 died at the hands of their spouses.
- In Papua New Guinea, 67 per cent of rural women and 56 per cent of urban women have been victims of spousal abuse, according to a national survey conducted by the Papua New Guinea Law Reform Commission.
- In Bangladesh, the killing of women by their husbands accounts for 50 per cent of all murders.

Social inequality between the sexes is one contributing factor to women's subordinate position within the family. As a result, many societies condone the "disciplining" of wives, and tend to ignore or trivialize even severe incidents of domestic violence.

In recent years, however, largely due to the efforts of NGOs, wife battering haas become an issue of importance. Women's NGOs, in particular,

- The **Women's Federation in Beijing,** for example, became concerned about the frequency of domestic violence in the three-generation families that make up two thirds of Chinese households. The Federation organized over 600 legal-knowledge training classes, reaching 90,000 women.[7]

RAPE

- In South Africa, a women is raped every 90 seconds, totaling approximately 320,000 women raped each year.[8]
- In the US, 16 women every hour are confronted by rapists; a woman is raped every six minutes. In 1991, the Federal Bureau of investigation recorded 106, 593 rapes in the United States.[9]
- In July 1991, a group of teenage boys attacked and raped 71 schoolgirls at a boarding-school in one East African country for refusing to participate in a protest strike against the local school administrators. Nineteen girls lost their lives in the attack.[10]

Statistics like this, from all around the world, demonstrate that sexual coercion is common in the lives of women and girls. Six well-designed studies from the US, for example, indicate that between one-in-five and one —in-seven of US women will be the victim of a rape in their lifetime. 11 Such US data are are consistence with studies of rape in other parts of the world.

Rape or sexual assault can be most damaging psychologically to a woman, leaving emotional scars that time and counselling often cannot erase. In addition to the rape of adult women, there have been increasing reports of incidents of incest and rape of young girls.

Instead of sympathy and support, male-dominated societies—especially those that emphasize virginity for unmarried women and sexual fidelity for wives—often blame the raped woman for the violence used against her. Far from being the victim in incidents of rape, she is treated as the accused.

Most countries have strong laws against rape and offer varying degrees of punishment to offenders. Several are now trying to set up systems that offer help and rehabilitation to the victims. However, some Governments still have repressive laws that make it possible for the victims of rape to be charged with criminal offences. Ordinances in at least one South Asian country equate rape with adultery. Thus rape is treated as a sexual lapse (on the part of the victim) and not as a crime. Rape victims charged with adultery can be sentenced to be publicly whipped, imprisoned or stoned to death[12] Thousand of women languish in jails under the law.[13]

SEXUAL HARASSMENT

While rape is the most obvious form of sexual violence against women , have to suffer on the streets and in the workplace; teasing, jeering, and unwanted touching and pinching of their bodies are common examples.

In some cultures, it is given delicate labels or euphemisms, or viewed with good humour and the psychological and emotional stress it causes its victims is ignored.

In recent times, increased attention to sexual harassment at the workplace, which includes sexual favours demanded of female employees in return for career advancement of job security, has led to changes and additions in the law.

- In the US, for example, amendments were made in 1991 to the existing Civil Rights Act that categorize sexual harassment as being discriminatory and allow targets of such harassment to recover compensatory and punitive damages.

As a result, women who have faced sexual harassment in the workplace now have recourse to the courts. In reaction, several US companies are taking active steps to establish a corporate sexual harassment policy to deter abusers and protect the victims of such harassment.

Female Genital Mutilation

Female genital mutilation (FGM), which affects million of women, primarily in parts of Africa, is recognized as a human rights issue and an act of violence against women, as well as a health concern.

Female genital mutilation is the collective name given to different traditional practices that involve the cutting of female genitals. Here, FGM is reserved to describe ritualistic practices where actual cutting and removal of sexual organs takes place.

FGM also known as female circumcision, can be divided into two broad categories:

- Clitoridectomy—which involves partial or total removal of the clitoris or removal of both the clitoris and the labia minora. About 85 per cent of all women who undergo FGM have clitoridectomies.
- Infibulation— which involves the removal of the clitoris the cutting off of some or all of the labia majora and incisions made in the labia majora to create raw surfaces. About 15 per cent of women who undergo FGM have infibulations.[14]

Most commonly, girls experience FGM at an age well before puberty, usually when they are between four and eight years old.

Women and girls experience pain, trauma and frequently severe complications, such as bleeding, infection, or urine retention, sometimes leading to death. The long-term physical and medical complications are numerous—in the case of infibulation, frequent recutting and stitching are often required—and there are substantial psychological effects on women's self image and sexual lives.

- Globally, at least two million girls a year are at risk of genital mutilation—approximately 6,000 per day. An estimated 85 million to 114 million girls and women in the world are genitally mutilated.

Most live in Africa, a few in Asia and, in recent years, cases have been reported in Europe, Canada and the US, where several immigrant African populations have settled.

It is important to note that FGM was also used by modern physicians in England and the US, as recently as the 1940s and 1950s, to "treat" hysteria, lesbianism, masturbation, and other so-called female deviances.[15]

According to Nahid Toubia, a Sudanese doctor who actively campaigns against FGM, it is a cultural practice, with no religious sanction attached to it. There is a wide misconception that it is an Islamic custom.

Recent efforts at the international level, particularly by UN agencies, have successfully placed FGM on women's health and human rights agendas. At the national level, several Governments and national leaders have condemned FGM , but few have translated their concern into laws prohibiting FGM.

- Egypt has had a Ministry of Health decree since 1959 that limits the types of FGM allowed and attempts to have them performed under medical supervision only.
- Kenya banned FGM in 1990.
- Burkina Faso has incorporated into its draft constitution a prohibition on female circumcision.

In 1984, the Inter-African Committee against Traditional Practices Affecting the Health of Women and Children was created by African women to combat FGM. It is now an international NGO, based in Geneva, with members in most countries where FGM occurs.

Aside from changes in laws, education on FGM is needed in the communities where it is practised. According to Nahid Toubia there is a pressing need for action on FGM, especially by using the mass media and popular culture to disseminate information, generate internal discussion and debate and present the basic health facts in an accessible manner among affected populations.

Missing Women

While abuse is a daily factor of many women's lives, there are others for whom it is fatal. Harvard University economist Amartya Sen shocked the world when he announced in 1990 that 100 million women were missing from global population figures, almost entirely from South and East Asia.[16] Sen's figure was later reduced to 60 million women by

Princeton demographer Ansley Coale.

The "missing women" are the victims of foeticide, infanticide, selective malnourishment, denial of health care and various forms of gender violence.[17]

In countries where most people have adequate health care and food, there are an average of 105 females to each 100 males. But in some of the world's poorer nations, the sex ratio is dramatically lower: 95 females to each 100 males.[18]

In several parts of the world, a mix of economic pressures and traditional beliefs gives preference to male children.

Boys' labour is needed in the fields in agrarian societies and, unlike girls, they bring in dowry to the household. Girls require the payment of dowry and parents fear the financial burden of their upbringing and marriage. As a Telugu proverb in India says, "Bringing up a girl is like watering a plant in someone else's countryard."[19] From the moment they are born, girls are considered the property of their prospective husband's household.

- In one survey in Bangladesh, 96 per cent of women said they wanted their next child to be a boy. Only three per cent wanted a girl.[20]

In communities where boys are preferred, women are blamed and made to feel guilty and ashamed for giving birth to daughters. As a result, the pressure to get rid of the female child can be intolerable.

Through a haze of heat and pain, the new mother hears the midwife mutter:"another daughter", and she bursts into loud sobs. Burdened with guilt for having two girls already, during this pregnancy she had prayed desperately for a son

—*Education of the Girl Child: Her Right, Society's Gain*, UNICEF, 1992

Gender-selective Abortion and Infanticide

Some girls are rejected even before birth. Several studies confirm that access to prenatal tests such as amniocentesis and ultrasound scanning, which detect the sex of the unborn child, is sufficiently widespread in many countries so that foeticide could, in fact, be responsible for skewing male-female ratios.[21]

Since the late 1970s, when this technology became widely available, thousands of female foetuses which were identified have been aborted.

Although genetic testing for sex selection has been banned in India under recent legislation [22] and in China since January 1995, it is still a lucrative underground business in these countries.

In spite of the relatively high cost of the procedure, most of the clients are women or couples from the middle and lower classes who would rather pay for the test and abortion than have to find the money for a dowry years later.

- In a chain to clinics offering sex preselection services in 46 countries in Europe, the US, Asia and Latin America, 248 out of 263 couples selected boys and 15 selected girls.[23]

Even when female babies survive the womb, they may not survive infancy:

- A World Bank report in 1990 said: "The deaths of young girls in India exceed those of young boys by almost one third of a million every year. Every sixth infant death is specifically due to gender discrimination.[24]

Dowry Deaths

The dowry was originally a wedding gift to a daughter from her family—of money, jewellery, clothing or household items. It was also a kind of insurance, some personal wealth in case of mistreatment by her new family or a failed marriage.

Now, it has become common for the groom and his family to demand a dowry of a large amount of money or goods at the time of marriage. In fact the prevalence of this custom is why many, especially poor, South Asian parents don't want to have a daughter.

Dowry-related abuse is common in many countries. The most extreme form is"bride burning"; wherein women are burnt to death (usually in the kitchen, in order to make it seem like an accident with the stove) by their husbands or inlaws.

Women in Areas of Conflict

Whilc all civilians suffer when war breaks out, it is women and girls who face the most risk and danger—not just the risk of being killed or injured, but also of being raped, sexually assaulted or abused.

Women have been subjected, throughout history, to especially brutal forms of rape as part of war. Rape is used as a symbolic weapon of war by combatants to humiliate their enemies and force submission.

In recent years, mass rape—as a systematic weapon of war—has been documented in the former Yugoslavia, Cambodia, Liberia, Peru, Somalia and Uganda.[25]

- A European Union fact-finding team estimates that more than 20,000 Muslim women were raped in Bosnia since fighting began in April 1992. Many were held at "rape camps" where they were raped repeatedly and forced to bear Serbian children against their will.[26]

A UNESCO report (CEDAW/C/1995/3/Add.3) on **"The Use of Rape as a Tool of War",** which examined the situation in Bosnia and Herzegovina, observed that in the Serb attacks on Bosnian Muslim villages, rape had been systematic, committed on the order of higher authorities and under their supervision, and thus had been used as a "tool of war" as part of a wider expansionist strategy.

The **International Tribunal of War Crimes,** set up by the UN Security Council in 1993 to consider the situation in the former Yogoslavia, considers mass rape as a "crime against humanity."[27]

The draft Platform for Action of the Fourth World Conference on Women takes a strong stand against the abuse of women during war and conflict. It asks Governments to condemn the use of war-related violence against women, such as mass rapes, forced pregnancies and other gender-specific abuses, and to consider them war crimes and crimes against humanity.

Refugees

Lien is 22 and from South-East Asia. Over two years ago, she boarded a flimsy fishing boat with 79 other people and set sail for a nearby country. The reserves of food and water were soon exhausted..twice they were attacked by pirates'........Lien was one of the several young women taken aboard the pirates' boat and repeatedly raped...... later she was rescued, and today is in a transit camp awaiting acceptance by a Western country.

—*United Nations High Commissioner for Refugees (UNHCR) and Refugee Women,* 1985

It is estimated that 80 per cent of the world's 23 million refugees are women and children—most exposed to poor nutrition or illness and many of the women and girls to violence, including rape.

- As the United Nations High Commissioner for Refugees reported: "Rape, abduction, sexual harassment, physical violence and the not infrequent obligation to provide "sexual favours" in return for documentation and /or relief goods remain a distressing reality for many women refugees."[28]

There are few available data to quantify the plight of women refugees, though the horror stories of attacks by soldiers, rebels, border guards and others with whom they come into contract have grown.

Studies have also noted a rise in domestic violence in the aftermath of a war; male refugees, having lost control over their own lives, are often known to beat up women in their families in an attempt to exercise control over them. In their host countries, refugee women often don't know the language or the laws and opt to suffer in silence.

UNHCR, UNIFEM, the UN Relief and Works Agency for Palestine Refugees in the Near East (UNRWA) and the UN Border Relief Operation in Cambodia have developed strategies to assist refugee women.

UNHCR has developed formal guidelines on preventing and responding to sexual violence, based on detailed recommendations by fieldworkers experienced with the rape and piracy attacks on refugees in all parts of the world.

The guidelines provide fieldworkers with practical advice on medical, psychological and legal ramifications of sexual violence. They are also intended to dispel the discomfort of many refugee workers with such crimes and counter any tendency to dismiss them as the inevitable by-product of social breakdown.

Ann Howarth-Wiles, UNHCR'S Senior Coordinator for Refugee Women, calls the guidelines " a fundamental primer" that should "immeasurably improve the sensitivity and skills of people who work with refugees.[29]

UNHCR has issued policy statements encouraging countries to consider that when rape or other forms of sexual violence are committed for reasons of race or political opinion, for example—and particularly when this is condoned by the authorities concerned—then the victims should be eligible for refugee status.[30]

Income-earning schemes can enhance the self-sufficiency of refugee women and leave them less vulnerable to violence and exploitation.

- More than 30,000 Afghan refugee women in Pakistan are producing bags, quits, school uniforms and carpets as part of a UNHCR income-generating programme.
- Refugee women are also involved in many other refugee camp programmes. In a refugee settlement in Zaire, the camp population has elected female coordinators.

The UN Development Fund for Women (UNIFEM) launched a programme called **African Women in Crisis** (AFWIC) in 1993 to promote the economic independence of refugee and internally displaced women in Africa. In Cote d'Ivoire and Ghana, for example, Liberian women refugees have learned skills, including surveying and construction, that are immediately useful and will also be vital for rebuilding Liberia.

Slavery and Trafficking

Trafficking in women is a global "industry" that transcends borders and cultures and is based on the sexual exploitation of women.

Women have been traditionally trafficked across borders for prostitution. In recent times, the traffic has often been disguised as mail-order brides and/or domestic labour schemes.

While it is difficult to estimate the number of women trafficked worldwide every year, there seem to be some clear patterns of movement—usually it is women from South-East Asia, South Asia, Latin America, Africa and Eastern Europe who are trafficked domestically and transnationally.

Often, they are brought from poorer countries to the economically more advanced ones, sometimes abducted from their rural villages and sold in big cities, both within their country and abroad.

Trafficking and prostitution both flourish because of the increasing number of women and families living in absolute poverty and the lack of real options for economic well-being and advancement. But trafficking is also flourishing because of the affluence of some countries and regions that allows men to buy sex and have access to a greater variety of sexual options.

Prostitution

A few girls may choose to work in the sex industry because it often pays better than other jobs available to poor women. But for many, the decision is beyond their control. Tens of thousands of young girls and women worldwide are forced into prostitution in order to save themselves and their children from starvation.

In poor areas where there are few job opportunities, some families pay "job agencies" to take their daughters and find work for them—only to find out much later that the agents are linked with the sex industry and that the work they found for the girls was as prostitutes. Many of these girls work in dismal conditions, working 10 to 12 hours a day. Often their employers or agents batter them and control their earnings. AIDS is now the new threat in their lives.

However, several NGOs are attempting to improve the lives of these girls. *The Thai Women of Tomorrow* programme run a at the Chiang Mai University in Thailand is proving educational and career alternatives to young women in order to protect them from being forced to enter prostitution and the sex industry. It has granted 1,000 scholarships worth US$120 each to sixth-grade girls in Pha Yao and Chiang Rai provinces. Another 500 young girls are being trained as dressmakers, health-care assistants, jewellery makers and secretaries in the programme.

Mail-order Brides

Mail-order brides is a flourishing trade in which there are increasing numbers of brokering agencies that arrange "marriages", primarily between women from the developing world and men from industrialized countries.

Although these women may voluntarily apply as mail-order brides with marriage agencies they often believe they will be able to choose their marriage partners. When they arrive in the country of their husbands-to-be, they often find limited choice and abuse.

Lost in their new country-with limited language skills, no knowledge of the local laws and culture, and most often without their passports, which are usually taken away by their new husbands—these brides find it difficult to get away.

Domestic Maids

Women who are recruited as domestic servants overseas can often face a fate similar to that of mail-order brides. Several work in Western Europe and the Middle East, working long hours with no breaks, often facing physical, sexual abuse at the hands of their employers.

They live in slave-like conditions in countries where they do not speak the language and their employer has control of their travel papers.

- According to the Human Rights Watch 1993 report: 1,400 Filipino maids in one Middle Eastern country fled to their embassy, seeking protection fro their employers, between April 1991 and April 1992.
- In 60 cases of abuse of Asian maids investigated by Human Rights Watch in that country,one third involved rape or sexual assault.

Child Prostitution

There is systemic and individual criminality, coupled with corruption which profiteers from prostitutes in general and child prostitutes in particular....... At the very worst, children are abducted, drugged and coerced by gangs and syndicates into prostitution both locally and across frontiers. They may also be killed or maimed in the process.

—Rights of the Children, Special Rapporteur,
UN Commission on Human Rights, January 1993

More than one million children are forced into prostitution every year, most are in Asia. While few country-based statistics are available, it seems clear that may of the women trafficked are actually mere girls aged eight to 16.[31]

- In Latin America, child prostitution—linked to poverty, the plight of street children. drug abuse and sex tourism— has been reported in virtually every country.

- In Brazil, there are reports of thousands of girls forced into prostitution in mining camps in the Amazon region.

Protection is guaranteed to children under the UN Convention on the Rights of the Child. However, until Member States enact adequate laws and take initiatives to protect children from brutality, little progress is possible.

Pressure from NGOs and the media has spurred responses from some Governments.

- Thailand has passed legislation to stiffen penalties against perpetrators, and its Prime Minister has announced a campaign to end child prostitution.
- The Philippines adopted a Child Protection Code in 1992 against child abuse.
- France and the Scandinavian countries have laws making sexual exploitation of children by their nationals in foreign countries illegal, and Germany is enacting a similar measure.

Sex Tourism

The sex tourism industry is the reverse of trafficking. In this case, clients travel abroad, particularly to South-East Asia, to meet prostitutes. Several small travel agencies in the West now operate "sex tours"—transporting men to the East on "erotic pleasure trips".

Sex tourism in fact is a significant foreign-exchange earner for countries such as Thailand, the Philippines, Malaysia, Singapore, Indonesia and several others in the developing world.

Obstacles, Trends and Goals

Violence against women is now recognized as a major issue of concern. However, much remains to be done to deal effectively with it. There is great need for educational programmes and legislation to be form formulated so that societies can change the way women are perceived.

The challenge is considerable. There exist many more types of practices that need to be eradicated.

- Early marriage, for example, thrusts a girl into the role of a wife and mother when she is still a child herself.
- The mistreatment of widows and elderly women is common in numerous parts of the world. In some cultures in South Asia, a widow is blamed for the death of her spouse and abused by her— inlaws and the local community: her head is shaved, and she has limited access to food and resources.

- In parts of northern India, the practice of "sati"— where the widow would commit suicide on the funeral pyre of her husband - is now increasingly rare.

The challenge ahead is not just in identifying violence against women in its many forms and taking action to prevent it, but also in educating the next generation to prevent its occurrence in the future. Children are often the first witnesses to incidents of domestic violence and many remain psychologically scarred for life as a result. Others suffer a worse fate.

- In the US, for example, more babies are now born with birth defects as a result of mothers being battered during pregnancy than from a combination of all diseases and illnesses for which pregnant women are now immunized[32].

Each different form of violence must be seen in its larger social context. Gender-based violence is the consequence of consistent social, economic and political inequality of women in society.

Cultural attitudes in all parts of the world need to change, as well the power relationships between men and women. Unless the unequal relationship between men and women is recognized, as well as men's power and control over women and their treatment of women as property in many societies, no amount of legal reform can reverse the phenomenon.

Other aspects, such as women's education, the building of self-esteem and economic empowerment, are equally critical issues. Some urgent measures include:

- More shelters and safe havens for battered women;
- Strengthened legislation;
- Reforming and sensitizing the criminal justice system to women's abuse, including the law, police, the courts and correctional services that can help safeguard women's rights and dignity;
- The discrediting of myths and misinformation, such as blaming the victim for "provoking" violence.

Notes

1. Report of the Canadian Panel on Violence against Women, 1993.
2. Heise, Lori, L. with Jacqueline Pitanguy and Adrienne Germain, "Violence against Women: The Hidden Health Burden", *World Bank Discussion Papers,* No.225, 1994.
3. MacLeod, L., *Women and Environment,* vol.12, No.10,1990, from the UNIFEM publication Battered Dreams, 1992, p. 5.
4. UN Centre for Social Development and Humanitarian Affairs, Division for the Advancement of Women, "Violence against Women in the family", 1989.
5. Biden, Joseph R.," Domestic Violence—A Crime, Not a Quarrel", *Trial* magazine, June 1993; see: "From the Surgeon General", US Public Health Service, 267 JAMA 3132, 1992.

6. See note 2, p. 25.
7. WHO, *World Health Statistics Quarterly,* vol. 40, No. 3, 1987, p. 261
8. "No to Rape", *Speak,* South African Women's Quarterly, No. 29, 1990.
9. Salzholz, E., and Clift, E., "Women under Asaault: Sex Crimes Finally Get the Nation's Attention," *Newsweek* magazine, 16 July 1990.
10. Perlez, J., *The New York Times,* 11 July 1991.
11. See note 2, referring to studies on rape by Koss (1993) and Kilpatrick, Edmunds and Seymour (1992). p 5.
12. "Rape and Sexual Abuse: Torture and Ill-treatment of Women in Detention", Amnesty International, 1991.
13. US *News & World Report,* 28 March 1994.
14. Toubia, Nahid, *Female Genital Mutilation—A Call for Global Action,* UNIFEM publication distributed by women, Ink, 1993.
15. See note 11,
16. Sen, A.,"More Than 100 Million Women Are Missing", *New York Review of Books,* 20 December 1990. Figure also cited in *Human Development Report,* 1993.
17. *Battered Dreams: Violence against Women as an Obstacle to Development,* UNIFEM publication distributed by women, Ink., 1992, p. 6.
18. *The world's Women: Trends & Statistics* 1970-1995, UN forthcoming.
19. World Vision of Australia, Information services booklet, "*Growing Up a Girl*", March 1993.
20. Rozario, Stephen, "Bangladesh" The Girl-Child Initiative", *Together,* a magazine of World Vision international, October-December 1992.
21. Study by Coale and Banister 1992, quoted in Heise, Lori L., *World Bank Discussion Papers,* No. 255.
22. The Pre-Natal Diagnostic Techniques "Regulation and Prevention of Misuse" Bill, India, 1994.
23. Patel, V., *Women in Action,* March 1988, p. 27; ISIS International, Latin American and Caribbean Health Network, *Women's Health Journal,* No.14. July-August 1989, p.12; *The Tribune: A Women and Development Quarterly, No. 44, March 1990, p. 17.*
24. *The World Bank Report,* 1990.
25. Study by Swiss and Giller, 1993, quoted in Heise Lori L., *World Bank Discussion Papers,* No. 255.
26. See note 2.
27. International Tribunal of War Crimes (ITWC), *Statutes,* Art. 4, para.45.
28. *UNHCR Annual Report, 1988.*
29. Marshall, Ruth "Protecting and Assisting Refugee Women", *Refugees Magazine,* UNHCR, P. 2.
30. *Ibid.*
31. *The Girl Child: An Investment in the Future,* UNICEF, 1991.
32. Whitehead, c., speech at "Within Our Reach: Second Annual Baby Love Conference", Office of Health Resources Development, North Carolina, 1989.

WOMEN AND POWER: WHERE WOMEN STAND TODAY

What we need are not just a few women who make history, but many women who make policy.

—Geraldine Ferraro, 1984 Vice-Presidential candidate in the United States, at the 1991 International Women's Day event at the UN

Women around the world share a common condition: they are not full and equal participants in public policy choices that affect their lives. The top decision-making positions remain largely male-dominated spheres where women have little influence.

Women's exclusion from power in the public arena is in sharp contrast to their ability to make crucial decisions relating to the survival of their families. Not only do millions of women manage scarce resources related to household consumption and health matters, but they organize, supervise, teach, heal, solve problems and make peace, providing our societies with the cohesion required for development.

Since the first world conference on women in Mexico City two decades ago, many women have entered the public arena, where they have become decisionmakers at all levels: in politics, business, industry, the civil service and the media. Many more have reached leadership positions in non-governmental organizations and community groups, effectively exercising or influencing power.

The names Aquino, Bhutto, Chamorro, Gandhi and Peron are associated with female leaders as much as men. However, while more women serve as heads of heads of State or Government, ministers, members of parliament, mayors and members of local councils than ever before, their members are usually too small to affect significantly the power structures that shape society. It is notable that many developing countries have made more progress in high-level political representation of women than some industrialized countries.

Nowhere is the gap between *de jure* and *de facto* equality among men and women greater than in the area of decision-making.

We see this in legislative chambers, in Governments, and in public service— equality for women in law is not mirrored by parity in representation.

—Secretary-General Boutros Boutros-Ghali at a gathering to mark International Women's Day in March 1994

In a period of increasing democratization on a global scale, women comprise more than half of the voters in almost all countries. They have had the right to vote and hold office in most countries for more than a generation. However, this has not translated into equal representation.

In only a few countries— mainly those in Scandinavia—are the proportions of men and women in decision-making and public policy-making more or less equal. On the whole, most countries are far from achieving the target of 30 per cent women in decision-making levels by 1995 set by the United Nations Economic and Social Council. The UN has set similar goals for its professional staff and has stepped up efforts to recruit and advance women within the Organization.

Still, women are largely absent from the leadership of international organizations, the top level of the diplomatic corps, the boards of transnational corporations and banks, and the higher ranks of the military and the police.

The lack of women's participation in political decision-making has important consequences. It deprives women of important rights and responsibilities as citizens, and excludes their perspectives and interests from policy-making and decision-making. Their voices are missing from key decisions on national budgets and setting of government priorities. Their skills and viewpoints often remain unheard, underrepresented or ignored.

Politics: National to International

In a male-led world reeling from one disaster to another, women in rich and poor countries alike are organizing to transform "old-boy" politics and win an equal role in fate-of-the Earth decisions.....

— Gloria Steinem, 1994[1]

In the Western world, only after countless demonstrations, hunger strikes and active lobbying did women obtain the right to vote, first in New Zealand in 1893. Two historical factors were decisive in women's securing the right to vote: their increasing participation in "male" jobs during the industrial revolution; and their substantial contributions in the world wars.

Beginning in the nineteenth century, women in several countries led prolonged struggles to obtain the right to vote. In Europe and North America in particular, a opposition to women's suffrage was based mainly on the assumption that women and politics did not belong together, that politics was a "non-feminine" activity.[2]

In other parts of the world, women earned their access to the modern political process through their active participation in the struggles against colonialism, for national liberation and in the formation of new States. In India, for example, women received the vote following independence as a natural extension of their active participation in the freedom struggle.[3] Wars, revolutions and independence movements brought waves of women into the voting booth.

By 1987, women had the right to vote in at least 115 countries, according to the **Inter-Parliamentary Union,** an NGO of national parliaments.[4]

In most countries, women won the right to vote and the right to stand for election at the same time. Although women have voted in increasing numbers in countries with democratic elections, the numbers of women in elective or appointive offices remain unacceptably low.

Few women, for example, reach the top levels of participation in national legislatures, even fewer reach major decision-making positions in government.

- On average, worldwide only 10.5 per cent of legislators and only 6.1 per cent of ministerial-level decision makers in 1994 were women.[5]
- In Norway, which has a female Prime Minister, 37 per cent of the cabinet and 39 per cent of Parliament consist of women.
- In the US, women in the current Congress comprise slightly over 11 per cent in the House and 7 per cent in the Senate.
- In other developed regions, participation rose from about 7 per cent in 1975 to about 17 per cent in 1994, with a high of 34 per cent in the Nordic countries.[6]
- In **Eastern Europe,** women's participation in parliament dropped sharply—from 22 per cent in 1987 to 6.5 per cent in 1993 — largely as a result of the collapse of communism and the elimination of quotas for women in parliament. However, a recent inter-parliamentary Union report (June 1994) shows an improvement in women's representation in 1994. In the Polish Senate, women's representation increased from 8 per cent in 1991 to 13 per cent in 1994; in Hungary, from 7.3 per cent in 1990 to almost 11 per cent in 1994.

In most countries of the world, women have not been—and still are not—candidates for leadership positions. Often they have limited access to the channels for achieving power at the top, especially in the executive bodies of political parties and trade unions.

In many countries undergoing dramatic political changes, women's active role in the process of democratization has induced significant political and legal changes. But the advent of democracy has not necessarily provided equal participation in politics and decision-making.

Prejudice, tradition and undemocratic regimes also hamper women in their quest for political power.

When women do achieve ministerial positions in government, they are usually put in change of such ministries as education, health, culture, social welfare, youth and women's affairs, and sometimes justice and legal affairs. Very few serve in such key sectors as finance, defence and internal and foreign affairs.

A Different Style?

If women share political power equally with men, will it change the way we live? While some argue that power defines the person regardless of gender, others believe women can wield power differently.

As women lead, they are changing leadership; as they organize, they are changing organization..... When women lead and articulate their purposes, it seems to me that they work together not only as individuals but with a sense of community and networking in a healthy way.... Women have fresh and imaginative skills of dialogue and are setting a more open, flexible and compassionate style of leadership.

—President Mary Rabinson of Ireland in a speech at the Global Forum of Women, 1992.

Very often, women bring a new agenda and more creative methods, and manage to make a difference n government polices.

- The strong presence of women in Norway's Government has made it a leading champion of human rights as well as women's rights, peace, environmental protection and development assistance.
- In Sweden, women working both within and outside Government prevented their country from entering the nuclear arms race and blocked efforts to continue use of nuclear power. [7]

Strategies to Address Inequities

Strategies for propelling women into leadership roles include:

Increasing women's participation in voting activity through education and information campaigns; and training in political and leadership skills, funding and campaign assistance for potential women candidates for political office.

Affirmative action (the steps to eliminate existing, remedy past and prevent future discrimination) can also encourage opportunities for women.

The purpose of affirmative action is to ensure that both women and men have an equal opportunity to compete for any decision-making or power-wielding position.

Quotas, or the reservation of a certain percentage of jobs for women in decision-making positions, are considered one such means of affirmative action.

Edith Cresson, the former French Prime Minister, said in 1991 that the only way to achieve a "massive increase in the number of women in all walks of political life" is through electoral systems which "make it possible to allocate to women a significant and compulsory percentage of senior party politicians and political commentators who are all men in the traditional mould."[8]

There is much debate today about the effectiveness of quota systems. In the former Communist countries of Eastern Europe, where quotas existed for women, it is argued that women had not more impact than in countries without quota systems. Women's representation in State legislatures was often mere "tokenism". This is widely thought to have resulted in unqualified and passive women filling the quotas which were allocated only to the official women's and other mass organizations, trade unions and ruling Communist parties.[9]

At an Inter-Parliamentary Union Symposium in 1989, however, participants focused on how quotas and other mechanisms to increase women's participation could provide more than token representation in multiparty systems as well as be a way to give women some leverage in authoritarian societies.

Participants agreed that at least 30 per cent female representation would provide the "critical mass" of gender balance needed to influence decision-making bodies by integrating the views, needs and concerns of women.

Quotas have been used as token percentages that segregate women into marginal positions, but also as larger percentages that genuinely expand women's access to political power.

What has, however, proved more effective in increasing women's representation in state legislatures is an electoral system with proportional gender representation. As part of it, political parties are encouraged to have a certain percentage of female representatives in their executive bodies as well as in their list of party candidates. Sweden was the first to try out quotas within its political parties, in 1972, with the result that female representation in the executive body of the Liberal Party reached 40 per cent. Political parties in Denmark, France and Norway have also introduced similar quotas.[10] Proportional representation is also a feature in Brazil, Greece and Hungary.

Another way of ensuring affirmative action is for Governments to define specific goals, timetables, targets and numbers that would help accelerate the pace of gender equality,. The UN set a goal for itself to place women in 35 per cent of its Professional staff positions overall and 25 per cent in higher-level posts by 1995. At the end of 1994, the proportion of women in all Professional posts stood at 33 per cent, and in higher —level posts, at 16 per cent.[11]

Affirmative Actions at the National Level

- The Sudan has established a 10 per cent minimum quota level for women's representation in all positions of local, municipal and state government.
- In 1992, the United Republic of Tanzania passed a law requiring that at least 15 per cent of all members of parliament be female.
- Antigua and Barbuda has set itself a goal of electing a minimum of seven women in parliament by 1999.
- In March 1993, Argentina implemented a law establishing quotas in the lists of political parties to guarantee a minimum of 30 per cent participation by women.
- Bangladesh attributes the increase of women in the civil services to the success of introducing quotas. Women's participation rose from 17 per cent of officers in the Secretariat in 1987 to 26 per cent in 1991 and from seven per cent of officers in the Directorates in 1987 to 20 per cent in 1991.

New Role as Civil Authorities

The number of women entering positions of civil authority and administrative and policy making jobs has increased considerably in the past few years.

Police Women

In many countries, according to data submitted to the United Nations Secretariat in national reports on the status and advancement of women as a December 1994, participation of women in police forces in terms of both numbers and level increased, especially over the last five-years. In one country in 1992, female cadets and trainees reached 33 per cent of the total. In another country, 13 per cent of the police chiefs were women.[12]

Most police women are specifically assigned to handle cases of violence against women, including rape or to supervise female prisons and prisoners. Although women's contribution in these areas has been considerable, the possibilities for promotion and career development are limited. Policewomen also face certain cultural difficulties with their male colleagues and with offenders who often do not recognize their authority.

Civil Service

Occupational segregation is a feature of most public administrations. While women on the government payroll are usually teachers, nurses or clerical employees or employed in departments like social welfare, men are employed in more critical departments such as defence or finance.

As a result, top positions in the civil service are still largely denied to women. One study identified impediments to women interested in a civil service career, including:[13]

- Socialization that instils and reinforces attitudes that stifle their aspirations;
- Gender stereotyping in jobs and in society as a whole;
- Lack of access to education and specialized training;
- Entry-level barriers and discriminatory promotion practices;
- Double burden of family and career responsibilities.

Private Sector

The growing presence of women in the global workforce and in almost every field of business and enterprise is one of the great demographic trends of the century. However, as in political life, positions in top management and decision-making in business elude women.

In the 1970s and 1980s, companies began to recruit women for management positions often because women could help them serve new markets and customers and become more profitable. Now women confront a new challenge: breaking through the "glass ceiling" that keeps many of them from being promoted to senior-management positions.

Regardless of whether organizations are public or private, large or small, national or international, women are entering the lower ranks of management, but rarely advancing to the top.

WOMEN AS LEADERS

Only a handful of women have reached the level of presidents or prime ministers:

PRESIDENTS

In the past:

Corazon Aquino in the Philippines;
Ertha Pascal-Trouillot in Haiti;
Isabel Peron in Argentina;
Lidia Geiler in Bolivia.

As of December 1994:

Violeta Chamorro in Nicaragua;
Vigdis Finnbogadottir in Iceland;
Mary Robinson in Ireland;
Chandrika Bandaranaike Kumaratunga in Sri Lanka.

PRIME MINISTERS

In the past:

Golda Meir in Israel;
Indira Gandhi in India;
Hanna Suchocka in Poland;
Edith Cresson in France;
Margaret Thatcher in the United Kingdom;
Maria de Lourdes Pintasilgo in Portugal;
Agathe Uwilingiyimana in Rwanda;
Kazimiera Danute-Prunskiene in Lithuania;
Milka Planinc in Yugoslavia;
Kim Campbell in Canada.

As of December 1994:

Gro Harlem Brundtland in Norway;
Eugenia Charles in Dominica;
Tansu Ciller in Turkey;
Benazir Bhutto in Pakistan;
Khaleda Ziaur Rahman in Bangladesh;
Siramavo Bandaranaike in Sri Lanka.

They represent an estimated 40 per cent of the workforce, but less than 20 per cent of management, and less than 6 per cent of senior management.

Women fail to make their mark in top positions in industry because they usually begin their careers in support positions as secretarial staff, or in human resources, accounting and public relations. They rarely gain experience in core areas such as manufacturing, marketing and sales, and, therefore, are later denied top positions in management.[14]

When women do rise to top positions, their potential is often underutilized. Stereotypes and misconceptions prevent organizations from appreciating the distinctive approaches that women bring to management and decision-making. Some research suggests that women managers may be better able to reconcile concerns for bottom-line results with a concern for people and to focus on both ends and means, and may be better planners and communicators.[15]

Female managers find it tough to break into the "old-boys network" of senior managers. But as their numbers grow, they are building networks of their won and adopting the mentoring system-by which successful female leaders guide the careers of junior women profesionals.

Media

Increasingly, the mass media are influencing the social and political agendas of the day. In addition to pursuing careers of their choice, women who establish careers in the media are in a better position to voice their concerns and opinions.

Ever since the United Nations Decade for Women (1976-1985), increasing numbers of women have entered the mainstream media as reporters and editors, producers and directors, as well as established a growing women's alternative media.

> *Almost everywhere an increase in the number of women working mainstream media has been recorded. But the power to develop media policy, and to determine the nature and shape of media content, continues to elude women.*
>
> —Margaret Gallagher and Lilia Quindoza-Santiago, eds., Women Empowering Communication, World Association for Christian Communication/International Women's Tribune Center, Bangkok, 1994

Women's overall share of jobs in the media remains low:

- Under 25 per cent in both broadcasting and the press in Africa, Asia and Latin America and the Caribbean; 30 per cent for the press and 36 per cent for broadcasting in Europe.

Women rarely occupy top media jobs:

- Out of 200 organizations studied in 30 countries for *The World's Women: Trends and Statistics: 1970-1995*, only seven were found to be headed by women.[16]

Across Asia, the number of women in the media has increased, yet this "has not made a significant change in the content, style of presentation of information. News decisions are still made by men even if news is increasingly reported and edited by women; the employment of women has not radically altered news agendas or priorities." In Asia, "most of the 'soft sections', the weekend supplements, the health, culture and education beats are now almost exclusively run by women; defence, commerce and foreign affairs are still largely male strongholds as are the editorships of most general and specialized publications", according to a media researcher, Vijayalakshmi Balakrishnan.[17]

BY 1990, more than one third of women employed in radio and TV worked in administration, and more than 40 per cent in Zambia, Japan, Chile and all European countries except Greece.

Yet, encouragingly more young women New want to make a career in the media. In fact, women form the majority of students of mass communication throughout the developed regions, in almost all of Latin America and the Caribbean, and in many parts of Asia and the Pacific.

Female-run alternative media, based outside State or public service broadcasting systems and mainstream commercial production, have witnessed a boom. A 1990 directory, *Third World Women's Publications,* listed over 300 such specialized periodicals.[18]Some other new publications include *Sister* in Namibia; *Speak* in South Africa; *Tamania Mars* in Morocco; and *Asmita* in Nepal.

Women's press services now include Depth News in Asia, the Women's Feature Service in New Delhi, WINGS (Women's International News Gathering Service) in the US and FEM PRESS in Chile.

The media are also used at the community and local level to develop skills and overcome fears, as with the Self-Employed Women's Association (SEWA) in India, which teachers women how to use video cameras to record their work and share information with other groups, or the introduction of video and radio among indigenous women in Bolivia and other parts of Latin America, like *Radio Tierra* in Chile and FIRE (Feminist International Radio Endeavour) in Costa Rica.[19]

Community-Based Organizations

In most of the world, women are becoming increasingly effective leaders of community-based organizations. The success of many such movements depends on the level of activism of women in the community.

Since the early 1980s, NGOs and community-based groups involved in development programmes such as literacy or health campaigns have become more gender-sensitive. They recognize women as primary nurturers and care-givers, health providers, and often responsible for the water, fuel and food needs of communities.

For example, the **Chipko (Hug-the-Trees)** movement in the Himalayas in the 1970s and 1980s was led largely by women. The Uttarkhand hill women were natural leaders of the movement, as they knew best the worth of the forests to their communities.

As leaders of community-based organizations, women usually strive to be democratic, emphasizing teamwork and individual responsibility.

- In Cameroon, the **Women's Networking Association** brings together 50 women's groups, carries out literacy campaigns and provides assistance, such as establishing cooperatives to purchase unsold produce marketed by village women.

- In Kenya, which has 23,000 women's groups, the **Green Belt** movement tackles problems of environmental degradation and poverty, encouraging women to use soil rehabilitation measures and natural fertilizers. With 50,000 women, it has planted 10 million trees and established training centres to increase women's employment opportunities.
- **The Alliance of Costa Rican Women** provides legal and health services to more than 4,000 low-income women.[20]

Women's organizations— grass-roots groups, professional associations, networks and other non-governmental organizations— have demonstrated success in mobilizing women, especially at the community level, in both rural and urban areas. Diverse in form, they help to advance women through advocacy, monitoring of public policies and rallying support.

Besides their local impact and their influence at the national level, community groups play an increasingly important role in international forums. At every major UN conference of this decade, active NGO forums and women's caucuses have led the lobbying efforts to influence the agendas and resulting programmes of action.

Obstacles, Trends and Goals

Since 1990, several changes have affected trends in the sharing of power and decision-making by women at all levels.

- The worldwide movement for democratization has created conditions for greater political participation, but has sometimes led to a decline in the number of women in decision-making positions as a result of the elimination of gender-based quota systems.
- The continuing rise of the global women's movement has sustained pressure on Governments and international organizations to increase women's participation in decision-making.

In many regions and in many fields— industry, media and politics— women still suffer both horizontal segregation (clustering in lower-paying, lower-status, staff and administrative jobs) and vertical segregation (occupying non-strategic areas).

Some believe that as women gain access to all fields, the weight of their numbers will change the conditions and opportunities. This has not always proved true. Lethargy inside organizations and institutional structures, and the influence of socialization and conformism, work to maintain the status quo.

Change requires active polices of equal opportunities, gender equality at every level of organization and the removal of "glass ceilings" that thwart advancement. Invisible barriers of attitudes and biases hinder women's advancement to positions of power and decision-making. Assertiveness training and support groups can help women feel less isolated and alienated, and empower them to make a difference.

Of the many remaining obstacles to women's advancement in decision-making, two stand out:

- Maternity: Working women usually face an either/or situation. Either they sacrifice their jobs and careers to become mothers, or they miss out on motherhood. Most women take on both roles with little support in child-care or flexible working conditions.

Often when qualified, professional women are poised to occupy top decision-making positions, they find their so-called "biological clocks" reminding them of motherhood. Those who choose maternity frequently find themselves taking a back seat in corporate, national or international decision-making bodies.

Motherhood is largely considered a women's burden and responsibility. In only a few countries is it considered society's responsibility to ensure that women and men both share productive and reproductive roles and responsibilities.

Governments and businesses are beginning to take action aimed at increasing women's participation in high decision-making positions: equal-opportunity programmes and the responsibilities of quotas; and support services such as day-care centres, creches and after-school services.

- Inequality in the public arena often reflects the pervasive inequality in the house-hold. With male and female roles firmly entrenched in most societies, women find if difficult to be taken seriously and step out of their traditional roles.

Women are pooling their efforts to influence public policy and rally support for women in political, social and economic decision-making. Only through united efforts can women bring about genuine change.

At the international level, several UN agencies are making a difference.

With UNICEF backing, an increasing number of countries are sensitizing government staff to gender awareness in planning and policy-making. In Kenya, training has been conducted for district-level officials.

In Ecuador, an inter-agency group made up of several UN agencies, including UNDP, UNFPA and WHO, prepared a common gender-training package for project managers, staff and beneficiaries.

Since 1986, the Food and Agriculture Organization of the United Nations (FAO) has helped train Honduran women, selected by local women's groups, to be active in rural development and organize their own groups.

UNIFEM offers leadership training to women in various parts of the world:

- A mentoring programme begun by the African Academy of Sciences in Kenya, which provides future female decision makers with leadership, technical, gender and advocacy skills through internships at national, regional and international institutions;
- The creation of a network of women involved in community development in Paraguay, to promote the design and implementation of gender-sensitive public policies;
- Funding the Gender-Watch Group in Thailand, nationwide network of NGOs, academic institutions and grass-roots female activists that monitors political activities and decision-making in the context of gender and lobbies to include women's concerns in national development plans.

According to Gertrude Mongella, Secretary-General of the Fourth World Conference on Women, "the level of participation of women in decision-making and sharing of power between men and women is still unacceptably low and calls in question the basic principles of democracy"[21] Unless women can fully participate in political and other decision- making, democracy cannot be achieved or effectively maintained.

Electing women to high office is a crucial role that women everywhere can accomplish. By casting their votes, women can bring about not only political change, but changes in public policy, in the economy and in society at large.

Notes

1. In a review of the book *Women and Government: New Ways to Political Power,* edited by Mim Kelber, 1994.
2. *Women in Politics and Decision-making in the Late Twentieth Century,* United Nations study 1992.
3. *Ibid.*
4. *Ibid.*
5. International Parliamentary Union; and *The World's Women: Trends and Statistics (1970-1995),* UN, forthcoming.
6. UN Statistical Division.
7. Kelber, Mim, *Women and Government: New Ways to Political Power,* Women USA Fund Study, 1994, introduction by M.Kelber and Bella Abzug.
8. Conference on "Women in Power" Athens, Greece, November 1992.
9. Einhorn , Barbara, *Cinderella Goes to Market-Citizenship, Gender and Women's Movements in East Central Europe,* Verso Books, 1993.
10. *The Situation of Women in the political Process in Europe,* Council of Europe, Strasbourg, vol. II, p. 113.

11. Gierycz, Dorota, UN Division for the Advancement of Women, paper on "Women in International Decision-making: Peace and Security Areas". For Expert Group Meeting on Gender and the Agenda for peace, UN, December 1994.
12. *Second Review and Appraisal of the Implementation of the Nairobi Forward-looking Strategies for the Advancement of Women,* UN.
13. Bayes, J., "Women in Public Administration: A Speculative Typology", presented at the International Political Science Association Roundtable for Sex Roles and Politics Research Committee, New York City. 1-2 June 1990.
14. Expert group meeting on 'Women and Economic Decision-making", Division for the Advancement of Women, 1994.
15. Research from the Center for Values Research, Dallas, Texas, a non-profit organization.
16. *The World's Women: Trends and Statistics* (1970-1995, United Nations, June 1995.
17. Balakrishnan, Vijayalakshmi, "Indigenous Social Norms and Women in Asian Media", pp. 42-43, in *Women Empowering Communication,* Gallagher, Margaret, and Quindoza Santiago, Lilia, eds., World Association for Christian Communication/International Women's tribune Center, Bangkok, 1994.
18. Adagala, Esther and Kiai, Wambui, "Flok, Interpersonal and Mass Media: The Experience of Women in Africa", in *Women Empowering Communication,* 1994.
19. Isis International, operating out of Santiago, Chile and Manila, Philippines, a non-governmental women's information and communication service.
20. See note 12.
21. *Human Development Report, UNDP,* 1993.
22. Report to the UN General Assembly's Third Committee, December 1994.

THE UNITED NATIONS AND THE STATUS OF WOMEN:

SETTING THE GLOBAL GENDER AGENDA

UN Action for Women

UN actions for the advancement of women began with the signing of the UN's founding Charter. In its Preamble, the members of the UN declared their faith "in fundamental human rights, in the dignity and worth of the human person, in the equal rights of men and women and of nations large and small.."

This happened 50 years ago, in October 1945, when the Charter entered into force and the UN was formally set up. Since then, the UN has been at the centre of a growing global movement for women's rights. By adopting international laws and treaties on women's rights, the UN has helped set a common standard for measuring how societies advance equality between men and women.

The Conventions, or international treaties, that the UN has adopted are legally binding for countries that recognize them. among such treaties are:

- The Convention on the Political Rights of Women (1952);
- The Convention on the Nationality of Married Women (1957);
- The Convention on Recovery Abroad of Maintenance (1956);
- The Convention on the Consent to Marriage (1962);
- The Convention on the Elimination of all forms of Discrimination against Women (1979);

The UN observed 1975 as International Women's Year and held the first world conference on women in Mexico City. Subsequently, two other UN conferences were held: Copenhagen (1980) and Nairobi

(1985). The Fourth World Conference on Women will be held in Beijing, China in September 1995.

The Forward-looking Strategies for the Advancement of Women to the year 2000, adopted at the Nairobi Conference, is a blueprint for women's advancement. Its 372 paragraphs deal with the entire spectrum of women's role in society. In Beijing, the countries of the world will review the advancement of women in light of these guidelines. They will also adopt a Platform for Action, addressing the challenges and demands of the next century.

In December 1993, the UN adopted the Declaration on the Elimination of Violence against Women, which defined what constitutes violence against women and outlined actions Governments and communities should take to prevent such acts. Earlier, in June 1993, the World Conference on Human Rights in Vienna, Austria, reaffirmed that women's rights are also human rights. One of the outcomes of the Conference was the appointment of a Special Rapporteur on violence against Women.The Rapporteur, who seeks and receives information on violence against women, its causes and consequences, and recommends means and ways to eliminate them, reports to the UN Commission on Human Rights.

The Convention on the Elimination of All Forms of Discrimination Against Women

The Convention on the Elimination of all forms of Discrimination against Women, adopted in 1979 by the UN General Assembly, is often described as an international bill or rights for women. Consisting of a preamble and 30 articles, it defines what constitutes discrimination against women and sets up an agenda for national action to end such discrimination.

According to the Convention, discrimination against women is.... "any distinction, exclusion or restriction made on the basis of sex which has the effect or purpose of impairing or nullifying the recognition, enjoyment or exercise by women, irrespective of their marital status, on a basis of equality of men and women, of human rights and fundamental freedoms in the political, economic, social, civil or any other field."

By recognizing the Convention, States commit themselves to undertake a series of measures to end discrimination against women in all its forms, including:

- To incorporate the principle of equality of men and women in their legal systems, abolish all discriminatory laws and adopt appropr/iate ones prohibiting discrimination against women;

- To establish tribunals and other public institutions to ensure the effective protection of women against discrimination; and
- To ensure elimination of all acts of discrimination against women by persons, organizations or enterprises.

The Convention provides the basis for realizing equality between men and women through ensuring women's equal access to, and equal opportunities in, political and public life—including the right to vote and to stand for election—as well as education and employment. States parties agree to take all appropriate measures, including legislation and temporary special measures, so that women can enjoy all their human rights and fundamental freedoms.

The Convention is the only human rights treaty which affirms the reproductive rights of women and targets culture and tradition as influential forces shaping gender roles and family relations. It affirms women's right to acquire, change or retain their nationality and the nationality of their children. States parties also agree to take appropriate measures against all forms of traffic in women and exploitation of women.

Countries that have ratified or acceded to the Convention are legally bound to put into practice its provisions. They are also committed to submit national reports, at least once every four years, on measures they have taken to comply with their treaty obligations.

The Convention, which entered into force on 3 September 1981, has so far been accepted by 139 UN Member States.

The Committee on the Elimination of Discrimination Against Women

The Committee on the Elimination of Discrimination against Women (CEDAW) was set up in 1982 to monitor the implementation of the Convention on the Elimination of Discrimination against Women.

The Committee is composed of 23 experts, who are elected by those countries that have ratified the Convention. Members of the Committee, who are person "of high moral standing and competence in the field covered by the Convention" serve for a term of four years and may be re-related. Though nominated by there Governments, the experts serve in their individual capacities and not as delegates or representatives of their countries of origin. Since its inception, and with only one exception, the Committee has always been composed entirely of women.

The Committee, which convenes once a year for a three-week period, reviews the reports of States Parties on the implementation of the

Convention on the Elimination of All Forms of Discrimination against Women and evaluates the progress made. It can suggest specific measures as well as make general recommendations to the States parties on eliminating discrimination against women. It may also invite UN specialized agencies to submit reports for consideration and may receive information from non-governmental organizations.

The Committee reports annually on its activities to the General Assembly through the Economic and Social Council, and the Council transmits these reports to the Commission on the Status of Women for information.

The Commission of the Status of Women

The Commission on the Status on Women (CSW) is one of the first bodies established by the UN Economic and Social Council. Set up in 1946, it monitors the situation of women and promotes their rights in all societies around the world. It prepares recommendations and reports for the UN on any issue affecting women. In case of urgent problems, the Commission can press for immediate international action to prevent or alleviate violations of women's rights.

In other words, CSW is the global advocate for equality between women and men.

The Commission, an intergovernmental body, has 45 members, each elected for four years. The membership of the Commission reflects the following geographical composition: 13 States from Africa, 11 from Asia, 4 from Eastern Europe, 9 from Latin America and the Caribbean and 8 from Western Europe and other States. The Commission meets annually for a period of at least eight days.

The central part of CSW's work involves setting universal standards regarding equality between women and men. It has also assumed a leading role in bringing women's concerns to the attention of the UN specialized agencies. Various UN Conventions, including the Convention on the Elimination of All Forms of Discrimination against Women, have set new standards in the area of human rights. Over the years, the Commission has dealt with issues such as women's participation in political life and in decision-making, and women's role in and contribution to development. It has put forward policy recommendations regarding women's rights in employment and in education, and their role in the economy and the environment. It has made recommendations on how to support women in their fight against poverty. Its work with regard to violence against women led to the adoption of the Declaration on the

Elimination of Violence against Women by the General Assembly in 1993.

CSW initiated the observance of International Women's Year 1975 and the world conferences on women. Following the adoption of the Forward-looking Strategies in Nairobi at the Third UN conference on women in 1985, the Commission has also been responsible for monitoring the implementation of these strategies.

In Beijing, at the Fourth World Conference on Women (September 1995), the Commission will present the review and appraisal of the Nairobi Strategies. Both CEDAW and CSW are serviced by the Division for the Advancement of Women (DAW) of the Department of Policy Coordination and Sustainable Development. DAW also acts as secretariat for world conferences on women. The Division carries out policy research and monitors implementation of programmes of action taken at world conferences on women. It maintains regular outreach with NGOs and academic and national institutions working for women's advancement. It is also the focal point for coordination of activities for women in the UN system as a whole.

Women in Development

The need for integrating women in the development process was placed on the international agenda in 1975, when the UN observed International Women's Year. Among the many concrete steps taken in this regard after the 1975 world conference on women was the creation of two UN bodies, UNIFEM and INSTRAW.

A result of the energetic advocacy of women at the first world conference on women, the United Nations Development Fund for Women (UNIFEM) was established by the United Nations General Assembly in 1976 to provide direct support to development projects for women. Originally set up as the Voluntary Fund for the Decade for Women, the Fund was asked to help improve the living standards of women in developing countries by addressing their concerns through providing direct technical and financial support and by promoting the inclusion of women in the decision-making process of mainstream development programmes. In 1985, the Fund became an autonomous body in association with the UN development Programme (UNDP) and was renamed UNIFEM.

Sometimes described as a bridge between international organizations, policy makers and disadvantaged women, UNIFEM is aid to and advocate for women of the developing world. Currently, UNIFEM works at the country level through its 10 regional offices. Among its priority areas are trade and industry, credit, science and technology, agriculture and food security, and policy -making and national planning. It also targets critical issues on the global agenda to ensure that gender is included in international policies such as those related to refugees and displaced persons, violence against women, human rights, global governance and environment. UNIFEM has recently established a women's human rights programme aimed at strengthening the capacity of women's organizations that work on human rights.

The United Nations International Research and Training Institute for the Advancement of Women (INSTRAW), established in 1975 by the General Assembly on the recommendation of the first world conference on women, is an autonomous body within the UN system with a mandate to carry out research, training and information activities worldwide to promote women as key agents for sustainable development.

Operating from its headquarters in Santo Domingo, Dominican Republic, the institute performs research projects to identify barriers that impede women's equality in the process of social, economic and political development. INSTRAW analyzes existing research material by interacting and working with Governments, UN agencies and academic institutions, as well as non-governmental organizations and other entities.

INSTRAW's experience has proved that the greatest problem affecting women in invisibility. With this purpose, INSTRAW develops new ways of understanding, new methodologies and statistics for training programmes and methods linked to issues such as:

- Economic empowerment;
- Collection of statistics and indicators on women's work in the formal and informal sectors;
- Availability of statistics on elderly women;
- Women and time-use;
- Statistics on women in the informal sector in industry, trade and services;
- Migration of women and the methodological issues involved in the measurement and analysis of internal and international migration;
- Women, water and sanitation and women and water management;
- New and renewable sources of energy;
- Women and environmental management;
- The role of women in environmentally sound and sustainable development;
- The image and participation of women in alternative and mass media;
- Gender and development studies, including training material.

THE UN SYSTEM AND WOMEN'S STATUS

- **General Assembly**: Highest intergovernmental body for the formulation and appraisal of policy, including rights of women and related issues.
- **Economic and Social Council**: Principal UN organ for coordinating the economic and social work of the UN and its specialized agencies, including the role of women in development.
- **Commission on Human Rights**: Main UN body on human rights; develops and codifies new international norms and monitors the observance of human rights around the world. A special Rapporteur on Violence against Women, appointed by the Commission, seeks and receives information on violence against women and recommends ways and means to eliminate it.
- **Commission on the Status of Women**: Main UN body dealing with policy decisions on women's status; monitors women's situation and prepares recommendations for the UN and its Member States.
- **CEDAW**: A committee of 23 international experts set up to monitor the implementation of the Convention on the Elimination of All Forms of Discrimination against Women.
- **DAW**: A division within the UN Secretariat: Services CEDAW and CSW and acts as secretariat for UN conferences on women
- **Specialized agencies and programmes**: Members of the UN system; play key role in stimulating and aiding technical cooperation for development, the key beneficiaries of which are women.
- **UNIFEM**: Autonomous body in association with UNDP, provides direct support to women's development projects.
- **Instraw**: Autonomous body within UN system; undertakes research and training activities for the advancement of women.

•

8 MARCH: INTERNATIONAL WOMEN'S DAY

International Women's Day (8 March) is not only an occasion marked by women's groups around the world. This date is also commemorated at the United Nations and is designated in many countries as a national holiday. When women on all continents, often divided by ethnic, inguistic, cultural, economic and political differences, come together to celebrate their day, they can look back to a tradition that represents almost a century of struggle for equality, justice, peace and development.

International Women's Day is the story of ordinary women as makers of history; it is rooted in the centuries-old struggle of women to participate in society and social change on an equal footing with men. In ancient Greece, Lysistrata initiated a sexual strike against men in order to end war; during e Fench Revolution, Parisian women calling for "liberty, equality, fraternity" marched on Versailles to demand women's suffrage.

The idea of an International Women's Day first arose at the turn of the century, which in the industrialized world was a period of expansion and turbulence, booming population growth and radical ideologies. Following is a brief chronology of the most important events:

- 1909: In accordance with a declaration by the Socialist Party of America, the first National Women's Day was observed across the United States on 28 February. Women continued to celebrate it on the last Sunday of that month through 1913.
- 1910: The Socialist International, meeting in Copenhagen, established a Women's Day, international in character, to honour the movement for women's rights and freedom and to assist in achieveing universal suffrage for women. No fixed date was selected.

From General Assembly resolution 32/142

The General Assembly,

.....*Taking into account* that secure peace and social progress, the establishment of the new International economic order as well as the full enjoyment of human rights and fundamental freedoms require the active participation of women, their equality and development,

Appreciating the contribution of women to the strengthening of International peace and security and to the struggle against colonialism, racism, racial discrimination, foreign aggression and occupation and all forms of fieign domination......

2. *Calls* upon all States to continue to make their contribution to creating favourable conditions for the elimination of discrimination against, women and for their full and equal participation in the social development, process and to encourage broad participation of women in the effort to strengthen international peace, extend the process of international detente, curb the arms race take measures for disarmament;.....

4. *Invites* all States to proclaim, in accordance with their historical and national traditions and customs, any day of the year as United Nations Day for Women's Rights and International Peace and to inform the Secretary-General thereon;.........

105th plenary meeting
16 December 1977

- 1911: As a result of the decision taken at Copenhagen the previous year, International Women's Day was marked for the first time (19 March) in Austria, Denmark, Germany and Switzerland, where more than 1 million women and men attended rallies. In addition to the right to vote and to hold public office, they demanded the right to work, to vocational training and to an end to discrimination on the job.

Less than a week later, on 25 March, the tragic Triangle Fire in New York City took the lives of more than 140 working girls, most of them Italian and Jewish immigrants. This event had a significant impact on labour legislation in the United States, and the working conditions leading up to the disaster were invoked during subsequent celebrations of International Women's Day.

- 1913-1914: As part of the peace movement brewing on the eve of World War, 1, Russian women observed their first International Women's Day on the last Sunday in February, 1913; elsewhere in

Europe, on or around 8 March of the following year, women held rallies either to protest the war or to express solidarity with their sisters.

- 1917: With 2 million Russian soldiers dead in the war, Russian women again chose the last Sunday in February to Strike for "bread and Peace". Political leaders opposed the timing of the strike, but the women went out anyway, and the rest is history. Four days later, the Czar was forced to abdicate; the provisional Government granted women the right to vote. That historic Sunday fell on 23 February on the Julian calendar in use elsewhere. International Women's Day has usually been celebrated on 8 March ever since.

Since those early years, International Women's Day has assumed a new global dimension for women in developed and developing countries alike. It has become a rallying point for coordinated efforts to demand women's rights and participation in the political process. Increasingly, Women's Day is a time to reflect on progress made, to call for change and to celebrate acts of courage and determination by ordinary women who have played an extraordinary role in the history of women's rights.

PLATFORM FOR ACTION

Since the United Nations held the first world conference on women 20 years ago (Mexico City, 1975), important progress has been made towards achieving equality between women and men. Women's access to education and proper health care has increased, their participation in the paid labour force has grown and legislation that promises equal opportunities for women and respect for their human rights has been adopted in more countries. As a result, important changes have occurred in the relationship between women and men.

Yet discrimination against women is still widespread. Violence against women remains a global phenomenon. Women's equal access to resources is still restricted and their opportunities for higher education and training are concentrated in limited fields. A "glass ceiling" continues to bar women's advancement in business, government and politics. Women are an overwhelming majority of the 1 billion people living in abject poverty and among illiterates. Decisions that effect women continue to be made largely by men.

The Beijing Declaration and Platform for Action, adopted unanimously at the Fourth World Conference on Women (4-15 September 1995) by representatives from 189 countries, reflect a new international commitment to the goals of equality, development and peace for all women everywhere.

The platform, divided into six chapter, identifies 12 "critical areas of concern" considered to represent the main obstacles to women's advancement. It defines strategic objectives and spells out actions to be taken over the next five years by Governments, the international community, non-governmental organizations and the private sector for the removal of the existing obstacles.

The platform was further reinforced in the Beijing Declaration. It reaffirmed the commitment of Governments to eliminate discrimination against women and to remove all obstacles to equality. Governments also recognized the need to ensure a gender perspective in their policies and programmes.

Mission Statement and Global Framework

Since the 1985 Nairobi Conference on Women, the world has experienced profound changes, with both positive and negative effects on women. A worldwide movement towards democratization has opened up the political process in many nations. The growing strength of women's organizations and feminist groups has become a driving force for change.

At the same time, widespread economic recession, political instability, heavy military spending, poorly designed structural adjustment programmes, the servicing of the external debt burden and continuing environmental degradation have had a disproportionately negative impact on women.

The Platform for Action, an agenda for women's empowerment, seeks to reverse this trend. It seeks to promote and protect the full enjoyment of all human rights and the fundamental freedoms of all women throughout their life cycle. It also calls for establishing the principle of shared power and responsibility between women and men at home, in the workplace and in the wider national and international communities.

The success of the Platform for Action will require a strong commitment on the part of Governments, international organizations and institutions at all levels. It will also require adequate mobilizations of resources at all levels as well as new and additional resources for the developing countries.

Poverty

Today, more than 1 billion people live in extreme poverty; the overwhelming majority of them are women. In the past decade the number of women living in poverty has increased disproportionately to the number of men, and the risk for falling into poverty is higher for women than for men. Poverty is particularly acute among women living in rural households.

Women are poorer because they have fewer economic opportunities and less autonomy than men. Their access to economic resources, education and training, and support services is limited. They also have very little participation in the way decisions are made. The rigidity of socially prescribed roles for women and the tendency to scale back social services have increased the burden of poverty on women.

THE PLATFORM RECOMMENDS ACTION TO:

- *Review*, abopt and maintain macroeconomic policies and development strategies that address the needs and efforts of women in poverty;
- Revise laws and administrative practices in order to ensure women's equal rights and access to economic resources;
- Provide women with access to savings and credit mechanisms and institutions;
- Develop gender-based methodologies and conduct research to address the feminization of poverty.

EDUCATION AND TRAINING

Education is a human right and an essential tool for achieving equality, development and peace. Though overall progress has been achieved in girls' enrollment at primary and secondary levels, girls in many countries still face discrimination due to customary attitudes, early marriages and pregnancies, lack of accessible schools, and inadequate and gender-biased teaching and educational materials. Girls continue to be denied quality education, especially at higher levels and in science and technology.

Investing in formal and non-formal education and training for girls and women has proved to be one of the best means of achieving sustainable development and economic growth.

THE PLATFORM RECOMMENDS ACTION TO:

- Ensure equal access to education. Governments are to commit themselves, by the year 2000, to universal access to basic education and completion of primary education by at least 80 per cent of primary-school-age children. They also agree to close the gender gap in primary-and secondary-school education by the year 2000, and to achieve universal education in all countries before the year 2015;
- Eradicate illiteracy among women. Governments are to reduce the female illiteracy rate at least to half its 1990 level;
- Improve women's access to vocational training, science and technology, and continuing education;
- Develop non-discriminatory education for training;

- Allocate sufficient resources for and monitor the implementation of educational reforms;
- Promote lifelong education and training and girls and women.

HEALTH

Women's health involves their emotional, social and physical well-being. it is determined by the social, political and economic context of their lives, as well as by biology. The enjoyment of the highest attainable standard of physical and mental health is vital for the life and well-being of women. It is also crucial to their ability to participate in all areas of public and private life. This right must be secured throughout their whole life cycle in equality with men.

The Platform defines reproductive health as a state of complete physical, mental and social well-being and sexual health whose purpose is the enhancement of life and personal relations. Equal relationships between men and women in matters of sexual relations and reproduction require mutual respect, consent and shared responsibility. The Platform recognizes that reproductive rights rest on the recognition of the basic human rights of all couples and individuals to decide freely and responsibly how many children they want to have, and when. They also have the right to obtain information and make decisions on reproduction free of discrimination, coercion and violence.

THE PLATFORM RECOMMENDS ACTIONS TO:

- Increase women's access throughout the life cycle to appropriate, affordable and quality health care, information and related services;
- Reduce maternal morality by at least 50 per cent of the 1990 levels by the year 2000 and a further one half by the year 2015;
- Encourage both women and men to take responsibility for their sexual and reproductive behaviour;
- Undertake gender-sensitive initiatives that address sexually transmitted diseases, HIVIAIDS and sexual and reproductive health issues;
- Increase resources and monitor follow-up for women's health.

VIOLENCE

In all societies, to a greater or lesser degree, women and girls are subject to physical, sexual and psychological abuse that cuts across lines of income, class and culture, in both public and private life. They often face rape, sexual abuse, sexual harassment and intimidation in the work place. They are particularly vulnerable to systematic violence during war.

Sexual slavery, forced pregnancy, sterilization and forced abortion, prenatal sex selection and female infanticide are also acts of violence. All such acts of violence violate and impair or nullify women's enjoyment of human rights and fundamental freedoms. Such groups of women as migrant workers require special attention because they are particularly vulnerable to violence.

Lack of preventive and protective laws, and lack of access or ineffective enforcement by public authorities of such laws where they exist, only perpetuate and increase violence against women.

THE PLATFORM RECOMMENDS ACTIONS TO:

- Adopt and implement legislation to end violence against women.
- Work actively to ratify and implement all international agreements related to violence against women, including the UN Convention on the Elimination of all Forms of Discrimination against Women;
- Adopt new laws and enforce existing ones to punish members of security forces and police or any other State agents for acts of violence against women;
- Step up shelters, provide legal aid and other services for girls and women at risk, and provide counselling and rehabilitation for perpetrators of violence against women;
- Step up national and international cooperation to dismantle networks engaged in trafficking in women.

ARMED CONFLICT

Peace is a prerequisite for the attainment of equality between women and men. Unfortunately, armed and other types of conflict still persist in many parts of the world. Aggression, foreign occupation and ethnic and other conflicts are an ongoing reality affecting women and men in nearly every region, aided by excessive military expenditures and the arms trade.

Though women rarely have any role in the decisions leading to armed conflicts, they work to preserve social order in the midst of the conflicts. They also make an important contribution as peace educators and resolvers of conflicts.

The Platform recognizes that rape, which is common during armed conflicts, is a crime, and under certain circumstances is an act of genocide. It condemns "ethnic cleansing" as a strategy of war and rape as one of its consequences. Such practices must be stopped and their perpetrators punished, it asserts.

THE PLATFORM RECOMMENDS ACTION TO:

- Increase the participation of women in conflict resolution at decision-making levels;
- Reduce excessive military expenditures and control the availability of armaments;
- Work towards the universal ratification of the anti-mine Convention and Protocol by the year 2000;
- Recognize the important roles and contributions of women in peace movements throughout the world;
- Recognize the need to protect women living in situations of armed and other conflict or under foreign occupation, or who have become refugees or displaced.

ECONOMY

Women contribute significantly to economic life everywhere. Their share in the labour force continues to rise, they are becoming more involved in micro-small and medium enterprises and their income is becoming increasingly necessary to all households.

However, women are largely excluded from economic decision-making, They face low wages, poor working conditions and limited employment and professional opportunities. Though women contribute to development through paid as well as unpaid work, their unpaid work, such aas domestic and community work, is not measured in quantitative terms and not valued in national accounts.

Discrimination in education and training, hiring, and remuneration and promotion, as well as inflexible working conditions, lack of access to productive resources and inadequate sharing of family responsibilities, contribute to restricted employment, economic and professional opportunities for women.

THE PLATFORM RECOMMENDS ACTION TO:

- Promote women's economic rights and independence, including access to employment and appropriate working conditions and control over economic resources;
- Facilitate women's equal access to resources, employment, markets and trade;
- Provide business services, training and access to markets, information and technology, particularly to low-income women;
- Strengthen women's economic capacity and commercial networks;
- Eliminate occupational segregation and all forms of employment discrimination;

- Promote harmonization of work and family responsibilities for women and men.

Decision-making

Women's equal participation in decision-making is not only a demand for simple social justice or democracy. It is essential for achieving transparent and accountable government. It will also provide a balance that more accurately reflects the composition of society.

Despite the widespread movement towards democratization in most countries, women remain largely underrepresented at most levels of government, especially in ministerial and other executive bodies or in reaching the target of having 30 per cent of decision-making positions held by women by 1995, as endorsed by the UN Economic and Social Council. They have achieved little progress in attaining political power in legislative bodies. Globally, only 10 per cent of legislative positions, and a lower percentage of ministerial positions, are held by women.

Similarly, the underrepresention of women in decision-making positions in the arts, culture, sports, the media, education, religion and law have prevented women from having a significant impact on many key institutions and policies.

The Platform recommends action to:

- Ensure women's equal access to and full participation in power structures and decision-making in governmental bodies and public administration entities, including the judiciary, international non-governmental organizations, political parties and trade unions;
- Increase women's capacity to paraticipate in decision-making and leadership positions.

Institutional Mechanisms

Most countries have established institutions for the advancement of women. These are diverse in form and uneven in their effectiveness. They are often marginalized in national government structures, without a clear mandate, and lack adequate staff and resources as well as support from national political leadership. At the regional and international levels, mechanisms and institutions for the advancement of women encounter similar problems.

Many organizations have developed methodologies for gender-based policy analysis. Unfortunately, they are applied either sporadically or not at all.

THE PLATFORM RECOMMENDS ACTION TO:

- Create or strengthen national machineries and other governmental bodies; ensure that responsibility for the advancement of women is vested in the highest possible level of Government;
- Integrate gender perspectives in legislation, public policies, programmes and projects,; ensure that before policy decisions are taken, an analysis of their impact on women and men is carried out.
- Generate and disseminate gender-disaggregated data and information for planning and evaluation; measure, in quantitative terms, unremunerated work that is outside national accounts.

HUMAN RIGHTS

All human rights are universal, indivisible, interdependent and interrelated. Their full and equal enjoyment by women and girls is a priority for Governments and the United Nations and is essential for the advancement of women.

Governments must not only refrain from violating the human rights of all women but work actively to promote and protect these rights.

Recognition of the importance of women's human rights is reflected in the fact that three quarters of the UN Member States have become parties to the Convention on the Elimination of All Forms of Discrimination against Women. However, the gap between the existence of rights and their effective enjoyment derives from a lack of commitment by Governments in promoting and protecting those rights and the failure of Governments to inform women and men alike about them.

THE PLATFORM RECOMMENDS ACTION TO:

- Promote and protect the human rights of women by fully implementing all human rights instruments, especially the Convention on the Elimination of All Forms of Discrimination against Women;
- Review national laws to ensure implementation of all international human rights agreements;
- Ensure equality and non-discrimination under the law and in practice;
- Achieve legal literacy.

MEDIA

Today, many women work in the media, but few have reached positions at decision-making levels. In most countries, the media continue to project a negative and degrading image of women and do not reflect women's diverse lives and contributions to society. Violent and degrading or pornographic media products in particular affect women negatively.

Everywhere the media have the potential to make a far greater contribution to the advancement of women. They can create self-regulatory mechanisms that can help eliminate gender biased programming. Women can also be empowered by having greater skills, knowledge and access to information technology.

The Platform recommends action to:

- Increase women's participation in and access to expression and decision-making in and through the media and new technologies of communication; Governments should aim at gender balance through the appointment of women and men to all advisory, management, regulatory or monitoring bodies;
- Promote a balanced and non-stereotyped portrayal of women in the media. The media organizations, NGOs and the private sector should promote the equal sharing of family responsibility and produce materials that portray diverse roles of women leaders;
- Develop within mass media and advertising organizations professional guidelines and codes of conduct and other forms of self-regulation to promote the presentation of non-stereotyped images of women, consistent with freedom of expression.

Environment

Through their management and use of natural resources, women provide sustenance to their families and communities. As consumers and producers, caretakers of their families and educators, women play an important role in promoting sustainable development.

The deterioration of natural resources results in negative effects on the health, well-being and quality of life of the population at large, especially girls and women of all ages.

However, women, who are rarely formally trained as natural-resource managers, remain largely absent from decision-making and have their experience and skills too often marginalized. Despite the leadership role played by women's organizations, institutional coordination with national bodies is very weak.

The Platform recommends action to:

- Involve women actively in environmental decision-making at all levels, including as managers, designers and planners, and as implementers and evaluators of environmental projects;

- Integrate gender concerns and perspectives in policies and programmes for sustainable development;
- Strengthen or establish mechanisms at the national, regional and international levels to assess the impact of development and environment policies on women.

The Girl-child

In many countries, the girl-child faces discrimination from the earliest stages of life, through childhood and into adulthood. Due to harmful attitudes and practices, such as female genital mutilation, son preference, early marriage, sexual exploitation and practices related to heath and food allocation, fewer girls than boys survive into adulthood in some areas of the world. Due to lack of protective laws, or failure to enforce such laws, girls are more vulnerable to all kinds of violence, particularly sexual violence. In many regions, girls face discrimination in access to education and specialized training.

More than 15 million girls aged 15 to 19 each year give birth and face pregnancy-related complications. Girls are also more vulnerable than boys to the consequences of unprotected and premature sexual relations, including HIV/AIDS.

The Platform recommends action to:

- Eliminate all forms of discrimination against the girl-child; enact and enforce appropriate legislation that guarantees equal right to succession and ensures equal right to inherit, regardless of the sex of the child;
- Eliminate negative cultural attitudes and practices against girls;
- Eliminate discrimination against girls in education, skills development and training;
- Eliminate discrimination against girls in health and nutrition;
- Eliminate the economic exploitation of child labour and protect young girls at work;
- Strengthen the role of the family in improving the status of the girl-child.

Institutional and Financial Arrangements

The Platform for Action establishes a set of actions that should lead to fundamental change. Immediate action and accountability are essential if the targets are to be met by the year 2000.

Governments are primarily responsible for their implementation. However, success depends also on various national, regional and international institutions, public and private, which require clear and strong mandates, authority and resources:

- At the national level, commitment at the highest political level is essential for the successful implementation of the Platform. By the end of 1996, all Governments should have their own national strategies or plans of action. Governments should establish or improve effectiveness of national machineries for the advancement of women, and seek the active support of a broad range of other actors.
- At the regional and sub-regional levels, the regional commissions of the United Nations should promote and assist national institutions. Regional institutions should develop and publicize regional plans of action for implementing the Platform within given time-frames and resources.
- At the international level, all entities of the United Nations system should have the necessary resources and support to carry out follow-up activities. International financial institutions are encouraged to review and revise policies to ensure that their investments and programmes benefit women.

To ensure system-wide implementation of the Platform and to advise on gender issues, the Secretary-General of the United Nations is invited to established a high-level post in his office. The Platform also calls for committing adequate financial resources from all sources and across all sectors.

UN MILESTONES IN THE ADVANCEMENT OF WOMEN

1945 The Preamble to the United Nations Chapter reaffirms "faith in fundamental human rights..... in the equal rights of men and women. "During the first General Assembly, held in San Francisco, female delegates demanded special attention for women's issues. The Economic and Social Council (ECOSOC) established a Sub-Commission of the Commission on Human Rights on the Status of Women.

1946 The United Nations Sub-Commission on the Status of Women becomes a full Commission. Its mandate is to promote women's political, economic and social rights. A Division for the Advancement of Women is set up in the Department for Policy Coordination and Sustainable Development, the same Division that is now acting as the Conference Secretariat for the Fourth World Conference on Women.

1948 The Universal Declaration on Human Rights opposes discrimination against women in Article 2: "Everyone is entitled to all the rights and freedoms set forth in this Declaration without distinction of any kind such as race, colour, sex......"

1949 The Convention for the Suppression of the Traffic in Persons and of the Exploitation of the Prostitution of Others is adopted by the General Assembly.

1951 The International Labour Organization (ILO) adopts the Convention Concerning Equal Remuneration for Men and Women Workers for Work of Equal Value.

1952 The International Convention on the Political Rights of Women is the first global endorsement of equal political rights under the law, including the right to vote. It is the first United Nations instrument in which states parties undertook legal obligations involving the principle of equal rights between women and men.

1954 The UN General Assembly recognizes that women are "subject to ancient laws, customs and practices" inconsistent with the Universal Declaration on Human Rights, and calls on governments to abolish them.

1955 The International Labour Organization issues a Convention on Maternity Protection.

1957 The Convention on the Nationality of Married Women is adopted, granting women the right to retain or change their nationalities regardless of their husbands' actions.

1960 The ILO Convention Concerning Discrimination in Respect to Employment and Occupation is adopted. UNESCO adopts the Convention against Discrimination in Education.

1962 The Convention on Consent to Marriage, Minimum Age for Marriage and Registration of Marriages is adopted to ensure, by national legislation, equal rights for both spouses.

1963 The UN General Assembly recognizes the dimensions of violations of women's rights and calls for a Declaration on the Elimination of All Forms of Discrimination Against Women (CEDAW).

1966 The UN Commission on the Status of Women submits the first draft of the anti-discrimination Declaration. The General Assembly adopts the International Covenant on Civil and Political Rights (and the Protocol on the Abolition of Capital Punishment) as well as the Covenant on Economic, Social and Cultural Rights,which calls for increased participation of women in public life, equal pay for equal work and the right to promotion.

1967 The General Assembly adopts the Declaration on the Elimination of All Forms of Discrimination Against Women "to ensure the universal recognition, in law and in fact, of the principle of equality of men and women".

1968 The Economic and Social Council of the United Nations initiates a reporting system on implementation of the provisions for the Declaration by governments.

1970 The General Assembly adopts its first resolution urging equal employment opportunities for women in the United Nations Secretariat.

1975 International Women's Year is celebrated throughout the world with events at the local, regional and international levels. Activities promote recognition of women's contributions to society and equal rights. The First World Conference on Women is held in Mexico City. The final Plan of Action calls for the preparation and adoption of an international convention against all forms of sex discrimination ad recommends procedures for its implementation. The General Assembly proclaims the first Decade for Women: Equality, Development, Peace. The United Nations Decade for Women (1975-1985) officially paves the way for a wide range of actions to improve women's status.

1976 The United Nations Voluntary Fund for Women is established to make financial resources available to further development projects aimed at women in developing countries. The United Nations International Research and Training Institute for the Advancement of Women (INSTRAW), based in Santo Domingo in the Dominican Republic, is also established by the General Assembly with a mandate to support the fuller participation of women in the economic, social political spheres.

1979 The General Assembly adopts the Convention on the Elimination of All Forms of Discrimination against Women (CEDAW,) which defines discrimination against women as any distinction made on the basis of sex which impairs women's equal enjoyment of fundamental rights.

1980 The Second World Conference on Women is held in Copenhagen to review progress made in the first half of the Decade on Women. It adopts a Programme of Action.

1981 CEDAW enters into force with the required ratification by 20 countries.

1985 The Third World Conference on Women in held in Nairobi, Kenya, at the end of the United Nations Decade for Women. The Nairobi Forward-Looking Strategies call for increased participation of women as equal partners with men in all political, social and economic fields, including their full access to education and training.

The United Nations Voluntary Fund for the UN Decade for Women becomes a permanent and autonomous organization in association with UN Development Programme (UNDP) and is renamed the United Nations Development Fund for Women (UNIFEM). It funds innovative development activities to benefit women especially in rural areas of developing countries.

1986 First World Survey on the Role of Women in Development is published by the UN.

1988 The Branch for the Advancement of Women is raised to the status of a Division, becoming the central UN unit on women's issues. WISTAT, the United Nations Women's Indicators and Statistics database, becomes operational as the focal point for the compilation of worldwide statistics on women.

1990 The Commission on the Status of Women reviews implementation of the Nairobi Forward-Looking Strategies and recommends convening he Fourth World Conference on Women.

1990- 1995 The system-wide Medium-term Plan for Women and Development adopted by the Economic and Social Council in 1998 begins. It identifies ways for promoting the advancement of women both within the UN system and through the work of the various agencies and offices of the UN system.

1991 *The World's Women: Trends and Statistics* is published, a compilation of data on the situation of women throughout the world.

1993 The Declaration on the Elimination of Violence Against Women is adopted by the General Assembly. It defines "Violence against women" as any act of gender-based violence that results in, or is likely to result in, physical, sexual or psychological harm or suffering to women, including threats of such acts, coercion or arbitrary deprivation of liberty, whether occurring in public or in private life.

1994 The Commission on Human Rights decides to appoint a Special Rapporteur on violence against women. The Special Rapporteur will seek and receive information on violence against women, its causes and consequences from Governments, treaty bodies, specialized agencies, non-governmental organizations and other bodies and recommend measures to eliminate violence against women.

1995 The Fourth World Conference on Women, scheduled for September in Beijing, will review and debate 12 critical areas of concern and adopt a Platform for Action. The UN celebrates its Fiftieth Anniversary with events throughout the year to highlight its achievements, including its contribution to the global women's movement.

1996- 2000 A Second System-Wide Medium-Term Plan for Women and Development is in the pipeline. The plan will outline further ways of strengthening the work of the UN for women's equality, including its own hiring practices, policies and programmes.